Intro 1-3 + epilogue

Progressive Intellectuals and the Dilemmas of Democratic Commitment

Progressive Intellectuals and the Dilemmas of Democratic Commitment

Leon Fink

Harvard University Press
Cambridge, Massachusetts
London, England
1997

To the memory of Herbert G. Gutman,
Christopher Lasch, and Edward P. Thompson,
three teachers who treated history
as the people's business

Library of Congress Cataloging-in-Publication Data
Fink, Leon, 1948–
Progressive intellectuals and the dilemmas of democratic commitment /
Leon Fink.
p. cm.
Includes bibliographical references and index.
ISBN 0-674-66160-5 (cloth : alk. paper)
1. United States—Intellectual life—20th century.
2. Democracy—United States—History—20th century.
3. Progressivism (United States politics) 4. Intellectuals—United States—
Political activity—History—20th century.
I. Title.
E169.1.F525 1997
973'.086'31—dc21
97-25506

Contents

Acknowledgments

I WAS FIRST drawn to the subject of this book by an invitation to comment on an excellent paper by George M. Fredrickson on intellectuals and the labor question at the American Historical Association annual meeting in December 1985. The occasion marked the first time since graduate school courses with Christopher Lasch that I had been forced to reckon seriously with the social role of intellectuals as a group. At the same time, without my fully realizing it, two other influences were pushing me in a similar direction. A sense of drift felt by many in my designated field of labor history raised my curiosity about the genealogy of this sub-discipline. And, also in 1985, my advisor and dear friend Herbert Gutman died. Altogether, I sensed a break in my own career and a heightened interest in the background of the profession I had chosen. Soon, plunged into research about the Wisconsin School of labor historians and fascinated with the materials and questions I was encountering, I began to expand my research into a free-ranging inquiry about the intellectual activists of the Progressive Era. By a curious serendipity, my personal quest coincided with the growth of a literature of academic self-scrutiny and disciplinary historiography, as symbolized most meaningfully by Russell Jacoby's *The Last Intellectuals* (1987) and Peter Novick's *That Noble Dream* (1988).

Over the next couple of years, I began to merge my continuing interest in the history of working people and democratic politics with this new stimulus from intellectual history, through interdisciplinary graduate courses on intellectuals and politics and the history of the social disciplines at the University of North Carolina at Chapel Hill alongside colleagues Donald Reid, Judith Farquhar, and Stephen Leonard. In addition, I enjoyed the advantage of three leaves from teaching responsibilities, including fellowships from the University's incomparable Institute for the Arts and Humanities (twice) and the Kenan Trust as well as the National Humanities

Center. During my year at the Center, I especially benefited from the wisdom and criticism of colleagues Henry Binford, Dan Carter, Steven Goldsmith, Linda Kerber, and Jeffrey Stewart. My own department at Chapel Hill has proved a nurturing as well as unusually good-humored base of operations. I am particularly grateful for partial readings of the manuscript by history colleagues Charles Capper, Peter Coclanis, Robert Gallman, Jacquelyn Hall, and Donald Reid, and for bibliographic suggestions from Lloyd S. Kramer and James Leloudis. From allied departments I received valuable counsel from Susan Bickford, Stephen Leonard, and Michael Lienesch (political science), Kenneth Janken (African and African-American studies), and Laurie Maffly-Kipp (religious studies). Finally, I have drawn on an exceptional group of graduate students—enjoying the most able research assistance from Georg Leidenberger and David Anderson and a variety of helpful suggestions from Andrew Arnold, Tom Baker, Michele Bowen-Spencer, Jefferson Cowie, Robert McDonald, and Adam Tuchinsky.

The fact that the chapters in this book deal with such diverse subject matter has led me to call on a wide-ranging list of scholars for further assistance, whether in the form of quick but crucial references or reaction to drafts of individual chapters. An undoubtedly incomplete list of those to whom I am so indebted includes David Carlton, John Brown Childs, Steven Cohen, Sarah Deutsch, Tom Dublin, Melvyn Dubofsky, James Epstein, Daniel Ernst, Ellen Fitzpatrick, Lacy Ford, Mary Furner, Julia Greene, Cindy Hahamovitch, John Higham, Walter Jackson, Joshua Miller, Christina Nelson, John Norman, John V. Orth, Peter Rachleff, Steven Sapolsky, Philip Scranton, Bryant Simon, Kathryn Kish Sklar, Judith Stein, James Stewart, David Strand, and Joe Trotter. Several academic events—including the Southern Labor Studies Conference, the British Society for Labour History, the University of Wisconsin's Perspectives on Labor History Conference, the Reynolda House Culture and Democracy Conference, and the Triangle Intellectual History Seminar—gave me the chance to try out pieces of the work in process before a stimulating audience.

I am grateful for permission to draw on previously published articles. "'Intellectuals' versus 'Workers': Academic Requirements and the Creation of Labor History" was published in the *American*

Historical Review 96 (April 1991), 395–421; and "Expert Advice: Progressive Intellectuals and the Unraveling of Labor Reform, 1912–1915" was published in *Intellectuals and Public Life: Between Radicalism and Reform,* edited by Leon Fink, Stephen T. Leonard, and Donald M. Reid, copyright © 1996 by Cornell University and used by permission of the publisher, Cornell University Press.

I also acknowledge my deepest appreciation to the librarians and archivists who helped me along the way, especially those at the Special Collections Department, Alderman Library, University of Virginia; the State Historical Society of Wisconsin; the South Caroliniana Library of the University of South Carolina; the South Carolina Department of Archives and History; and the Manuscripts and Archives Department of Yale University Library. My home during most of my research and writing was Davis Library at the University of North Carolina at Chapel Hill, where I have long depended on the consistent combination of cheerfulness and professionalism from the staff at the research, interlibrary loan, and circulation desks. In addition, fellow scholars Will Dunstan and William S. Powell proved valuable and supportive library neighbors.

Historical research is inevitably a collaborative enterprise, but sometimes the sense of cooperation (and indebtedness) is especially acute. In the course of my work I effectively stumbled on three scholars with whom I was at least in part plowing a common field. In each case—Jack Stuart on the Wallings and Mary Mac Motley and Harvey Neufeldt on Wil Lou Gray—my partners welcomed me, giving generously of their own research and insights.

The special situation of Mary Mac Motley—as the great-grandniece of her historical subject—raises another group to whom I owe thanks. I have been immensely aided by the special exertions as well as candid recollections of the descendants of the central characters in this book. Anna Walling Hamburger, Peter B. Lauck, and Mark Perlman have also greatly enriched my effort by their understanding of their parents' lives and their commitment to the historian's enterprise.

As this book moved toward completion, I was most fortunate to have support and instruction from the editors at Harvard University Press. Aïda D. Donald and Elizabeth Suttell offered vital encouragement and tough but valuable guidelines, while Donna Bouvier proved a masterful manuscript editor.

Although this project has in many respects represented a diffuse and far-flung adventure, one woman's gaze has helped to keep it and its author in order. Susan Levine has read and reread the multiple drafts of the work and, as ever, has made its writing worthwhile.

I dedicate this book to three people who died during the course of the project but whose lives sustain me still. Different in intellectual focus and political as well as personal styles, they shared a willingness to induct a young recruit into the mysteries of the craft and convince him that history must be a part of any noble dream.

Introduction

IN HIS provocative volume of 1987, historian and cultural critic Russell Jacoby lamented the disappearance of what he labeled "public intellectuals," that is, "writers and thinkers who address a general and educated audience." Due to a host of changes—the decline of bohemian urban centers, the rise of a self-insulated academic professionalism, selective repression of academic free spirits, and assimilation of once-dissident Jewish voices—a tradition of engaged, left-wing social commentary (most closely associated in Jacoby's mind with such post–World War II New York writers as Alfred Kazin, Lewis Mumford, C. Wright Mills, Edmund Wilson, Irving Howe, Dwight Macdonald, Daniel Bell, and Lionel Trilling) appeared to have all but exhausted itself. A younger generation of educated radicals, moreover, had not only failed to occupy the cultural space of its progenitors, but had also appeared to have traded in its own earlier commitment to social and political change for the blandishments of academic tenure and the prestige associated with specialized journals and conferences.[1]

Yet no sooner than it took to say Kaddish for the public intellectual did the figure vigorously, and self-consciously, reappear. The combination of outside attack on the universities, internal self-scrutiny (including Jacoby's volume), and wider social polarization and politicization led many academics in the 1980s and 1990s to seek new outlets for their work and greater contact with a variety of extra-academic publics. The phenomenon of the new public intellectual (most notably associated with a prominent, if diverse, group of African-American writers and critics) has been duly noted in the nation's press: indeed, according to one computer archive, no fewer than 248 stories appeared on the subject between the end of 1987 and the beginning of 1995 in major newspapers and magazines.[2] The impulse for connectedness, moreover, echoed not only in individual authors who managed to escape professional journals in favor of mass-circulation outlets but also in institutional initiatives, such as citizenship education, service, and applied learning programs, which were intended to reunite thought and action on college and high school campuses and to link the campus to the world outside.[3]

Since Jacoby coined the term "public intellectual," concern for the academic's social function has become a matter of widespread scrutiny. For humanities and social science scholars on the nation's campuses, two related trends have been apparent. First, there is an administrative preoccupation with a "return to [undergraduate] teaching" as a necessary corrective to the perceived self-indulgent and professionally driven "research" focus of university faculties. Second, among the scholars themselves there is a renewed search (and renewed cache) for effective connections with a larger audience. While both tendencies in my view hold promise, they may prove disappointing as sources of democratic cultural renewal. (The teaching role I will not emphasize here, except to note that there is obviously a built-in tension between demands to concentrate one's intellectual attention on—versus beyond—the classroom.)[4]

Quickly shorn of its oppositional political trappings, the idea of the public intellectual has all too easily emerged as simply a new and preferred style of scholarly self-presentation. Connection to an audience, or a public, today pretty well exhausts the common understanding of what the public intellectual is about. Interpreting Jacoby's text as an unnecessarily pessimistic "jeremiad" on academic narrowness, historian Neil Jumonville concludes his own book-length treatment of the postwar New York intellectuals with the cheerful assurance that "future generations of intellectuals will find or found new outlets for work in the generalist vein." And indeed, other commentators have already found the species in full bloom. In one recent citation, for example, even former President Jimmy Carter is viewed as "more engaging in his other role as a public intellectual, the accessible yet cerebral commentator who eschews academia's only-for-specialists approach to writing." Similarly,

But it's no longer oppositional.

about two prominent African-American scholars we learn that "the *Atlantic* and the *New Yorker* have branded [Henry Louis] Gates [Jr.] and [Cornel] West America's new breed of 'public intellectuals,' because they're as comfortable inside walls of ivy (Harvard, where they both teach) as on Ted Koppel's set or the pages of every important periodical."[5]

The problem with such definitions is that they beg the question of purpose. Market share and celebrity, rather than any serious message or project of social transformation, risk becoming the new standards of intellectual significance.[6] This is surely not what the author of *The Last Intellectuals* had in mind when he warned that "younger intellectuals have responded to their times, as they must; they have also surrendered to them, as they need not."[7] At least to the extent that Jacoby (and the rest of us) would address a *political* (and not just a communicative) problem facing radical democrats, we must look beyond the constraints of styles of expression and focus on the basic relationships—or lack thereof—between the intellectuals and their would-be coalition partners.

Like Jacoby, I believe that such an analysis requires a historical perspective, yet I prefer to extend the time line of social group formation to emphasize those we might consider the nation's first, rather than its so-called last, generation of public intellectuals. The pre–World War I American intellectuals, as I selectively review them in the following pages, certainly attempted to engage with a larger public. Indeed, as I see them, a sense of responsibility, even stewardship, of a democratic mass citizenry defines these progressive reformers—accounting at once for their compelling messages as well as their peculiar predicaments. The gap between democratic theory and social practice has long disturbed idealistic Americans, but perhaps never with greater urgency than in the first decades of the twentieth century. Progressive intellectuals characteristically combined individually persuasive forms of expression with specific institutional strategies and political projects of redress. A missionary sense of public service marked their lives; they aimed for more than placing clear prose in commercially accessible outlets. In short, their degree of effort—if not success—I think was greater than that of most of their latter-day counterparts and thus worthy of close inspection by those who would wish to reawaken a public intellectual vocation.

Those I shall call intellectuals—that is, those who play a socially interpretive role as speakers, writers, or group leaders based on their own advanced learning—have wrestled since the early days of the Republic with their separation from the mass of their fellow citizens. On the one hand, the power of democratic ideology, a binding nationalism, and/or an evangelical faith in the redemptive spirit have led a significant number of these uncommonly well-educated men and women to identify with the circumstances and aspirations of ordinary working people. On the other hand, misunderstanding, condescension, and outright disappointment are often the most visible legacy of their initiatives. Intellectuals have played a crucial part in every democratic reform wave in American history; yet just how to advance the ideal of democratic culture and how to act as a cultured democrat remain troublesome questions.

As early as 1837, Ralph Waldo Emerson gave eloquent voice to basic dilemmas facing the socially conscientious American scholar. Concerned to transcend the increasingly narrow specialization of roles imposed on ministers and other professionals by a spreading marketplace economy, Emerson sought out a vocation as lyceum lecturer and writer that left him free to address the common good from a position of relative independence. Aiming to reconcile public and private spheres of insight as well as colliding social factions, Emerson's self-reliant scholar would discover the keys to the impartial common good, serving as a kind of moral compass for an undisciplined democracy.[8] Yet the very standards of judgment that Emerson set for himself, in particular his refusal to be compromised by worldly temptation, inevitably set him up for disappointment from that part of the public which did not or could not practice his chosen virtues:

> One has patience with every kind of living thing but not with the dead alive. I, at least, hate to see persons of that lumpish class who are here they know not why . . . The worst of charity, is, that the lives you are asked to preserve are not worth preserving. The calamity is the masses. I do not wish any mass at all, but honest men only, facultied men only, lovely & sweet & accomplished women only; and no shovel-handed Irish, & no Five-Points . . . or 2 millions of paupers receiving relief, miserable factory population, or Lazzaroni, at all.[9]

Emerson's impatience with the lumpish masses.

theme

From the beginning, therefore, the American intellectual had chosen a paradoxical vocation: a social critic committed at once to identification with the whole of the people and an elitist whose own mores and life situation would prove somewhat alienating from the very public he or she had chosen to serve.

To be sure, there were intellectuals after Emerson who sought conscientiously to avoid self-alienation from the "lumpish class" or "mass." Walt Whitman, for one, offered a lyrical, if carefully impersonal, embrace of the democratic crowd.[10] In a ringing defense of the "popular democracy" that had willingly performed a "labor of death" to defeat the "secession-slave-power," Whitman, in *Democratic Vistas* (1871), defended the masses from outside skeptics as well as their own debilities. Taking note of the long-laid "repugnance between a literary and professional life and the rude rank spirit of the democracies," Whitman acknowledged the defects of his heroes: "I myself see clearly enough the crude, defective streaks in all the strata of the common people; the specimens and vast collections of the ignorant, the credulous, the unfit and uncouth, the incapable, and the very low and poor." In the end, he argued, it was precisely the role of government (and by inference scholars too) to educate the masses—"not merely to rule . . . but to develop, to open up to cultivation, to encourage the possibilities of all beneficent and manly outcroppage, and of that aspiration for independence, and the pride and self-respect latent in all characters." Democratic civilization, he believed, must not rely on "the rule of the best men, the born heroes and captains of the race (as if such ever, or one time out of a hundred, get into the big places, elective or dynastic)" but on the capacity of government "to train communities through all their grades . . . to rule themselves."[11] Whitman eloquently outlined a vision of democratic intellectual practice; a poet, he left it to others to fill in the details.

In a more strategic manner, Harvard graduate and antislavery agitator Wendell Phillips had similarly beseeched college students for years "to leave the heights of contemplations [and] come down to the everyday life of the people."[12] In 1881 he returned to the Harvard forum of Emerson's "American Scholar" address to offer his own instruction to "the Scholar in a Republic." The "book-educated class of the North," Phillips thundered, had ever a betrayed a "chronic distrust of the people." Succumbing to pedantry and elitism if not the direct blandishments of antidemocratic political patrons, professional academics had all too often missed out on the liberating moments of "true education" as in the exploits of a John Brown. Yet Phillips, like Emerson, looked to the independent intellectual as a positive, even potentially redemptive, democratic force. While the politician and the cleric perforce defended their own selfish interests, the scholar might stand "outside of organization with . . . no object but truth—to tear a question open and riddle it with light." A democratic culture ultimately depended on its intellectuals "to refine the taste, mould the character, lift the purpose, and educate the moral sense of the masses on whose intelligence and self-respect rests the state."[13]

For decades to come, other educated men and women, in the spirit of Emerson, Whitman, and Phillips, would act out the heroic social role of popular tribune and moral prophet. By the late nineteenth century, however, particularly as workers, farmers, and other previously marginalized groups including women and African-Americans organized themselves into tangible political blocs, the image of the "movement intellectual" offered an alternative to the lonely, if independent, voice of democratic sympathy. Labor editors such as John Swinton in New York and Phillips Thompson in Toronto acted out a new wave of democratic culture creation from within the meteoric life of the Knights of Labor. Temperance and women's rights advocates similarly built new communicative networks even as they attended to practical political measures.[14] Educated sons and daughters of the American middle or upper class, such as Henry Demarest Lloyd, Henry George, George Bellamy, Frances Willard, and Florence Kelley, likewise attached themselves to the democratic ferment of their times.[15] In each case, the activist-intellectual's role contained something of the figure of the Emersonian moral critic and something of the Phillipsian agitator, but something new as well. The promise of a democratic mass movement suggested the possibility of a more intimate and permanent connection between ideas, organization, and power: more than a mere catalyst of protest, the scholar might even serve as a leader of the people.

The potential for such a populist bloc uniting intellectuals with

Soon fizzled to be replaced with (20th specialization

more plebeian social elements in a face-to-face democratic space dimmed considerably by the turn of the century. The collapse of visionary and broad-based social movements like the Knights of Labor and the People's Party narrowed the operative social space at once for independent radicals and middle-class "friends of the workingman." The intellectual-worker alliances that continued were either localized, limited to educational initiatives, and/or increasingly top-down if not paternalistic in execution.[16]

But beyond such contingent influences also lay the irrepressible force of an expanding social division of labor. Education itself, an increasingly formal process, fitted the graduate with an occupation and daily work environment physically removed from industrial neighborhoods. The spreading white-collared middle class sought protection from, not solidarity with, the disorderly elements of immigrant-dominated central cities.[17] Moreover, the core elements of nineteenth-century popular democracy were all coming under suspicion. The new, science-oriented universities, like the efficient business corporations that partially sustained them, typically nourished values diametrically opposed to such tradition-centered and patronage-bound institutions as political parties, craft unions, and ethnic families.[18] Not group loyalty and community welfare but individual merit and "objective" standards of performance were the watchwords of the technocratic institutions that both trained and absorbed the nation's brainpower. In the circumstances, "democracy" became less a description of an egalitarian social order and more an abstract alternative—to be debated—of governmental and civil order.

Cut off as they were from any immediate and obvious agent of social transformation, a significant stream of American intellectuals nevertheless not only clung to democratic ideals but developed vigorous forms of both political and cultural intervention. To be sure, such forms varied widely. At one extreme were those who rejected the accoutrements of intellectual privilege and adopted a life of permanent agitation among the common people. Such a spirit, for example, was Morrison Isaac Swift, Williams College graduate and Hegelian scholar who adopted the cause of the urban unemployed in the late 1880s and early 1890s. Attempting to charter a "social university" as a kind of counter-institution for the industrial working class, Swift in 1891 tried in vain to return his Ph.D. to Johns Hopkins and to have his name "erased from the list of graduates of the university."[19] In his vicarious identification with the working class, Swift placed himself among that rebellious minority of middle-class intellectuals who would redirect their talents in open defiance of their own social backgrounds.

Another form of intellectual distrust and alienation from American centers of power was manifest in the tradition of "moral criticism" perhaps most closely associated with the philosopher-psychologist William James. It was James who imported the very term "intellectual" into the American lexicon after it had been revived in France amidst the Dreyfus Affair of the 1890s.[20] As Ross Posnock has argued, James articulated "the burden of the modern intellectual as the obligation to express *moral* outrage against modernity, what James repeatedly called 'all big organizations.'"[21] In the language of the Puritan jeremiad, James summoned a society increasingly steeped in materialist accumulation and political corruption back to its simpler republican moorings.[22] The heroic intellectual, according to this script, might lead the people away from selfish and jingoistic indulgence and toward the fulfillment of America's democratic promise.[23] Perhaps the most direct twentieth-century descendants of the romantic-democratic James were the "Young American" critics—Randolph Bourne, Van Wyck Brooks, Waldo Frank, and Lewis Mumford—who, like James, harnessed aesthetic and even spiritual values to the search for a "revitalized democratic community."[24] Together, this moralistic tradition of democratic criticism best exemplifies what sociologist Edward Shils has called the "penumbral culture" of American intellectuals: "a society in which the intellectuals—literary, humanistic, and academic—for a century were alienated in sentiment and imagery from the nonintellectual elites, both national and local."[25]

Most democratic intellectual activists of the early twentieth century, however, fell outside both the rebel and the romantic categories sketched above. Neither fully forsaking their educated or professional pedigrees in favor of pure rank-and-file-ism nor opting for an aesthetic distance from the corruptions of bourgeois society, they engaged—as intellectuals—in practical projects of what they most often called "progressive" political and social reform. Such projects, however, inevitably bore the weight of problems that stemmed at once from social conditions in America and from the social position of the intellectuals themselves.

As far as the nation went, the issues for reform-minded intellectuals were twofold: *Could* the people prevail? The very material changes wrought by industrial capitalism—urbanization, mass immigration, concentrated power, poverty amidst progress—posed a formidable theoretical as well as political obstacle to democratic values. Many of the initiatives undertaken by populist, socialist, progressive, or later New Deal reformers—whether to municipalize public transit, to secure labor rights, or to provide the modicum of a welfare state—explicitly attempted to redress the problems of inequality and powerlessness in a machine age. Yet there was no obvious or enduring vehicle that would translate progressive ideas into progressive measures, and the obstacles—corporate power, political bossism, the courts—often proved overwhelming.

But another concern followed on the first. *Should* the people prevail? Those who enlisted from above in popular political struggles quickly encountered the frustrations of moving the masses in the direction of what was seen as their logical best interests. Ignorance, fear, cupidity, prejudice—all stalked every effort to rally the People against their Enemies. As early as the turn of the century, many self-styled democrats could not imagine democratic change arising spontaneously from the people; at best, it would need to be carefully laid on or at least brokered and managed by sympathetic experts allied to democratic constituencies.

Aside from the daunting internal complexity of the nation's social problems, the intellectuals' own circumstances also conditioned their response to the perceived crisis of democracy. Twentieth-century reform initiatives drew in large measure on a vast new pool of college graduates and postgraduates who had been at least temporarily freed from inherited social-economic roles. Together, urban-bohemian circles, independent newspapers and magazines, and college campuses provided new spaces for the consideration and amelioration of social ills. From such redoubts a host of new ideas soon helped to transform American education, social policy, and the law, and even—as pragmatic relativism—challenged conventional ideas about knowledge itself. Yet the very buoyancy of this creative intellectual network also proved somewhat self-limiting, inducing an insularity both from centers of political power and from the daily life of the people whose interests the intellectuals sought to serve. Many erstwhile reformers would ignore this problem, drifting without qualm into a self-isolating culture of twentieth-century academic professionalism. Yet others of the educated classes maintained a more practical worldly engagement, attempting to extend a vision of intellectual involvement with working people hatched in the early years of Progressivism well into the coming decades. It is their journey in particular that concerns us here.

Progressive Intellectuals and the Dilemmas of Democratic Commitment explores the actions of a select group of democratic activists against the larger temper of their times. Through the experience of one or more key characters, each of seven chapters examines a dilemma inherent in the search by intellectuals to contribute to a more democratic society: the Wisconsin labor historians (Richard T. Ely, John R. Commons, and Selig Perlman) and the problem of defining the worker-academic relationship; Charles McCarthy and the tension between expertise and advocacy; William English Walling and the problem of intellectual self-marginalization; Anna Strunsky Walling and the test of democratic ideals in daily life; A. Philip Randolph and the contradictions of democratic leadership; W. Jett Lauck and the harnessing of both state and economy to democratic ends; and Wil Lou Gray and the enigma of adult education as liberation or social control. Forming two bookends around these case studies, the opening and concluding chapters take a synthetic approach, documenting the ebb and flow of twentieth-century confidence in the very idea of a common culture connecting educated opinion to the world of the ordinary citizen. To this end, Chapter 1 follows the creation of a progressive intellectual vision and its subsequent challenge by an increasingly skeptical social science, while Chapter 9 picks up the renewed fashion of the public intellectual, comparing present-day examples to the models of an earlier era.

One problem with embarking on an exploration of these early-twentieth-century figures lies in our confidence that we already have the answers to the problems they raise. To be sure, much thoughtful consideration has already been given to the internal problems and weaknesses of the Progressives' reform impulse and,

their weaknesses

in particular, the pragmatic streak that was its most distinctive philosophical legacy. An uncritical embrace of "science" and "progress" as levers to a better future, naive reliance on administrative (and ultimately bureaucratic and manipulative) solutions to social problems, and, more abstractly, commitment to knowledge and growth at the expense of wisdom and values undoubtedly contributed to a growing tendency towards social engineering among the twentieth-century American liberal intelligentsia.[26] Yet there are problems with this standard "history of ideas" approach to the intellectual reformers as a social group. A tone of glib condescension all too often sneaks into critiques of Progressive reformers, as if from newfound heights of wisdom we have somehow resolved the classic issues of democracy and industrial civilization that they first confronted.

Nothing, of course, could be further from the truth. At a political level the issues with which early-twentieth-century intellectuals grappled remain remarkably, if all the more disturbingly, alive today. Only their form and context have been altered. Whereas our forebears dealt with the chaos and dislocation of a newly consolidated industrial economy, so do we face the impact of a postindustrial division of labor. Whereas they challenged the investment in market forces of immutable laws of nature, we encounter those same forces masquerading as the only "efficient" and "affordable" answers to every conceivable social policy question. Whereas they confronted technologies of consumption and cultural control that were newly national in scope, we live in a fundamentally transnational world of media images and consumer yearning. Whereas, in many cases, they entered the academy (creating modern social science disciplines in the process) in order to address the problems of industrial civilization, we search for ways to *transcend* the academic boundaries of critical social discourse.

But it is at the cultural level that the dilemmas initially addressed by the Progressive intellectuals perhaps remain most perplexing. Indeed, perhaps never has doubt about the quality of mass democratic culture so abounded as in the contemporary United States, the regnant superpower in a newly democratic world order. At home, the very concept of a democratically inspired state—with the capacity to establish minimal standards of welfare and opportunity as well as to disseminate a common set of civic values—is at once discred-

us now compared to them then

ited by an ascendant political right as both inefficient and inimical to individual initiative and shunned by an identity-obsessed left as a vestige of an outmoded and intolerant universalism. As politics attracts an ever-shrinking sector of the electorate to ritualistic participation in the democratic process, commentary rages over the abuse and impoverishment of its constituent powers. References to a "nation of nitwits," the "dumbing of America," "talk-show fascism," as well as psychological analysis of a "panic culture" suggest, at the very least, a crisis of faith about the capacity of the mass public to engage productively in decisions affecting the nation's future.[27] Following the 1995 Oklahoma City bombing of government offices and the Unabomber attacks, one commentator warned that Americans may "lack the necessary habits of mind and a sphere of common reference" necessary for democracy.[28]

In such circumstances, today's educated elite might profitably reexamine the experience of those who first coped with the problems of culture-building in an industrial civilization. Encountering challenges no less daunting than our own, they nevertheless found both the social and psychic space to identify with America's industrial rank and file, uphold the banner of universal education, and contest the political status quo even in the face of gnawing doubts. Instead of rushing to judge them on the basis of later results (a crude test not without its poetically pragmatic sense of justice for those who called themselves pragmatists), we would do better to reconstruct their initiatives with a sensitivity to the temper of *their* times.

Surely the most important problems to study are precisely those that remain unresolved. Can the American intellectual community act (once again) as a rallying point in defense and extension of popular self-rule and mass welfare? It is almost a cliché to note that today's campuses, rather than its workplaces or inner cities, hold a premium on radical discourse about fundamental social change. What are we to make of such a cleavage? Against the background of a long record of high expectations and dashed hopes, it seems prudent that any new attempt by those whom Christopher Lasch has called "the thinking classes" to take up democratic cudgels should at least be accompanied by a trail map.[29]

1 Progressive Reformers, Social Scientists, and the Search for a Democratic Public

AMERICAN intellectuals at the beginning of the twentieth century preferred to adopt an optimistic view of their relation to the larger public. Products of an expansive higher education system, reared with Protestant moral values but rejecting the ministry in favor of the new professions, and confronting the industrial city (and especially its immigrant masses) with the cheerful curiosity of the middle-class ingénue, the Progressive generation of reformers boldly positioned themselves as agents of social change.[1] To these writers, social scientists, and social workers (and for a time the terms were nearly synonymous) the problems of poverty, inequality, racial and ethnic intolerance, women's rights, even war, were all thought solvable, or at least ameliorable, by a combination of applied reason and active citizenship. The favored phrases of progressive reformers—"industrial democracy," "new nationalism," "new commonwealth," "new democracy"—pulsed with heady expectations that expansive decision-making and widespread social power-sharing would produce the most healthy body politic.

If the people were to seize their democratic birthright for the greater good, however, it followed that they must engage their higher faculties of reason. The inertia of ignorance, superstition, and blind custom could be overcome only by embracing the powers of the scientific method. Whereas the privileged few might readily exploit the lethargy of the masses or feverish frenzy of the crowd for selfish purposes, the success of democratic self-rule depended at bottom on the conscious and rational participation of an informed public. If the crowd was the people in the rough, the democratic public were the people schooled in a sense of civic duty. It was no wonder then that education ranked so high on the agenda of Progressive reformers. Acknowledging the many thorough-going criticisms of machine civilization, philosopher Horace M. Kallen noted that one feature of modern life was universally exempted from condemnation: "Education is the one institution of industrial society to which its sachems and sages 'point with pride,' its rebels and prophets with hope."[2]

At the same time education implied a heroic, tutelary role for the public-spirited intellectuals themselves. Their functions of thought, investigation, and criticism were, in this reckoning, not marginal activities but central to the public's own regeneration. Turn-of-the-century publicists took up with enthusiasm the Enlightenment view of the intellectual. As economist E. R. A. Seligman would write of the intellectual's role, "The scholar must possess priestly qualities and fulfill priestly functions, including political activity. His knowledge, as Fichte says, 'should be truly applied for society's use; he should get people to feel their true needs and acquaint them with the means of their satisfaction.'"[3] William James similarly offered a heroic view of the scholar-democrat. The constant danger of democracy, he advised, was that the people "will choose poorly." Yet the antidote to such democratic "self-poisoning," according to James, was just as surely available in the form of a leadership class drawn from the college-educated: "Individuals of genius show the way, and set the patterns, which common people then adopt and follow."[4] Even an avowed socialist who disparaged the "enormous waste of intellectual potentialities" evident in a society divided between "idlers" and "drudges" might find fulfillment in the vision of universal education, "at once labourious and leisurely."[5] Perhaps never before or since have American scholars felt themselves, as a group, so confidently bound and allied to the interests not merely of Truth, but of the Multitude, and in particular the working classes and the dispossessed. If America's future lay unavoidably with the awakening of its urban, immigrant millions, then the intellectuals, via the chemistry of education and enlightened public policy, would be the bell-ringers. "Publicity," Progressive intellectuals would readily have agreed with Britain's Jeremy Bentham, "is the very soul of justice."[6]

Yet the confidence of the Progressive intellectual generation (here defined as those thinkers who came of age between 1890 and 1918)

truth + the dem multitude via education.

would be sorely tested. On both intellectual and political grounds, they would discover that it was one thing to mouth democratic principles and quite another to demonstrate that they could work in daily life. Moreover, their own role in the pageant of democratic citizenship would prove equally problematic. What responsibility, if any, did the best educated owe to those with less learning, and by what means could they discharge such an obligation? In this book I hope first to pursue such issues at the broad and synthetic level, then to deepen the exploration with more intimate studies of individual cases. In this first chapter, I sketch an overview of the problem, documenting the early (if naive and contradictory) faith of intellectuals in democracy, examining the several streams of disenchantment that crystallized in the 1920s, and concluding with the mixed experience of the most ambitious attempts to create a common enterprise among workers and intellectuals.

PERHAPS THE earliest harbinger of democratic optimism among the Progressive intellectual generation was Lester Frank Ward. This Civil War veteran, whose professional credentials included fieldwork for the U.S. Geological Survey and a chaired professorship in sociology at Brown University from 1906 until his death in 1916, is undoubtedly best known as the champion of "reform Darwinism." Insisting that human development could control rather than be controlled by the social environment, Ward's ideal of "sociocracy" represented the summa of systematic governmental planning on behalf of human welfare. To get there required, above all, sweeping educational reform. "The great demand of the world," declared Ward, "is knowledge. The great problem is the equalization of intelligence, to put all knowledge in possession of every human being." Without rejecting the idea of individual hereditary differences, Ward stoutly rejected all assumptions of group differences based on race, class, or sex superiority: a difference in "mental equipment," not a difference in "intellect," separated the "intelligent class" from the "intellectually disinherited":

> Or, to state it more clearly, if the same individuals who constitute the intelligent class at any time or place had been surrounded from their birth by exactly the same conditions that have surrounded the lowest

Ward strong for nurture

stratum of society, they would have inevitably found themselves in that stratum; and if an equal number taken at random of the lowest stratum of society had been surrounded from their birth by exactly the same conditions by which the intelligent class have been surrounded, they would in fact have constituted the intelligent class instead of the particular individuals who happen actually to constitute it. In other words, class distinctions in society are wholly artificial, depend entirely on environing conditions, and are in no sense due to differences in native capacity.[7]

Among a new generation of radical social scientists, Ward's personal influence was most deeply stamped on Edward A. Ross. Ross, who like Ward grew up in rural Iowa, took a Ph.D. in political economy under Richard T. Ely at Johns Hopkins but "gazed with awe" at the author of *Dynamic Sociology* when he first met him at American Economic Association meetings in 1890. Ross married Ward's niece two years later, dedicated his major work to "my Master," and went on to name two of his children after "Uncle Lester."[8] Published a year after Ross's dismissal from Stanford for unacceptable political expressions, *Social Control* (1901) combined a zeal for reform with a functional description of the agents of order in an industrial society. Ross was particularly anxious to distinguish the possibilities of a rational and democratic ordering principle (what he called "social control") from the brute force and coercion of "class control." Familiar with the irrational-crowd theories of European psychologists such as Gustave Le Bon and Scipio Sighele, Ross, following Ward, believed that democratic political structures and positive government could counteract the danger of popular rule: strengthened by the intellectuals' guidance, the "public" would keep the "crowd" or mob mind at bay.[9]

If secular humanism offered one prop to democratic educational change, a more widespread stimulus was religion. In his interpretation of progressivism as "a climate of creativity," historian Robert M. Crunden has highlighted the diffusion of Protestant moral values into secular professions including social work, journalism, academia, the law, and politics.[10] Creative individuals from middle-class backgrounds, Crunden argues, found conventional outlets inadequate for the quest for religious perfectionism instilled in them during childhood and thus transformed middle-class occupations along a socially conscientious or "progressive" axis. The influence of religion for many such figures—including such influential thinkers as philosopher-psychologists William James, George Herbert Mead, and John Dewey as well as settlement house founder Jane Addams—as adults might be no more than implicit but, in Crunden's words, "it was always there."[11]

Whether secular or religious in nature, the ethical inspiration of a new generation of intellectuals pulled them inexorably towards commitment to a democratic culture. Best developed in the pragmatic philosophy of the period, an emphasis on experience connected knowledge not to formalist abstractions or dogma but to a realm of voluntary action, resting on the imperative of active citizenship and inclining almost as a corollary toward the democratic process and veneration of the public sphere.[12] If knowledge (as Dewey argued) was a function of association and communication, not formalist abstraction, then the freedom and vitality of the public sphere, from basic educational institutions through political decision-making, were the ultimate measure of a society's achievement.[13]

The development of a democratic culture, for example, drove John Dewey's much-celebrated ideas about educational reform. For Dewey the school perhaps most intimately connected the lives of the intellectual reformer and the citizen-to-be. In keeping with his larger democratic vision, he thus called on the public schools to be unhooked from their "medieval" moorings and become reconnected to the experiential life of the community:

> The introduction of active occupations, of nature-study, of elementary science, of art, of history; the relegation of the merely symbolic and formal to a secondary position; the change in the moral school atmosphere, in the relation of pupils and teachers—of discipline; the introduction of more active, expressive, and self-directing factors—all these are not mere accidents, they are necessities of the larger social evolution . . . When the school introduces and trains each child of society into membership within such a little community, saturating him with the spirit of service, and providing him with the instruments of effective self-direction, we shall have the deepest and best guaranty of a larger society which is worthy, lovely, and harmonious.[14]

What Dewey called the "spirit of service" echoed broadly in the appeals of contemporary reformers. Rule by the people could work, such thinking suggested, to the degree that individual citizens lifted both their heads and their hearts to concern themselves with the common good.

For Progressives, therefore, democracy depended on the self-cultivation of the citizen as active student. "No man and no mind was ever emancipated by being left alone," wrote Dewey.[15] Not only external constraints but also habit—what James called "the enormous fly-wheel of society"—limited the application of rational inquiry to new ways of living. "We dream beyond the limits of use and wont, but only rarely does revery become a source of acts which break bounds."[16] As Dewey argued, hope lay in the forms of scientific inquiry. Its more self-conscious and more technical vocabulary at once rendered it more promising than "floating, volatile, and accidentally snatched up opinions" yet, for the same reasons, required "more ability to use and understand it than to get skill in any other instrumentalities possessed by man."[17] Dewey's own early failed experiment with *Thought News*—a collaboration among social scientists to get beyond the superficialities of newspaper headlines and apply sociological theory to current affairs—and historian James Harvey Robinson's commitment to the popularization of science education reflect the priority that a generation of reformers placed on the medium of public opinion and popular education as keys to democratic progress.[18]

Even when working outside his immediate influence, many writers of the period shared Dewey's commitment to democratic intellectual citizenship, to truth as less a form of discovery than a form of association and communication in the solving of practical problems.[19] The classics of both social science and muckraking journalism for the period—including Charles Beard's *An Economic Interpretation of the of the Constitution*, John R. Commons's *Documentary History of American Industrial Society*, Ida Tarbell's *History of Standard Oil Company*, Jacob Riis's *How the Other Half Lives*, Lincoln Steffens's *Shame of the Cities*, Florence Kelley et al.'s *Hull House Maps and Papers*, W. E. B. Du Bois's *The Philadelphia Negro*—were all distinguished by their emphasis on facts over general interpretation. In each a passionate spirit of advocacy was submerged in a confident

expectation that the public could learn, and draw appropriate conclusions, from a scientific treatment of the facts.[20]

Dewey's University of Michigan colleague Charles Horton Cooley
offered theoretical justification for such confidence. The son of a distinguished jurist and professor of law, and a man who spent virtually his entire life on the Ann Arbor campus, Cooley read widely in
economics and philosophy before settling on a career as professor of
sociology.[21] In *Social Organization: A Study of the Larger Mind* (1909)
Cooley determined to refute critics of democracy, those who cast aspersions on "the organized sway of public opinion." "No mere ag-
gregate of separate individual judgments," public opinion was to
Cooley a rational and positive thing, "a cooperative product of communication and reciprocal influence." Distinguishing transient
"popular impression" from "mature opinion," Cooley believed people capable of reaching a sound, "organic social judgment" after sustained discussion and debate. It was democratic practice itself, he argued, that offered the best defense against the "wild impulses of a
rabble," a veritable "training in judgment and self-control." In upholding the capacity for democratic rule, Cooley likewise echoed the
disdain of many of his social science contemporaries for the worship
of the free market: "It would be fatuous," he wrote, "to assume that
the market process expresses the *good* of society. The demand on
which it is based is a turbid current coming down from the past . . .
To accept this stream as pure and to reform only the mechanism of
distribution would be as if a city drawing its drinking water from a
polluted river should expect to escape typhoid by using clean
pipes."[22]

Popular political commentary shared basic assumptions with the
scholarly research of the period. Not surprisingly, the three most famous political journalists of the Progressive Era—Herbert Croly,
Walter Weyl, and Walter Lippmann, who together organized the
New Republic in 1914—all borrowed from a fund of pragmatist assumptions in elaborating variations of a prewar social democratic vision. If Croly's *The Promise of American Life* (1909) juxtaposed a call
for a pragmatic, experimental state with an appeal for "exceptional
fellow countrymen" to give the common citizen "acceptable examples of heroism and saintliness," his *Progressive Democracy* (1914),
with a positive nod toward the dreams of contemporary radical syn-

dicalists, expressed a more full-hearted faith in the ordinary citizenry.[23] Weyl's *The New Democracy* (1912) was, even more than Croly's original effort, a pragmatic critique of earlier liberal orthodoxy. Political progress in the United States, he argued, was hindered "by ancient political ideals which still cumber . . . modern brains, by political heirlooms of revered—but dead—ancestors." Out of America's relative abundance, however, had come the belief in "a full life for all the members of society," and this idea offered a new "impetus for action."[24] Of all contemporary writers, journalist Walter Lippmann, who like Croly had encountered William James while a student at Harvard, ultimately offered the most discerning application of the pragmatic method to politics. "Every abstraction," wrote Lippmann in *A Preface to Politics* (1913), "every rule of conduct, every constitution, every law and social arrangement, is an instrument that has no value in itself."[25] A year later, in *Drift and Mastery*, Lippmann abandoned his previous psychological aestheticism, which rooted individual choices in a wave of Bergsonian feeling, in favor of a "scientific experimentalism" that owed much to Dewey.[26]

If John Dewey best expressed the precepts for democratic commitments among intellectuals, Jane Addams likely offered their most thorough-going example. Indeed, the two intellectual activists openly acknowledged a mutual debt. Dewey was a collaborator with Addams's Hull House, serving on the board of directors and completing field work under the auspices of the settlement house. His *School and Society* (1900), published two years before her own statement of social philosophy, *Democracy and Social Ethics*, had an immediate impact on her thinking. That "little yellow-covered book," she noted, "made so clear the necessity for individualizing each child that it is quite fair, I think, to say that his insistence upon an atmosphere of freedom and confidence between the teacher and pupil, of a common interest in the life they led together, profoundly affected all similar relationships, certainly those between the social worker and his client."[27]

Dewey, for his part, recognized in Addams's "primitive affection" for the common people a practical egalitarianism previously missing from formal democratic theory. "Miss Addams," he wrote, "had a deep feeling that the simple, the 'humble' peoples of the earth are those in whom primitive impulses of friendly affection are the least spoiled, the most spontaneous. Her faith in democracy was indissolubly associated with this belief. It permeates what she wrote because it was part of the life she lived from day to day."[28]

Beginning with the pragmatists' insistence on knowing through experience, Addams may be said to have further democratized Dewey's theories on two grounds. First, she insisted that social knowledge—vital to both the "intellectual classes" and the worker-citizen—could not be adequately gleaned from a formal tradition of academic training tied to genteel lifestyles. This point, of course, was related to Addams's initial concern with "a fast-growing number of cultivated young people who have no recognized outlet for their active faculties . . . They hear constantly of the great social maladjustment, but no way is provided for them to change it, and their uselessness hangs about heavily." The settlement house, Addams declared in 1892, was thus "an attempt to relieve, at the same time, the overaccumulation at one end of society and the destitution at the other."[29] The experiment of the settlement, moreover, served not just to create a useful function for the conscientious upper middle class, but to devise a new standard of "social learning." Addams argued that the very tools that the educated classes might bring to the industrial laborer had been hopelessly tarnished by the remoteness of intellectual work from ordinary life. "The same tendency to division of labor [as found in the workplace] has also produced over-specialization in scholarship, with the sad result that when the scholar attempts to minister to a worker, he gives him the result of more specialization rather than an offset from it. He cannot bring healing and solace because he himself is suffering from the same disease."[30] Rather than sit in studies and meditate, the new scholar-activists would "drink at the wells of human experience."[31] The Hull House project, concludes historian Dorothy Ross, pointed towards an "interpretive sociology" that would combine domestic and romantic influences as well as Deweyan pragmatism and that would be distinct from the "scientistic" tendencies of the discipline's mainstream academic discourse.[32]

Second, in celebrating the capacities and the emergent social standard visible among urban working people, Addams broadly identified the task of the settlement activists in immigrant neighborhoods with labor-centered political alternatives in England and the United States:

> These quarters continually confound us by their manifestations of altruism. It may be that we are surprised simply because we fail to comprehend that the individual, under such pressure, must shape his life with some reference to the demands of social justice, not only to avoid crushing the little folk about him, but in order to save himself from death by crushing . . . We are often told that men under this pressure of life become calloused and cynical, whereas anyone who lives with them knows that they are sentimental and compassionate.[33]

The so-called fighting rabble or quarrelsome mob of conventional middle-class opinion were transformed in Addams's gaze into potentially world-saving "kindly citizens" "through the [democratic] pressure of a cosmopolitan neighborhood."[34]

Once given the ethical field of force Addams prescribed, the social role of the intellectual became obvious. If the laboring poor were society's diamonds in the rough, the intellectual's task was to offer just enough polish of education to help workers recognize their inherent social value and raise their expectations "to imagine, to design, [and] to aspire."[35] It was no accident, therefore, that of all her far-flung initiatives, Addams's personal favorite was the Working People's Social Science Club established at Hull House. Here was the unity between Thought and Action, Science and Democracy, to which the true pragmatist aspired.[36] Similarly, progressive ideas on education, in Addams's eyes, reached fulfillment in the Hull House Labor Museum, where Russian women garment workers displayed to visitors the various historical stages of spinning and weaving: "Far beyond its direct educational value, we prize it [the museum] because it so often puts the immigrants into the position of teachers . . . [F]rom having been stupidly entertained, they themselves did the entertaining."[37]

The settlement house offered institutional expression to the ideal of symbiotic relationships between science and democracy, intellectuals and workers. Vida Scudder, Wellesley College literary scholar and social reformer who helped establish the College Settlement Association in 1887, gave voice to the moral imperative that accompanied such ideals in her novel, *A Listener in Babel* (1903), in which Hilda Lathrop, a young woman trained by the settlement experience, decides to forsake a genteel future in favor of entering factory work, aiming to redesign it to human scale:

> I do believe at times that the intellectual classes, so-called, will never be healthy again until they return to a more natural life, including some productive labor with their hands. My belief is intermittent, however. But when it fails, another takes its place. If manual work is a blessing, not a curse, I want my share of it; if it is a curse, not a blessing, I ought to take my turn . . . Horror of our industrial conditions has deepened on me as I came near them . . . but I cannot content myself with general theory . . . still less with general attack . . . The beautiful only exists as it is found in use, as it springs from the common life of all and ministers to the common life of all. That is the kind of beauty for the lack of which America perishes.[38]

Altogether, a distinctive women's intellectual culture perhaps best preserved the democratic and reform-oriented purpose of social science pioneers into the early twentieth century. To be sure, the women's culture emerged in part by default and was not without its own blemishes. On the one hand, middle-class female intellectuals, shut out of the upper echelons of academic social science, generally connected to institutions (such as settlement houses and government agencies) that involved more continuous, direct contact with working people—particularly the working poor—than their male colleagues. When the Hull House staff assembled for what they labeled only partly in jest "faculty meetings," they were practicing a kind of intellectual activism that would become increasingly rare in university circles.[39] While women graduates were finding positions either entirely outside or on the margins of academic life, Marion Talbot, the University of Chicago's dean of women, would regret in 1916 that the "University itself does not take up more actively the social needs of the community and use [women's] skills in connection with them."[40]

On the other hand, women as intellectual reformers often tended toward an immodest respect for their own understanding of the needs of immigrants and the working poor. As historian Ellen Fitzpatrick has commented on the attitude of University of Chicago graduate and immigration reformer Frances Kellor, "If social policy was best formulated by experts, average citizens could do little more than attend to the superior judgment of those in command."[41] Similarly, Sophonisba Breckinridge, from her position at the University of Chicago's School of Civics, would counsel Hull House against direct handouts to tramps: "It is of course a very easy thing to give a man who asks for a meal some food and send him on, but it is very bad for the man. If we are going to feed him, we ought, of course, to find out why he is tramping, and after investigating put him in a way of getting work. This requires, however, a good deal of specialized knowledge and organized effort."[42] In short, among American social work and social settlement reformers, as among their British progenitors, the colonial metaphor of teaching the "natives" how to behave, however rationalized within prescriptions of neutral expertise, insinuated itself into a discourse of neighborliness, self-sacrificing service, and social partnership.[43]

It was not only social settlements but socialists (sometimes overlapping categories, to be sure) who took as their chief task the educational awakening of the working-class public. Ex–iron molder and leading Chicago socialist lecturer Arthur M. Lewis popularized the wisdom of such contemporaries as Lester Frank Ward, Richard Ely, and Karl Marx. Regularly drawing overflow crowds to his Sunday lectures on science in Chicago's Garrick Theatre between 1907 and 1915, Lewis was only one of many contemporaries who sought to transfer the fruits of a higher learning to a laboring audience.[44] For such thinkers the educational process, whether formal or informal, beckoned as an open door to radical, even revolutionary, social transformation. The hopes of many such middle-class radicals were summed up by a Miss E. F. Andrews of Montgomery, Alabama, writing in the *International Socialist Review* in 1901. Refuting the aspersions sometimes cast upon the abilities of the industrial masses, Andrews lamented the "enormous waste of intellectual potentialities of the race" lost to long hours and lack of educational opportunity. "Intellectual achievement," Andrews insisted in terms little removed from Ward's own, "is a matter of opportunity as well as of ability and requires a reasonable amount of leisure and well-being for success. Imagine a street railway conductor working eighteen hours a day and actually not seeing enough of his children to know them by sight, producing a work of genius! . . . . Imagine

Shakespeare set to driving a nail machine at twelve years of age; where would Hamlet's soliloquy be?"[45] Assuming common aspirations as well as common capacity among the populace, progressive intellectuals set for themselves a clear, if naive, agenda: discover the truth (or, in a more pragmatic sense, the *process* of truth-finding), communicate this knowledge to the people, and let the people (by freedom of association and the suffrage) thereby change the world.

naive

Indeed, for some Progressives the gap between popular capacity and popular enlightenment seemed already to have narrowed remarkably. In Chicago, for example, where approximately half the city's wage earners were organized in trade unions by 1903, teacher and student might even change places. Chicago settlement leader and theologian Graham Taylor exulted in 1904 in the mass movement of trade unionists who formed the vanguard of an effort to municipalize the city's streetcars: "Far from being ignorantly inconsiderate, these workmen voters are practically the only organized bodies of citizens who made any consecutive effort to understand and publicly discuss the [transportation-related] issues involved. They have been threshing out . . . the points of general public policy . . . for three or four years in every labor union and in open public meetings."[46] Journalist Hutchins Hapgood agreed: "Take any Chicago personage of importance whatever his profession or his position, and somehow or other he has been influenced by the spirit of the intellectual proletariat."[47]

Perhaps belief in the power of education more than any other single factor defined the Progressive Era intellectuals' hopes for a democratic future. No matter what one's background or occupation, so the logic went, common sense equipped with the "facts" prepared one for full and active citizenship. Even at its most generous, as we have seen with the female political culture of the settlement house, such faith in education carried with it the dangers of condescension. In other circumstances, the "education" test for citizenship could go beyond arrogance to categorical exclusion of whole groups of people. Thus it was that progressive intellectuals tended to vacillate on issues of nativism and racial exclusion.

The case of Edward A. Ross is particularly suggestive here. During the early years of the twentieth century, Ross's descriptions of the immigrant working class, while always race conscious, reflected a

widespread faith in education + the facts.

strong confidence in the assimilative capacity of the culture. Yet evidence of the stubborn persistence of immigrant community mores ultimately dismayed Ross, tipping the balance in his analysis of forces affecting American life from environmental (i.e., subject to education) to hereditary (i.e., permanent) ones. By 1912, he had entered the front ranks of immigration restrictionists, convinced that the unrestricted flow of southern and eastern Europeans would lead to Anglo-Saxon "race suicide."[48]

Whatever the long-term conceptual shortcomings of the early Progressive social scientists and political commentators, their efforts generally reflected a confidence that they could communicate and connect with a democratic public dominated by an ethnically polyglot working class. Whether drawing on actual social experience (via movements such as the Knights of Labor, settlement house programs, public lectures, and the streetcar municipalization crusade) or projecting their own rationalist or millenarian hopes for the future, these reform-minded intellectual leaders upheld a remarkably sanguine view of the potential of industrial society. For such activists, "public intellectual" would doubtlessly have seemed an oddly redundant term.

THIS CONFIDENT embrace of the democratic public among reform-minded intellectuals, however, was soon interrupted. Beginning before World War I and continuing through the decade of the twenties, a cloud of disillusionment with the processes of popular self-government and even the very concept of the democratic will spread thickly over the centers of higher learning in America.[49] The causes were several, but they had a common denominator. Images of mass behavior, as reflected in electioneering, war fever, Army intelligence tests, postwar reaction, or simply the display of "lowbrow" tastes reflected in commercialized popular culture, convinced many observers that public opinion was not the stuff of which dreams of progress could be made.[50] The tone of intellectual pronouncements gradually shifted from a confident (if somewhat presumptuous) association with the democratic public to feelings of concern, revulsion, and even open resistance to the will of the nonintellectual multitude.

From the beginning, the process of disillusionment carried a certain inner ironic logic. The rise of Progressive Era intellectuals had

intells lose faith in the masses c. 1914-30

in part depended on the decline of an earlier politics of ritual partisan loyalty as the determining force in political behavior. In particular, the fracturing of the anti-ideological Third Electoral System—catalyzed by the 1890s depression and accompanying rise of Populism and antimonopoly sentiment—created an opening for more issue-oriented, information-centered political campaigns.[51] As expressed in labor-progressive municipal alliances of the 1890s and continuing through the claims of the La Follette campaign in Wisconsin, Roosevelt's New Nationalism, and even Wilson's New Freedom, appeal to the direct political voice of the people (through petition, referendum, recall, direct election of senators, and ultimately the direct presidential primary in 1912) complimented or, perhaps more accurately, sustained a wide-ranging and diverse set of agitations for economic, regulatory, and social welfare reforms. The "consent of the governed," as Stow Persons once neatly explained, had long been "veiled" by America's constitutional republican system. Now, however, horrified reaction to political bossism and the abuses of industrial capitalism combined in renewed appeal to the inherent powers of the People.[52]

The very invocation of the larger public interest, of course, was mediated by those with communication skills. As publicists, educators, and muckrakers (a role initially praised and later criticized by Theodore Roosevelt), the intellectuals at once advocated for a transfer of political and economic power to the people and unselfconsciously tutored the public in its proper responsibilities as a sovereign power. A fetching innocence (or was it merely self-delusion?) thus surrounded the prewar ideal of public opinion and intellectual opinion-shapers as the natural allies of the common people.

Even before the war, there were intimations that the democratic revival within the Progressive political culture had come at a certain cost. The very channels by which intellectual reformers made their way into the public sphere also nourished other powerful actors. According to George Kibbe Turner in the reform-minded *McClure's*, Theodore Roosevelt had first perfected the pattern of "manufacturing public opinion":

> Roosevelt, schooled in publicity for twenty years in New York and Washington and Albany, called in the reporters, and, from that time

on, through his two terms, ruled the newspapers of the country from their front pages. He was the great impressionist in national news; every day he threw the color that he wanted on the minds of the newspaper-reading public . . . The democracy of the printing press had come; and Roosevelt was its founder.[53]

The success of "democratic" reforms, coolly reported Turner, actually advanced the patterns of manipulation. The presidential preference primary of 1912, for example, first accommodated the professional press agent, a figure who heretofore had practiced promotional arts in the theatrical and literary worlds.[54] In the new political circumstances, "candidates, not parties, must introduce themselves directly to the voters—and incidentally finance the machinery for doing so." The Progressives assumed a vanguard role in this process. The campaign of Senator Robert La Follette, for example, aided by Gifford Pinchot, "a master and promoter of political publicity," and the money of Chicago multimillionaire Charles R. Crane cranked up an unprecedented publicity operation, occupying "a dozen rooms and forty to fifty employees." And La Follette's campaign was nothing compared to the subsequent "million dollar" fracas within the Republican Party between Taft and Roosevelt. The system, argued Turner, clearly depended on big individual backers doling out huge sums of money. "Now everybody who reads understands what this means. It means simply the underwriting of presidential candidates for hundreds of thousands of dollars—exactly as a bond issue is underwritten before it is offered to the general public."[55]

Turner's alarm at the market in political information touched a common nerve among radical progressives. That public opinion could be bought and sold, or treated by private interests as an investment like any other, threatened the integrity of the democratic process. This antimonopoly critique of the corruption of the public sphere reached its peak in the report of the Commission on Industrial Relations, 1912–1915, which denounced both the "lies" of public relations men, who served corporate interests, and even the potential corruption of scholarly research, reflected in universities endowed by private foundations.[56] Yet in presenting the people as an innocent lamb before the depredations of outside interests,

Rise of irrationalism theory. People can't be trusted

such critiques remained faithful to the basic early Progressive faith in the virtues of the public and the democratic process.

To be sure, democratic-progressive appeals to a rational public ignored a substantial body of accumulated intellectual commentary that cast doubt on the very capacity of plebian self-rule. British conservative thinkers from Edmund Burke (1790) to Walter Bagehot (1872) and Sir Henry Maine (1885) had assailed the bedrock concept of the will of the people as an illusion or worse.[57] Building further on irrationalist psychology at the turn of the century, continental theorists such as Gustave Le Bon, Georges Sorel, Vilfredo Pareto, and Gaetano Mosca adopted openly elitist political models, supposedly more in keeping with the realities "behind the fictions of political action."[58] If American political scholarship (as produced both by native and foreign talents) was less likely to venture down such tracks, its empirical findings nevertheless also lent credence to grave doubts about the efficacy of the democratic process. Even the more sympathetic of earlier nineteenth-century observers from Alexis de Tocqueville to James Bryce had contrasted the self-images of America's democratic institutions with its effective working principles.[59] Subsequent analyses, whether by liberal commentators like E. L. Godkin (1896) or comparative political scientists such as Moisei Ostrogorski (1902), furthered the development of a new realism in the study of political behavior.[60] On the whole, as historian Martin J. Wiener has summarized, the new scholarship revealed gaping holes in democratic theory: "the excessive faith in elections, the lack of provision for the necessity of organizing the electorate, the lack of foresight about the increasing difficulty of generating public interest in an ever larger and more complex society."[61] Harvard's patrician president, A. Lawrence Lowell, drawing on the new realism and the psychological insights of William James on political behavior, concluded by 1913 that ordinary citizens were incapable of coping with an increasingly complex society:

> The amount of knowledge needed for the administration of public affairs is increasing more rapidly than the diffusion of such knowledge, and . . . this is lessening the capacity of the ordinary citizen to form an opinion of his own on the various matters that arise in conducting the government . . . This is particularly true where the special knowledge

of experts is involved, because it is not easy for the community at large to weigh expert opinion. Few things are, in fact, more difficult, or require greater experience: and yet the number of questions on which the advice of experts is indispensable grows with every advance in technical knowledge and mechanical invention.[62]

A more formidable challenge to the classic democratic faith of the Progressives, because it emanated from a source remarkably like themselves, were the writings of the British Fabians. These middle-class radicals—most notably Sidney and Beatrice Webb, George Bernard Shaw, Graham Wallas, and briefly H. G. Wells—by the late 1890s had already begun to turn away from their youthful trust in the enfranchised proletariat toward a harder-edged commitment to a collectivism of experts. Discouraging election turnouts and the subsequent jingoism of the Boer War convinced Wallas, in particular, of the fundamental inadequacy of the rational-Enlightenment view of politics. A visit to the United States combined with his extended reading of political science on both sides of the Atlantic revealed to him a basic delusion common to democratic culture: the assumption "that all eyes can see the stage of public action, and, consequently, that each voter can at any moment, pronounce an unbiased opinion on any point required."[63] Wallas's Fabian colleague Leonard Hobhouse put it more bluntly: "The man-in-the-street is the man in a hurry; the man who has not time to think and will not take the trouble to do so if has the time. He is the faithful reflex of the popular sheet and the shouting newsboy."[64]

Within American Progressive ranks, Walter Lippmann was the first to bundle such criticisms into a sustained challenge to the democratic faith. Studying at Harvard (his class of 1910 also included John Reed and T. S. Eliot), the young Lippmann struggled to reconcile his socialist ardor with the intellectual skepticism he imbibed directly from Lowell, William James, and the visiting Wallas. Yet after a brief stint as an assistant for Rev. George Lunn, the socialist mayor of Schenectady, Lippmann resigned, disgusted by both the pettiness and the caution of Lunn's realpolitik. Like his college mentors, however, Lippmann also felt that the source of the problem was deeper than mistaken strategy or weak-kneed leadership. How connected were the ideals of middle-class socialists with the perspective of the ordinary worker or voter? Lippmann likened the radical reformers to "Peer Gynt struggling against the formless Byg . . . we were struggling with the unwatered hinterland of the citizens of Schenectady." He was put off by the "great dull mass of people who just don't care." This astringent critique of the popular political culture took more formal shape in *A Preface to Politics* the following year. In this book the bravado of the young radical intellectual, in full embrace of the modernist sensibility, pointedly conflicted with the clichés of the democratic creed; already, Lippmann was extolling the cool reason of scientific managers and experts over the tyranny of the majority.[65]

World War I and its aftermath turned Lippmann from radical curmudgeon to neoconservative. As did several of his young Progressive colleagues, Lippmann worked as a propagandist in charge of publications for the information office of Newton Baker's War Department, a kind of in-house competitor to George Creel's Committee on Public Information. Let down like most "war intellectuals" with the terms at Versailles (Lippmann joined the rest of the *New Republic*'s editors in a bitter break with President Wilson in 1919), he emerged from government service seemingly determined not to be taken in again.[66] In three books—*Liberty and the News* (1920), *Public Opinion* (1922), and *The Phantom Public* (1925)—Lippmann delivered what Dewey judged "perhaps the most effective indictment of democracy as currently conceived ever penned."[67] Beginning with a condemnation of the role of the wartime press for its "manufacture of consent," Lippmann entered ever deeper waters, ultimately questioning the capacity of a democratic citizenry truly to govern themselves. In contemporary life, according to Lippmann, the individual citizen was no longer a real participant in public affairs but "rather like a deaf spectator in the back row, who ought to keep his mind on the mystery off there, but cannot quite manage to keep awake . . . In the cold light of experience he knows that his sovereignty is a fiction. He reigns in theory, but in fact he does not govern."[68]

The susceptibility of the mass public to outside manipulation challenged the early ideals of a growing number of intellectual reformers.[69] Even the irrepressible George Creel by 1924 had come to despair of reaching a serious public: "The very *existence* of a forceful, effective public opinion is much to be doubted," he admitted, adding, "It is these joined causes—the indecencies of partisanship, the noise and unintelligibility of a large portion of the press, the lack of trust-worthy information, the dreary routine of mud-slinging that passes for political discussion—that have killed public opinion, or rather deafened it, confused it, bored it, disgusted it."[70] The apparent indif-ference of the public to the appeals of reform intellectuals convinced the latter of the depravity of the former. A forerunner to the theo-retical critique of mass culture later associated with the émigré intel-lectuals from the Frankfurt Institute for Social Research, the criticism of the postwar intellectuals characteristically seized on the develop-ment of propaganda, public relations, and the art of the "ballyhoo" as confirmation of popular depravity. "Publicity, the hope of the Pro-gressive Era," as historian Lee W. Heubner has written, "became pro-paganda, the scourge of the twenties."[71]

Cultivation of this new, disenchanted view of the public was aided by the claims of opinion manipulators themselves. The self-reflection of public relations visionary Edward L. Bernays, for ex-ample, offered abundant confirmation of Lippmann's worst fears. The son of Ely Bernays, a wealthy Viennese-Jewish grain merchant, and Anna Freud, sister of the great psychoanalyst, Edward Bernays parlayed a career of specialized writing and press agentry into great wealth. Rather than a source of later regret, Bernays's service on the Creel Committee during World War I (after managing the U.S. tours of Diaghilev's Russian Ballet and the great Caruso) revealed to him the unlimited potential of the instruments of public relations: "It was the war," he stated proudly, "which opened the eyes of the in-telligent few in all departments of life to the possibilities of regi-menting the public mind."[72] Bernays quickly entered the front ranks of corporate promoters, with Ivory Soap, the American Tobacco Company, and Thomas Edison among his many celebrated clients. Bernays, moreover, was not merely a doer but a philoso-pher. Seeking to set his work within a larger context, Bernays cited Lippmann as well as the earlier French psychologists for discovering the dynamics of mass behavior in industrial society. "These discus-sions of public opinion," Bernays noted, wanted only "the applica-tion of their findings to everyday use. None had taken up the work-ing relationship between private policies and practice and public opinion."[73] No one, that is, until Bernays, in *Crystallizing Public Opinion* (1923) and *Propaganda* (1928).

Where Lippmann and others had expressed foreboding before the decline of the autonomous individual, Bernays saw not only the means of professional opportunity but also a substitute path to social order. While democracy had initially "uprooted kings" and "put power in the hands of the people," "reaction," he stated matter-of-factly, "has set in." A minority "has discovered a powerful help in influencing majorities"; it was now "possible to mold the mind of the masses that they will throw their newly gained strength in the desired direction." Propaganda, in short, had emerged as "the executive arm of the invisible government." Moreover, "in the present structure of society, this practice is inevitable." Summarizing an extended literature with an unperturbed, even cheery, cogency, Bernays concluded that "instead of a mind universal literacy has given [the common man] rubber stamps." The "mind of the people" is "made up for it by the group leaders in whom it believes and those persons who understand the manipulation of public opinion. It is composed of inherited prejudices and symbols and clichés and verbal formulas supplied to them by their leaders."[74] Instead of quaking before the irrationalism of the masses (or looking, as Lippmann did, for awkward substitutes to formal democratic authority), Bernays looked happily to the harnessing of public opinion by public relations professionals in the service of established interests.

The view of the public as manipulable consumers gained wide currency in the 1920s.[75] Historian T. J. Jackson Lears, for example, has skillfully dissected the career of advertiser-evangelist Bruce Barton, who found a kind of missionary moralism in converting the masses to his message of therapeutic self-fulfillment. What seems most striking, however, is less the message itself than the new emphasis on the arts of the messenger. In his classic *The Man Nobody Knows* (1925), Barton extolled Jesus Christ primarily as a great salesman, "the most successful advertising man in history."[76] In a similar manner, historian Ralph Volney Harlow pursued the career of Founding Father Samuel Adams as "promoter of the American Revolution," the most important of a group of agents "devoted to the task of convincing the people that they were oppressed, and in

Bruce Barton

organizing them so that they could give point to their feelings." Within such a framework, the leader became less the representative of the people than master manipulator. "The Revolution," in Harlow's terms, "was not a spontaneous movement, the result of a genuine popular uprising, but rather the product of something not so very different from agitation and propaganda."[77]

In certain respects, the new attitude was not unconnected to the initial progressive thrust, which emphasized the enlightened role of reformer vis-à-vis the people—a view of the intellectual as a kind of electrical tripwire, whose purpose was to activate the citizenry to a sense of its responsibilities. Yet there was an important difference. In seeking to tap, as George Creel put it, the "anger of an aroused people," the prewar muckraker (or progressive educator) assumed a basic commonality of thought process between teacher and student. Increasingly, the progressive's postwar counterpart affected a more distanced ennui and scarcely disguised contempt for the "impulses, habits, emotions" characteristic of Bernays's group mind.[78]

It was almost inevitable that John Dewey should respond to the postwar disenchantment with the democratic public. Associated more than anyone else with optimistic hopes for education and social change among both prewar progressives and socialists, Dewey was himself obviously shaken by both the war and the discomforting new intellectual climate. In two brief reviews of Lippmann's writing and then in a series of lectures published as *The Public and Its Problems* (1927), Dewey attempted to resolidify the foundations of a democratic, reform faith. The weakness of his effort testifies to the strength of the countervailing winds, and to the ultimate loss of direction of democratic theory in the hands of American intellectuals.

While acknowledging that Lippmann had "thrown into clearer relief than any other writer the fundamental difficulty of democracy," Dewey struggled to salvage the baby of democracy from the bathwater of consumer culture.[79] Yet in his general open-mindedness, tolerance for dissent, and respect for Lippmann's intelligence, Dewey also betrayed a Panglossian capacity to underestimate an intellectual threat to his own principles. Such a hypothesis, at least, helps to explain how Dewey could read Lippmann's explicit attack on popular rule as "in reality a statement of faith in a pruned and

[handwritten note: Dewey grudgingly admits that Lippmann has a point!]

temperate democratic theory" and even compare Lippmann's trust in the management of public affairs by nonpolitical insiders to the model of guild socialism! Sticking doggedly to his faith in the basic structures of American society, Dewey was on stronger ground in questioning Lippmann's solution to the influence of "stupidity, intolerance, bullheadedness and bad education" on public affairs. Could (and did) not such perversions of rationality as easily emanate from church or monarchical (or any other elitist) authority as from the people? But in the end, Dewey fell back for solutions on the development of scientific methods of rational inquiry and their assimilation via an unspecified process of education by a "wider public."[80]

Just how much, despite his objections, Dewey had learned from Lippmann became clear in *The Public and Its Problems*. From the beginning of his analysis, Dewey accepted the proposition that the fundamental problem in American life lay in the adaptation to a scientific age. Older forms of thought, especially the individualism at the root of traditional liberal democratic political theory, were as ineffectual in making sense of the complexity of modern life (what Dewey called the "Great Society") as old national borders had been in containing the outbreak of the Great War. "Is the public a myth?" he wondered. "Is not the problem at the present time that of securing experts to manage administrative matters [rather] than the framing of policies?"[81] Unable to offer a direct refutation of his rhetorical questions, Dewey resorted to an appeal to general hopes and utopian dreams. While ceding a large ground of "technical matters" (including sanitation, health, transportation, housing, city planning, regulation of immigrants, scientific management, and taxation) to trained technicians, Dewey clung stubbornly to a field for democratic action that encompassed questions "which have to be composed and resolved before technical and specialized action can come into play."[82] The very pace of technical change and the widening set of material forces pressing the human condition, he suggested, required a revitalized public—new structures of understanding, communication, and social interaction that he called the "Great Community."[83]

In important respects, however, Dewey no less than Lippmann had passed the baton of sovereignty to a "scientific" model of human progress. Like Lippmann he dismissed the idea of the "omnicompetent individual" as a historically proven "illusion." He had learned that "man acts from crudely intelligized emotion and from habit rather than from rational consideration."[84] Fortunately, according to Dewey, among the plurality of group habits had developed the "scientific habit," characterized by the "development of a critical sense and methods of discriminating judgment," though unfortunately "this apparatus is so highly specialized that it requires more labor to acquire ability to use and understand it than to get skill in any other instrumentalities possessed by man."[85] By this reckoning the immediate task for democratic activists lay not in any immediate empowerment of the public (or "outsiders") but in transferring scientific method and know-how into popular culture.[86]

In making mass communication (even above power-sharing) the basis for the modern order, Dewey tiptoed close to but then self-consciously backed away from the provocative subject of propaganda. On this matter, he insisted, the required volume must be "written by one much more experienced than the present writer. Propaganda can accordingly only be mentioned, with the remark that the present situation is one unprecedented in history."[87] In the meantime Dewey placed his faith in the deus ex machina of the Great Community, a world where "the highest and most difficult kind of inquiry and a subtle, delicate, vivid and responsive art of communication must take possession of the physical machinery of transmission and circulation and breathe life into it." In this communicative universe foreseen by Walt Whitman, "democracy will come into its own, for democracy is a name for a life of free and enriching communion."[88]

That Dewey's democratic commitments asserted themselves in a moralistic, almost mystical, add-on to the substance of his findings only hinted at how beleaguered his earlier beliefs had become within academic circles. His liberal democratic values now appeared, at best, a transcendent projection from the social evolutionary process he had always championed. The democratic Dewey thus strained as hard as he could against what he judged to be the educated person's common impression of Middletown America—that the people "generally speaking [are] morons and boobs [who] must

Dewey retains some kind of mystical democ. faith.

be expected to act out the part to which they are assigned."[89] But the "scientific" facts clearly argued against the democrat's reliance on the genius of the people.[90]

In the face of sociological evidence, the only way Dewey could save a belief in equality was to fall back on an environmental explanation of behavior for, as he put it, "the more one knows of history the more one comes to believe that traditions and institutions count more than native capacity or incapacity in explaining things."[91] Democracy might be saved, Dewey implied, if the people were put through the right hoops. Enlightened social policy and rational institutions (that is, the infrastructure for the Great Community), he suggested, were the sina qua non of a workable democracy. But now ends and means had effectively exchanged places in his argument. Instead of being the conveyer and the ultimate repository of scientific vision, the democratic public could only hope to be its recipient or, at best, its consultant. In the face of an inevitable modern disintegration of the traditional nodes of community—"family, church, and neighborhood"—the revival of working democracy awaited a perfected machinery of communications.[92] As an active agent, the public, Dewey might almost have said, must be destroyed in order to be saved.[93]

DEWEY'S RETREAT did not occur in a vacuum. The effective transformation of the public from active agent of social change to passive object of outside forces had emerged as a commonplace of social science thought. "To an intellectual class that watched their native religion turn to fundamentalism, patriotism to chauvinism, and politics to reaction," argues historian Dorothy Ross about the 1920s, "science appeared to be the one pure and sustaining discipline in the modern world."[94] Ross suggests that the distinctive ideology of the new social science expert represented a reappropriation of the turn-of-the-century notion of social control. What had once been a relatively loose-fitting garment intended to cover both democratically designed social change and the instruments of collective social discipline, however, now took on "greater insistence and harder contours, stressing objective, quantitative methods and behaviorist psychology."[95] Less directly, Ross implies that the new consciousness,

combined and indeed stimulated as it was by "the growing power of professional specialization," effectively distanced the practitioners of social science from their subjects.

Trends in political science and sociology, two key disciplines whose primary business was to understand the American public, confirm a connection between what Ross labels "scientism" and democratic disenchantment. Within the Chicago school of sociology, for example, the Christian meliorism once favored by Albion W. Small and Charles R. Henderson all but disappeared into the categorical analysis of America's pluralistic masses.[96] In addition to its "scientific" array of primary documents, William I. Thomas's monumental five-volume study *The Polish Peasant in Europe and America (1918–1920)*, written in collaboration with Florian Znaniecki, displayed the social scientist as a kind of omniscient evaluator of backward cultures. Obtaining the then-enormous sum of $50,000 from Hull House benefactor Helen Culver for a study of the new immigrants, Thomas first searched for the appropriate target population: "I first of all went over to Europe to locate a suitable group, where good materials were available. The choice was between the Italians, the Jews, and the Poles. The Poles are very repulsive people on the whole, but there had been a movement for 'enlightenment' and freedom that had developed many documents and masses of material on the peasant, so I decided to bore in there."[97]

Despite previous personal contact with Hull House, Thomas as well as his Polish collaborator, Znaniecki, developed a more positive image of and better contacts with the distant European Poles than with neighboring Polish-Americans in Chicago.[98] The reason for this, in part, had to do with the authors' fear of the uneducated, undirected masses. Concentrating on the flux of social organization and disorganization within the peasant community, Thomas and Znaniecki credited the Polish clergy and native intelligentsia with helping the native Poles toward a remarkable "evolution" in attitudes. From a "mental horizon limited to his immediate social environment," with thinking and acting defined by "tradition and custom," the peasant had emerged as a "conscious patriot" in just "one or two generations."[99] The diaspora community, by contrast, had succumbed to social breakdown. In addition to the lack of effective incorporating structures in the host community, the émigrés suffered from the absence of "an educated class":

> The intellectual leader here is thus an isolated individual, often economically dependent on those whom he attempts to lead; unless he is a priest, his prestige is usually rather low and even if he could maintain his standards without proper social encouragement, he would still have to adapt himself to the demands of the masses rather than impose his ideals on the masses.[100]

Left to themselves, the immigrants tended to vacillate destructively between the extremes of the "Philistine" (whose attitudes had congealed too early) and the "Bohemian" (whose attitudes had never congealed), unable to locate the golden mean of the "Creative Man."[101]

The very meaning of the term "popular attitude," as applied in academic studies, signaled a rising skepticism about the culture of the democratic masses. Proceeding from the work of Thomas and his University of Chicago colleagues through Elton Mayo's experiments on industrial efficiency at the Hawthorne Works of the Western Electric Company in the late twenties to the "public opinion research" of the Gallup polls in the mid-thirties, use of the concept, as historian Donald Fleming has documented, shifted drastically from its original emphasis on the "libertarian ideal of the individual's reasoned participation in recasting his own attitudes." Highlighted in the sampling techniques of the 1920s sociological classic *Middletown*, public opinion emerged as the "overt data" from which inferences about deeper "attitudes" could be derived. The very ascription of group attitudes by social scientists applied only to the "other," like the "raw peasant," not "people like themselves." Essentially a strategy for dealing with the masses, who had so dramatically inserted themselves into the public affairs of the world, "attitude" became a mechanism for the intellectual control of those perceived as culturally primitive. The intrusive outsider, concludes Fleming, "could hardly be dignified with the familiar name of 'ideas,' with the implication of a coherent position arrived at by rational processes and lucidly formulated."[102]

The practical implications of the less-than-autonomous self were most quickly developed within the nascent science of industrial psy-

Mayo

chology. Led by Harvard's Hugo Munsterberg, experimenters closely attached to large industrial interests sought to combine economic and technological stimuli to influence and control workers' psychological impulses. Positing the obsolescence of free will and more specifically the inability of ordinary workers to judge their own productive capacities, Munsterberg's *Psychology and Industrial Efficiency* (1913) justified the replacement of worker initiative by managerial authority in the service of efficiency. The new science, beamed one practitioner in the mid-twenties, "discover[s] the usable and nonusable qualities in each of us."[103]

It is not surprising that profound political disillusionment on the part of ex-Progressives contributed to the image of the benighted citizen within the postwar framework of the social sciences. As Thomas wrote of the urban immigrant public in 1921, "They are politically disfranchised while retaining the ceremony of a vote. No longer able to act intelligently or responsibly, they act upon vagrant impulses. They are directed by suggestion and advertising. This is the meaning of social unrest . . . It is a sign of a baffled wish to participate."[104] To be sure, such gloomy images of the larger public only brightened the prospects for social engineers. Equipped with new theories and methods, sociologist Frederick Lumley confidently set out to update Edward Ross's ideal of social control. In *Means of Social Control* (1925), Lumley called on Americans "to abandon the individual as the measure of all things social and fix upon the group"; in the highest state of social organization, scientists would rule, dispensing with the outmoded "democratic gratification" of the individual.[105]

More commonly, however, the disenchanted Progressive-cum-social scientist did not so much preach to the multitudes as measure them. Robert E. Park, the leading sociologist of the postwar decade, for example, adopted a characteristically circumspect view of the possibilities for social change. Recruited to the University of Chicago after years spent working with Booker T. Washington at Tuskegee Institute, Park displayed his political mentor's distaste for meddling intellectual radicals and moralistic reformers. Believing, like Washington, in the dominant role of the marketplace in shaping the quality of life, Park counted on the invisible functionalism of human conduct: "as members of society, men act as they do elsewhere from

Robert Park had apprenticed at Tuskegee with BTW.

motives they do not fully comprehend, in order to fulfill aims of which they are only dimly or not at all conscious."[106] Although incremental change based on the careful cultivation of new attitudes was possible, Park believed, advocacy usually proved not only misguided but a violation of "scientific neutrality."[107]

The academic's cultivated objectivism and preoccupation with the irrationality of the body politic achieved its quintessential expression in the person of Park's Chicago colleague and the doyen of interwar political science, Charles Merriam. Like so many of the disappointed reformers, Merriam's flight from progressivism had been sealed by service with the wartime Creel Committee. "Society is dissolving every moment," he wrote in 1921, "and the question is, How shall the reconstruction of authority in the minds and lives of men be made?" Merriam's initial answer centered on a classic Progressive goal of "civic education" with the primary goal of inculcating the scientific method; by 1925, however, his tone was less one of conversion than control as he announced in *New Aspects of Politics* that modern forms of mass communication placed a premium on "two great mechanisms . . . that have never before existed . . . with the same possibilities of effective use. These are [universal] education and eugenics."[108]

Merriam's *The Making of Citizens* (1931), a comparative study of the relation of education to political processes, revealed just how far political science had traveled in its definition of "civic education" from the crusading democratic tones that Dewey's early work had given to that term. Merriam's emphasis was not on change but on the sources of political cohesion and stability:

> The loyalty of the individual to his church, to his class, to his race, to his locality, blend into a loyalty to the state; or divide and disintegrate into conflicting allegiances and attachments. How these conflicting interests, loyalties, cohesions are combined, and how they are united in a particular territorial state . . . is a matter of profound interest to the political scientist and to the maker of states.[109]

For the scientist of politics, as opposed to the intellectual reformer, the citizen was less an agent than an object acted upon by many subjects. As a source of legitimacy and power the state itself now possessed greater proximity, greater intimacy than its confused and infinitely malleable inhabitants.

Merriam's prize student, Harold D. Lasswell, perhaps the greatest contributor to modern political psychology, went even further. Early experiences as a high school debater and encyclopedia salesman combined with his own dissertation research published as *Propaganda Technique in the World War* (1927) led Lasswell toward a characteristically hard-boiled view of popular motivations.[110] The romantic democrat filled with dreams of a beneficent public will inevitably be disappointed, he asserted. If General Foch had proved the "great generalissimo" on the "military front," so President Wilson had been the equivalent on the "propaganda front": "to illuminate the mechanisms of propaganda is to reveal the secret springs of social action, and to expose to the most searching criticism our prevailing dogmas of sovereignty, of democracy, of honesty, and of the sanctity of individual opinion."[111]

In less than twenty-five years, American social science had become deeply disenchanted with the dream of an informed, rationally self-governing public. One might suggest, moreover, that this "group attitude" became engrained in the very making of American higher education. Education historian Lawrence R. Veysey has noted the strong connections between the development of university sanctioned "liberal culture" and a self-conceived isolation from the "largely uncivilized" "materialistic" world outside campus gates. Social, political, and religious controversies especially threatened a natural-science ideal of objectivity. The comparatively autonomous, even self-isolated, models of the British and German universities beckoned invitingly at the turn of the century to many architects of the new American graduate schools.[112] In addition, although U.S. institutions of higher learning had in the late nineteenth century been engulfed in controversies about their rightful purpose and governance, they had generally righted themselves on the basis of a "bureaucratized, administrative chain of command." The neutral language of scientific fact, which covered a retreat from the values of social advocacy and service, sustained the more microcosmic interests of institutional stability and interdisciplinary tolerance. Only an extraordinary campus, like the University of Wisconsin, counterposed a serious alternative to such developments.[113]

In such a setting even lip service to democratic commitments gave way to more cynical reflections. With characteristic irony, Harvard philosopher George Santayana surveyed the academic scene: "There are always a few men," he pointed out, "whose main interest is to note the aspects of things in an artistic or philosophical way. They are rather useless individuals, but as I happen to belong to the class, I think them superior to the rest of mankind."[114]

TO BE SURE, the starkly "realist" opinion that dominated academic and much extra-academic commentary about the fate of democracy in the 1920s was not all-inclusive. In the teeth of postwar disillusionment with the possibilities of an egalitarian culture, radical hopes for a democratic sphere of public dialogue and communication still inspired a dedicated few. Grouped around the labor movement or explicitly socialist vehicles such as the Socialist Party, the Communist Party, or *The Liberator*, left-wing Progressives ignored or rejected soured postwar judgments in favor of creating tangible, if more strategic, connections to a democratic public. Like antiwar socialist Randolph Bourne, the radical democrats were inclined to exempt "the people"—"the sluggish masses, too remote from the world conflict to be stirred, too lacking in intellect to perceive their danger"—from blame for the war and instead attacked the "war intellectuals" for succumbing to an "itch to be in the great experience."[115]

Largely outside the framework of the established universities, a variety of institutions attempted to extend the earlier ideal of citizen and worker education as a source of democratic renewal. In one of the most ambitious of such initiatives, in 1919 James Harvey Robinson resigned his professorship at Columbia to launch the New School for Social Research, designed, as he put it, "to bridge the gap between the intellectual and capitalistic classes and the so-called working classes." Drawing on such talents as Charles A. Beard, John Dewey, Alvin Johnson, Wesley C. Mitchell, and Thorstein Veblen, Robinson hoped to create a democratically self-governing research and teaching community in a setting outside the "factory-like buildings of the usual repulsive character associated with education." Unbeholden to elite benefactors, social science might be freed from its class affiliation to play an emancipatory social role. Almost as quickly as it began, however, fiscal reality annulled the grandiose dreams for a "democratic" alternative to the research university; forced to depend on the tuition of enrolled students, the New School soon occupied an honorable if less revolutionary niche as a center of adult education, a conduit more than a creator of new knowledge.[116]

Even as the New School tried and failed to activate an intellectual-worker alliance, "labor education" offered a concrete example of just what could—and could not—be done during the period. While education had always been a significant theme within the Anglo-American labor movement, a new variety of intellectual-worker contact developed at the turn of the century. Curiously, of the early initiatives perhaps the most famous was Ruskin Hall, a workingman's school established at Oxford University by visiting American students Walter Vrooman and Charles Beard in 1899.[117] In the same year the immigrant-socialist culture of New York City produced the Workers' School (later Workers' Education League); a more famous socialist effort followed in 1903, with the formation of the Rand School of Social Science. Within the trade union movement, the Jewish Waist and Dress Makers Union (International Ladies Garment Workers Union), Local 25, asked the New York Public Library to open a special branch for union women; and as early as 1915 Barnard instructor Juliet Stuart Poyntz was hired to head education classes at the union's summer Unity House. Consolidating the ILGWU's leadership in this field, union vice-president Fannia M. Cohn in 1917–18 chartered the Workers' University at Washington Irving High School in Manhattan.[118]

Yet it was not until the end of the war that workers' education reached full flowering as an organized movement. Variously established by trade unions (including the AFL-coordinated Workers' Education Bureau and the Workers' School of the Amalgamated Clothing Workers led by J. B. S. Hardman), universities (the Wisconsin School for Workers, the Bryn Mawr Summer School for Women Workers, the Boston Trades Union College, and the University of California's extension service for trade unions), and independent, associative efforts (the Work People's College, Brookwood Labor College, Commonwealth College, the Southern Summer School for Women Workers), worker schools and union education programs promoted diverse contacts between university-trained faculties and working people.[119]

Brookwood Labor College in Katonah, New York, launched in 1921 just as the antilabor Americanization crusade had broken out at the end of the war, offered a good example of the combination of educational utopianism of the Deweyite pragmatists and a more hardened, class-conscious resistance to state-business control of public education and media that influenced labor education pioneers. As director and president of the board respectively, A. J. Muste, labor activist from a radical Quaker perspective, and James H. Maurer, worker-socialist and president of the Pennsylvania Federation of Labor, reflected Brookwood's melding of philosophical and practical purposes.[120] A student of theology and philosophy (having taken classes with James and Dewey at Columbia University) who had followed the social gospel into leadership of the victorious Lawrence, Massachusetts, textile strike of 1919 (emerging as executive secretary of the Amalgamated Textile Workers), Muste placed considerable faith in the independent power of workers' organizations and the integrity of workers' own culture. In words that might have been spoken by Jane Addams, for example, he encouraged the dramatic arts at Brookwood on grounds that "there is material for drama in the experiences and thoughts and emotions of workingmen and women that other people do not know and that the workers themselves do not really appreciate because they are too close to it."[121] Typically, the workers' schools combined an appeal to Progressive pedagogical principles—"respect for facts . . . ability to determine relevant facts to solve problems"—with a socialist ideology enabling the student to break out of "uniformity of thought and conduct," which, according to Maurer, characterized the "penal system" of bourgeois education. Communist Party worker-education activist Max Bedacht thus openly urged Brookwood "to create proletarian consciousness and anticapitalist convictions."[122]

Of all the apostles of worker education, no one waxed more enthusiastic than eclectic scholar Herbert Ellsworth Cory. Beginning his academic career as an assistant professor of English literature at the University of California, Cory in turn gravitated to psychology, biology, aesthetics, and educational theory during research and teaching appointments at Johns Hopkins and the University of Washington. It was in California where Cory likely first encountered economist and labor theorist Carleton H. Parker, to whom he dedicated *The Intellectuals and the Wage Workers: A Study in Educational Psychoanalysis* in 1919. Inspired by the contemporaneous radicalism of the Russian bolsheviks, the British, French, and Italian syndicalists, and the American Wobblies, Cory offered an original blend of Deweyite education theory and Freudian psychology in an appeal to a new social order. Surpassing even Jane Addams in his confidence in the innate capacity of the laboring classes, Cory foresaw a happy convergence between militant workers and "radical scientists of human nature."[123] Contrasting the progressive school's emphasis on creative play with the "classical educationalists" ("who believe in drudgery for drudgery's sake"), Cory leapt to associate the doctrines of pragmatism with the advance of the workers' movement. Unions, in his eyes, became "vast laboratories of the first really vital sociology," general strikes the locus of "sublime instances of the release of love and magnanimity," and the "dictatorship of the proletariat . . . the first type of government honest enough to admit itself to be transitional and not eternal."[124]

Cory's modest "program for the American university" implied nothing less than an "inevitable convergence" of intellectuals and wage workers by "the most thorough reconstruction of educational methods." At its core was the addition to the faculty of "psychoanalytic advisors":

> We must work towards a psychoanalytic co-operation between each student and certain expert faculty advisers for the purpose of the experimental organization of these courses into the student's life with all its conflicts. We must work towards a rejection of recitation and lecture in favor of something more like the proletarian forum. Let all teachers form industrial unions and affiliate with the wage-workers to signalize the identity of the Copernican revolution in education with that in the labor-movement.[125]

No less transformative hopes for American labor education were entertained by the visiting Belgian socialist and worker-education leader Hendrik de Man when he surveyed the U.S. scene in 1921. The German-educated, cosmopolitan son of an Antwerp business family—whose travels to the United States included a brief sojourn among Wobblies in Puget Sound and a politically interrupted ap-

Cory's
Blend of Freud,
Marx + union
worker radicalism

pointment at the University of Washington—was much impressed by American institutions such as the Workers' University in New York City, the Boston Trade Union College, the Chicago Workers' Institute, the San Francisco People's Institute, and the Seattle Workers' College. Although they represented different types of organizations and educational goals, all of them, de Man noted approvingly, "mean some degree of departure from the traditional type of extension work where ex cathedra lecturers condescend to go slumming in the 'lower' intellectual spheres, and 'uplift' the workers by feeding them on crumbs from the academic table—a kind of surrogate of the real stuff, administered in smaller doses, too." The new venues, de Man believed, were the true incubators of a new and better society, a kind of counter-hegemonic imprint of a future order. He asserted, "When labor strikes, it says to its master: I shall no longer work at your command. When it votes for a party of its own, it says: I shall no longer vote at your command. When it creates its own classes and colleges, it says: I shall no longer think at your command. Labor's challenge to education is the most fundamental of the three."[126]

It must have been figures like Cory and de Man whom New School philosopher Horace M. Kallen had in mind in 1925 when he linked the "recent swift efflorescence" of labor education to "utopian fantasies about [postwar] reconstruction." More modest in his own expectations, Kallen nevertheless positively associated labor education with an "era of moral hope" and an "exalted mood of service" in which sympathetic intellectuals applied Deweyite doctrines of the autonomy and self-development of the child to the working class. Whereas the public schools and even the nation's colleges were providing a "grammar of assent, not a logic of inquiry," new, progressive institutions would ideally "require an immersion of the [student] from the beginning in the immediate data of the social setting."[127]

The problem, as Kallen saw it, lay in breaking through the decorative, imitative, and socially safe versions of higher learning toward a Baconian ideal of knowledge as purposive control or power. Anticipating the Gramscian concept of hegemony Kallen wrote of an "iron ring" that "chains and channels the spirit of man":

By and large . . . the actualities of power and wealth and well-being wherein society at points comes to fruition are realized vicariously, through the substitutes and symbolism of the arts and literature and through the acquiescence in their being and the desire for their possession which constitute the persistent mental set of the great body of workers. This generates and sustains the social atmosphere they breathe and defines the personal objectives they seek. Altogether, they round out a circle in which the consumption of the leisure classes defines the ideal of the working classes, the production of the working classes sustains the practices of the leisure ones. Work nourishes waste; waste directs work.[128]

In place of formal classes, which maintained a separation of "education" from "life" (and attacking even the socialist "proletcult" as a merely "compensatory" gesture with respect to bourgeois cultural norms), Kallen anticipated a more practical integration of knowledge with the experience of real-world social "direction." He found suggestive models in the British consumer cooperative movement and in American industrial experiments with "worker's control," as in the B&O railroad plan for workers' shop committees. Full integration of educational standards into the labor movement would result in civil service exams for trade union leaders, "a nucleus from which the educational process could ultimately radiate into every shop." Trade unions themselves, thus oriented to both knowledge and control, would take on functions "analogous to schools of business administration."[129] Like the informed citizen in Dewey's cosmos, Kallen's idealized labor movement beckoned as the preferred vehicle to connect science with democratic planning.

Unfortunately, the ebullient projections of advocates like Cory, de Man, and Kallen—so reminiscent of the prewar social science idealism of Cooley, Dewey, and Addams—proved short-lived. For the radical intellectuals of the postwar period, the labor and socialist movements had become a lifeboat, a kind of public in miniature, a vicarious replacement for the larger democratic community championed by their prewar counterparts. Instead of its being a rising star as these theorists had anticipated, however, the workers' movement of the twenties turned out to be a lumbering oxcart.[130]

Nowhere was less enthusiasm exhibited for the more daring in-

[handwritten note:] Kallen et al. soon to be disillusioned by the labor movt.

unions themselves / grimly practical

tellectual schemes of the reformers than within the trade unions themselves. The trend was set among the pacesetting ILGWU, when more practical types dismissed as "sentimental" Fannia Cohn's broader adult education goals in favor of a specifically labor education approach that would equip union stewards with collective bargaining skills. The earlier aim of preparing workers via education for a new social order came under added suspicion when the Communist Party challenged garment workers' leadership in the mid-twenties.[131]

Within the AFL high command, as well, the die was cast as early as 1918 in the speedy rejection of a proposal by War Labor Board staff member Charles Sweeney to study worker education programs in London as a blueprint for preparing American labor to "manage its own affairs" and "develop its own voices." "Democracy," Sweeney argued, "will spread only as education spreads, and democracy in industry is no exception." Although the proposal had the endorsement of Felix Frankfurter, a friend of labor, AFL representatives on the tripartite Council on National Defense would have none of it. In addition to discountenancing any connection with the Marxists, who were infesting the British programs, AFL vice-president Matthew Woll (the future chairman of the Federation's educational arm) asserted that "the greatest fundamental error and immature judgment manifested in the development of this proposal lie in confusing the higher educated man with leadership." Ending his prosecutorial brief with a paean to the native good sense of self-taught AFL chieftain Samuel Gompers, Woll suggested that too much learning was a dangerous thing.[132] Given AFL leadership worries about the intellectuals' proclivities towards socialism and communism, it is not surprising that they wished to keep all educational programs on a short string.[133]

Fighting the prevailing political winds, the dreams of radical educators for the labor movement generally proved misplaced. Wisconsin-trained economist and labor educator David Saposs in 1932 would look back wistfully on the aspirations of the 1920s: "In this sphere [i.e., worker education] some [intellectuals] even became known as leaders and enjoyed considerable prestige and independence. But not for long; reorganization of WEB and attack on Brookwood is carrying out [the] historic policy of the A F of L to squelch and smother intellectuals."[134] Herbert Ellsworth Cory was more emphatic in dismissing his early commitments as mere youthful fantasies. In an autobiographical account published in 1943, he ruefully looked back on *Intellectuals and Wage Workers* as "a manic performance of which I became heartily ashamed." Indeed, a decade earlier he had self-consciously given up faith in progress and science altogether and converted to Roman Catholicism.[135]

The cycle of postwar disillusionment experienced among American intellectuals carried even more serious repercussions in Europe, nowhere more tragically exemplified than in the career of Hendrik de Man. After twenty years of directing Belgian worker-education experiments, de Man grew weary of the "outworn primitive democratic adoration of the crowd" ensconced in social democratic theory. In contrast to their would-be intellectual leaders, de Man concluded by 1926, "the civilization which the working class wants to have opened is only bourgeois civilization . . . We must see the culture of the proletarian masses as it really is, namely a culture of substitutes for or imitations of petty-bourgeois culture." In the circumstances the best the labor movement could do, argued de Man, was "to create for the masses certain material conditions which are essential preliminaries to all [higher] civilization."[136] By the 1930s, de Man gradually turned away from the incrementalism of the parliamentary process and towards the power of a state executive and the mobilizing power of nationalist ideology as means to overcome mass inertia. Backed into both an ideological and political corner by the rise of German Nazism, this erstwhile champion of labor education (and titular head of the Belgian Labor party) was alone among Belgian political leaders in defending King Leopold II's decision to surrender to the invading German army.[137]

IF DE MAN'S career represents a fall from democratic faith and action more extreme than that of his Progressive American contemporaries, it nevertheless points to a central dilemma in twentieth-century democratic cultural development. No simple solution has beckoned for creating a public sphere where the claims of enlightened social science could be debated, assimilated, and translated into public policy. No grand plan for a dialogue between intellectuals and a mass audience has ever been put into practice. While the division of labor in twentieth-century society has continued to multiply (a recent U.S. Secretary of Labor, for example, has written of the chasm separating the prospects of manual workers from those he calls "symbolic analysts"), the task of finding common communicative ground for collective action has grown ever more daunting.[138] As renewed fears about the modern-day crowd abound, we seem bereft of an earlier confidence that democratic citizenship might serve as a source of wisdom as well as political legitimacy.

Yet if early-twentieth-century intellectuals did not produce a solution to the problem of cultural as well as industrial democracy, they surely offer examples of commitment from which we might learn. Both in the academy and outside it the new century nurtured a great variety of practical efforts to connect the insights and resources of higher learning to the needs and interests of the great democratic majority. If we are to understand such efforts—for their ambition and insights, as well as their failings—we need to reconstruct them with close attention to the nuance of individual efforts in specific contexts. The trail of such examples—to define a mutually beneficial relation with working people, to practice democratic virtues in private as well as public spaces, to discover the tools of investigation and publicity, to raise the poor and illiterate into an educated citizenry, to lead workers into powerful trade unions, and to secure a public policy with democratic and even redistributionist ends—not only reintroduces us to a set of historical actors but challenges us to ask new questions of ourselves.

2 Defining the People

The Wisconsin School of Labor History and
the Creation of the American Worker

T HE WRITING of labor history reveals much about the shifting patterns of intellectual activism in American life. The academics who first documented the struggles of American trade unionism were themselves part of the action. Writing during a time of tremendous ferment within the labor movement, the intellectuals inhabited an academic world in flux, a world that placed substantial pressure on those who would define their progressivism in both political and intellectual ways. Offering a kind of sociology of knowledge for the most important of these pioneering labor historians, I argue that the intellectuals' personal experience materially shaped a definition of worker and labor union interests, and that this definition had long-term repercussions for public policy as well as scholarship. Or, to put it more provocatively, when intellectuals set themselves up as spokespersons for workers (as labor historians necessarily do), their own self-image plays a large (and usually unexplored) role in the histories the intellectuals write.

THE FIRST treatises on workers' organized activity appeared in the 1880s, an era that economic historian Mark Perlman has aptly called "The Awakening."[1] On the one hand the term evokes the clamor of the decade's Great Upheaval—the tide of strikes, protest, and national organizing activity by workers in the exploding ranks of the Knights of Labor and emerging federations of skilled trades, each of which challenged the power of capital to dictate the terms of an industrial future. But the term applies equally well to writers—the reform-minded intellectuals, especially political economists, who experienced the social crisis of industrialism and the advance of specialized knowledge as not merely coincident but connected events. Indeed, the first commentators on the labor movement included some of the most brilliant lights of a new generation of educated Americans, individuals who would go on to make their mark within, and in several cases to dominate, their chosen academic or professional fields.

Products of both the unprecedented expansion of university enrollments and the development of postgraduate programs at several elite schools, the pioneer scholars were men (and a few exceptional women) who generally had inherited a religiously derived moral sensibility for which the poverty as well as unrest of the industrial city was a new and troubling experience.[2] If American social problems pricked their Christian social conscience, their diagnosis was in turn filtered through a strong European, especially German, intellectual lens. Experience for many in research universities abroad not only offered a model for future American higher education, it also exposed these young Americans to a more historical, contingent, and pluralistic view of the world than that suggested by an unbending faith in individualism and the iron laws of classical political economy.[3]

To be sure, prior to the awakening of academic intellectuals, there had been no dearth of intellectual interest in radical social reform and industrial democracy. Political-intellectual "advocates," such as Ira Steward, John Swinton, Henry George, Edward Bellamy, and later Henry Demarest Lloyd and Clarence Darrow, had each articulated a pro-labor and indigenous American radicalism.[4] But a gulf separated them from the new academic generation. The former lived outside the university setting; their findings were less self-consciously connected to an "objective," scientific, or scholarly quest for truth. They were, generally speaking, citizen-activists appealing to a broad republican audience as writers, editors, and attorneys—and, as such, were throwbacks to a preindustrial world with a less searing division between skilled workers and the educated classes. A few among them, including Steward, William Sylvis, and later Terence Powderly, Edward King, and George McNeill, were in fact worker-intellectuals who slid comfortably into prominent roles within the unions and labor reform organizations.

These labor agitators had also been aided by a few professionals who toiled more quietly for workers' welfare. For example, much of importance had been accomplished since the late 1860s in the way of collecting information and statistics on wage rates and working conditions, particularly via a growing circuit of state labor bureaus. The most prominent center for such work had been Massachusetts, where the irrepressible advocate George McNeill had served as state labor commissioner (until forced to resign for political reasons in 1873). McNeill's less obstreperous and more painstakingly professional successor, Carroll Wright, established the basis for a permanent government role in monitoring the national labor force, heading the first federal labor bureau (within the Department of the Interior) in 1884. Although relatively restrained in his social judgments Wright (and a few other empiricists like him) gave vent to a growing economic revisionism, referring scornfully, for example, to the "hard, unsympathetic nature" of the "so-called science of political economy."[5]

What pushed the new economists of the 1880s forward, however, was not only religious sympathy and educational pedigree but also the visible mobilization of the workers themselves. A movement of unions, cooperatives, and political action, loosely grouped around the sprawling presence of the Knights of Labor, initially presented itself as a possible engine of fundamental social change. Willingly dissolving the barrier between campus and community, the young academic radicals welcomed the arrival of this rational, yet morally charged and broad-gauged, social movement. Like breathless late arrivals onto a departing train, the academics threw caution to the wind; saluting the movement for labor reform, they openly identified with its aims and principles while implicitly casting themselves as its chief interpreters abroad and tutors at home.

The first and clearest exemplar of this tendency was Richard T. Ely, perhaps the most influential academic reformer of his generation. Ely, the son of well-read but struggling Presbyterian farmers from western New York, had secured a position at Johns Hopkins after imbibing the social gospel at Columbia and pursuing a graduate degree at Heidelberg under the historicist economist Karl Knies.[6] Ely wrote *The Labor Movement in America* in 1886 at the height of the academic and political radicalism of the Gilded Age. Decrying the extremes of the old-school "conservative trade unionist" who accepts the "fixed bounds" of "natural laws" as well as the revolu-

Ely

Ely overrated possibilities of the Knights of Labor [handwritten annotation]

tionary socialist, Ely identified a "midway" position that "begins within the framework of present industrial society, but proposes to transform it gradually and peacefully, but completely, by abolishing a distinct capitalist class of employers." The labor movement was to play the leading role in this process.[7] Gradually replacing the formal church as a source of human brotherhood, the Knights of Labor, proclaimed Ely, was "preparing the way for a moral regeneration of the American industrial system and for the establishment of the 'ideal' system, the union of capital and labor in the same hands, in grand, wide-reaching co-operative enterprises."[8] Rather than promoting social divisions, the Knights promised an inclusive moral unity with which even the academic might identify: the Knights of Labor "did not emphasize class war; in fact in certain instances they would admit teachers, preachers, other intellectuals and even employers."[9] Amazed at the integration within the Knights' ranks of diverse occupational groups (and even groups of Confederate and Union Civil War veterans), Ely romanticized the Order as the practical working out of a Hegelian unity of opposites and invested in it his hopes not only for domestic progress but ultimately for ending wars through international parliaments.[10]

To be sure, even in his rhetorical swoon before the movement of the masses, Ely did not surrender a constructive social role for people like himself. His own genteel manners and even a measure of cultural condescension showed through his egalitarian sympathies. To assuage a skeptical middle-class readership, Ely acknowledged the apparent illogic of a political enlightenment arising from "below." "Strange is it not! that the despised trades-union and labor organizations should have been chosen to perform this high duty of conciliation! But hath not God ever called the lowly to the most exalted missions, and hath he not ever called the foolish to confound the wise?" Ely's personal contact with Terence Powderly, general master workman of the order, likewise inverted the normal condescension bestowed by the leader of more than a half-million citizens on a private petitioner. Honored to meet with the university professor, Powderly humbly addressed his correspondence to "Richard T. Ely, Ph.D.," closed it "Very Respectfully Yours," and readily apologized for his own inattention to economic literature: "I am so busy I seldom get the chance to read the daily papers. I know that this is wrong and that a man in my position ought to have the time to scan the doings of the day . . . but our members do not think that way and I must keep at the drudgery of letter writing and reading all the time."[11]

Ely set an example that others quickly followed. Next to him in the front ranks of the labor-oriented intellectual awakening was Henry Carter Adams, perhaps best known as an early theorist of the regulatory state and a moderate reformist within the academic economics establishment.[12] But Adams's earliest contributions, like Ely's, reflect a more radical cast of mind. Another rebel from midwestern small towns and theological orthodoxy, Adams completed his doctorate at Johns Hopkins in 1878, headed for Germany, and returned to juggle part-time teaching positions at Cornell and the University of Michigan.[13]

Adams's views on the labor problem were distinguished not only by an original elaboration of a worker's property rights in a job but by his exploration of such issues in the midst of a charged political climate. In Cornell's Sibley College Lectures delivered during the Knights' violence-plagued Southwest Strike in April 1886, Adams resolutely and passionately defended organized labor as "the greatest and characteristic movement of the present century." While censuring the disorder accompanying the strike, Adams accepted the basic logic of strikers who had walked off their jobs to protest the arbitrary dismissal of union members: "What the Knights of Labor say is, that they desire to exercise some of the rights of proprietorship over the industry to which they give their skill and their time. And it's certainly true that concession to their demands would deprive men now controlling industries of the right to control and operate their property 'under well defined rules of law'; but we will not add '[under] common sense,' for that is the question at issue."[14]

Ely and Adams may have been the most intellectually precocious of the Young Turk economists, but both their sympathies and broad analysis of the labor problem were shared in the mid-1880s by colleagues who would later elaborate the more conservative principles of twentieth-century economic thought. Perhaps the most prominent was John Bates Clark, the father of modern marginal utility theory.[15] When he was called home from Amherst College to take over his ailing father's plow manufacturing business in Minnesota, Clark witnessed the hard times of surrounding farmers. He passed

John
Bates
Clark

up a career in the ministry after graduation and turned to economics. Following study in Germany, Clark taught part-time at Smith, then divided his time between Amherst and Columbia before securing a permanent position at Columbia in 1895. In his early scholarship Clark tried to combine the moral ends of Christian social reform with the workings of the competitive marketplace, an effort crowned by the publication in 1886 of *The Philosophy of Wealth: Economic Principles Newly Formulated.*

Clark was convinced that "individual competition," which had regulated an earlier era, was now "incapable of working justice," and he looked to new forms of "solidarity" by employers, government, workers, and the church for "the beginnings of a reign of law." In his defense of labor unions and even boycotts as commensurable resources against an unjust distribution of the economic product, and an identification with the Knights of Labor as the chief hope for the unskilled, Clark hoped to contain social conflict by a new institutionalization of economic interests. Beginning with arbitration, then advancing to profit-sharing and ultimately to the "full cooperation" preached by English Christian socialists, society would be "redeemed" when men voluntarily accepted the fraternal principle. "Christian socialism," declared Clark, "is economic republicanism; and it can come no sooner, stay no longer, and rise, in quality, no higher than intelligence and virtue among the people."[16]

The distinguished later career of another Columbia economist, E. R. A. Seligman (who made his reputation in the field of public finance), likewise overshadowed his earlier enthusiasms. While no refugee from the Christian hinterlands (his father was a wealthy Jewish businessman), Seligman nevertheless shared much with his generational peers. Following European study and completion of a doctoral dissertation on medieval guilds, Seligman in 1885 helped Ely found the American Economics Association (AEA). "The paramount question of political economy," the young Seligman argued, "is the question of distribution and in it the social problem (the question of labor, of the laborer)—how, consistently with a healthy development on the lines of moderate progress, social reform may be accomplished."[17]

In a celebrated parlay over Henry George's proposed single tax before the American Association for Social Science in 1890, Seligman well reflected the simultaneous identification of the New Economists with academic objectivity and social reform. Declaring that there was "not a single man with a thorough training" in economics who advocated the single tax, Seligman complained that while the specialist was universally respected in the natural sciences, "every man whose knowledge of economics or the science of finance is derived from the daily papers or one or two books with lopsided ideas, thinks he is a full-fledged scientist, able to instruct the closest students of the markets or of the political and social organism." Henry George responded energetically to Seligman's attack, at once linking academic economists to the exploiting classes and condemning Seligman's claim to expertise as insidious elitism ("if we cannot all study political economy . . . then democratic republican government is doomed to failure, and the quicker we surrender ourselves to the government of the rich and learned, the better"). Most interesting for our purposes is that Seligman, in final rebuttal, chose to stand not merely on scientific grounds but to argue pointedly, "It is grossly unjust to ascribe to professors of political economy a truckling or even an unconscious subservience to the powers that be." Indeed, not without a degree of hyperbole, Seligman further insisted that "in the United States, to mention only one instance, almost the entire support which the labor-unions receive is at the hands of the college professors—a course which has drawn on them not a little opprobrium."[18]

Even in his early, "radical" phase, however, Seligman undoubtedly seemed tame compared to the firebrands around him. Edmund J. James and Simon Nelson Patten, for example, who had helped reorient Ely during his first European trip, also led the fight for a reform-oriented professional association. As director of the Wharton School of Finance in 1886 James, who would shortly thereafter turn away from social issues towards a career in commercial education and administration (winding up as president of Northwestern University and then the University of Illinois), vigorously endorsed labor unions and attacked ruthless owners for producing mass discontent.[19]

WE MAY WELL take the creation of the American Economics Association (AEA) in 1885 as the first official recognition of an in-

AEA 1885   strong labor - intell link.

tellectual-labor entente in American public life.[20] For a brief moment, at least, the possibility of what many of the AEA organizers called a "Christian social science" seemed the obvious intellectual corollary of a social and political movement seeking to redefine political economy on moral principles.[21] The first volume of AEA *Publications* in 1886, for example, included an argument by Edmund J. James for municipal ownership of utilities, Albert Shaw on associations among the Minneapolis Knights of Labor, Edward W. Bemis on producer and consumer cooperatives in New England, and Henry C. Adams's classic justification for government control of monopoly in "The Relation of the State to Industrial Action."

Exactly this juncture between critical scholarship and the social gospel attracted Oberlin College senior John R. Commons to begin a lifelong path of labor studies. Another Midwest refugee from ministerial ambitions, Commons even as an undergraduate had decided that "the educated man should not become linked to an aristocracy of intellect, but should be a guide the army of discontented may trust and follow."[22] Following Ely to Hopkins in 1888 and soon helping his mentor to found the reformist Institute for Christian Sociology, Commons quickly emerged as the most determined, as well as the most talented, representative of the new economic thinking.[23] In the 1890s, even as other colleagues turned away from philosophical and political issues, Commons maintained a reputation as an academic "hothead."[24]

A characteristic outburst occurred during a public exchange with the conservative Yale economist Arthur T. Hadley in 1899. In his presidential address to the AEA, Hadley, a defender of the liberal marketplace as instrument of the common good, urged economists to function above the din of political and social conflict as a kind of far-seeing policy elite—"representatives," as Hadley put it, "of nothing less than the whole truth." In rebuttal, Commons, who was speaking without an academic position of his own, caustically dismissed Hadley's presumptions as a mask for bourgeois privilege by denying the fundamental nature of social antagonisms: "As economists I believe we would stand on safer ground if, when our conclusions lead us to champion the cause of a class . . . or to expose another class, we should come squarely out and admit that it is so;

John R. Commons

not because the class interest is foremost in our minds, but because the class is the temporary means of bringing about the permanent welfare of all."[25]

Of course, the impact of the stirrings of reform-minded academics should not be exaggerated. Youthfully confident and enthusiastic, they were, to be sure, a distinct and finite subset of social-science-oriented professionals. During a period of widespread labor unrest and an organized mass movement, however, when both serious social reforms and more apocalyptic transformations of the social order appeared possible, the visions of the radical idealists made an impression even on more traditional, conservative colleagues. For example, Francis A. Walker, superintendent of the federal census and president of the Massachusetts Institute of Technology, initially reacted violently against the labor upheavals of the 1880s, heaping abuse on strikers, foreign laborers, and radical dreamers such as Henry George and Edward Bellamy.[26] Walker's election as president of the AEA in 1887 has been cited as evidence of the organization's budding emphasis on public respectability at the expense of radical reform. But it is worth noting that Walker, a moderate critic of laissez-faire dogma who had years before attacked the Malthusian wages-fund doctrine (which predicted an inevitable approach of wages to near-starvation levels), took pains to conciliate the labor movement (and thus also to reassure his professional left flank) in his presidential address of 1888. In "Efforts of the Manual Laboring Class to Better Their Condition," Walker joined his colleagues in a remarkably even-tempered treatment of the rise of the Knights of Labor and its social implications. He referred to the "revolution" in economic thought that had followed the revolution in political thought during the preceding one hundred years. From a "general consent of economic opinion that all distinct efforts of the laboring class, directed to the advancement of their own interest, must at the best be useless" he moved to "the present time when . . . it is fully recognized that the self-assertion of the laboring class importantly contributes to the equitable and beneficial distribution of wealth; and that such self-assertion, within proper limits and by proper agencies, is not more for the interest of the laboring class than of the employing class, or of the community as a whole." Obliquely, Walker even buttressed the case for direct intellectual-worker con-

F. A. Walker moves left in late '80s

tacts by implying that the insights on wage theory of British economist Henry Fawcett were due in part to the fact that "one-half of his
actual intimate daily companions were laboring men."[27]

The "Awakening" of the 1880s offers ample testimony to the
quality of labor-oriented engagement by a generation of socially
conscious intellectuals. Whether by joining in forums with labor
leaders and social reformers, establishing professional associations
through which to maximize their influence on public opinion, or
training a younger generation of citizens and scholars, the new-
school economists etched in the possibility of a formal intellectual
counterpart to labor-populist currents in workplaces and electoral
politics. Perhaps most significant, these intellectuals imagined that
the "scientific" development of their own field of knowledge was intimately bound up with the welfare of working people. As Richard
Hofstadter and Walter P. Metzger concluded, "the strategies of the
new political economy and of organized labor . . . seemed to coin-
cide."[28]

Yet overall, between 1890 and 1910 the ardor of the labor-oriented academics perceptibly cooled. In place of public identification
with workers' aspirations and open advocacy of social transformation, the young social scientists either withdrew from advocacy altogether or channeled their reform energies into more publicly acceptable roles as policy "experts"—a process that Mary Furner has
labeled "practical research."[29]

Suspension of a politically engaged, anticapitalist critique by the
labor economists likely had several causes, reflecting changes within
as well as outside the academy. Part of the problem was intellectual.
Lacking a developed social theory (while generally disdaining revolutionary socialist models as well as the "amateurish" heterodoxy of
a Henry George), the academic radicals found it difficult to establish
their social claims on anything but subjective moral foundations.[30]
Scientific integrity as well as the demands of academic respectability impelled many of the new economists toward accommodation
with the developing marginalist revolution in economic thought, a
theoretical universe in which workers appeared less as visionary citizens than as integers of material self-interest.[31] Marginalist theory,
moreover, carried a persuasive descriptive brief in an economic
world where corporate capital had secured its institutional and legal

moorings. In this respect, the collapse of both the Knights of Labor by the end of the 1880s and the defeat of subsequent labor-populist political challenges in the early 1890s left few options for theorists who had seriously contemplated a different political economy.

A more immediately revisionist goad to erstwhile academic radicals, however, was supplied by university administrators. Four of the most prominent of the labor-oriented economists—Adams, Ely, Bemis, and Commons—faced either the threat or the fact of dismissal for their intellectual commitments. These actions were part of a larger housecleaning of heterodoxy in the universities that climaxed in the mid-1890s; the survivors of this "intellectual Haymarket" learned the contemporary limits of academic freedom each in his own way.[32]

Henry Carter Adams was dismissed in 1886 from his half-time position at Cornell, following publication of his Sibley College lecture "The Labor Problem." Adams had been unlucky enough to have as official commentators on his talk both Cornell University president Charles Kendall Adams and the president of Cornell's board of trustees, lumber millionaire Henry Sage. While the university president publicly offered his understanding that labor troubles "partly arise from the old familiar weakness of human nature which inclines every man to get all that he can . . . and from the inclination to get large pay for little work," Sage declared emphatically that strikes derived "mainly from our foreign population" who "neither believe in God nor government." Sometime following the debate, Sage reportedly marched into the president's office and declared, "This man must go, he is sapping the foundations of our society."[33]

With his career saved by a full-time tenured appointment at Ann Arbor, Adams maintained a lower public profile even as he continued to elaborate a defense of collectivist, democratic regulation of the marketplace. It was not through association with popular movements that Adams subsequently advanced his ideas, however, but through state administrative agencies. Chief statistician in the late 1880s for the Interstate Commerce Commission, Adams pushed for expansive investigatory and regulatory powers and against restrictions increasingly imposed by the courts. While Adams's intellectual curiosity alone may have steered him from the labor question toward other issues, his career is indicative of a more general gravitation among the new economists away from controversy and toward applied expertise.[34]

In any case, Adams's experience proved a harbinger of the troubles the more outspoken "Elyites" would face in the following decade. In 1894, during the nationwide railroad strike precipitated by the Pullman boycott, Ely himself, by then a full professor at Wisconsin, endured an administrative trial before that university's Board of Regents for alleged support of local strikers as well as for theories that supposedly undermined a society based on private

University of Wisconsin economist Richard T. Ely, circa 1900–1910. Photo by E. R. Curtiss. (State Historical Society of Wisconsin, WHi X3 41451)

property. To prove his innocence, Ely presented himself as a conservative and a scientist with no interest in public agitation or direct contacts with the working class.[35] His case ended in his personal exoneration and in a ringing endorsement of the principle of free inquiry by the university trustees. Although personally vindicated, Ely's ordeal left him deeply wounded.[36] He effectively withdrew from all reform activity for the next five years. In 1902, facing financial stress from his wife's illness, Ely sold his magnificent labor history collection and used the proceeds to invest in real estate. Although Ely did reassert his reform credentials during the Progressive Era (chartering the American Association of Labor Legislation in 1906), his biographer locates a passion for respectability in his actions well before his open political souring in the 1920s, when he campaigned against public utilities while maintaining extensive industry connections.[37]

Edward Bemis fared less well. He was forced out of a tenured position at the University of Chicago in 1894 on formal grounds of incompetent teaching, an excuse for the pressures brought to bear on President William Rainey Harper by Bemis's call for municipally owned utilities and criticism of railroad owners. Except for a short stint at a Populist-dominated college in Kansas, Bemis did not regain academic employment.[38]

The pressure on Commons was more subtle. In 1895, Indiana University authorities, having impatiently borne his heresies for three years, "urged" him to take a full professorship extended by Syracuse University. In 1899, however, the same propensities led Commons to outright unemployment when Syracuse abolished his position. There followed five years of academic unemployment; in 1903 Ely referred to Commons as having been "practically blacklisted." When he finally found a position at Wisconsin, Commons referred to the feeling as being "born again . . . after five years of incubation."[39]

Commons's rebirth also occasioned the flowering of what has been called the Wisconsin School of labor history, which culminated in the momumental ten-volume *Documentary History of American Industrial Society* (1910–12) and four-volume *History of Labour in the United States* (1918, 1935). Combining research on labor history, industrial relations, and economic theory with an active concern for

Ely shrinks back,
Bemis fired
Commons pressured

public policy, Commons and his students at Madison contributed significantly to the Progressive political thrust of the state in the La Follette years and beyond. In addition to the industrial relations field, such areas as civil service law, utility regulation, workmen's compensation (as it was then known), and later unemployment and monetary policy all received sustained, creative attention from the "Wisconsin crowd."

It is worth noting, however, that in order to rescue institutional labor studies from academic oblivion, Commons had to reposition himself as both scholar and thinker. In Commons's case, the shift from academic bad boy to mature and influential professional involved both a gradual evolution of perspective and a self-conscious learning experience. Commons retrospectively acknowledged a causative link between academic deprivation and his personal and intellectual development. His dismissal at Syracuse, he wrote, helped reorient his theoretical focus from abundance to scarcity: "I figured that a 'chair' in political economy was not physically pulled out from under you, it was economically pulled out by withholding the funds . . . At least, I knew, after 1899 at Syracuse, that holding and withholding were not the same, and the latter was more important."[40] The notion that the scarcity value of labor and property was a key determinant of economic behavior became a hallmark of Commons's labor history as well as his more theoretical writings. In his view, skilled trade unionists, for example, characteristically sought to restrict entry into the labor market—an idealism of the job rights of the individual worker and occupational interest group—rather than foster a larger classwide solidarity.[41]

Commons's move to Wisconsin also reflected new political understandings. Beginning with a diplomatic leave-taking at Syracuse, Commons, both in his writing and personal decorum, increasingly earned the respect of colleagues for assimilating professional mores. Endorsing Commons's fitness for an academic appointment, conservative Harvard economist T. N. Carver insisted, "Whatever may in the past have been said against his so-called indiscreet utterances can not now be said because he has published nothing for a number of years so far as I have learned, which would not stand the severest scientific criticism."[42]

Commons in fact had learned more than a lesson in academic

manners. Thanks to connections with a few self-made men of broad social vision, his academic hiatus proved a most productive and intellectually creative period. A series of contract research assignments—with the Democratic National Committee, the Industrial Commission of 1900, and the National Civic Federation (NCF)—laid the groundwork for continuous ties to public research projects. From his campus base in Madison, Commons spearheaded drives in the state for expansive civil service reform, an industrial commission, and workmen's compensation laws; through the Commission on Industrial Relations (1912–15), the American Association for Labor Law Reform, and informal networks, he remained for years a signal national influence for labor law reform and social welfare legislation.[43] Like Henry Carter Adams, the career of John R. Commons illustrates the general turn taken by social scientists from the moral and agitational stance of the critical outsider to a position of technical expertise and influence among policy-making elites.[44]

His growing contact with institutions of social mediation—both government bureaus and the tripartite bodies of business, labor, and public representatives that he long favored—led Commons to a revised understanding of the relationship, and boundaries, between intellectuals and workers. A necessary reliance on the "public interest" (those "two-thirds of the voting population" who were but "spectators" to the inevitable industrial disputes) in particular required a disciplined self-restraint by the labor-oriented intellectual.[45] At the NCF, in personal contacts with United Mine Workers president John Mitchell and American Federation of Labor president Samuel Gompers, Commons learned that the "place of the economist was that of adviser to the [trade union] leaders, if they wanted him, and not that of propagandist to the masses."[46] Socialist ideologues, he believed, all too often set themselves on a collision course with the leadership of the trade union movement. "I do not, of course, hold that trade unions are the ultimate goal," he told Henry Demorest Lloyd, "but at the present stage they are absolutely essential, and I do not like to see anything thrown in their way."[47] Disinterested empirical investigation rather than open advocacy was the intellectual's modern weapon.

Commons's approach was in accord with the dominant tenor of the contemporary labor movement. Out of the nadir of the 1890s

How Commons changed.

depression, labor unions had revived not on the basis of the inclusive, antimonopoly platform of the Knights of Labor but through the self-protective and politically conservative craft unionism of the American Federation of Labor. Its leaders, Samuel Gompers and Adolph Strasser, who had been grounded in European Marxism, chose early to present themselves as practical men opposed to theorists, or "fool friends" of labor. Inherently inhospitable to rabble-rousing reformers, declared Gompers characteristically in 1898, trade unions "are not the creation of any man's brain" but rather "organizations of necessity . . . of the working class, for the working class, by the working class."[48] Such bread-and-butter unionism at once provided a legally defensible position from which to extend the province of collective bargaining and offered internal ideological protection from the advocates of independent labor or socialist political initiatives, both within and outside the labor federation. Whereas experts might still be sought and even needed for specific functions (legal defense, bill drafting, and public relations, for example), the AFL, unlike the Knights of Labor, sought no broader alliance with men and women of letters. AFL secretary-treasurer Matthew Woll in 1919 characteristically responded to criticism from an intellectual "friend of labor": "The A F of L does not take its inspiration from those who sit and peer at it through microscopes in contemplation, nor yet from those who pick and pull at its being with scalpel and forceps in heavy-browed analysis. The A F of L takes its inspiration from the needs of the men and women who toil."[49] Indeed, John Frey, self-taught editor of the *Iron-Molders' Journal* and trade union conservative, happily quoted Gompers as saying, "God save us from our intellectual friends. All I ask is that they get off our backs."[50]

In ways he doubtlessly did not anticipate, Gompers's formulation of workers' psychology and interests found ready acceptance in the academic world. The postulation of the labor movement as a force born of economic necessity rather than intellectual or moral vision justified a stance of scholarly objectivity (as opposed to overt union advocacy) by academics, which was in any case a political imperative within the university. The twin doctrines of sovereignty of the labor leader and autonomy of the academic serendipitously fulfilled the needs of both parties.[51]

Together, the contemporary academic and political contexts help to explain the special self-consciousness on the part of the Wisconsin School economists about the relationship of intellectuals to the labor movement. In his introduction to the multivolume *History of Labour* (1918), for example, Commons identified intellectuals as "a miscellaneous class of men and women, taking more or less part in labour movements, yet distinct from manual workers." Commons readily allowed that this group had played a major role in the development of the American labor movement—from Frances Wright and Robert Dale Owen to Horace Greeley, Henry George, John Swinton, Henry D. Lloyd, and George McNeill. But, by a kind of unspoken evolutionary process, the influence of such people was sharply reduced within "the organization or management of the 'wage-conscious' trade unions."[52]

Professor John R. Commons in his study, 1925. (University of Wisconsin–Madison Archives, X25 1923)

Commons sharpened his argument in an entry in the *Encyclopaedia of the Social Sciences* (1935). Here he integrated American developments into larger trends, identifying the intelligentsia as the "natural leaders" of the first "desperate" stage of labor movements, "the stage of Marx, Lassalle, Lenin, Powderly, Louis Blanc or Proudhon." He wrote, "They have a formulated social philosophy and an ability to articulate what the others feel but cannot tell." Then, as the possibility of stable and successful organization develops, new "rank and file" leaders ("a Gompers, an Applegarth, a Legien, a Jouhaux") take over. In Commons's view, such a development was natural and fitting. The intellectual's "proper place" was "not as a leader in forming policies" but "as a technician in details and adviser against mistakes."[53] This prescription set Commons apart from the more doctrinaire socialist and communist intellectuals; by the time he wrote his autobiography in 1934, Commons had lost all patience with a social class he now identified with the extreme political left: "I always look for them [intellectuals] and try to clear them out from all negotiations between capital and labor, and from the councils of labor."[54]

If his own accommodation to the realities of academic and trade union politics inclined the mature Commons to a dim view of the critical intellectual, he left further elaboration of this perspective to his student, Selig Perlman. Perlman, far more than Commons, made the issue of the intellectual's role a central feature of the Wisconsin view of labor history.

Perlman's first account of the subject, as presented in Commons et al.'s *History of Labour*, ventured little beyond Commons's own assertion that intellectuals tended "to direct the manual workers away from the strict and narrow interest of wage-earners as a class, and to lead them towards affiliation with other classes."[55] Perlman applied this dictum in particular to the Knights of Labor's infatuation with the "panacea" of cooperation—the very topic that had attracted economists of an earlier generation to the labor movement—distinguishing the "middle-class psychology" of the Knights' leaders from the more down-to-earth "wage-consciousness" of the trade unions.[56]

Even more pointedly, Perlman's magnum opus of 1928 defined the continual struggle of "organic labor" against "dominance by the intellectuals."[57] Instead of an "American exceptionalism" à la

Selig Perlman

Sombart, Perlman's intellectual-versus-worker paradigm implied a "Soviet" exceptionalism, with "backward" Russia the one country where the "will to power" of intellectuals within the workers' movement had prevailed. Outside the Soviet Union, argued Perlman, built-in tensions between the two social groups persisted (with the intellectual element weakest of all in the United States), but the trade union element, mature and well-organized, tended increasingly to stamp both industrial and political action in its own pragmatic, nonrevolutionary image.[58] Published as *A Theory of the Labor Movement*, Perlman's work was as much an analysis of intellectuals as workers. He himself noted to a friend that the "Macmillan people . . . made me . . . abandon my more laborious title of 'Capitalism, Labor, and Intellectuals.'"[59]

Aside from empirical observation and political context, contemporary social science and philosophy seem also to account for the dualism separating Perlman's workers and intellectuals. In one of the major sociological works of the period, for example—Robert Park and Herbert E. Miller's *Old World Traits Transplanted* (1921)—the intellectual is treated as the immigrant type most often "misadapted to American society."[60] More generally, post–World War I disillusionment with reform movements had set off a wave of academic recriminations against radical ideologues. While working-class leaders of working-class birth tended to be "realistic" and economic-interest-oriented, argued young sociologist and statistical methodologist Stuart A. Rice in 1923, the "intellectual" types were more likely to be driven by "suppressed tendencies and emotions, and not because of reasoned conviction or the practicability of their aims or promises."[61] An even more likely influence on Perlman was the continental sociologist Robert Michels, whose *Political Parties* (1911), with its emphasis on the oligarchical tendencies of democratic institutions, offered a sober corrective to romantic intellectual dreams. Indeed, by 1932 Michels extended his earlier analysis into a stage theory of intellectual-worker interaction remarkably reminiscent of those already published by Commons and Perlman.[62] At a slightly further remove, Perlman's categories also resemble those of Deweyan pragmatism. Perlman's attack on the left intellectual's "social mysticism," the reduction of human goals and destiny to a matter of abstract faith, for example, appropriates the turn-of-the-century pragmatic critique of religious idealism and its ultimate replacement by the scientific study of human experience.[63] Similarly, the "organic" psychology (or "job consciousness") that Perlman attributed to the trade unionist shared the essential qualities of problem-solving, instrumental learning favored by the pragmatists.[64]

A further clue to Perlman's broader philosophical bent derives from his close friendship with Max Kadushin, the famous Hebraist who served as Hillel rabbi in Madison from 1931 to 1942. Kadushin's early works, including *The Theology of Seder Eliahu, a Study in Organic Thinking* (1932) and *Organic Thinking* (1938) make explicit reference to an "organismic approach to social science," associating concepts drawn from Dewey, Alfred North Whitehead, and anthropologist Lucien Levy-Bruhl with the logic of rabbinic theology. In particular, the complementarity Kadushin finds between "logical" (abstract and systemic) and "organic" (essentially context-related) thought closely corresponds to Perlman's basic dualism, suggesting a common contemporary climate of intellectual discourse.

But Perlman's argument may also be open to a deeper, more personal reading. Like the work of Ely and Commons before him, Perlman's masterpiece reflected an implicit commentary on his own relation to his subject. As a member of what might heuristically be considered the third generation of labor historians, Perlman represented an important departure from his predecessors in one vital respect: he was an immigrant Jew in a non-Jewish and often anti-semitic academic world. Born in 1888 to a small merchant family in the Russian town of Bialystok, Perlman, a shy child afflicted with a stutter, threw himself into his studies at *cheder*, or the local Jewish day school. Winning a scholarship to the city's science-oriented gymnasium, where an influential teacher introduced him to Georgii Plekhanov and a new world of intellectual and political radicalism, Perlman then followed other Russian émigrés to Italy, studying medicine at the University of Naples.[65]

A fortuitous set of events brought Perlman to America in January 1908 at age nineteen. The radical bohemian poet Anna Strunsky was gathering a new wardrobe in New York in anticipation of a European trip with her future husband, wealthy American socialist William English Walling. Her seamstress turned out to be

Perlman's Jewish exile experiences

Perlman's aunt, and talk eventually turned to her brilliant young nephew who read Marx. After a meeting in Naples, Perlman accepted Wallings's invitation to come to New York to do translations. His first impressions of his new home were not particularly auspicious. Witnessing a police attack on a rally of the unemployed and the subsequent panic unleashed by an anarchist bomb in Union Square within three months of his arrival, Perlman wrote Mrs. Walling in his halting English that "if not the clubs instead of the nagaikas [whips] in the hands of the blue coats, I could think I stay on Russian ground." While rejecting the reckless actions of anarchists in New York as he had done in Russia, the young Perlman nevertheless vicariously joined the Walllings in mourning the death of Russian populist (Social Revolutionary Party) leader Gregory Gershuni, who had earlier sanctioned the assassination of the czarist minister of the interior and proposed a revolutionary alliance between peasants and intellectuals.[66] Alone and likely feeling vulnerable on both personal and political grounds, Perlman identified with the Union Square marchers: "And who can feel the acuteness of the unemployed more than I? I am going out every day in search of any position, but in vain . . . In Russia, my belonging to the Jewish nation prevented me from [the] finishing of my studies, and here my belonging to the nation of the poor creates just the same conditions."[67] Within a few months Walling again came to Perlman's rescue, this time by facilitating his admission for the following year to the University of Wisconsin to work with Wallings's friends, Ely and Commons.[68]

At Wisconsin, Perlman quickly emerged as a brilliant, uncommonly cosmopolitan student. Completed after one year of coursework, his undergraduate thesis on the history of socialism in Milwaukee outwardly reflected how the young revolutionary partisan had moderated into a careful and mature student of political possibility. Espousing the revisionist opportunism of Eduard Bernstein, Perlman's thesis extolled Victor Berger and the Milwaukee socialists for the triumph of "realism" over "revolutionism" in labor and political circles.[69] Privately, he half-apologized to Anna Strunsky Walling for such retreat to moderation: "Temperamentally, I am in absolute disagreement with opportunism, but treating the matter objectively I feel obliged to admit

Selig Perlman as a graduate student at the University of Wisconsin, Madison, 1912. (Courtesy of Mark Perlman)

that the opportunist kind of socialism is *the* kind which stands a chance in this country."[70]

Even as he imbibed the heady new intellectual influences of his Wisconsin mentors, Perlman, just as at gymnasium, never lost the self-consciousness of being an outsider. Part of the difficulty lay in the transition from political advocacy to professional-academic culture. After completing his thesis in 1910, he privately wrote of feeling "sick and tired of school" and complained of "too much petty jealousy and horizontal gradation . . . I have very many friends, but I'm on poor terms with Prof. Ely and his staff. In our seminary [with Ely and Commons] on Karl Marx, I lead the attack upon the Ely forces. I assure you that the only object of this seminary [sic], as far as I can see, is to fight with your personal opponents. Nobody gives a swap for the truth. Arguing is all we are after."[71]

Much of Perlman's sense of alienation was connected to his Jewishness. Nor was his discomfort attached merely to surroundings he found unfamiliar and customary Upper Midwest references to Jews as "sheenies." On a formal level, and by any contemporary comparative measure, Commons's approach to his students was uncommonly tolerant and inclusive. In a later reminiscence for the State Historical Society, Perlman called his advisor "a formal man, rather difficult to get acquainted with . . . [but] exceedingly generous in his intellectual life . . . I have always maintained that I owe everything to Professor Commons."[72] Yet according to his son, Perlman privately expressed frustration at what he experienced as Commons's residual cultural anti-semitism, which Perlman felt limited the depth of their friendship.[73] One of Perlman's most embarrassing moments came when he brought his parents to live in Madison, after their economic position in Russia had collapsed. Now he was revealed before his mentor not only as a "Jew", not only as an "immigrant with a Yiddish accent," but worst of all, a "poor Russian Jew."[74] Moreover, it pained Perlman that the dedication of his *Theory*— "To J.R.C. and N.D.C." (Mrs. Commons)—never prompted an acknowledgment from his mentor. The worst moment came in 1931 when, before the usual crowd of Friday Nighters gathered at the Commons house, Commons declared that Edwin Witte had been named his successor at Wisconsin and openly expressed relief at not having to place Perlman in that position. Perlman did not get out of bed for days after this slight and broke off contact with Commons for an extended period.[75]

It was only at the end of his life, it seems, that Perlman expressed to anyone beyond his own family his profoundly mixed feelings about his Wisconsin experience. Writing to his dear friend and early benefactor, the then-widowed Anna Strunsky Walling, during a trip to Israel in July 1957, Perlman treated an obviously painful issue with characteristic wit and detachment.

> I brought to the University [of Wisconsin] a set of rare books as a gift and I told them that after I retire in June 1959 from the J. R. Commons Research Professorship [to which Perlman had just been appointed] I'll also bring my library, which includes the one [Commons] had left me, to the Hebrew University [in Jerusalem]. I can well imagine his enigmatic Anglo-Saxon smile . . . if someone in

Commons's residual
anti semitism + slights
against Perlman!

the upper sphere, where I am sure he is now abiding, brought to him this bit of news that the books of his library with their many marginal annotations by himself will find their permanent resting place at the Hebrew University, for with all of his affection for me personally he was never free of serious misgivings about Jews as such. Maybe that's why I am so pleased to have had the University of Wisconsin create that "name" professorship for me and to have the Administration have done it without my knowledge—so that I have really not "put any-thing over" on dear John R., a so-called "Jewish" trait he had fre-quently adressed [sic] to me.[76]

For all his accomplishments, Selig Perlman often experienced the academic profession—at least outside his own classroom—as cold, unrewarding, and inhospitable. Both by temperament and for lack of invitations, Perlman rarely left Madison. Unlike others in the Wisconsin School, he did almost no direct public service work and had little contact with labor leaders or public figures or, outside Madison, even policy-oriented academics.[77] It is noteworthy that the man who left the most indelible impression of twentieth-cen-tury worker ideology—the notion of the basic common sense of the laboring "Tom, Dick, and Harry"—never met Samuel Gompers, Matthew Woll, William Green, or John L. Lewis and never ad-dressed a union meeting or convention.[78]

Perlman's brief but demanding venture beyond the university's walls—field work in 1913–14 for the U.S. Commission on Industrial Relations—offers a revealing glimpse of his imaginative yet limited contact with American workers. The young Perlman was first dis-patched to New England textile towns gripped by fear and repres-sion following a wave of organizing drives inspired by the radical syndicalist Industrial Workers of the World. Traveling incognito in order not to arouse employer suspicions, Perlman sought to gather evidence of industrial conditions and popular feeling.[79] Unable to gain entree to workers' homes, Perlman devised an ingenious strat-egy for acquiring candid and spontaneous opinion. He relied on local Jewish storeowners ("they are as a rule excellent observers of men and conditions and coming into very intimate contact with the

[handwritten note: Perlman didn't mix with workers or unions]

Perlman's "undercover" work in Jewish shops + among immigrant miners

laboring people . . . they are in a position to form correct opinions of the manner of thinking of the various elements of the population") and casually chatted with customers in their stores.[80]

In a second report from the field, this time from the Pennsylvania anthracite region, Perlman reflected directly on the tension between the emotions of the raw, untutored immigrant miner and the practical-mindedness required for trade union survival. The immigrant miner, Perlman discovered, readily parroted in interviews the view of his district organizers and officers "that trade agreements should be sacredly observed; that no one having a grievance should arbitrarily quit work, but should report to the union." Yet the situation changed abruptly as soon as the informant returned to his mates in the mine or attended a meeting of the local: "When one member after the other gets up and states his grievances, our apparently confirmed believer in the trade agreements is most likely to get up and shout 'Strike.'" The wisdom of the trade unionist, Perlman observed, likewise lay along a differentiated path of ethnic particularism.

> With regard to the position in the union, the Poles can show the highest attainment, probably about ¼ of the presidents of the locals being Poles. The Poles would have achieved still greater prominence in the official circles in the union had it not been for their extreme sensitiveness to abuse. Thus, it is not [un]usual for a Polish officer in a local to throw up his office [i.e., quit] as soon as he comes in for abuse from any of the members. The English speaking officers, either because they rarely understand the uncomplimentary epithets hurled at them by the foreign speaking members, or because they are less sensitive, are in a better position to attend to their duties in a calm mood. The Lithuanians are far less sensitive to insult, but are inferior to the Poles in capacity for leadership and are therefore generally led by the Poles . . . The Italians not only lack the high capacity of the Pole[s] for organization, but are just as sensitive to insults and slights.[81]

Rather than an inherited trait, Perlman suggests, the reasoning of the trade union leader was an acquired capacity, a third stance somewhere between the emotional reactions of the raw immigrant on the one hand and the overdeveloped ratiocinations of the intellectual on the other.

It is likely that Perlman's experiences both in Russia and the

United States led him not only to a clear delineation of intellectuals as a separate social group but to a deep ambivalence, connected to his own bittersweet fortunes, about the intellectual's social role. Dating from his early education, Perlman conceived of a heroic intelligentsia who offered a moral but politically ineffectual critique of worldly power. Perlman himself more closely cut the modern image of the intellectual as college professor—a humane and philosophical man of letters who had many well-formed opinions about the world but who was totally ill-equipped to act within it. The social gap suggested in *A Theory of the Labor Movement* between workers and intellectuals accurately reflected the world Perlman had known in Europe; it was reproduced on the Madison campus, where few manual laborers could be found. Yet, as thoroughly socialized as he was into the intellectual world, the marginalism Perlman felt as a Jewish academic made it difficult for him to feel comfortable in the company of the campus elite. Unlike many of his more technocratic-minded contemporaries to his right and left, Perlman had no reason to entrust the world to intellectuals.[82]

THOUGH FERTILIZED by intimate and even idiosyncratic circumstances, the labor economists' distinction between workers and intellectuals was nevertheless broadcast over a wide field. On the whole it met political as well as academic requirements. The historic preponderance of employer power together with an inherent antagonism to collective economic action in American law had sent defenders of workers' welfare searching for a durable shelter.[83] Wisconsin School reformers believed they had found a defensible home for organized labor in the theory of labor relations that became known as "industrial pluralism." Connecting collective bargaining not to the destruction of the capitalist order but to its reinvigoration, industrial pluralists pressed for legally sanctioned mechanisms of managed conflict between employers and workers. A champion of the doctrines of his mentor John R. Commons, William M. Leiserson noted as early as 1926 the difference between the relatively new term "industrial relations" (which implied mutual accommodation and adjustment) and turn-of-the-century discussion of the "labor problem" (which implied "a solution" in terms of rights and wrongs). The change, in Leiserson's view, had by no means banished ethics from the considerations of reformers; rather, the frozen mentality of Labor vs. Capital had been replaced by appeal to "an awakened social conscience" and a larger "public mind," and "new moral tests are [henceforth] applied to both management and workers."[84] A shrewd political and social compromise, the model of collective bargaining sanctioned by industrial pluralism depended on the rational accommodation of conflicting, but equally legitimate, interests. Even as union rights, therefore, were defended on grounds of "public interest" (that favorite resort of the Progressive generation), they would, of course, also be subject to the limitations that that interest might impose.

The Wisconsin scholars' ideal of the pragmatic worker—self-interested, self-protective, and essentially incrementalist in orientation—set against the abstract intellectual indeed helped to define the regulated freedom ultimately accorded labor unions in the era of the Wagner Act. Not only did the National Labor Relations Board (NLRB) draw in its very creation on Commons's own efforts on the prewar Commission on Industrial Relations, but Commons' students, Leiserson and Harry A. Millis, personally presided over the administrative consolidation of the Board beginning in 1939. Not surprisingly, Leiserson analyzed the problem of left-wing influence within the newly founded Congress of Industrial Organizations (CIO) and the resultant political backlash against the NLRB within the classic terms of the "intellectual" problem: "Communists and social reformers of various kinds [who] have attempted to capture the movement, control its policies, and divert the power of organized labor into social politics or revolutionary channels and away from collective bargaining and the institutions of stable industrial government which are its normal aims."[85] An early application of the Leiserson-Millis doctrine of administrative objectivity was the dismissal of NLRB secretary and alleged Communist Party member Nathan Witt. Secretary of Labor Frances Perkins captured the prevailing view that Witt represented "one of those intellectuals who was in love with labor, who thought that labor was always right and never could be wrong."[86] The comments of these policymakers recall the story of another Wisconsin labor historian, Philip Taft, about his teacher, Selig Perlman, for whom "'intellectual' . . . became a pejorative label for anyone whose views he did not share":

institutionalization of incrementalism + against Labor intellectuals.

When I taught summer school in 1949 at Madison, there was a meeting of the School for Workers at which the Secretary-Treasurer of the UAW, Emil Mazey, spoke, advocating the formation of a labor party. Going home Professor Perlman asked me, "Who was that intellectual?" I had to tell him that this was a man who participated in the sitdown strikes, who was one of the finest of the new trade unionists, and who defied the Detroit gangsters who sought to interfere with the union.[87]

Intellectual prescription and government action thus ultimately joined hands. Altogether, the political triumph of labor reform thought must rank as one of the most impressive examples of social change ever emanating from academe. While banishing the disabling injunction and unmitigated employer authority as the modus operandi of American industrial relations, public policy by the 1940s formally accepted the "pragmatic" trade unionist (focused on acts of immediate, incremental material improvement) as a worthy industrial citizen, even while banning his "intellectual" counterpart (liable to the delusions of political radicalism or solidaristic acts, such as sympathy strikes and secondary boycotts) from the door.[88]

However politically efficacious, preoccupation with the intellectual as a threatening outsider and factional foe resulted in a notable blind spot. For all their voluminous and monumental exploration of American labor relations, the Wisconsin scholars avoided self-scrutiny. The industrial relations model discountenanced the meddling radical and restricted both business and labor to horizons of commonsense materialism. It offered little analysis of its own mediating figures or intent. Without apparent irony, some of the best scholars, the most subtle ideologists, and the most effective social reformers of the early twentieth century wrote themselves out of their own history.

3 The People's Expert

Charles McCarthy and the Perils of Public Service

C.I.R

PRESIDENT Woodrow Wilson's appointment of a federal commission in 1912 to recommend solutions to "a state of industrial war" represented an unprecedented opportunity to address the nation's most contentious domestic issue. Relying as it did on several of the era's leading public intellectuals, the Commission on Industrial Relations (CIR) implicitly tested the social influence of a larger labor reform community of academics, social investigators, and political activists as well as the chances for a progressive policy agenda on the labor question. "If they do their work with imagination and courage," Walter Lippmann predicted, "they will do more than any other group of people in this country to shape our history."[1] Volunteering his assistance, Wisconsin's legislative librarian, Charles McCarthy, saluted the project as "the greatest work ever undertaken in America."[2]

Yet within two years a fight between the chairman and the research staff effectively split the commission into feuding camps. Unable to reach a consensus in its final report, the commission squandered much of its external goodwill as well as its budgetary appropriation. Though its final recommendations may well have been, as some observers have said, the most radical social wisdom ever emanating from an official federal authority in American history, the militant rhetoric fell largely on deaf ears.[3] Except for a few pieces of ameliorative legislation with tangential connection to the commission's mission, little came of the "twenty-two months of investigation, hundreds of hours of well-publicized hearings, and thousands of pages of testimony."[4] The commission generally received a brushoff from Congress and, at best, served organized labor as a propaganda tool rather than a serious strategic ally.[5] Although the coming of World War I did indeed witness a dramatic increase in state labor regulation, the moment proved less a triumph of pre-war reform fervor than an emergency measure to be jettisoned for its very coercive origins.[6]

But even before outside factors like the war came into play, the commission's internal strife had muffled its message and blunted its impact. The head of the commission's women's research division, Marie L. Obenauer, experienced the internal upheaval as "painful and disheartening beyond description." John A. Fitch, editor of *Survey*, labeled the unraveling of the commission's promise "one of the saddest spectacles of this generation." With some justification, therefore, the journal of the National Association of Manufacturers fairly crowed, "We are not disappointed with the product of the Commission's labors: nothing constructive was expected of it and nothing constructive has been produced."[7]

What went wrong with the CIR? While a full answer to the question would encompass the peculiar mechanics of American politics and state reform as a whole, the relevant issues here have to do with the role and behavior of the labor reformers themselves. In particular, the CIR exposed competing visions about the very function of intellectual activism: What purpose did social investigation serve? In what relation to government and the people did investigators stand? Such queries, inextricably caught up in the contemporary conflicts of policy and personality, in the end lay bare not only obstacles to industrial democracy but key dilemmas within the social history of American intellectuals.

CONCEIVED under President Taft, chartered by Congress, and staffed by appointments of President Wilson, the Commission on Industrial Relations was a direct result of a determined campaign by a coalition of reform-minded businessmen, social workers, academics, and religious leaders.[8] Conviction of the McNamara brothers for the bombing of the building that housed the *Los Angeles Times* amid a bitter struggle over the city's open-shop policies proved a final public spur to action. Following closely upon a presidential campaign waged in a climate of growing dissatisfaction with laissez-faire economics (in which three candidates identified with progressivism and the fourth with socialism), the political climate could hardly have been more conducive to proposals for industrial reform. Finally, dissatisfaction with prior commissioned research that had been all but ignored by legislators convinced the new commission from early on not merely to collect information but to "be interpretive and remedial."[9]

From the beginning, the CIR assumed a determinedly didactic posture. Structured on the model of the corporatist National Civic Federation (with its nine members equally divided into public, labor, and business representatives), the commission generally followed the lead of its chairman, Kansas City attorney Frank P. Walsh, and its most distinguished public member, Professor John R. Commons of the University of Wisconsin.[10] Appointment of these two well-known labor reformers consolidated support from both organized labor and the intellectual community. Even the ever-suspicious Samuel Gompers suspended his initial criticism of "intellectuals on a sociological slumming tour."[11]

Superficially, the alliance of Walsh's political skills with Commons's scholarly expertise offered bright prospects for the commission's effectiveness. Both the integrity of his convictions and his energy in pursuing them recommended Frank Walsh to many in the reform community as the perfect captain for a radical-progressive assault on the battlements of industrial privilege. Journalist George Creel, for example, lionized him as "a great lawyer, a persuasive speaker, and the most authentic liberal I have known."[12] Selected after legal scholar Louis Brandeis declined to serve, Walsh combined extensive labor contacts with impeccable radical reform convictions. A loyal Democrat, he had organized a "social workers for Wilson" brigade in 1912; he also possessed a more personal connection to the White House via Margaret Wilson, the president's daughter, who cultivated a number of Progressive reformers.[13] The one chink in the Walsh armor was perhaps a product of his very combativeness. When in the spring of 1915 Creel jokingly addressed the CIR chairman as "Mr. Francis 'Poleon Walsh" and "Dear 'Poleon the Greatest," many of Walsh's colleagues and erstwhile admirers were no longer smiling.[14]

Politically, Walsh exhibited a crusading populist spirit alongside a bare-knuckled realpolitik born of his Missouri background. Born in

Frank P. Walsh, chairman of the Federal Commission on Industrial Relations, 1912–1915, pictured here as co-chair of the National War Labor Board, 1918. Photo by Western Newspaper Union. (State Historical Society of Wisconsin, WHi X3 50580)

1864 to a poor Irish Catholic family in St. Louis, Walsh held a succession of laboring jobs until teaching himself law in 1889 and entering the rough-and-tumble world of Kansas City machine politics. The young George Creel (who himself had climbed from déclassé southern roots into a professional career) quickly lined up with Walsh, the brains behind the local anti-Pendergast political faction and chief reform strategist in corruption-ridden Missouri.[15]

Together Walsh, Creel, and a coterie of reform-minded writers and small businessmen articulated a self-styled antimonopoly politics resting on hostility to the corporations, radical tax doctrine, and generous social welfare spending. Both inside and outside the courtroom, Walsh attacked the corruption of the political parties, railroad influence over legislators and judges, and the shameful plight of the urban poor. A big, athletic man with a booming voice and commanding courtroom presence, Walsh regularly dueled Pendergast loyalist and future U.S. senator James A. Reed in cases across the state, including the successful defense of Jesse James, Jr., on charges of train robbery.[16] Few persons selected to federal governmental responsibility had developed a less respectful attitude towards the trappings of office or the niceties of procedure than Walsh. When legal ambiguities arose in connection with the work of the pioneering Kansas City Board of Public Welfare, for example, Walsh responded with a chuckle, "To [hell] with the law. Let us go ahead and do it and we will take care of the law later."[17] Creel characterized him as "an agitator outside," not "a plodding administrator inside."[18]

A self-styled champion of the underdog, Walsh displayed especially friendly relations with organized labor. Receiving early endorsement as CIR chair from President Gompers and continuing cooperation from the commission's three moderate labor representatives, Walsh also quickly won over more radical figures, such as "Big Bill" Haywood and Eugene V. Debs, and drew warm praise from Mother Jones. Perhaps Walsh's closest contact in labor circles was Chicago's militant and politically minded Federation of Labor chief, John Fitzpatrick, with whom he would collaborate for years to come.[19]

Walsh made no pretense to neutrality on the labor question. In correspondence with the editor of the *Christian Socialist* in 1915, he called himself a political independent and "so far as social and

Walsh — combative attorney
w/ labor friends

economic effort is concerned . . . ready to go with any person or group traveling in the direction of human justice."[20] Awaiting Congressional confirmation of the CIR panel in the summer of 1913, he listened sympathetically when his hometown friend L. A. Halbert advised that the commission seek to "give the people power over industry and not be hindered by the ancient fetish of the rights of private property." Though such a purpose could not be openly avowed, allowed Halbert, he nevertheless urged Walsh to develop the "data to establish this position so that it can become the dominant ideal for all time."[21] During the same period Walsh wrote Creel that "we will call our little meeting of 'conspirators' in New York early this Fall for the purpose of finding out exactly what we want and going after it." Already, reported Walsh, "this Commission has put me in touch with a number of people around the country of genuine radical views and undoubted sincerity . . . I will try to establish a sort of quarters for own people . . . [If] writers such as we could get together, there is no telling where we would stop."[22]

Of all Walsh's early moves to set the CIR on solid footing, none seemed more astute than his recruitment of the University of Wisconsin scholar John R. Commons as a fellow commissioner.[23] Not that the appointment was a surprise. Indeed, an investigation of industrial life without a Madison imprimatur would have been startling. Since the 1880s, the state university had championed the rhetoric of public service and aligned itself with the social gospel critique of free-market capitalism. The happy coincidence of La Follette progressivism and the social policy orientation of university president Charles R. Van Hise (who was himself considered for the CIR chair) secured Madison's reputation in the early twentieth century as a laboratory for progressive legislative measures. For nearly two decades, intellectual research, reform political strategy, and legislative bill-drafting commingled as never before in American society. Toward this end, Van Hise took no more important step than his acquiescence to the recruitment of controversial labor economist John R. Commons in 1904. In addition to a distinguished reputation for social research, Commons by 1910 had inspired pioneering state legislation for civil service extension, an industrial commission, and workmen's compensation. With an encyclopedic grasp of American labor history and experience on both the U.S. Industrial

Commission of 1902—the last federal survey of industrial conditions prior to the CIR—and the pathbreaking Pittsburgh survey of 1907–1909, Commons was easily recognized as the nation's leading authority on the problems of industrial society by the time the CIR was created. Walsh's promise to Commons "to rely heavily on such experts as you" symbolically paid tribute to (and, in turn, won support from) the entire sector of contemporary social service and social science professionals. In concrete terms, Walsh looked to Commons to organize the commission's research work, while the chairman himself concentrated on the public hearings.[24]

Much as it was in the world of scholarship, Commons's influence on the CIR was ultimately secured through the efforts of his students, broadly defined. His direct role was limited from the outset by an obligation to return to teaching after a two-year leave with the Wisconsin Industrial Commission. With only his summers available for full-time focus on the project, Commons relied on a brilliant young stable of students, former students, and intellectual acquaintances.[25] The early months of investigation, however, proceeded slowly. With little coordination between hearings and research and a lack of clear goals, thirty-four-year-old economist and commission staff member W. Jett Lauck struggled to coordinate work on a disparate set of topics, ranging from coercion in company towns to the legal framework for collective bargaining to working women's welfare. Only when Charles McCarthy answered an urgent call from Commons and Walsh to assume direction of the research in June 1914 did the investigation really snap into shape.[26]

Charles McCarthy was already a skillful and renowned professional policymaker when he joined the CIR. Having transformed the Wisconsin Legislative Library from a hole in the wall into the country's first research and bill-drafting service, he had played an integral part in the Progressive transformation of Wisconsin government. Indeed, McCarthy himself popularized the state's reform legacy in *The Wisconsin Idea*—a virtual ode to the marriage of democratic idealism and administrative efficiency, commissioned by Theodore Roosevelt to aid the Progressive cause in 1912.[27] Preoccupied with political matters in Madison, McCarthy initially fended off appeals to act in any more than a consultant role to the CIR. When he finally accepted Chairman Walsh's plea for help, however, McCarthy entered the scene with the confidence of one used to reorganizing things. Among his first communications to Walsh was a gentle chiding of the chairman for being "altogether too good-natured—you allow everybody to impose themselves upon you . . . You can't even get through your mail without interruption."[28]

Although McCarthy, like Walsh, emerged from a poor Irish working-class background—the son of a factory worker and a boarding housekeeper from Brockton, Massachusetts—McCarthy's ascent traversed a different geographic and educational plane and engendered a different approach to government and politics. Accepted as a special student at Brown University after following the theatre circuit as a stage hand to Providence, Rhode Island, McCarthy flourished under the tutelage of Brahmin historian John Franklin Jameson. As physically daring as he was intellectually ambitious, the wiry young McCarthy also excelled at football; he was nominated to all-America teams and was the first Brown man to score against both Harvard and Yale. His reputation on campus was sealed in the special friendship that developed between the shoeworker's son and John D. Rockefeller, Jr., McCarthy's classmate and assistant football team manager.[29]

Even collegiate fame, however, did not separate McCarthy from the burden of his humble social roots. Unlike most of his Brown classmates, McCarthy worked his way through college; indeed, in order to graduate, he required special faculty dispensation for coursework missed while working. After graduation, McCarthy coached football at the University of Georgia for two years, supplementing his income with research service on Southern history for Professor Jameson. Finally, he was able to enter graduate school at the University of Wisconsin, where he was attracted both by the reputation of the history department and the reform thought of economist Richard T. Ely. McCarthy took his Ph.D. in history, economics, and political science in 1901, writing a prizewinning thesis under Frederick Jackson Turner on the Anti-Masonic Party.[30] Even with solid intellectual credentials, however, he fell short of full academic qualifications. Rough of speech, awkward in personal style and dress, and, most important, unmistakably Irish, McCarthy was apparently judged a poor social risk for a university position both by Turner and his old friend Jameson. Fortunately for McCarthy, a position as chief documents clerk for the state's Free Library Commission opened shortly after his graduation, and Turner pushed McCarthy into the position with enthusiasm and relief. Professional placement coincided with personal commitment when McCarthy married his landlady's daughter, a schoolteacher of German Protestant background.[31]

McCarthy's odyssey of hard work and modest upward social mobility equipped him at once with a thirst for cultural refinement and an abiding sympathy for those who had not enjoyed his own good fortune. Once in Madison, he displayed a fierce idealism about social service and social justice. Even while doggedly pursuing his dissertation travels in various eastern cities, for example, he regularly wrote his wife, Lucile, of the hardships of the working people he saw around him: "The electric went by the docks and I could see the sailors at work, the stevedores hauling and tugging, could hear loud orders, curses and all the hum and rattle and roar of business . . . What a loafer I am! What an easy time we have compared to them!" Journeying through Pennsylvania, he contrasted the "crashing of modern machinery" to the "thousands of creatures ground down and brutalized in all this."[32] McCarthy would later recall his early sense of mission: "I had an idea in my head that there was somebody needed between the great mass of workers and the educated people and I tried in every way to prepare myself to be that somebody if I could."[33]

Rather than a populist agitator like Walsh, however, the educated McCarthy emerged as a skillful technician of the machinery of government. In what one contemporary called "the accidental meeting of an opportunity and a shrewd Irish intellect," McCarthy had almost single-handedly developed the prototype for state legislative reference services. Self-consciously drawing on the examples of earlier British reformers like Francis Place, who had developed an influential private library of political tracts, and Jeremy Bentham, who had insisted on a practical test for all reform ideas, the young McCarthy simultaneously answered contemporary demands for efficiency in government and growing calls for ameliorative legislation. McCarthy became a particularly valuable accomplice for activist Wisconsin governors, especially during the administrations of two progressive sons of the university, Robert La Follette (1900–1906) and Francis McGovern (1910–1914). McCarthy also made a mark in national political circles, violating his declared non-partisanship in the heady reform climate of 1912. Courted by both Wilson and Roosevelt after La Follette's candidacy suffered ir- *Bull* reparable setback, McCarthy joined the platform committee at the *Moose* Bull Moose convention and coauthored the famous antitrust plank, whose excision by conservatives from the published platform ultimately dampened Roosevelt's independent appeal.[34]

McCarthy's "radical progressivism," two terms he comfortably applied to his own thinking, differed in one important respect from Walsh's labor populism. On top of traditional democratic egalitarianism, the "Wisconsin Idea" heaped a new social welfare statism. Thus, while the Wisconsin program continued to depend for its rationale on antimonopolism—"unequal conditions of contract" over the necessities of life and industry, the swamping of individual capacity and initiative by "predatory wealth"—the remedy, suggested McCarthy, was "not so simple."[35] The Wisconsin Idea required less an understanding of workers and farmers under capitalism (whose universal plight was assumed) than an appreciation of the experience and insight of a remarkable group of university-based reformers. The arrival of Richard T. Ely in particular, who had studied in Germany before finishing his graduate work at Johns Hopkins, brought the "inspiration of New Germany" back to "the German university of the German state of Wisconsin." This institutional connection, combined with the social impact of depression, facilitated a successful transcendence of liberal individualism and classical political economy.[36]

While naive (if not a trifle racist) in his comparative sociology, McCarthy's Teutonic idealism served a rather shrewd set of observations about American society.[37] As determined reformers had discovered since the Gilded Age, neither the legislature nor the courts could be looked to as an effective instrument of social welfare in the United States. Like other Progressives, McCarthy placed ultimate blame on a patronage-based political system: "Good administration is impossible unless combined with ordinary business methods and the latter are not compatible with the policy 'to the victors belong the spoils.'"[38] Nor, however, had "non-political" courts helped matters. By narrowing the constitutionality of both regulatory and welfare measures and by granting a rule by injunction in industrial relations, the judiciary had proven even more insensitive to the condition of the "man in the street."[39]

What was missing from the public sphere was the continuity—and flexibility—of dispassionate administrative authority. "Good laws," declared McCarthy, "are ineffective unless accompanied by good administration." In the circumstances, the German model heralded an alternate path to social democratic initiatives via administrative action. Lacking a reliable civil service structure, Wisconsin reformers led by John R. Commons had developed the public commission as an alternative administrative apparatus.[40] McCarthy was not unaware of the paradox of a philosophical radical defending a system of government by appointment. "It may seem strange," he allowed, "that the system of appointive offices meets with so much approval in a state where there is such confidence in democracy and where the direct primary election is in favor."[41] McCarthy nevertheless expressed confidence that a vigilant public could at once take full advantage of highly trained government "experts" and at the same time hold them to democratic accountability.[42]

Selectively invoking the contributions of diverse social architects—Bismarck, the civil service, radical intellectuals, the socialists—McCarthy turned Germany (and occasionally other countries as well) into a veritable cafeteria for American progressive measures. "Shall we always hear the returning travellers' tale of the improvements throughout the entire world with a provincial and smug spirit and be foolish enough to believe that we can learn nothing, while right in our midst are problems which have confronted every nation at some time in its history?" Adopting the via media arguments of his European social democratic contemporaries, McCarthy sought to preempt an ideological rebuff: "Shall we always be deceived by the cry of 'Socialism' whenever it is necessary to use the state to a greater degree than formerly? When it comes to the attainment of any reasonable legislation for the true betterment of human beings, the only way to beat the Socialists 'is to beat them to it.'"[43]

His whole educational and professional experience imbued McCarthy with an infectious enthusiasm about the possibilities of rational reform action. Called in the first group of expert witnesses in late December 1913 to advise the CIR, McCarthy spoke with utter confidence and perhaps a touch of insolence about extending the

We'll only get decent democ by appointive commissions!

Charles McCarthy, circa 1910, in his office at the Wisconsin Legislative Library.
(State Historical Society of Wisconsin, WHi X3 61)

Wisconsin experiment to the national level: "We had this situation in Wisconsin: They had that reform movement in the state, headed by Mr. La Follette. It was a question of what should be done, just the thing that you people are up against, and a question of how they could do it, and we hit upon a way of working that thing, which might be useful to you here." Essentially, McCarthy's proposed method—one that he would soon be in a position to act upon—amounted to a national commission of applied brainstorming.[44]

McCarthy and his Wisconsin-trained staff exemplified what Commons had called "utilitarian idealism," a social democratic faith that "constructive research" might lead to the "gradual reconstruction of society."[45] Dedication to the exacting standards of social investigation, they were convinced, went hand in hand with radical social change. In private communications they regularly referred to themselves as "radicals," penetrating critics of the social order, yet equally saw themselves as professionally respectable "experts."[46]

Tensions between the philosophical radicalism and pragmatic reform practice of this group of labor investigators were neatly registered in the views of William Morris Leiserson. Deputy director of the Wisconsin Industrial Commission and barely thirty years old when summoned to the CIR as assistant research director under McCarthy, Leiserson still managed to inhabit both the idealistic world of his radical socialist youth and the more technocratic province of government administration that would define his future career. A Jewish immigrant from Estonia, Leiserson arrived in Madison in 1905 as a revolutionary socialist, but quickly tempered his views under the influence of undergraduate teachers like Commons as well as Milwaukee municipal socialists Victor Berger and Daniel Hoan, to whom he quickly gravitated. Even after graduation, however, Leiserson and fellow Commons students such as Ira B. Cross and David J. Saposs maintained contact with the local socialist club. As late as 1912, Leiserson was in indirect negotiation with Friedrich Sorge about the proper translation of Marx, and as late as 1915 he was still writing articles for the socialist newspaper the *Milwaukee Leader*.[47]

Something of the division in Leiserson's soul was apparent in his first contact with the CIR. Summoned as a witness before joining the staff himself, Leiserson, in good Wisconsin fashion, first urged the panel not to get bogged down in the general problem of unemployment but to focus on getting "something done right now." Proposing a national chain of public employment offices, Leiserson momentarily allowed that the idea "may look like dealing with palliatives that are not getting at the fundamental thing." When labor commissioner James O'Connell pursued the issue, asking for the underlying remedy in finding work for the unemployed, a revealing exchange took place:

Mr. Leiserson. If you want to know how to remedy that proposition, I may state, that, for example, all industries in the country ought to be owned by the Government, and everybody ought to get a month's vacation the way I do . . . that is the fundamental remedy in my opinion. If you recommended that, where would you get? You would get nowhere.

Divided minds + souls. e.g. Leiserson.

Commissioner Delano. We would get it in the neck.

Mr. Leiserson. Yes; that is why I say you have got to get down to the practical proposition of what you can do now . . .

Commissioner Lennon. If you would come in every day we would all be Socialists, the first thing you know.

Mr. Leiserson. Well, I would not object.[48]

If the young Leiserson was more cavalier than most in revealing his ultimate political sympathies, his basic outlook—deep-seated social democratic commitments combined with an eye for detailed and defensible policy initiatives—fit the Wisconsin pattern. Together, McCarthy and Leiserson clearly believed they were riding a radical reform juggernaut. The adrenalin fairly flowed between them in early December 1914, for example, when McCarthy described a sleepless night from which he had profited by rereading Beatrice and Sidney Webb on the rise of British new unionism in the 1880s.[49] Convinced that if they sized up their situation properly, the pace of social progress in America might truly match that of Europe, the CIR directors inspired a young and ill-paid staff with a spirit of happy sacrifice.

It was not long before national versions of the Wisconsin-style strategy—striking social initiatives veiled by their very administrative machinery—were emanating from the research wing of the commission. Perhaps McCarthy's most far-reaching proposal was one calling for a federal industrial council, a body modeled on Wisconsin's industrial commission but considerably expanded in scope. Through the industrial commission form (justified by the welfare clause of the Constitution) reformers could achieve "what we have so often talked about in the past—the expansion of the constitution." Generated in discussions with Commons, who for years had conceived of various such plans, the idea was ultimately set down in a bill drafted by young commission staffer Selig Perlman "to bring about an approximate equality in the bargaining power of labor and capital in unorganized industries." Proposing state intervention on a scale more massive than even later New Deal reformers ever contemplated, Perlman's plan offered basic protection for labor's right to organize and strike, with an extensive list of unfair labor practices. It further stipulated that an industry in any locality that remained unorganized six months after passage of the act constituted "prima facie evidence that employers have prevented organization" and authorized the council in such a case to "step in and fix the conditions of employment, viz: wages, hours, etc. subject to review by the courts."[50]

A sense of complementarity initially bound Walsh and McCarthy in harmony within the life of the commission. McCarthy enjoyed a relatively free hand on the research side, while the chairman viewed his role less as conducting a legislative research bureau than a trial before "the great jury of the American public." In dramatic and well-publicized forays across the country, the commissioners bore striking witness to the rawest scenes of industrial warfare—the attack on the Wobblies in Paterson, New Jersey; threats to the Protocol of Peace in the New York garment industry; the crushing of the shop crafts' federation on the Illinois Central Railroad; the routing of the Fulton Bag Mill employees in Atlanta; and, most dramatically, the Ludlow Massacre, which obliterated the coal miners' strike against the Rockefeller-owned Colorado Fuel and Iron Company. Altogether, the Walsh-led commission provided a continuous, blistering exposé of industrial tyranny in the United States. With public advocacy his main mission, Walsh tended to look on McCarthy's research and bill-drafting responsibilities as "technical matters," the business of tying up administrative ends. Still, for months he willingly deferred to the Wisconsin-led brain trust in order to surround his own convictions with the force of scientific legitimacy and, ultimately, added political weight. He seemed generally impressed by McCarthy's political brainstorming, including his proposal to use the tariff laws to enforce fair labor standards on protected industries—"like everything else you present to me it looks good." Similarly enthusiastic about an idea to investigate the "gun men" (private police forces) employed in industrial disputes, Walsh specified that the investigators be drawn "from among your students at Madison . . . I don't believe I would entrust it to anybody in the U.S. except yourself." His own results-oriented thinking led McCarthy naturally to invert the chairman's priorities; he tried to subordinate, or at least coordinate, hearings with less flashy investigations of his research staff. Yet however peripheral he found them to the concrete work of bill-drafting, McCarthy also recognized the educational value of public hearings, particularly under the direction of such a skillful public advocate as Walsh, a man whom McCarthy respectfully described as "a Wendell Phillips type, essentially an agitator."[51]

It was outside pressure that first drew their contrasting styles and skills into conflict. A rump group of largely southern, conservative congressmen who had sought to sabotage the investigation from the start forced Walsh to return intermittently to Congress for necessary appropriations.[52] As early as the summer of 1914, uncertainty of funding was producing occasional backbiting between the administratively lax and cavalier Walsh and the scrupulous and efficient McCarthy.[53] Walsh regularly waved off McCarthy's attempts to impose a stringent timetable on the project. "You have always worried too much about the finances of this Commission," Walsh insisted after McCarthy complained of dwindling funds in December 1914. "I feel almost as though I could do all I care to do without any financing from a public source. You stick to me . . . and we will come out all right."[54] But the resources were simply not sufficient to sustain such a liberal managerial approach. Proceeding unchecked on all fronts, the commission hit dire straits by February 1915. Finally forced to reckon with fiscal reality (and fearing denial of a last request from Congress), Walsh, at a Chicago meeting on February 28, ignored McCarthy's advice and ordered draconian cuts in the research budget, including wholesale staff layoffs. When McCarthy strenuously objected, Walsh effectively relieved his chief lieutenant of command.[55]

While the money question touched the raw nerve of the chairman's authority, a more insidious issue had alienated Walsh from McCarthy before their public confrontation. An unexpected conflict had arisen amidst the investigation of the Rockefeller interests in Colorado. The work of the CIR had roughly coincided with the escalation of one of the nation's most violent industrial disputes, the coal miners' strike against the Rockefeller-controlled Colorado Fuel and Iron Company (CFI) in southern Colorado. Beginning in September 1913, the strike pitted an ethnically diverse workforce of some 10,000 families against a virtual industrial barony. Owning the lands and homes of their laborers, controlling courts and county government, paying wages in scrip valid only in company stores, contributing to a mine death rate twice as high as any other state in the nation, and enforcing their rule with a heavily armed private police force, the CFI was a catalog of the horrors of unregulated capitalist power. National Guard troops, initially ordered in by Colorado governor Elias M. Ammons in late October as a strictly neutral force to quell growing skirmishes between strikers and company police, in the end only added to the company's muscle power. Billeted on company property, supplied through the company store, and freed from earlier restrictions by an intimidated governor, militia officers openly protected strikebreakers. Tragedy followed on April 20, 1914, when a machine-gun attack on the strikers' tent colony at Ludlow engulfed the entire encampment in flames. Among the fifty-three persons killed in the onslaught were two women and eleven children, who had suffocated in a dugout tent cellar. Widespread unrest followed what became known as the Ludlow Massacre until the U.S. Army intervened on April 28, ending the violence and effectively crushing the strike.[56] Walsh's good friend George Creel, who was covering the Colorado story at the time, immediately fingered the Rockefellers as "traitors to the people" and "accessories to the murder of babes."[57] While the CIR assembled an impromptu hearing (and Congress established a separate mediation panel), Frank Walsh determined to go after the system that could produce a Ludlow.[58]

For Walsh, like Creel, the embodiment of that system was John D. Rockefeller, Jr. More than any other witness before the CIR, Rockefeller received the full force of Walsh's prosecutorial passion. Outfoxed by his subject's well-coached and evasive encounter with the commission in January 1915, Walsh pursued him again in a furious, unrelenting examination the following May.[59] His exposé of Rockefeller's complicity in the CFI's elaborate and unbending anti-union campaign (utterly contradicting Rockefeller's own carefully constructed alibi of ignorance and distance from the affair) constituted for Walsh a glorious final chapter of the commission's work, dramatic proof of the populist argument that a democracy could not allow economic power to fall into too few hands.

From the beginning Walsh and the CIR staff saw the evil of Rockefeller power not only in its ramifications at the workplace but also in its impact on American democracy. For this reason, they expended considerable effort in documenting the direct corruption of public officials and other, more insidious forms of corporate influence buying, including the dismissal from the state university of an outspoken anti-Rockefeller law professor.[60] Rockefeller's hiring of Ivy L. Lee, ex-journalist and public relations pioneer, as corporate publicity director after the massacre also came in for close scrutiny. Grilled on two extended occasions, Lee seemed to arouse a special ire among the commissioners (as well as the larger progressive community), in part out of righteous indignation over his manipulation of images, in part perhaps because he employed his intellectual skills on behalf of the archvillains of the reformers themselves. Upton Sinclair, for example, rechristened him "Poison Ivy"; Carl Sandburg judged him "below the level of the hired gunman and slugger."[61]

But it was the outwardly most benevolent of the Rockefeller cultural projects that most intrigued the members of the commission, especially Walsh and McCarthy. W. L. Mackenzie King, the former Canadian Minister of Labor, had accepted a contract just after the massacre to undertake a "far-reaching study of industrial problems" for the Rockefeller Foundation.[62] A new industrial relations department of the foundation, which had previously shied away from controversial social questions, was created for the occasion. Despite the general philosophical mandate for the project, King was rushed to Colorado to devise a grievance system (later unveiled as the famous "Colorado Plan" of company unionism) in lieu of collective bargaining. Although Rockefeller himself ultimately drew public, and even presidential, praise for his industrial penance, King and the foundation's industrial relations department did not so easily pass muster before the CIR.[63]

It was McCarthy himself, it appears, who first suggested to a receptive Walsh that the commission use the King investigation to open a general inquiry into the role of private foundations in matters of education and social research. As a zealous and idealistic advocate of public education, McCarthy had for some time entertained doubts about the growing role of private philanthropies in educational matters, opposing on principle, for example, even the much-celebrated Carnegie pension program for university professors. Unless philanthropists like Carnegie and Rockefeller presented their gifts in one great bundle, no strings attached, McCarthy worried, they would come to exercise undue influence over supposedly democratic bodies. He thus coached Walsh in October 1914 that regarding great

V. suspicious of corporate philanthropy.

foundations "the world will . . . and should distrust them." As an alternative to the foundations, McCarthy endorsed an idea popular among Madison reformers—a national research body, perhaps even a "national university" as advocated by President Van Hise.[64]

Frank Walsh required little encouragement to take on the foundations. As early as 1913 he had voiced support for the replacement of all privately funded social work by political action and public funding. If, for academics such as McCarthy and Commons, private money posed a *potential* problem for public institutions, for Walsh it was more like a gushing stream of pollutants. In January 1915, when the commission entered the second phase of its Colorado investigation, it thus turned an unparalleled investigatory light on the cultural counterparts of corporate power, ultimately devoting more than a thousand printed pages of testimony to the subject in the section of its final report entitled "The Centralization of Industrial Control and Operation of Philanthropic Foundations."[65]

For Walsh the hegemonic influence of the foundation suggested the ultimate, terrifying expansion of monopoly power from economic control to thought control. In words dripping with venom, Walsh would later conclude:

> Mr. Rockefeller is taking money obtained through the exploitation of thousands of poorly nourished, socially submerged men, women and children, and spending these sums, through a board of personal employees, in such fashion that his estate is in a fair way not only to exercise a dominating influence in industry, but, before many years, to exact a tribute of loyalty and subserviency to him and his interest from the whole profession of scientists, social workers and economists . . . No argument is needed to convince a sensible American of the subtle and pervasive and irresistible power that is wielded autocratically by men who control the disbursement of huge sums of money. It is a power that goes straight to our instincts, to our points of view, to the raw materials of which our opinions and judgments are made.[66]

Walsh's convictions on the subject of the foundations were so strong as to provoke a split within the Progressives' ranks. *Survey* magazine, the leading contemporary exponent of reform-minded social research and an early crusader for the CIR, in an October 1914 editorial, welcomed the newly announced Rockefeller Foundation initiative while at the same time offering a rather critical assessment of the industrial commission's first year of work. Lauding the "disinterested" record of Mackenzie King in labor controversies, *Survey* expressed a willingness to accept the foundation's intention "at its full face value—an attempt to take up the 'most complicated and at the same time the most urgent question of modern times,' and to grapple with it 'for the well being of mankind throughout the world.'" Contrasting the administrative autonomy of the foundation with the cumbersome bureaucratic machinery which had slowed the CIR's work, *Survey*'s editor, Paul U. Kellogg (who had earlier directed the Pittsburgh Survey for the Russell Sage Foundation) went so far as to suggest that "the limitations of a private inquiry, undistracted by divergent points of view, with unlimited resources and time, with no patronage assaults to stave off, are less obvious than those of such a public commission."[67]

The irrepressible Walsh quickly fired back. In a series of published exchanges with Kellogg, the commission chair not only defended the CIR's work against its private competitor (including an especially vigorous tribute to its research director) but also attacked the editorial as "cunning and dishonest," concluding that the editors must have been "compelled to publish the same . . . by your patrons and masters, and that you are ashamed of it." Walsh's shot (and another soon fired by Creel in an article entitled "How Tainted Money Taints") was a clear reference to *Survey*'s endowment by the Russell Sage and Carnegie foundations.[68]

Although the particular controversy was soon muted, the *Survey* altercation set an ominous example for the intellectual reformers at the commission. With his courtroom bluster, Walsh implicitly opened fire on an entire generation of intellectuals, targeting them as apologists for monopolists. Financial insecurity and uncertain social standing had in fact made many social scientists and social investigators of the early twentieth century rely on the philanthropic extensions of the great corporations as well as wealthy individuals. John R. Commons's appointment at the University of Wisconsin, for example, depended on a package of philanthropic grants and gifts, including a modest subvention from the Carnegie Foundation.[69] At the time he opened up on Kellogg, Walsh could not have known how deep into his own ranks the logic of his attack might extend. It is unlikely he would have altered his course in any case.

For McCarthy the CIR crusade against his old schoolmate, Rockefeller, might have provoked conflict and discomfort from the beginning. Surprisingly, it did not. Indeed, for some months Charles McCarthy served Walsh as a willing and effective instrument of the campaign to confront John D. Rockefeller, Jr., with his social responsibilities. When Walsh chose the investigation of foundations as the vehicle for hauling Rockefeller and other company officers before the CIR (perhaps because Rockefeller had already appeared before another congressional body that focused more narrowly on Colorado strike issues), he looked to McCarthy for support. "I expect you can give us a lot of assistance in getting young Mr. Rockefeller and Mr. Green [Jerome Greene, secretary of the Rockefeller Foundation] before the Commission," Walsh wrote in early October. Two days later, Walsh again pleaded with McCarthy to get Rockefeller "of all others" to cooperate. "Use all your good offices and ingenuity to bring this about." McCarthy seemed perfectly willing to do his part. Cheering on Walsh before his first encounter with John D., Jr., McCarthy agreed that there was "a great case to be won." As late as mid-December he agreed that the gathering evidence from Colorado "confirms all your program in relation to the Rockefeller matter. Inevitably abuses will come unless these big endowments are under some kind of public control. All the way through there is a confirmation of my idea about JDR, Jr. as the same man I knew, far away from people, good intentions personally but enmeshed and educated in a system which is entirely wrong."[70]

But it was precisely his direct personal contacts with Rockefeller that made things more complicated for McCarthy than for Walsh. McCarthy did not suddenly exhume an old friendship in contacting Rockefeller from his CIR position. Rather, ever since the miners' troubles broke out in Colorado, he had conducted a frustrating private campaign to "reform" Rockefeller's thinking and behavior on industrial matters, communicating at once with the stiff and aloof Rockefeller and a small circle of old school friends and Rockefeller confidants.[71] As part of this effort, McCarthy had tried in vain at least since March 1914 to expand the foundation's interests in the areas of social and industrial welfare.[72] When, after the Ludlow

McCarthy was an ex-college friend of Rockefeller — complicating factor!

events, Rockefeller referred vaguely in congressional testimony to the contemplation of an industrial inquiry, McCarthy encouraged him further, writing in August, "*Now* would be the time for it when the Commission is in being. If you could coordinate your work with that of the Commission the result would be perhaps a sane and wise program which could be brought out a year from now."[73]

To be sure, the format and composition of the Mackenzie King project—tightly controlled by the foundation officers—was not what McCarthy had had in mind. As soon as the King venture was announced, McCarthy urged their mutual friend John Murdock to warn Rockefeller that "it is necessary to have a Democratic Organization. A Complete One." The money, he insisted, ought to be given outright to an industrial body with labor and business representation. "If that is done this money will be a great blessing." If not it "may be a great curse." Yet Rockefeller and his emissaries turned a deaf ear to such entreaties, claiming that a thoroughly "scientific" investigation could not be compromised by mere public "opinion." Privately, Mc-Carthy despaired that Rockefeller was "not in contact" with the real world and needed a public jolt to wake him up. Always trusting Rockefeller as a man of "good intentions," McCarthy determined to break through the "wooden" people around his old friend. Still hoping that in the heat of the Walsh hearings, Rockefeller would willingly surrender the King investigation to "popular control," McCarthy told Murdock that "this great investigation may be the best thing that ever happened to John D. Rockefeller, Jr."[74]

But the errand for Walsh complicated McCarthy's task. He now took the lead in securing Rockefeller cooperation with the government panel. Seeking a conference in early October with Jerome Greene, for example, McCarthy masked his real doubts about the Mackenzie King project behind a screen of benign curiosity: "I think it is of tremendous importance to the country. Great foundations are going into philanthropic work and other work which has a bearing on the great question of industrial unrest . . . Such a conference will be of the greatest value to you." Similarly, in encouraging a hesitant Rockefeller to meet with the commission, McCarthy emphasized the positive public relations that might come from such an apppearance: "The more you keep explaining and the more approach you make to the American People . . . the better they will understand your motives." In the end, McCarthy flattered Rockefeller, the industrial project would bring him well-deserved appreciation. "It will probably be side by side with your health work and your agricultural work in the South the greatest work your institution will be known by." When his sweet talk to the Rockefeller entourage was short-circuited by a subpoena issued independently by a commission staffer to Rockefeller in Providence, McCarthy apologized profusely, distanced himself from the maneuver, and pleaded that as research director he had "nothing to do with the hearings of this kind." The apology was largely disingenuous, however, for McCarthy himself had already worked up a set of tough questions for Rockefeller to confront on the witness stand.[75]

However well-intentioned, McCarthy compromised his position with regard to the Rockefeller case. Over the course of a very few months he had acted towards the Rockefeller industrial mission alternately as promoter, tutor, and prosecutor. His own faith in his consistent effort to respect a valued friendship while at the same time serving the public interest was entirely sincere—and attested to by the deposit of all his correspondence with the Rockefeller people in the CIR files. In the process, however, he opened himself (and potentially the entire commission) to the appearance of double-dealing and hypocrisy.

But who would have the interest—and the nerve—to strike at McCarthy? On January 14, 1915, McCarthy first expressed alarm that malicious rumors were circulating about him at the Rockefeller headquarters at 26 Broadway in New York City. Suspecting Jerome Greene, who, McCarthy believed, had never appreciated his ideas and blocked his personal access to Junior, McCarthy appealed to his old friends and Rockefeller confidants J. S. Murdock and Lefferts Dashiell to affirm his integrity. "I want those who knew me when I was a boy," McCarthy pleaded, "to know now that I am the same person with the same purposes, the same objects, the same standards that I had when I was in college." Dashiell responded by telegram, "Your fears are groundless. Friendship absolutely unaffected." Three months later, however, Murdock let slip that "John D. was very indignant at being summoned here in Providence and he laid it all to your door." On January 15, 1915, only ten days before the first Rockefeller hearing, McCarthy received an urgent summons from Walsh to come to New York. Walsh had just been told by Rockefeller that, according to the records of the foundation, "only one" outside person had encouraged them to begin a study of labor conditions, and his name was McCarthy. There was further insinuation, hinted at by Rockefeller and apparently magnified by others, that McCarthy's original interest in the Rockefeller project had been pecuniary, that he had applied to direct the inquiry himself. Rockefeller also produced for Walsh the early letters from McCarthy that documented his claim.[76]

Stung by the revelations, Walsh nevertheless proceeded with the Rockefeller investigation. Faced with McCarthy's strenuous and self-righteous denial of any wrongdoing (including a refusal to dignify the charges by defending himself before a special commission meeting), Walsh temporarily pocketed the issue. The hearings went as scheduled except for one particular: while focusing on the structure and activities of the foundation, Walsh all but ignored the Mackenzie King research project, with which the government's own research director might easily be linked.[77]

The proud Walsh, however, never forgave McCarthy the embarrassment his friendship with Rockefeller had caused the commission. When McCarthy dared to challenge Walsh's authority during the commission's budget crisis of February 1915, Walsh deftly turned the tables on him, making McCarthy's (rather than Walsh's) unscrupulous conduct the pivotal issue. "There is no doubt in my mind," Leiserson explained to McCarthy, "that the reason Walsh fired you was to shift the issue from the budget to you personally." Despite the protests of John R. Commons and most of the staff, Walsh won endorsement of his actions before a special CIR executive session by "foxily [trying] to show how you were treacherous to the Commission."[78] *Survey* editor John Fitch, who had earlier been the victim of Walsh's taunts, was outraged. "It would appear that he intends to scream Rockefeller at everybody who crosses his path."[79]

For Walsh, however, the Rockefeller issue served as more than an expedient tool with which to rid himself of a bureaucratic rival. It seemed to confirm a deeper suspicion of the aims and methods of the intellectuals with whom he had been making common cause. How else can one explain the sense of triumph with which he reported the initial dismissal of the Wisconsin brain trust to George

Creel? "The most complete cleaning out . . . that the Wisconson idea has ever received in its long and tempestuous career," he crowed, citing other research experts (besides McCarthy) "whose heads [will] fall with a distinctly dull thud within the next two weeks . . . It was the biggest intellectual victory I ever won any place."[80]

In the weeks after McCarthy's dismissal, Walsh and Creel fashioned a thoroughgoing repudiation of ideas and people they had once admired. To St. Louis publisher William Marion Reedy, for example, Walsh offered a scathing dissection of the Wisconsin Idea. Its so-called "large, constructive programs," wrote Walsh, required cooperation with the "principal despoilers" of workers' rights (that is, the Rockefellers) and involved "interminable 'bill-drafting'" and an administrative machinery "which should throw the legal profession into spasms of delight and the proletariat into hopeless despair."[81] Creel voiced even more viscerally the resentment that "independent" radicals like himself and Walsh felt for those they called the "professors." Smarting from a *New Republic* editorial critical of his earlier attack on Paul Kellogg, Creel responded with a vivid contrast between himself and his detractors:

> For fifteen years I have devoted myself to a task of agitation in politics and industry, trying always to stay close to what may be termed the "underdog." During this time I have seen oppression, exploitation, corruption, treachery and betrayal in all their forms, and it may well be that these experiences have made me less than judicial, overquick to suspect and denounce. You, on the other hand, are academic products who have come to be commentators by self-election, based upon self-valuation, aided, I believe, by an endowment fund that spares you the fear of existence. The antagonism between us, therefore, is as instinctive and inevitable as that of the house cat for the street dog.[82]

McCarthy, for his part, had lost all respect for the direction of the commission. Initially he and Leiserson believed that they could outmaneuver Walsh, who they agreed was "absolutely weak when it comes to knowledge of the subject." All they had to do, they thought, was expose his ignorance of "scientific work" before his fellow commissioners.[83] When even the remonstrance of Commons proved futile, however, McCarthy accepted his defeat. While encouraging the young researchers who looked up to him to stay and

Commission's irrevocable splits + multiple reports = powerlessness

extract "some ray of light" from the commission, McCarthy now privately judged Walsh "absolutely incompetent and untrustworthy."[84] McCarthy's role on the CIR had come to an ironic end. The person who had most idolized the state as an agent of rational and judicious social change had come face to face with the underside of bureaucratic power.

In view of such personal bad blood and recrimination within its activist core, it is not surprising that the CIR failed to reach internal consensus or effective outside support. In the end Congress shut its ears to the cacophony of the commission, manifest in three conflicting reports along with a host of individual disclaimers and supplemental opinions among the nine commissioners. The major cleavage was that splitting Walsh and the three labor commissioners, who signed an eloquent anticapitalist and antistatist report drawn up by Basil Manly, from a loose coalition of the five other commissioners, who endorsed in principle Commons's plodding, and rather dispirited, version of Wisconsin ideas.[85] Still shadow-boxing with his intellectual adversaries (while also seeking allies among his fellow commissioners), Chairman Walsh tacked, in the end, toward a radical version of AFL "voluntarism." Seeking a British-style immunity to legal prosecution for labor unions (a proposal also endorsed by Commons), the Manly report was spare in its demands of action from government, calling for stringent inheritance taxes, public ownership of utilities, and a confiscatory tax on unimproved land. Indeed, the "official" report warned explicitly against unnamed advocates of a "huge system of bureaucratic paternalism such as has been developed in Germany." In a supplemental statement to the Manly report, Walsh dissented even from Manly's call for a "special commission" on mediation, a much-diluted version of the Commons-Perlman plan for state and national industrial commissions with extensive administrative powers. Violating "the habits, customs, and traditions of the American people," such a "ponderous legal machinery," scoffed Walsh, would subject business and workers equally to "the whim or caprice of an army of officials, deputies, and Governmental employees."[86]

The commission's chairman did not neglect a related area of concern: the unregulated power of foundations in general and the depredations of Rockefeller money in particular. In the last of several "additional findings" submitted to Congress, Walsh and two of the labor commissioners described the $100 million Rockefeller trust as "wages" "withheld by means of economic pressure, violation of law, cunning, and violence." Excoriating Rockefeller and Mackenzie King for failing to answer questions put to them on the stand (even recommending that they be summoned for further questioning before the House of Representatives), Walsh and company called for liquidation of the foundation and expropriation of its assets for purposes "directly beneficial to the laborers who really contributed the funds." It was a grand, if largely futile, denouement.[87]

WHILE ROOTED in a complicated and by no means inevitable chain of events, the internal impasse of the CIR reflected a basic, built-in dilemma for twentieth-century radical reformers. Generally operating in the absence of (or at some remove from) popular mass movements, intellectuals played a prominent role as advocates for issues of popular welfare or democratic rights. But how could intellectuals best represent the people and their interests? The alternatives sharply delineated during the CIR experience almost uncannily anticipated two dominant pathways of intellectual advocacy during the rest of the century. On the one hand, intellectuals have acted as agitators of a working-class public. On the other hand, self-styled social planners or engineers have sought social deliverance less in the stirrings from below than in a rational discourse among themselves or with articulate representatives of interested parties.[88]

The CIR offered a forum for both intellectual roles: a vehicle for advocacy by agitators behind Walsh and a laboratory for rational policy formulation by Commons and McCarthy. In his role as commission chairman Walsh shared in the development of the arts of mass communication with both friends and foes. Public relations experts like the notorious Ivy Lee, for example, who made the corporate image itself the subject of advertisement, effectively mediated the relationship between the mass producer and the mass market. By joining government investigation to the exposé style of muckraking journalism, pro-labor radicals like Frank Walsh and George Creel fashioned a counterbalance on the side of mass advocacy.

Alongside these contending agents of popular persuasion—reach-

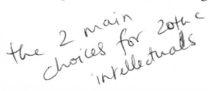

the 2 main choices for 20th c intellectuals

ing out in his own way to corral, cajole, or excite a distant public—stood another brand of intellectual activist: the planner or social engineer. No less political or partisan by inner conviction, planners nevertheless trusted more to the forms of administrative agency than to the white heat of public opinion. Planners, like publicists, came in different political shapes. Mackenzie King served as an able social engineer within the post-Ludlow Rockefeller camp, recruiting Junior to a lifelong crusade for company unions (or nonunion employee representation plans), even as Charles McCarthy and John R. Commons perfected the same skills in public bodies for more liberal ends. As Leiserson consoled Commons near the end of the commission's work, "You have no sympathy with so-called learned reports, to be stored away in libraries, but on the other hand . . . you have less respect for loud protestations against well known industrial evils . . . instead of trying to get at fundamental causes and working out permanent remedies."[89]

But for all those intellectuals who identified as democrats and self-conscious agents of radical social change (and these included both Walsh and McCarthy) the limitations of their position—either as agitator or engineer—seem in retrospect all too clear. None of the CIR protagonists was able to wrest from his work the results that he had wanted. To be sure, Frank Walsh commanded the political spotlight momentarily, as registered by his contribution to a labor-oriented reelection strategy for President Wilson in 1916, including passage of the Adamson Act, which provided an eight-hour day for railroad workers.[90] Walsh, as David Montgomery suggests, might well have had the makings of a great social democratic legislator, but he needed a mass following to press home his eloquent message.[91] Failing in the end to arouse the wrath of the workers as an alternative to bureaucratic control of industrial relations, Walsh became the chief agent of governmental administrative intervention under wartime exigency as co-chair of the War Labor Board. Without apparent embarrassment, he managed a disputes adjudication machinery remarkably like the one he had earlier scoffed at from the hands of his more "academic" CIR colleagues.[92] Walsh's friend George Creel also entered wartime government service, but he did it by elaborating on the very techniques of popular persuasion that he had originally practiced as a journalist. The similarity of method between radical reform education and corporate advertising was perhaps never better exemplified than by the assimilation of both into Creel's Committee on Public Information, the wartime propaganda machine responsible for unifying a doubting public around Wilson's war aims.[93] In another sense, Creel's self-righteous moralism had simply been applied to new ends. A fellow muckraker once noted, "To Creel there are only two classes of men . . . There are skunks, and the greatest man that ever lived. The greatest man that ever lived is plural, and includes everyone who is on Creel's side in whatever public issue he happens at the moment to be concerned with."[94]

Compared to such natural agitators, the intellectual engineers kept to an outwardly more consistent but inwardly more troubled course. Following his commission work, Commons fell into the most severe of his periodic depressions, collapsing before the spring exam period in 1916 and not returning to his academic post until February 1917. Many years later, Selig Perlman recalled that the conflicts within the commission "made a tremendous impression upon Professor Commons, it robbed him of his sleep and peace of mind." Commons would again consult for federal and state authorities around employment and other issues, but never at his prewar pace. McCarthy, for his part, recuperated from his commission experience by throwing himself into a dollar-a-year position with the wartime Food Administration. Separated from his family and living in near-penury in Washington, D.C., when not visiting war-torn Europe, McCarthy seemed utterly driven by a sense of patriotic service. When he died in 1921 at age forty-eight, more than one friend lamented that he had simply "burnt himself out."[95]

The painstaking plans for labor reform advanced by both Commons and McCarthy proved political nonstarters, championed neither by the labor movement that might most have benefited nor by public officials, who were unwilling (outside of wartime exigency) to challenge the marketplace regulation of labor relations. In this sense the CIR project displayed the isolation of intellectual activists and reformers from local and state-based political leverage, the common frustration of early-twentieth-century state builders by America's peculiarly decentered political authority. Reformers could research and advocate all they wanted, but such activity did not necessarily swing votes or assure tangible political influence.[96] With no way to mobilize an independent constituency for their ingenious governmental programs, social engineers such as McCarthy and Commons were captives of their reigning public patrons. Unfortunately for them, there was in the United States no Bismarck (and only the occasional La Follette) capable and prepared to turn their intellectual handicraft into political-administrative reality. A consumer democracy may have bestowed unprecedented attention on a growing class of academically trained, critical intellectuals without necessarily buying their brand of public policy.[97]

But it was not only in the political realm that one senses the insecurity of the intellectual reformers. Charles McCarthy offers a revealing case study in this regard. Here was a man of remarkable creativity driven by an intense psychic striving related both to economic and social marginalism. These considerations may help to explain the quality of McCarthy's fateful relationship with his college classmate John D. Rockefeller, Jr.

Why had McCarthy kept up his largely one-way initiatives and illusions of influence with Rockefeller since their college days together? The first and rudest explanation appears to be money: on several occasions since his graduation McCarthy had solicited Junior for financial support, initially for himself, later for his friends or favored causes. Despite Rockefeller's ready offer as an undergraduate "to help [McCarthy] in this way anytime [he] asked," such gifts likely carried more baggage than either solicitor or provider openly acknowledged or fully appreciated. Strain was evident as early as 1899, when, for want of prompt payment for his coaching duties at Georgia, McCarthy found himself "stuck" and compelled to seek help from Rockefeller in order to continue his graduate education. As a "business proposition," he appealed for a $200 loan with interest. Three months later, however, expressing shame and open discouragement over his continuing poverty (and acknowledging that he was "paying a pretty high price for my ambition"), he humbly requested another $100. While Rockefeller's extant communications to McCarthy are spare in both number and content, the substance of his response is clear enough: in each case, Rockefeller extended McCarthy exactly half the funds requested.[98]

Rockefeller lent money to McCarthy.

The difference in means between the two men remained a significant, if largely unspoken, issue between them. Mutual embarrassment was again acute as they congratulated each other on their marriages in 1901. While McCarthy excused himself for not sending a gift to the new couple (indeed, within the same week he was asking Rockefeller for suggestions regarding university employment!), Rockefeller was equally maladroit in gracing McCarthy's nuptials with the "present" of forgiving McCarthy's $150 loan. For over a year after their wedding, Rockefeller beseeched the McCarthys in vain to accept some token of his esteem (not only had McCarthy refused Rockefeller's offer and repaid the loan in full, but he adamantly rejected any thought of a gift he could not reciprocate). Money never disappeared from the relationship between the two men. As late as March 1914, for example—only a few weeks before his sustained campaign to alter Rockefeller's Colorado policies and foundation priorities—McCarthy openly solicited a contribution for the sister of a deceased friend.[99]

This is not to imply that McCarthy, in any extended sense, felt dependent on Rockefeller. Rather, what is remarkable is McCarthy's stubborn presumption of social equality and even a degree of intellectual condescension toward his wealthy friend. Despite attaining a publicly respectable professional position, McCarthy always lived in straitened circumstances.[100] Yet neither in his relations with Rockefeller nor with anyone else did McCarthy ever appear to backtrack or flinch from the affirmation of his own opinions. Regarding Rockefeller, in particular, he appears to have convinced himself that he was every bit Junior's social equal: on the basis of old school ties and the meritocracy of brainpower, McCarthy readily and unabashedly presumed to counsel the man of wealth on matters large and small. Characteristically, after they had each experienced a separate wringing from the CIR, McCarthy extended his sympathy to Junior, counseling him that "humiliation once in a while" might be "a good thing." A year later, it was McCarthy who again picked up the thread of correspondence, expressing joyous satisfaction in his work, wishing Rockefeller could share in his discoveries, and implicitly offering his counsel to the philanthropist in matters of public policy. Again, Rockefeller politely begged off.[101] Years after the CIR events, Rockefeller reportedly eulogized McCarthy in a Bible class as a man who had started with "little before him except to drag out his life in a shoe factory" but who had gone on to accomplish "great feats."[102] Yet, as attracted as they might be by an intellectual Horatio Alger figure, people like Rockefeller did not willingly cede control of the marketplace—even the marketplace of ideas—to such upstarts.

If there is a certain pitiable and even desperate quality in McCarthy's determination to prove his worth and utility in Rockefeller's eyes, we might best connect that urge to the formative social experiences—and basic ambivalence—of the new intellectuals' social position. Thus, even as a man like McCarthy trusted his intellectual expertise, subjecting social problems to reasoned analysis, he knew the weight of birthright as well as the pull of political power over the legitimation of social knowledge. By one means or another the politically committed intellectual had to take account of such distortions of idealized rational discourse to accept, as Max Weber put it, a "trained ruthlessness in viewing the realities of life, and the ability to face such realities and to measure up to them internally."[103] To succeed, McCarthy not only had to excel on a meritocratic level, he also had to master the informal rules of the game.

Indeed, the game metaphor is particularly appropriate in relation to McCarthy. It was through sports, after all, that he had first distinguished himself in college and thereby also encountered John D. Rockefeller, Jr. As with many college men for whom competitive sports served as a critical socializing experience—combining fierce individual striving and selfless cooperative effort—the metaphor of the playing field came easily to McCarthy. Once, for example, fearing an impending legislative attack on his reform program, he wrote a college friend, "The great corporation power in this state has tried to smash me and will eventually smash me, if I stay. I will not squeal if it comes, but will take my medicine as I did on the field of football at your side in the old days." Or again, when his younger cousin, writing from prep school, sought his worldly advice, McCarthy quoted Theodore Roosevelt's canonical football philosophy: "Do not flinch, do not foul, but hit the line hard."[104]

Such, at least, were the classic metaphors through which American higher education socialized a new generation of male professionals. Connecting scions of great wealth with striving sons of

His sports metaphors

the middle and even working classes, the playing field concocted an image of fair dealing and meritocratic social reward.[105]

Or did it? To young muckraker George Creel, the themes on the college football field mirrored the grosser social division of labor in the larger society. Determined to refute *Survey*'s initially favorable reaction to Rockefeller's planned industrial investigation—which had begun by linking McCarthy and Rockefeller as "two old football colleagues"—Creel had contrasted McCarthy's "honest toil" as a player with Rockefeller's role as team manager. Far from sharing in the "blows and bruises and indomitable courage that made 'Charlie' McCarthy a football hero at Brown," Rockefeller "never got any nearer the football field than the ticket office. He was the manager of the team, counting the dimes while McCarthy took the punishment."[106]

Although McCarthy would doubtless have written off Creel's diatribe as crude propaganda, his own approach to the gridiron exposed a set of working principles not contained within favored homilies to the game. Thus, in those premodern days of American football, with the rules still in a state of flux, this scrawny substitute quarterback (he usually played halfback) in 1895 successfully challenged custom, and fooled Dartmouth, with a "quick kick" from center. Another proud moment came while coaching the University of Wisconsin against Minnesota in 1907. Prior to the game McCarthy discovered that Minnesota had sent a spy to Wisconsin practices. As football then was played without standard uniforms, Coach McCarthy during practice focused the plays on an end who was wearing a white jersey and on the quarterback, who had donned a white cap:

> Then in the gymnasium I showed them how the second man, the man behind the man with the white cap and white jersey, would take the ball. I calculated that Minnesota would be so positive that they would put out the man with the white jersey and the white cap and take no notice of the other men. When the game was started my men were so confident that they pulled off a forward pass right away. Sure enough, five Minnesota men downed the man with the white jersey and the other man, untouched, ran the whole length of the field. We pulled up 17 scores by crossing it over before Minnesota knew where they were.[107]

The impish cleverness that McCarthy applied to football strategy he likely associated with his Irish roots: it was the quick, if subversive, intelligence that the immigrant underdog needed to survive. McCarthy once quipped that the ideal football team would be composed of ten Germans and an Irish captain. Placed against his own tireless attempts to adapt German social welfare measures to American soil, the joke perhaps carried a larger meaning. The intellectual as activist was never in a position to go it alone. It would take some very clever piloting as well as a sturdy craft to bring substantial industrial reform to the United States. In these terms perhaps McCarthy's problem on the CIR was the presence of too few Germans and at least one Irishman too many.[108]

4 Joining the People

*William English Walling and the Specter
of the Intellectual Class*

INTELLECTUALS have long served as a scapegoat in American
politics. Revenge against the avant-garde is best recognized in the
post–World War II world: anti-intellectualism, what Arthur
Schlesinger, Jr., called the "anti-Semitism of the businessman,"
flourished during the McCarthyism of the early 1950s, and it has
made notable curtain calls in the Nixon-Agnew attack on the "nat-
tering nabobs of negativism" and, more recently in former Vice-
President Quayle's indictment of the "cultural elite" for their purported subversion of right-thinking "family values."[1] Such examples
tend to sustain historian Richard Hofstadter's classic 1962 argument
that a persistent, even pervasive, strain of anti-intellectualism in-
habits American public life, stretching, as he saw it, from the
Puritans through the Populists and then on to the anti–New
Dealers.[2] A primitive egalitarian spirit, Hofstadter argued with both
conviction and wit, spread from a foundation in religious and business attitudes to dominate educational as well as political culture.[3]

Curiously enough, however, in his enunciation of the theme,
Hofstadter specifically exonerated those American intellectuals who
have themselves fashioned full-blown attacks on their own kind.
According to Hofstadter, one should not confuse the inner dialogue
among intellectuals—however "quarrelsome" and "ill-mannered"—
with the blanket "suspicion of the life of the mind" which has all too
often swept up the "common culture." "The criticism of other intellectuals," he explained, "is one of the most important functions of
the intellectual, and he customarily performs it with vivacity."[4]

I wonder about this basic separation of the Billy Sundays and
even the Joe McCarthys from writers, professors, and better-edu-

cated political activists. When intellectuals condemn their peers *as a group or class* and *on the basis of group characteristics,* do they not also contribute in important ways to a culture of anti-intellectualism? Granted, we still know precious little about the inner historical relationships between populist and elitist species of intellectual loathing, but there is no reason to dismiss the connection out of hand.

In this chapter I trace one of the more curious early-twentieth-century genealogies of anti-intellectualism. The environs of the pre–World War I American Socialist Party provided at once a breeding ground for critical intellectuals and a nesting place for bitter, internecine warfare among these same intellectuals. Passions aroused by the war and the concurrent Bolshevik Revolution catalyzed earlier disagreements into vitriolic, systematic condemnation of political antagonists. In this climate there arose a sustained, formal indictment of the middle-class intellectual as a threat to the health of the republic or the party, depending on one's perspective.

I focus on the turbulent career of William English Walling. Perhaps the most cerebral and well-read of active American socialists, Walling played a pivotal role in liberal, labor, feminist, and socialist causes. Best known as convener and first executive chair of the NAACP in 1908–1909, Walling joined Mary Kenney O'Sullivan to found the Women's Trade Union League in 1903 and co-chartered the Intercollegiate Socialist Society in 1905. Blessed with the financial means and political understanding to travel in Eastern Europe, his writings from Russia after 1905 first riveted the attention of American radicals on a new model of revolutionary action. With five books and numerous articles to his credit, by 1916 Walling had established himself as a formidable, if unorthodox, representative of the intellectual left, confidently taking his place in the movement's factional wars by bitterly assailing an alleged alliance of Fabians, "state socialists," and the "careerists" in the party's National Executive Committee with the skilled labor "aristocrats" of Samuel Gompers's American Federation of Labor (AFL).[5]

By 1917, however, Walling at age forty began to reverse his political course. The coming of World War I, while generally traumatic for the socialist cause, utterly scrambled Walling's political compass. From a caustic critic of liberal reform and conservative trade union-

William English Walling, American socialist and author, circa 1905. (Courtesy of Anna Walling Hamburger)

ism, he became a champion of win-the-war-first Wilsonianism, a scourge of antiwar pacifists, and a political friend of Samuel Gompers. The Bolshevik Revolution, both for its renunciation of the fight in Europe and for its internal repressions, consolidated Walling's march to the American political center. A close ally of Gompers during the war, he emerged from the international conflict as a fixture in the AFL's subsequent propaganda battles against the Communist and Socialist Left. An unsuccessful Democratic candidate for Congress from Connecticut in 1924, Walling surfaced in Fiorello La Guardia's losing 1929 campaign for mayor of New York with a public attack on the Socialist candidacy of Norman Thomas. As an oft-used minister without portfolio for the AFL in international affairs, Walling's last mission at age fifty-nine was an attempt to make contact with the German trade union underground in 1936.[6]

A prominent theme in Walling's extensive political writings was his recurrent evaluation of the social role and influence of intellectuals. Walling's approach to intellectuals as a group evolved in four stages and was roughly congruent with his own personal and political development. Initially, Walling represented what might be termed a socialist-idealist stance, drawn from a mixture of middle-class progressive and classical socialist thought. By 1909, he had adopted his better-known left-wing position, a "new intellectual" caustically dismissive of the bureaucratic tendencies of his peers. The Great War, in turn, put an end to his revolutionary fantasies and marked the beginning of his assessment that the biggest threat to American liberties came from misguided members of the cultured classes. Finally, reaction to Bolshevism polished Walling's revisionist course. Walling's evolving critique of intellectuals prefigures more recent neoconservative attacks on the New Class not only as a cultural elite out of touch with the organic sensibility of the common people but as a dangerous group that can infect the masses with an alien ideology.

THE NEWLY CREATED American Socialist Party into which Walling stepped just after the turn of the century had inherited a rich half-century of dispute about intellectuals from its European progenitors. In a movement dedicated to social equality via the mobilization of the working class, the very presence (often in important places) of persons of middle-class background and uncommon formal education—John Spargo, Robert Hunter, J. G. Phelps Stokes, A. M. Simons, and William J. Ghent, to name but a few—was bound to excite concern. What should socialists make of this fact? The paradox was self-evident; the tension, obvious. But responses to the problem were varied and multitextured.

The very foundation of the modern socialist movement was replete with arguments about the proper role of intellectuals. Donald Drew Egbert and Stow Persons have drawn attention to the "implied paradox" within Marxism of "a revolutionary movement of the working class . . . and a highly rationalized, articulated, and comprehensive ideology." While Marx in the 1864 *Communist Manifesto* indicted salaried writers as "paid wage laborers" of the bourgeoisie, he elsewhere vacillated, never offering a categorical assessment of the intellectuals' relation to the revolutionary process. Generally speaking, the rationalist-universalist values underlying Marxist social analysis resisted political excommunication based on social origins, be they sociological, national, or racial in nature. At the same time, its claims to scientific and philosophical rigor clearly enhanced the value of scholarly adherents to the cause.[7] Perhaps the most eloquent gloss on the relations of workers and intellectuals had come from the great nineteenth-century German socialist, not Karl Marx, but Ferdinand Lassalle. Defending himself in court on charges of arousing class hatred, Lassalle committed himself to the union of the "two polar opposites of modern society, science and the workingman . . . when these two join forces they will crush all obstacles to cultural advance with an iron hand."[8]

Their own finesse of the question of the intellectuals, however, by no means spared socialists from contemporary political polemic on the issue. The very entrée of Marx and Engels into the tempest of German workingmen's organizations in the 1840s, for example, immediately elicited the riposte from the conspiratorialist Wilhelm Weitling that Marx was a "mere theorist" and "closet philosopher." At the first congress of the International Workingmen's Association (or First International) at Geneva in 1866, the disciples of Pierre-Joseph Proudhon tried in vain to restrict membership to bona fide wage earners. But the fiercest attack on the Marxist "bourgeois intellectuals" came from Michael Bakunin's anarchists; their threat to Marxist hegemony was sufficient for Marx and Engels to move the International headquarters to New York in 1872 and effectively to save their movement by temporarily dismembering it.[9]

Bakunin's critique of the International's Marxist intellectual leadership was no mere matter of tactical positioning but rather was linked to a competing vision of workers' democracy. For Bakunin, intellectuals themselves were less the problem than was their de facto alliance with the state. In Bakunin's view, the state remained inherently exploitative and coercive. Even under presumed social-democratic control, it substituted the tyranny of a purely abstract liberation for a real "social revolution." A state-centered elite, in Bakunin's nightmare vision, would erect a "despotism savant . . . penetrating into the very spirit of men and corrupting their thought at the source." A "new class" of "real and counterfeit scientists and scholars" would divide the world "into a minority ruling in the name of knowledge, and an immense ignorant majority. And then, woe unto the mass of ignorant ones."[10] That Bakunin reflected a more purely working-class version of the socialist vision was of course disputed by Marx, who turned the tables on his critic, accusing Bakunin in 1872 of assembling a dictatorship with a "general staff of literary bourgeois exercised over the revolutionary proletariat in the name of the Idea."[11]

By the time of the formation of the Socialist Party of America in 1901, the international socialist movement, which had been resurrected in a Second International centered in the German Social Democratic Party (SPD), had swallowed, if not fully digested, its doubts about the intellectual. As suggested in the writings of Karl Kautsky, the most influential theoretician of the period, the revolutionary social scientist might find a happy and appreciative home within the ranks of what has come to be known as "classical Marxism." Kautsky's exposition of the SPD's foundational Erfurt Program in 1892 tentatively divided middle-class intellectuals into the reactionary mass that would follow their property-holding interests and the few "idealists" who possessed "not only the requisite theoretical insight, but also the courage and strength to break with their class." However small in number, these socialist intellectuals would form a crucial link in the revolutionary process, connecting a proletariat "thirst[ing] for knowledge" but "without means to instruct itself" with the liberating "science" of socialism.[12] In subsequent work, Kautsky's categories became even more flexible. Breaking with the bipolar model of class development, Kautsky stressed the rapid growth of a white collar sector and welcomed "in particular the various important roles in politics of the intellectuals who constitute no class at all."[13] Austro-Marxist Max Adler would extend Kautsky's selective invitation into wholehearted embrace of a workers' education model, linking workers and intellectuals in common practice. Socialism, in Adler's view, constituted the material expression of the philosopher J. G. Fichte's educational idealism; but just as the socialist movement offered enlightenment to the masses, so it allowed the intellectual to think and act freely: the party thus ensured the intellectual's raison d'être.[14]

A second testing ground for intellectuals and socialism developed in London. Part of the revival of British socialism in the mid-1880s, both the Social Democratic Federation led by H. M. Hyndman and especially the Fabian Society of Sidney and Beatrice Webb, George Bernard Shaw, Annie Besant, H. G. Wells, and others had created an efficient transmission belt connecting discontented liberals of the educated classes with self-educated trade unionists and impoverished urban laborers. By defusing the socialist vision of the unpleasantness of class war and stressing instead the tools of research and education, the Fabians had made a comfortable home for the reform-minded social scientist. In its most striking anti-Marxist formulation, as A. M. McBriar has summarized, Fabian doctrine implied that "not only was socialist theory itself the product of middle-class thinkers in revolt against the environment in which they had been brought up; the lines of the struggle for and against Socialism did not run between the classes, but cut right through them, from richest to poorest."[15] To be sure, such revisionism burst the boundaries of orthodox adherence to class analysis and revolutionary social change. Yet, while otherwise sharply at odds in their political analysis, the Marxist and Fabian models of socialist practice alike stressed careful social analysis and understanding of social theory as prerequisites for intelligent political action. As an heir to the Enlightenment, attempting to incorporate science into a veritable "arsenal of ideas," the socialist movement presumed a significant and honorable space for intellectuals.[16]

American socialist circles at the turn of the century generally attested to this positive (and positivist) faith. With near unanimity, as historian Mark Pittenger noted, American socialist thinkers were Spencerian optimists, trusting that the world was evolving along a path of material progress and ever greater social interdependence. The challenge—and hence the support for the movement intellectual as well as education for the masses—lay in properly assessing the potential of the current moment for political and institutional innovation.[17] Commitment to a discourse of rational social-political analysis, and more specifically to the formalism of social-evolutionary thought, set a characteristic tone among socialist activists. Even the company of the movement's most irrepressible left-wingers—Emma Goldman, "Big Bill" Haywood, and Walling among them—at Mabel Dodge's salon in 1913 led anarchist Hippolyte Havel to quip disparagingly, "They all talk like goddam bourgeois."[18]

If they deferred to formal traditions of learning, however, American socialists insisted that such knowledge be distributed beyond the favored few. For many, in fact, socialism itself implied a democracy of learning, with society envisioned as one great schoolroom in which all citizens could fulfill their full capacities as thinkers and knowers. There existed no more blithe and full-hearted exponent of this view, for example, than self-taught Chicago lecturer and erstwhile molder Arthur Morrow Lewis. A fixture at the Garrick Theatre, where he regularly translated the latest social science research into an endorsement of Second International orthodoxy, Lewis attributed his own learning to a simple "systematic" reading of "good books." While "studiously avoiding" technical terms and openly addressing his remarks to "a class of readers who have not yet been reached by the sociologists of university chairs," Lewis emphatically denied any necessary tension between the culture of the manual and the mental laborer. Indeed, by Lewis's reckoning, in logic borrowed from Kautsky himself, the evolution of industry was building a kind of intelligentsia of the assembly line:

> The communist worker of today, in all that relates to social philosophy, thinks more clearly than the professional intellectuals of the schools. His environment brings him into daily contact with the latest results of science in the field of mechanics and this is delivering him

from the superstition inculcated in infancy. The professional intellectual, bred to the occupation, is constantly engaged in ideas that have their roots in former modes of wealth production and his mind turns in vicious circles from which he finds no avenue of escape. Should he take up Socialism and enter the movement, his first and greatest surprise is to find himself surrounded by hundreds of workmen who are fundamentally and undoubtedly his intellectual superiors.[19]

AS A YOUNG "professional" intellectual, William English Walling was no less eager than the self-taught Lewis to uncover the diamond in the rough of the common folk. The son of a wealthy Kentucky physician who had served as U.S. consul to Edinburgh and maternal grandson of William Hayden English, former Democratic Party vice-presidential candidate, Walling fulfilled the ardent wish of his successful, old-stock American family (which even claimed Daniel Boone in its lineage) to have one "brain educated" prodigy.[20] At age nineteen in 1897, Walling graduated from the University of Chicago, and after a year at Harvard Law School he returned to Chicago to study economics and political science with Thorstein Veblen. But his commitments were less academic than political, and Walling abandoned his studies to serve as an Illinois factory inspector for two years before moving to New York City in 1902 to take up residence as a writer and social worker at the University Settlement. It was during these years that Walling joined the X Club, a group of radical progressives and socialists who regularly met for discussions at a midtown Italian restaurant. Soon, amid the company of John Dewey, Charles Beard, Lincoln Steffens, Morris Hillquit, and others, Walling established himself as a serious movement intellectual.[21]

Walling's early socialism was an eclectic blend of European Marxism, the American equal rights tradition, and a romantic populism flavored with a Russian Narodnik twist.[22] Overall, one senses in his early efforts both a personal rebellion against his own genteel upbringing and a search for connectedness with that vast "other" of the immigrant working class. Not unlike other "settlement socialists" such as Jane Addams or Lillian Wald, his class analysis was as much a personal as a political declaration. Walling, for example, counseled the newly arrived resident Ernest Poole to "make friends with these settlement people and listen, listen all the time. They've got a lot to teach us boys, so for the love of Jesus Christ don't let's be uplifters here!"[23]

In the context of turn-of-the-century settlement work (especially in New York and Chicago), moreover, the Christian social gospel enjoyed a substantial encounter with Judaism through the surrounding working-class immigrant community and its manifold cultural and political institutions. Certainly, the impact on Walling of such engagement was profound. Through contacts with the Jewish community he further developed his thoughts on labor and socialism, extended his sympathies toward revolutionary Russia, and met his future wife, the radical poet Anna Strunsky.[24]

The Russian connection, facilitated by his Jewish contacts, proved especially important to Walling's development. For one, willful identification with the common people was likely enhanced by Walling's reading of the Russian masters Gorky and Tolstoy, whom he would come to know personally. Even more important, however, his two years of travel in the turmoil of the postrevolutionary Russia of 1905–1907—an adventure that included brief detention in a czarist prison—firmly oriented his early political idealism. As one of the few direct English-language commentators on contemporary Russia, Walling parlayed his financial resources (through his hiring of translators and ethnic guides) and wide-ranging curiosity into both a comprehensive and an influential review of political and social developments.[25]

Walling's accounts of his Russian trip, first filed in regular dispatches to the liberal periodical *The Independent,* then re-edited for his book *Russia's Message* (1908) made him, according to one recent commentary, "the leading American exponent of the Russian revolutionary mystique." Among the most compelling features of the Russian revolutionary developments for the young American observer was the "spirit of democracy" that he found exhibited in the peasant villages and that appeared to him to bind together the radical idealist and the masses. The *mir,* or traditional village communes, wrote Walling, "are ruled by a pure spirit of democracy not only in political but in economic affairs. Public life is not a thing apart as in some externally democratic countries, where private business overshadows public affairs and politics are a mask for private interests and the greed for office."[26] A partisan of the populist Social Revolutionary Party (SR) rather than the Mensheviks or the Bolsheviks, who equally disdained the peasantry, Walling wrote of a Russian movement "bent on finding a common ground for the best parts of the doctrine of Marx and Henry George." His highest praise was reserved for the organizers of the SR-friendly Peasants' Union—whom he called "the leaders of the people"—mainly teachers and other members of the middle classes who showed a proper respect for the self-government of the peasantry. "The majority of the founders of the union," he wrote, "were what may be called independent Socialists: most of them were inspired by the Socialist

"A Group of Village 'Intellectuals.'" Walling's orientation to the Russian political scene post-1905 revealed much about his own democratic idealism and the projected place for a person like himself in a popular movement. Photograph for article by William English Walling, "The Real Russian People," in the New York Independent 63 (Sept. 26, 1907), 732.

Revolutionary program, but they did not feel that it would be just or practical to urge their ideas on the peasant delegates and left them entirely free to work out their own programme with a few stimulating suggestions." Beneath a photograph of what Walling labeled "a group of village 'Intellectuals'," he identified "a woman doctor, her assistant, the school teacher, his wife, an agricultural expert and a visiting student." "In city and village alike," he continued, "the educated classes have succeeded in establishing the most cordial and intimate relations with the people."[27]

His particular orientation to the Russian situation revealed much about Walling's own democratic idealism and the projected place for a person like himself in a popular movement. On the one hand Walling upheld the model of the writers and professionals who founded the Peasants' Union as "democratic leaders"—"that is they were helping the people to go where they themselves desired." As a son of Hull House and the University Settlement, Walling believed that he had found in Russia a politicized laboratory for a democratic dialogue with which he was already familiar. "It is as if the whole country were an endless series of social settlements in which the settlement residents had not merely sacrificed a few luxuries and pleasures, but had accepted the risk of imprisonment, exile, and execution."[28] On the other hand Walling was wary of those who he sensed would make revolution from above or outside the will of ordinary people. Such concern placed him at odds at once with Marxist revolutionaries and Fabian technocrats, whom he associated with economic determinism and a blueprint for change heedless of popular consensus. "Attach[ment] to Socialism (collectivism) rather than to democracy," he feared, "leads at once . . . to the idea of a domination of some minority, usually some part of the middle class. The Socialism then proposed is not any fundamental change of society but only a State Socialism, the extension of the functions of the government."[29]

Just as Walling brought his distinctly American idealism to bear on his observations of Russian events, so he returned to the United States with the conviction that "Russia has a message for humanity." He left Russia certain not only that what he called the "second act" of the Revolution was "inevitable," but also that the "Russian struggle is not far away, as we sometimes imagine, but nearer to us in the end than any of the smaller spectacles that are taking place in front of our own doorways."[30] It is not surprising that Walling, the educated, upper-class socialist agitator, should be drawn to an ideal of mutual and practical interaction between peasantry and intelligentsia. Onto the complicated and tenuous political alliances existing in prerevolutionary Russia, he projected his own dreams for an intimate, organic reconciliation of Science and the People.

But neither Russia nor the America to which he returned in 1907 lived up to Walling's euphoric expectations. Revolutionary advance, whether through peasant-worker-intellectual alliance or social democratic party, appeared less and less a sure thing. In Russia the czar's armed henchmen clung tenaciously to power; in Europe no amount of revolutionary theory could cover the reality of socialist compromise with bourgeois parliamentarians; and in the United States, early socialist enthusiasm was dampened by both a spirit of reform within the old parties and general resistance from the trade union federation. Even the most determined activists were compelled, by the end of the decade, to reckon with the general "breach between the premise of active human liberation and the frustrating reality of opportunistic legalism."[31]

In particular, Walling's dream, to which he had paid homage in Russia, of intellectual-populist alliance was cruelly shaken by eruption of the Springfield, Illinois, race riots in August 1908, a rampage of murder and destruction that forced more than two thousand black people to flee the city where Lincoln had lived and was buried. Rushing to the scene directly upon his return from Europe, Walling and his wife, Anna Strunsky, were moved to call a series of emergency meetings of Negro rights supporters on their return to their New York apartment, which resulted in the founding of the NAACP.[32] Particularly in the context of his Russian epiphany, what appeared to have most disturbed Walling, as evident in his published account of the Springfield events, was that the common people of the town apparently condoned the action of the mob.[33] It is noteworthy, moreover, that in the strategic development of the NAACP, the radical Walling did not just agree with his liberal collaborators but took the lead in separating the political defense of black rights from the class-centered project of the labor and socialist movements to which he was ideologically committed. Within the new organization's inner council, he argued that the attitudes of both white labor leaders and the rank and file rendered them useless as allies on the race issue. Clearly, the existing instruments and strategies for popular mobilization from the Left had failed. The inevitable evolutionary logic of social democratic reform had become murky indeed.[34]

Within the worldwide socialist movement, frustration inevitably led to tension and even outright division among erstwhile comrades. On the Left, for example, a diverse group of discontented spirits turned from the painstakingly slow path of socialist electoral work toward the fresh winds of syndicalism.

Associated most commonly with Georges Sorel, Hubert Lagardelle's *Le Mouvement socialiste,* and the early writings (1905–1907) of cosmopolitan sociologist Robert Michels, syndicalist doctrine reappropriated the direct-action emphasis of the anarchists but set it within a union and workplace-centered framework.[35] Politically, syndicalism first became a significant force in France with the founding of the Confederation generale du travail (CGT) in 1895 and an unprecedented strike wave, which took advantage of boom times in the first decade of the new century.[36] In a period heady with the possibility of relatively autonomous advances at the workplace, impatient young radicals readily took on the comparatively lumbering structures and gradualist ideologies of socialist political parties. Attacking the stultifying effects of party bureaucracy (he would soon temper his criticism with a more distanced analysis of all organizations, including trade unions) Michels declared in 1907 that the SPD had become "an end in itself, a machine that one perfects for its embellishment, and not for the services it could have rendered."[37]

Crucial to this workerist turn within the socialist movement was the rekindling of a sociological (as well as ideological) critique of the state and state-oriented political praxis, with a sharp distinction implied by syndicalists between worker and intellectual interests. Such conflict, according to Lagardelle, might even be "likened to an actual class struggle if it were not an abuse of terms to give the name of class to the group of professional thinkers." The contradiction arose from the fact that workers' efforts toward emancipation were "necessarily directed against the modern hierarchy embodied in the state and its disputing parties," while the intellectuals "have a ten-dency on the contrary to increase the part played by government."[38] Attacking the archetype of socialist parties, the SPD, Sorel proclaimed that the party was, "in the last analysis, an organization of workers under the direction of orators; it is an oligarchy of demagogues, governing the working class, providing its reading matter, telling it which candidates to support in elections and living off its profession as directors of the people . . . The true vocation of intellectuals is the exploitation of politics."[39]

Nor was the antistatist, antitechnocratic tone of socialist discourse in this period entirely the province of ideological syndicalists. In the same period, ex-Fabian dandy and malcontent H. G. Wells produced his own influential critique of the dull, plodding reformism he associated with his former colleagues. His widely read political satire *The New Machiavelli* (1910) offered a brilliant parody of the state-making dream among middle-class intellectuals:

> Order and devotion were the very essence of our socialism, and a splendid collective vigour and happiness its end. We projected an ideal state, an organized state as confident and powerful as modern science, as balanced and beautiful as a body, as beneficent as sunshine, the organized state that should end muddle for ever; it ruled all our ideals and gave form to all our ambitions.[40]

Radical American intellectuals eagerly assimilated the European critiques of social democracy. Although possessed of no bureaucracy on the scale of the SPD, too little influence to be co-opted by bourgeois parties as in France, and no self-constituted intelligentsia as in England, the Socialist Party of America (SPA) had its doubters on both the left and the right. In the first few years of its existence, the Party had balanced its polarities by insisting on an independent political organization on the one hand, but deferring to the craft-centered conservatism of the AFL in organizing the workplace on the other. By 1909, especially after disappointing national electoral showings and the growing challenge to the AFL by the militant Industrial Workers of the World (IWW), or "Wobblies," only the symbolic leadership of Eugene V. Debs (who was uninterested in theory and strategy) kept the potentially warring factions in their place.[41] To electoral strategists on the right, the determinedly independent, ideological stance of the SPA damaged relations with trade unions and other potential allies (thus forgoing the British Labour Party model). Among the younger critics on the left, however, the party appeared to have already temporized too long.

In the United States, the neo-syndicalist left wing gathered around the IWW. Following his colorful role in the Colorado mine wars of 1904 and subsequent exoneration in the Steunenberg murder case, IWW leader William Dudley ("Big Bill") Haywood rivaled Eugene V. Debs as a celebrity in socialist circles.[42] A simultaneous revulsion from the tepid and exclusionist principles of the AFL and infatuation with the Wobblies' message of universal class solidarity attracted a coterie of intellectual supporters. As socialist moderates determined to stamp out violent rhetoric after the disastrous McNamara case of 1911 (in which much of the labor movement had been defamed by the confession of a union leader in a dynamite attack on the Los Angeles *Times* building), IWW sympathizers took up the cudgels in defense of revolutionary socialism. Reaching its apogee following the successful Lawrence textile strike of 1912, a Wobbly–New York intellectual entente extended to Haywood's participation in Mabel Dodge's salon (which included Walling) and the famous "Workers' Pageant" at Madison Square Garden organized by John Reed, Margaret Sanger, and other Greenwich Village radicals during the 1913 Paterson silk strike.[43] When Haywood was officially expelled from the party's National Executive Committee for advocating violence in 1913, among those who signed a resolution of protest were the intellectuals Max Eastman, Rose Pastor Stokes, Louis B. Boudin, Walter Lippmann, and Walling.[44]

The split among former comrades was formalized in the socialist press. When *International Socialist Review* publisher Charles H. Kerr fired editor A. M. Simons in 1908 for lack of sympathy with the Wobblies, this party organ became the exclusive property of left-wingers, including Louis B. Boudin, S. J. Rutgers, and Walling. The Left also dominated newer publications, such as the *New Review* (1913–1916) and the radical bohemian *Masses* (1911–1917), edited after 1912 by Max Eastman.[45]

Into this cauldron of swirling conflict and engaged expression, Walling briefly emerged as the "enfant terrible of the American socialist movement," the leader of a group of so-called New Intellectuals, outspoken radicals who would challenge all conventions, including socialist ones.[46] In his European travels, Walling had struck up a friendship with British Marxist H. M. Hyndman, and he quickly adopted Hyndman's antipathy for the ideologically nebulous Independent Labour Party (ILP) and the exclusionist skilled trades unions that sustained it. To Walling, whose commitment to the movement had initially developed from sympathy for the interests of immigrant workers and racial minorities, trade union politics carried with it the threat of a retreat to national chauvinism and race hatred. Assailing a British proposal for a socialist congress of English-speaking peoples as "tainted with imperialism and the possibility of race prejudice," Walling took a revolutionary internationalist line, rejecting a "narrow-based state socialism" in favor of what he called "the actual class war." Not surprisingly, Walling in this period was particularly critical of the AFL. "In America," he explained to Hyndman in 1909, "we find the greatest obstacles to the spread of this class war are the organized skilled workers with their agreements and combinations with the capitalists."[47]

Laborist and state-socialist politics most alarmed Walling for their racist and exclusionist potential. In *Progressivism—and After,* he saved some of his strongest words for a dissection of "socialism and the race problem," castigating the Socialist Party's right wing for its Asian exclusion policies and open assertion of Aryan chauvinism. Walling ridiculed the argument, which he associated with Robert Hunter and Ernest Untermann, among others, that because immigrants "have been deprived of a vote by the existing capitalistic government of this country they occupy a politically servile position and that their presence is therefore a menace to Socialism":

> The same argument of course would result in allotting an inferior position to negroes in the Socialist movement, and also to hundreds of thousands of disfranchised foreigners and white Southerners. It would also suggest to the Socialist's enemies that it is only necessary to disfranchise parts of the working class in order to get the Socialist Party to forsake them. [Adolph] Germer said that the Governor of Alabama had used all the power of the State to prevent the negro working men from being organized and that it was therefore impossible to do any-

thing with them. This reminds one of the Irishman's explanation that the people were ready to revolt, only the police would not let them.[48]

Yet Walling was no orthodox Marxist. Sounding at once like a left revolutionary and a nostalgic American republican (a tension that accurately reflected his ambivalent nature), he described himself to Hyndman as "a democrat and not in any sense a Collectivist or a State Socialist."[49] Even as he upheld the principle of revolutionary class struggle, Walling also embraced a liberal democratic "spirit of revolt" that he associated as early as 1913 with Deweyan pragmatism.[50] Resisting all encumbrances on human freedom, Walling happily enlisted Marx to attack "individual capitalism" while simultaneously summoning iconoclasts H. G. Wells and Hillaire Belloc and even Friedrich Nietzsche to assail "state socialism" (which he variously associated with the Fabians, the Labour Party, and the SPD).[51] Any subordination of the individual to organizational or bureaucratic ends—from the "machine methods" of SPA leaders to IWW disdain for internal procedure—was apt to draw Walling's ire.[52] Politically, Walling sought to carve out a middle ground of "revolutionary socialism" between the bourgeois reformism of social democracy on the one hand and the "backward"-looking project of syndicalism on the other.[53]

The themes of workers' democracy and individual autonomy that echoed from the prewar Left also awakened older doubts about the intellectual's role in the socialist movement. After all, if the working classes were capable of revolution, why they had not yet undertaken the task? Who had led them astray? The first blast on this front may have issued from Boudin, a Russian-Jewish immigrant of middle-class upbringing with an interest in legal studies and economic theory. Despite the abuse he himself had taken at the inaugural 1905 IWW convention for daring as a practicing attorney to seek voting credentials in a "wage earners" organization, Boudin held firm to workerist ideals of revolution.[54] His *ISR* essays, collected into a 1907 volume entitled *The Theoretical System of Karl Marx*, made clear that the position of the intellectual in the movement was at best marginal. "Capitalistic ideas and habits of mind," he stressed, were normally "inculcated" into the working class via a bourgeois "lower stratum" of teachers, journalists, and the like—a "new class" who existed either as the "'hangers on' of some other class" or were "[suspended] in the air entirely, where they obtain their income from wind."[55]

Not surprisingly, moderate party leaders were horrified by such intellectual-bashing. In a classic exposition of the tutelary posture of the Second International—and a direct response to syndicalist attack—John Spargo insisted that it was "hardly possible to conceive that there could have been a Socialist movement or a Socialist literature at all but for the 'intellectuals' . . . It is to the 'intellectuals' that the proletariat owes whatever understanding it has of its position in social evolution, its mission and its opportunity."[56] The American Fabian and Rand School director, William J. Ghent, grew positively apoplectic at the thought, implicit in syndicalist writings, that socialist revolution would dissolve intellectuals as a category and redistribute work and thought throughout the population. The very notion, he wrote in 1909, filled him with "repulsion and disgust," as it would anyone "to whom civilization has any meaning."[57]

But even many left-wing thinkers hesitated to take the full plunge toward syndicalism and self-abnegation as intellectuals. An *ISR* editorial generally praising Lagardelle's "exceedingly clever presentation" nonetheless identified syndicalist writers as "members of this same despised class of 'intellectuals' and this to an even greater extent than the 'parliamentarians' at whom they hurl such fine scorn."[58] The paper also printed Robert Michels' reconsideration of intellectuals and socialism in 1909 in which he contrasted, among others, the "heroic" role of intellectuals within the Italian party with the "corruption" of an "all-proletarian" organization like the AFL.[59] In 1908, *ISR* correspondent Charles Dobb was disturbed by the "peculiar phase of recent thought and discussion in the socialist movement in America" evident in the "more or less heated attacks upon those of our comrades who are included in the classification 'intellectuals' . . . and the cognate idea of 'leaders' and 'leadership.'"[60]

Walling himself at first rather stumbled into the issue in the midst of factional warfare. In the fall of 1909, just as he was privately rehearsing his opposition to the Labor Party idea with Hyndman, he received an apparently naive letter from Algie Simons soliciting his support within the SPA's National Executive Committee (NEC) to move the party—following the British Labour Party model—toward a more ideologically moderate stance through an electoral alliance with the AFL. Walling reacted with fury. Selectively quoting from Simons's letter to friends and newspapers across the country, Walling exposed Simons's self-description of the party's divisions as one between "on the one side . . . intellectuals like myself" and "on the other side a bunch of never-works, demagogues, and would-be intellectuals, a veritable Lumpenproletariat."[61]

Release of the Simons letter touched off what John Spargo described as a "near riot" among the party's leaders, not only polarizing Left and Right factions but also casting especially bitter aspersions on the personal character of the party's intellectual activists. While the incident had no lasting political effect—the right wing remained in control of the NEC even as the AFL utterly ignored Simons's attempt at rapprochement—it guaranteed Walling's isolation from the party leadership. His former friends did not easily forget Walling's personal betrayal: Simons wrote that it had "pained me as nothing I have had happen to me during my work in the Socialist movement," while Spargo smeared Walling as "mentally unbalanced," "erratic," and "an outsider . . . who never did a day's work in his life."[62]

But if Walling's first swipes at the SPA high command were both personal and partisan, he quickly moved to a more abstract (if no more disinterested) plane of attack. His adoption since 1908 of the left-wing critique of state socialism left open the question of which social groups sustained a statist regime. In Sidney and Beatrice Webb's classic exposition of socialism (*What Is Socialism?*, 1912), Walling uncovered his bête noire:

> Astonishing as it may seem, the Socialist State pictured by the Webbs presupposes (l) the dominance of the "intellectual" class and the "aristocracy of labor" and (2) the permanent subjection of the unskilled workers . . . It is these two classes, minor professionals and aristocracy of labor, that are expected by the Webbs to inaugurate in Great Britain not merely State Capitalism (in which the small capitalists dominate), but also State Socialism (where the small capitalists are subordinated to these two classes).

For Walling, the entire reformist-socialist project smelled of a *class* project: "What the intellectuals look forward to is really a beneficent rule of—the intellectuals."[63]

Yet beyond its initial polemical flourish, Walling's critique of the denizens of state power did not travel far. If not the intellectuals around the state, who would provide the political and administrative leadership for the socialist project? Who would possess the freedom, knowledge, and power to serve as instigators of change? In the years immediately preceding the Great War, Walling seemed to shrink politically before such questions. That he had in fact backed himself into a quandary is revealed in the contradictions in his writing of this period.

On the one hand, his last major work of prewar political analysis, *Progressivism—and After* (1914), all but dispensed with the problem of historical agency. Despite his prior nod toward a Deweyan political free will, Walling here fell back into a stepladder approach to socialism. Apparently bowing before the inevitability of a growing governmental presence in domestic life, he now anticipated regimes of "progressivism" or "state capitalism" (in the interests of small capitalists) followed by "laborism" or "state socialism" (in the interests of labor aristocrats and intellectuals) as necessarily preceding the distant proletarian revolution to which he had earlier committed himself. Walling's contemporary, the skeptical Progressive Walter Lippmann, was likely his most astute and even-handed reader. Defending Walling from orthodox Marxist criticism, Lippmann lavished praise on Walling for the honesty of his inquiry. "When all is said," he wrote, "Walling is perhaps the only American Socialist of standing who keeps inquiry alive, the only one who doesn't rewrite the same book every year or two." Yet Lippmann also discovered a "perplexing fatalism" in Walling's perspective, a one-dimensionality that contradicted the author's rhetorical embrace of pragmatism. Exposing the core of Walling's own dilemma, Lippmann noted, "For all real purposes, Socialists are reduced to being people who know what is going to happen, but that knowledge helps them not at all, because they can't change what is going to happen. Whatever is to come is to be in the interest[s] of a ruling class, and it's the ruling class that will carry them out." In misunderstanding the true spirit of pragmatism, Lippmann lamented, Walling neglected the "possibility of altering events that lie before us . . . fatalism cannot lead to action; it is a way of observing the world, not of dealing with it."[64]

But on the other hand, even as his political will retreated before a mechanical determinism, Walling continued to express a blithe, almost apolitical faith in the power of the free-spirited individual. The socialist vision, by this reckoning, represented the collective empowerment of such spirits, freed from class and other oppressions. This romantic faith, virtually unattached to political program of any kind, was best exemplified in Walling's 1916 tribute to Horace Traubel, a socialist poet and ardent admirer of Walt Whitman. Walling lionized Traubel for breaking through the evolutionary logjam of social development, projecting the socialist agitator as a "vital factor" rather than "dead tool" of evolution. Against even his own logic, Walling willed a sphere of individual autonomy that he associated with the democratic poets: "Like Whitman," he wrote, "Traubel distrusts all institutions and systems, past, present, and future. But he goes beyond Whitman in his distrust of ideals and ideas—which may tyrannize over the individual as much as institutions and systems . . . Traubel, a democrat on all sides, recognizes no authority—either existing or to come."[65]

But Walling had clearly perched himself on the horns of a dilemma. The intellectual, it seemed, had either to choose a metaphysical realm of artistic freedom or technocratic service to a burgeoning welfare state. In the face of such bleak (and historically static) options, the self-doubting intellectual now all but required an outside force to restore a sense of political direction.

The historian Arthur Mitzman has justly labeled the Great War "a turning point in the history of the psyche as well as the polity of the West."[66] For the subset of American socialist intellectuals to which Walling belonged, the psychic turbulence of the era was particularly profound, encompassing three major tremors, each of which was quite capable of spinning an individual out of his or her assumed political orbit. First came the collapse of international socialist solidarity in the face of nationalist war-mongering, a disillusionment most dramatically signaled in the August 1914 support for German war credits by SPD leadership in the Reichstag. The second shock emerged in the powerful U.S. mobilization around the war effort, initially resisted by most left-wing and Progressive figures but championed after 1916 by the intellectual president, Woodrow Wilson, along with an intense appeal to patriotic service. Finally, and perhaps most critically, the Bolshevik Revolution of 1917 projected a

new and provocative socialist face, a militant mien that all but demanded total identification or adamant rejection.

Walling, like many of the native-born SPA intellectuals, was not
only buffeted by these events but ultimately deposited into an entirely new political space. His transformation began in bitter reaction to the German socialist sell-out of the antimilitarist cause. Still
professing left-wing intentions, Walling attacked Kautsky as a "nationalist" in early 1915, chided European socialists for pursuing
peace with Germany "at almost any price," and argued for prolon-
gation of the war "until the people of Russia, Germany, and Austria
are driven to revolt."[67] Nationalism, not militarism, he had concluded by 1916, was "the enemy," and socialism (as opposed to
"bourgeois pacificism") "demands the support of some but not all
defensive wars."[68]

How quickly the ideology of self-defense can become its own nationalistic crusade seems borne out in Walling's experience of the
war era. Within a twelve-month period, Walling had thrown in
with President Wilson's war-for-democracy line, while severing his
connection with the officially antimilitarist SPA and its supportive
organs the Intercollegiate Socialist Society (ISS) and the *Masses*.[69] A
draft manifesto written by Walling for the Social Democratic League
(an ad hoc collection of prowar socialists) called for U.S. intervention two months before the April 1917 declaration of war.[70] Indeed,
in only one particular did Walling diverge from his newfound allies
from the old socialist right in his prowar sentiments. Unlike Charles
Edward Russell and to a lesser extent John Spargo, Walling never
conflated the "Germanism" of antiwar SPA leaders like Morris
Hillquit with their Jewishness.[71]

Although old frictions with his ex-comrades on the socialist right
denied Walling an executive position in the League or the other
prowar progressive lobby, the American Alliance for Labor and
Democracy, he more easily made up with one powerful former an-
tagonist: Samuel Gompers. The writer-activist and the labor leader
shared not only a general enthusiasm for the war effort but also a
particular passion to contain the Bolshevik element in Russia.
Repeatedly and frantically, in the months before October 1917, the
two tried to bend U.S. policy to forestall the Soviet threat; subsequently, they lobbied hard to toughen the western diplomatic and

military posture towards the new Russian regime.[72] In the process Walling emerged as a kind of unofficial minister of foreign affairs for the AFL, a status recognized as he accompanied the American labor delegation to Europe at the personal invitation of Gompers during the peace negotiations and later for the foundation meeting of the International Federation of Trade Unions.[73]

In the immediate postwar years, Walling continued his collaboration with the AFL's high command. While never recapturing either the public notoriety or the influence of his younger years, Walling was frequently tapped by Gompers both for his knowledge of international affairs and for his skill in addressing a wider audience. On the home front, Walling's anti-Bolshevism remained a stock in trade. The ex-bohemian openly supported the National Civic Federation's crusade against such dens of subversion as the *New Republic*, the American Civil Liberties Union, and even the American Library Association, while his newly calibrated political activism included a defense of the expulsion of socialists from the New York legislature in 1920.[74]

Throughout these efforts, Walling still considered himself very much a progressive internationalist. His defense of Mexican presidents Alvaro Obregon and Plutarco Calles from U.S. business calls for intervention in the mid-twenties, for example, drew on his still-strong aversion to economic imperialism, and he accused the Coolidge administration of hiding behind "100 per cent patriotism and flag-waving" in order to facilitate "every form of reaction and profiteering at home."[75] Similarly, his defense of AFL domestic policy, whether distributed through the labor and mainstream press or collected in his 1926 volume, *American Labor and American Democracy*, still assumed a distinctly social democratic outlook. Against the backdrop of official Federation support for the La Follette presidential bid of 1924, Walling argued strongly for a reconciliation of traditional trade union voluntarism with a "progressive" regulation of business in the interests of both producers and consumers.[76]

Yet while maintaining a generally critical outlook on public affairs, the postwar Walling breathed not a word of criticism—either in public or in extensive business correspondence with Gompers—

of the labor federation that he had once excoriated as a bastion of reaction and exclusion.[77] His about-face was completed when in 1929 he publicly defended iron-molders' leader John Frey, who had asserted that "with perhaps a few exceptions in a few localities, the American trade-unionist is more eager to organize the negro than the negro is to become a member."[78] When the moderate NAACP's leader (and Walling's old friend) Walter White called Frey's remarks "a casuistic defense of the exclusion," Walling jumped to reassure Frey that labor "has nothing to be ashamed of" on the "color question." Moreover, according to Walling, it was the NAACP, particularly the "nasty reds" gathered around W. E. B. Du Bois, who needed to be "straightened out."[79]

Despite such dramatic repudiations of former loyalties, one coordinate remained fixed across Walling's pre- and postwar political telemetry: the intellectual as impediment to democratic culture. In resurrecting this old nemesis, albeit from an opposite angle, Walling remained sure of his footing. Thus, the same social group that had once threatened—as Fabians—to collaborate with exclusivist skilled workers to further its own bureaucratic and statist agenda now appeared in its Bolshevik guise to be manipulating the unskilled proletariat in a totalitarian seizure of state power. "Sovietism," Walling argued in 1920, depended on an alliance of the "intellectual proletariat" with the "unskilled and "unconscious mass," a union cemented by the demonic power of propaganda.[80] As such, the intellectual-as-Bolshevik extended political error into social pathology: "The Bolshevists," Walling allowed, "undoubtedly have some first-class minds among them—but they are minds of the peculiar and abnormal type of persons who are willing and able to abandon themselves utterly to securing leadership of the ignorant by any and all means that will achieve that end."[81]

The chastened sensibility of the ex-revolutionist regarding the threat of the intellectual class placed Walling in good company with the AFL's contemporary academic boosters, the labor economists of the Wisconsin School led by John R. Commons and Selig Perlman.[82] Indeed, in its virtual disavowal of the need for intellectuals, Walling's *American Labor and American Democracy* sounded a distinctly Wisconsin-like note:

Organized labor's social philosophy, its system of ideas . . . is comparatively less fundamental in America than in other countries because our labor-unionism is based not upon ideas, but upon experience. In other countries labor organizations have been founded largely on general ideas and an effort has been made to base economic and policies on those ideas. In America, on the contrary, general ideas have arisen exclusively out of labor's daily experience in collective bargaining.[83]

This position of anti-intellectual pragmatism was even more explicit in a contemporary defense Walling wrote of the AFL's nonpartisan politics. The first lesson a successful American labor movement had learned, proclaimed Walling, was "that labor can not afford to admit non-labor 'intellectuals' into leadership either in its economic or in its political organizations."[84]

Reconciliation of the former left-wing leader with the apostles of American exceptionalism was more than literary. Commons, for example, personally stamped Walling's 1926 text with his seal of approval, labeling it "as nearly an authoritative statement of the principles and policies of the American organized labor movement of the past forty years as any statement that could be issued by any person not an active official or working member of an American union."[85] The Selig Perlman connection was even more intimate. Years before, Walling's personal largesse had subsidized the radical young Russian's emigration to New York to translate Marx and subsequently facilitated his enrollment at Wisconsin. The parallel political trajectories of the two men is recognized in this 1936 eulogy by Perlman addressed to Walling's widow:

I recall my overnight stay at your Westport home in the summer of 1925 when he told me of his wonderful relations with Samuel Gompers who had just died, and how perfectly willing he was to continue to take his orders from organized labor rather than to play the Messiah to labor.

And finally I recall our chance visit together at Chicago in 1934, when, over a glass of beer, we marveled with mutual delight at each of us having arrived independently at an identical analysis of the labor situation—even to the point of employing the same expressions.[86]

Alas, the onset of the Depression and the threat of international fascism in the early 1930s prompted one more shift in Walling's positions, including a new take on old themes. Thus, after years of determined attack on the British Labour Party model, Walling opined in an untitled, undated manuscript from the early thirties (presumably for delivery under AFL auspices) that "labor favors any form of political action that is effective." Supporting the consumer-demand, high-wage logic of Labor–New Dealers, Walling declared that "uncontrolled private operation is no longer practical without sacrifice of the interest of labor and mass of the producers and consumers of the nation. Where private initiative remains practicable it must submit to an increasing public control . . . The government is taking on so many and so far-reaching economic functions of a permanent sort that we are doubtless in the midst of an economic and political revolution, building the foundation of a new social order." Such "revolutionary developments" would necessitate "an immensely greater attention to legislation and to governmental departments and commissions and in many instances to the active participation of labor representatives in their administration."[87] Ironically, Walling's domestic stance resembled that of the meliorative state reformer, the nationalistic social democrat, and the Fabian—exactly the perspectives that he had once foresworn. On the international front, Walling's fears likewise shifted from communism to fascism. In the summer of 1936, he journeyed to Europe as executive director of the Labor Chest for the relief and liberation of European workers. Despite an aggravated arthritis condition and high fever, he proceeded to Amsterdam in September to meet representatives of the German labor underground. Before the meeting he suffered a fatal heart attack.[88]

WILLIAM ENGLISH Walling's political journey is an instructive one. Beginning with high hopes of joining the working-class struggle, socialist intellectuals such as Walling generally found themselves something of a breed apart. Nestled uncomfortably in a hothouse of revolutionary thought somewhere between the liberal-statist reformers on the one hand and rank and file workers on the other, how were they to reconnect to the "real" world? The theories, visions, and principles of old comrades stood on one side; call of country, sense of service, and lure of influence stood on the other. Yet, in dashing from the Scylla of the romantic Left to the Charybdis of establishment liberalism, Walling remained equally frustrated by those intellectual "others" who followed their passions to different conclusions.

Nor was this profile of what might be called the "anti-intellectualism of the intellectuals" unique to Walling; it seems to fit a much larger contemporary cultural pattern. The issues that preoccupied Walling—of reform, revolution, the role of the state, and the role of the intellectual within the democratic process—loomed large for all those entrusted with functions of analysis, theory, education, and organizational leadership in the era of the Great War. Perhaps what is most remarkable about the contemporary verdict on such issues, however, is that regardless of where one stood politically and ideologically, a finger of blame tended to point in the end at some version of the *trahison des clercs*.

On the left, for example, the Communists adopted a kind of mirror image of Walling's caricature of intellectual disloyalty, but applied to their own "class enemies." By nature, this argument went, intellectuals represented outposts of bourgeois culture, and even those who became critics lacked sufficient iron in the belly for revolutionary action. To Louis Fraina, once Walling's editor at the *New Review*, their prowar "sell-out" proved that intellectuals composed "a corrupt and corrupting influence [whose] petty bourgeois souls scent the flesh pots of Imperialism . . . In every imperialistic country it is precisely these 'workers of the brain' who manufacture and carry into the ranks of the workers the ideology and the enthusiasm of Imperialism."[89] S. J. Rutgers, a Dutch left-winger and civil engineer who had emigrated to Brooklyn in 1915 and subsequently joined the international leadership of the Comintern, waxed similarly caustic on the untrustworthiness of the intellectual's basic socialization.[90]

> The environment and the education of the intellectual have this for their one aim. The idiotic school system, which all but absolutely bars general culture in order to waste time upon all kinds of irrelevant information which, if eventually needed, may be had from any handbook; the burden of lessons to be learned by rote and work to done at home which prevents future intellectuals from gathering any experi-

ence of life in their leisure hours; the promoting of an exaggerated and consequently senseless sport; all this, as a system of education, compares only with military drill . . . The little world of the University undergraduate, fenced off from real life, outwardly and seemingly "free" and the secluded circle, animated by an arrogant caste-spirit, in which army officers move, are means to one and the same end: the maintaining of exploitation.[91]

Only the strictest vigilance by justly suspicious workers—what Lenin defined as the "dictatorship of the proleteriat"—Rutgers wrote, could win the "titanic war . . . against monopoly, whether monopoly of money or monopoly of mind."[92]

The animus that Fraina and Rutgers expressed toward intellectuals for their reactionary historic roles blossomed within the culture of the Communist Party into full-fledged anti-intellectualism. As one of the "God that failed" generation of ex-Communists, Arthur Koestler remained in 1954 most perplexed by the contempt for learning to which he had succumbed as a "special feature of Party life":

> It is relatively easy to explain how a person with my story and background came to became a Communist, but more difficult to convey a state of mind that led a young man of twenty-six to be ashamed of having been to a university, to curse the agility of his brain, the articulateness of his language, to regard such civilized tastes and habits as he had acquired as a constant source of self-reproach, and intellectual self-mutilation as a desirable aim. If it had been possible to lance those tastes and habits like a boil, I would gladly have submitted to the operation.[93]

For some, the Communists appeared to make an intellectual lifestyle unbearable, while for others Bolshevism itself represented a kind of coup d'état by and for the intelligentsia. Ironically, the Bolsheviks' contempt for the defiant individualism of the intellectual equally found echo in distinctly anti-Communist commentary in the postwar period. It was in these years that the left-wing intellectual was identified as a distinctly "bad citizen," constitutionally unable or unwilling to follow society's norms. The social democrat William J. Ghent thus identified the key threat of the postwar period (actually, he dated their emergence to the Lawrence Strike of 1912) as the revolutionary intellectuals whom he christened the "Super-Radicals, scorners of conformity and restraint, devotees of difference." These "addicts of alterity" strive constantly to be different—"different from the bourgeoisie and different from one another"—but, in practice, "in susceptibility to every fresh contagion of unrest they are almost of one blood." "Mistaking their own emotions for public movements," the super-radical intellectuals by their rantings and ravings ultimately make a mockery or worse of the serious, pragmatic Left and thus hasten the "Reaction of the Right." By way of explanation of this lunatic fringe, Ghent surmised that "perhaps it was the result of a long series of Freudian repressions." By way of control, Ghent defended criminal syndicalist laws.[94]

John Spargo, too, reacted to the wartime era and particularly the Bolshevik threat with a deep mistrust of intellectual radicalism. How could men and women "who have thought long and earnestly upon the social question" and "of the highest rectitude in their personal lives" end up applauding a policy "so inherently illiberal and undemocratic" as Communism, Spargo wondered. To answer, he, like Ghent, turned to psychology, in particular to a "fairly well defined form of psycho-neurosis" previously associated with religious fanaticism, labeled "hysterical hyperesthesia." Blinded by an ecstatic faith, the rational powers of the "typical Bolshevik Intellectual" regularly succumb, according to Spargo, to

> exaggerated egoism, extreme intolerance, intellectual vanity, hypercriticism, self-indulgence, craving for mental and emotional excitement, excessive dogmatism, hyperbolic language, impulsive judgment, emotional instability, intense hero-worship, propensity for intrigues and conspiracies, rapid alternation of extremes of exaltation and depression, violent contradictions in tenaciously held opinions and beliefs, periodic, swift, and unsystematic changes of mental attitude.[95]

Part of the psychopathology of the radical agitator, Spargo argued, derived from gender inversion. The stigma of effeminacy had long attached itself to social reformers, but this (perhaps because he was a male reformer himself) was not Spargo's point. Indeed, while acknowledging a sociological link between pro-Bolshevik sentiment and the leisure of well-educated upper-class men and women, Spargo took pains to refute the popular view of Bolshevism as a mere fad among "society butterflies."[96] It was less dilettantism than full-time commitment that worried Spargo, and his worst fear centered on the unsexed, revolutionary woman. In particular, he identified one type "among serious and high-minded women" of the Left who were utterly "unemotional, creatures of pure intellect, whose minds work with mechanical precision and regularity."

> Generally . . . their sexual life is either arrested or abnormal. They have been thwarted in love and remain unmarried, their normal desires being starved, or if married they are sterile. Such people come as near attaining "the passionless pursuits of passionless knowledge" as human beings may. The type is hard, dried-up, brilliant, and capable of great callousness and cruelty.[97]

In Spargo's case, fear of such social mutants, a new play on the old Amazon women theme, not only reinforced a personal renunciation of socialism but later carried over to open attacks on the New Deal.[98]

Americans, we should note, had no monopoly on the growing vituperation surrounding the intellectual's political role. The spirit of self-accusation, or at least of bitter disillusionment with whole sectors of one's intellectual peers, readily crossed national boundaries. In retrospect, Julien Benda's *Trahison des clercs* (1927), with its attack on the entire tradition of intellectual engagement, proved a relatively benign form of disillusionment-cum-disengagement. From the ranks of the Left, perhaps the most systematic critique of the intelligentsia from within was fashioned from Siberian exile in the 1890s by the renegade Polish Marxist Jan Waclaw Machajski. Machajski argued that socialism, for all its proletarian protestations, effectively served a new middle class of intellectuals and professionals who would employ political democracy, government ownership, and their educational "capital" to rise to social domination.[99]

With little political impact on the contemporary Left, Machajski's doctrines (which resembled those of Sorel) were later popularized in the United States by Austrian immigrant Max Nomad (born Nacht), whose writings from the 1930s through the 1950s contributed to a rich vein of literature on the "new class." The potential of this term (which was used by liberal analysts in the early post–World War II period as an economic category) for social criticism (for this purpose it was often transformed into "cultural elite") blossomed with the neo-conservative reaction to the social agenda of the 1960s.[100]

In the end, little more than a half-century and a few rhetorical adjustments separated the fulminations of the pre–World War I Left of William English Walling et al. and the post-Vietnam Right of Spiro Agnew, Irving Kristol, and Dan Quayle. From the internal preoccupations of the bohemian Left at the turn of the century to more recent thunderings by a neo-populist Right, the problem of the intellectuals endures within American political discourse.

We are left with Hofstadter's basic curiosity about the sources of the problem. For me, the fact that socialist writers as much as others should wrestle with the intellectual's social role suggests that the issue may be less one of the exceptionalism of American evangelical and business-saturated popular culture than Hofstadter imagined. Rather, at least part of the dilemma seems to inhere in the democratic ethos itself. For while commitment to "democracy" (especially left-wing democracy) readily summons up appeals to the broad public and the collective good, the necessarily attending logic of agency and leadership is conceptually ill-defined and often unacknowledged. In the American case, at least, a culture proclaiming a simultaneous dedication to "democracy" and "progress" thus guarantees recurrent friction over the would-be agents of their improbable delivery. Whoever steps forward to lead the people has, in a fateful sense, already put on airs. The subsequent deflation and fall are predictable. In commenting on the "philosophical method of the Americans," De Tocqueville noted:

> As to the influence which the intelligence of one man has on that of another, it must necessarily be very limited in a country where the citizens, placed on the footing of a general similitude, are all closely seen by each other; and where, as no signs of incontestable greatness or superiority are perceived in any one of them, they are constantly brought back to their own reason as the most obvious and proximate source of truth. It is not only confidence in this or that man which is

then destroyed, but the taste for trusting the *ipse dixit* of any man whatsoever. Every one shuts himself up in his own breast, and affects from that point to judge the world.[101]

What the Walling story shows is that the trouble arises as much from the top of the intellectual pyramid as from the bottom. In the case of the American socialists, the proposal of group marriage between intellectuals and masses, so exuberantly enchanting to socialist architects, first fell victim to self-estrangement among the intellectuals themselves. Soon thereafter, antisocialist guardians of the republic readily stigmatized the intellectuals as pariahs to protect the workers from unwelcome suitors.

5 A Love for the People

Anna Strunsky Walling and the Domestic Limits of Democratic Idealism

THE QUEST for democracy among early-twentieth-century radical intellectuals extended from designs for social change and even revolution to the intersection of two sympathetic hearts. While romantic love had become a staple of middle-class yearning since the mid-nineteenth century, Progressive Era political activists endowed the concept with special force. Decades before the feminist aphorism "the personal is political" gained currency, American intellectuals willfully attached political significance to their private lives and relationships. As Christopher Lasch first noted in 1965:

> The new radicalism differed from the old in its interest in questions which lay outside the realm of conventional politics. It was no longer his political allegiance alone which distinguished the radical from the conservative. What characterized the person of advanced opinions in the first two decades of the twentieth century—and what by and large continues to characterize him in the present time—was his position with regard to such issues as childhood, education, and sex; sex above all.[1]

Anticipation of and commitment to a passionate life—a life fired not only by democratic idealism but also by intimate romantic and sensual fulfillment—was indeed one of the hallmarks of many of the young writers and activists, both women and men, of the pre–World War I years. Yet how to weave love into the fabric of one's work and political activity? And how to sustain it through the burdens of daily life? As with the larger political project of industrial democracy, so with companionate marriages—between the intent and the deed stood a myriad of obstacles and many struggles. And given both the social division of labor and the emotional economy of the contemporary middle-class family, women were apt to play the leading role in the trials on the home front.

When wealthy socialist journalist William English Walling met writer Anna Strunsky in New York City sometime in 1905, both were running from—as well as toward—love. That each had suffered from earlier, impetuous entanglements lent greater self-reflection to their discovery of each other's attractions and more determination to their commitment to a shared life course.

ANNA STRUNSKY, the fourth of six children born to Russian Jewish parents (her mother was the daughter of a Belorussian rabbi), arrived with her family in New York City in 1893 at age fourteen. Soon established in San Francisco, where her father pursued a lucrative liquor business, Anna grew up in both a worldly and an intellectually ambitious household where all the children were encouraged to educate themselves and to act on their abilities.[2] Among Anna's siblings, Albert entered real estate and helped develop Greenwich Village, Max became an orthopedic surgeon, Hyman a writer for the New York *Call,* Morris a journalist, and Rose—Anna's lifelong confidante—a Lincoln scholar, a translator of Tolstoy, and a fellow revolutionary socialist.[3] Both Anna and Rose attended Stanford University, and it was during her college days that Anna became a fixture in a bohemian set of writers, artists, and political bon vivants—largely from upper-class Protestant families—who called themselves "the Crowd."[4]

Anna was clearly a young woman of quick wit and independent expression as well as dashing, dark beauty. A favorite story of her years at Stanford concerned an encounter with visiting philosopher William James after he listened approvingly to a paper she had read in one of her classes. David Starr Jordan, president of the university, invited Anna to breakfast with the distinguished guest and then to accompany him to the train station. As Anna retold the story many years later, she had noticed that the meal had left a spot of egg on the distinguished guest's beard. Should she interrupt to say, "Dr. James, would you like to use my handkerchief to get the egg off your beard?" or "Dr. James, would you want to use your handkerchief . . . " No, that was totally impossible. She would have to allow

Anna Strunsky Walling, American socialist and poet, circa 1905. (Courtesy of Anna Walling Hamburger)

him to get on the train unimproved. "Now what would you have done?" she would gaily interrogate her own children.[5]

Like others in her set, Anna combined her ardent political interests with intense, emotionally demanding personal relationships.[6] It was through the Crowd that Anna met Jack London at a Socialist Labor Party lecture in the fall of 1899.[7] At twenty-two, already a published author and a veteran of both General Charles T. Kelley's Industrial Army of 1893 and his own explorations of the Klondike, London possessed a certain vagabond celebrity. He was immediately taken with the earnest young writer of both verse and prose. Jack and Anna soon engaged in a serious, if physically delimited, affair of the heart. Taking the romantic lead, Jack addressed Anna as "Comrade Mine," admonished her to stop calling him "Mr. London," confessed "to sitting here, crying like a big baby" after finishing *Jude, the Obscure,* and even reported on taking hashish "as a matter of sin investigation."[8] Anna later recalled her own excitement at their acquaintance: "It was as if I were meeting in their youth, Lassalle, Karl Marx or Byron," she wrote;

> a pale face illumined by large, blue eyes fringed with dark lashes and a beautiful mouth which opening in its ready laugh revealed an absence of front teeth, adding to the boyishness of his appearance. The brow, the nose, the contour of the cheeks, the massive throat were Greek. His form gave an impression of grace and athletic strength . . . He was dressed in gray, and was wearing the soft white shirt and collar which he had already adopted.[9]

According to one reminiscence, Jack and Anna were "constantly together," exchanging manuscripts, meeting at her family's home overlooking Jefferson Square, or dining with friends at Coppa's Italian restaurant, after which at a friend's attic studio Anna might "recite poetry in her rich, low voice, and youth's eternal arguments on life and love and art wore away the hours till the candles guttered out in their sockets."[10]

The London-Strunsky arguments about love and life, initially growing out of spontaneous conversation, took on an extended and self-consciously serious form in an elaborate exchange of correspondence. The very contrast in their temperaments acted as a powerful magnet between them. "I came to you like a parched soul out of the wilderness, thirsting for I knew not what," Jack wrote Anna. "What have you been to me? I am not great enough or brave enough to say . . . Above all, you have conveyed to me my lack of spirituality, idealized spirituality."[11]

Yet the very intensity of his feeling for Anna, a force that threatened his vaunted self-reliance (together with a residual anti-semitism) made London an unlikely suitor.[12] Still, it must have been a shock to Anna when in April 1900, Jack London abruptly married Bessie Maddern, an old friend from Oakland who had utterly conventional ideas about a woman's duty to a successful husband. The marriage, admittedly without passion on Jack's part, broke down within four years, when London fell in love with Charmian Kittredge and left his wife and two young daughters. In the face of infuriated public opinion, London and Kittredge married in 1905 and lived together until his death in 1916.[13]

Anna Strunsky was not untouched by the wild saga of London's personal life. His marriage to Bessie, it appeared, only sharpened the tension between them. Drawing on their earlier arguments in conversation, London and Strunsky hatched a thinly veiled fictionalized correspondence (the only collaborative intellectual enterprise in which London ever engaged), which was published anonymously in 1903 as *The Kempton-Wace Letters*.[14] The letters accentuated the differences between the two authors on love and romance, with London attempting anonymously to defend his own, utilitarian approach to marriage.

The *Kempton-Wace Letters* takes the form of an extended correspondence between a young, ambitious Berkeley student named Herbert Wace (London) and an elderly male poet, Dane Kempton (Strunsky), who had once loved and lost Wace's mother and now serves as mentor to her son. Wace announces plans to wed young Stanford student poetess Hester Stebbins, but he offends Kempton— and ultimately loses Hester—because of his narrowly "efficient" and coldly "scientific" approach to romance. Wace contrasts his own world of "things and facts" to the romantic illusions of Kempton's "ideas and fantasies." "I have already classed you as a feeler, myself as a thinker."[15] Identifying with what he insists is the basic reproductive logic of the universe, Wace dismisses love as a mere "convention."[16] Unmasking the polite distinction between the "respectable" sentiments of romantic love and the "illicit" passions of the "garmented beast," Wace concludes that the race instinct for "progeny" is the most honest and basic rationale for marriage: "the slug must procreate its kind, or its kind will perish; and so I."[17] Perceiving marriage as a "race" obligation otherwise more important to a woman's than a man's life, Wace opts for an intellectualized approach to "conjugal love" as distinct from "romantic love," which he sees as "a disorder of mind and body . . . produced by passion under the stimulus of imagination."[18]

In response to his young friend's cynical and prosaic approach to love, Dane Kempton (Anna Strunsky) refashions the case for modern romance. Disdaining Wace's sexual division of character types, Kempton insists, "Men are not either intellectual or emotional; they are both. It is a rounded not an angular development which we follow." The compatibility with another soul sought through romantic love, Kempton argues, is not the lowest but the highest of human faculties. "We live most when we are most under its sway, and it is for such self-promised sparks that we live at all. Romance quickens and controls as does nothing else, and because of this it is not only a means but an end in itself. It is stirred-up life."

Moreover, modern-day feminism promises to lift the imperfections and double standards of traditional romance. "Woman is newborn in strength and dignity, and the highest chivalry the world has ever known is in blossom. She is an equal, a comrade, a right regal person. She is no longer a means but an end in herself, not alone fit to mother men but fit to live in equality with men . . . Because of the greater and more general emancipation of woman the subtlety of modern love has become possible."[19]

In the end, the poet's logic of love carries the day against the "mad scientist" Wace. A sadder but wiser Hester Stebbins rejects Wace out of loyalty to her own (and Kempton-Strunsky's) ideals, which combine love and equality: "Before everything else in the world I pray that knowledge of love come to the man over whom the love of my girlhood was spilled. Do you ask what is left me, dear friend? Work and tears and the intact dream. Believe me, I am not pitiable."[20] The modern woman, Anna Strunsky implies, will insist on a partnership of mutual respect, even if she still awaits her own Prince Charming.

In real life, the *Kempton-Wace Letters* caused some problems for both of its authors when it appeared in 1903. Only months after the book's publication, London walked out on Bessie Maddern, and she was quick to blame Anna Strunsky for disruption of the marriage, even naming her in a legal separation petition. Jack vehemently denied that Anna played any role in his decision, but he hesitated to admit his dalliance with Bess's close friend Charmian Kittredge, and a divorce was not arranged until 1905.[21] Many years later, Anna would confess that once, in 1902, while they were working together on the book, Jack London had indeed proposed that they run away to New Zealand or Australia and get married. Initially, she had whispered "yes," but after thinking it over and consulting with her mother, Anna demurred, and the matter was never raised again.[22]

Anna Strunsky left Jack London with her romantic principles intact, if still uncertain of how to act upon them. To escape unwanted publicity, she traveled to New York and Europe in 1903. In London she met the great Russian anarchist Peter Kropotkin; back home later that year she was introduced, through the intercession of radical San Francisco publisher Gaylord Wilshire, to a glittering new cast of literary and political figures. These included two men who would later loom large in her life, left-wing socialist William English Walling and anarchist Leonard Abbott. She also drew closer to another friend from among the Crowd, the young socialist law clerk Cameron King. As the left-wing community cheered the news of revolt in Russia in early 1905, a smitten Cameron King, who had apparently worshiped Anna for years, tried to place her traumatic adventure with Jack London in bold relief:

> The years that have past, years of pain and sorrow, are past. Let the memory of their miseries pass with them. Forget regrets and fold to your heart the work and joy to come . . . The old order changeth! For you and for me there is work, achievement, salvation. I hold you close and long. I look into your eyes, I kiss your lips—and then—Fling wide the gates . . . and usher in the multitude of tasks and duties.[23]

But it was not Cameron King who would share the coming exhilarating years with Anna Strunsky. When he wrote she had already accepted an invitation from Walling to join him on a journalistic investigation of St. Petersburg and other sites of smoldering revolutionary ferment in Russia. Within four months she sent back word of her engagement. Poor King was crushed. In his bitter first reaction to her alleged "deceit," King questioned whether the "romantic and obligatory circumstances of your meeting have unduly influenced your naturally impulsive heart." Did she truly "love [Walling] for himself—not because he made Petersburg possible for you, not because he has become unwarrantably confused with the romance of the struggle for freedom, not because you are lonely and he is the only friend within 5000 miles?"[24] But King soon calmed down and wished the new couple well. To Anna he admitted his hurt after what he labeled "years of futile courtship." "Your revolution in personal life," he confessed, "has meant a sort of anarchy for me."[25]

Amidst the backdrop of earth-shaking political events, the Walling-Strunsky match burst into flame. In January 1906, Walling wrote from Russia that he was experiencing "a very serious heart affair—my 'finish' we all believe." Preparing his conventional, Midwestern Protestant parents back home for news that would undoubtedly surprise and disturb them, he offered a succinct portrait of his bride-to-be. Anna Strunsky, he began, had already acquired a reputation as a literary "genius" and the "best known speaker on the coast."

> She is loved, sometimes too much by everybody that knows her—literary men, settlement people, socialists. She is young (26), very healthy and strong. Of course she is a Jewess . . . (but I hope to improve that—at least in private life—but we haven't spoken much of such things). She believes in everything I do and what is most important, she believes in me.[26]

It had been a fast-blooming romance. Apparently taken with Anna's charm from their first meeting, Walling had initially concealed his emotions behind a businesslike if friendly exterior. Mistakenly thinking that she was still attached to Jack London, he was content to praise her political work with the Friends of Russian Freedom, to offer contacts in New York or Washington with other "girl Socialists," and finally, to urge her to join him abroad as part of a "news bureau project" to "meet the revolutionists" in Russia.[27] Once reunited abroad, the two—frequently joined by Anna's sister, Rose—were swept up in a dramatic series of journalistic adventures, including a brush with hostile authorities in 1906 and later arrest and brief detention in St. Petersburg.[28] During their travels, including visits to the sites of anti-Jewish pogroms and a private meeting with Tolstoy, their growing feelings are captured by simple notes and telegraphic transmissions: "[Having] the time of my life dearest" or "Dearest love, I love you!"[29] Anna would confess to her future mother-in-law that the couple "were as surprised at our love as you were when you received [word of it]. We had had no idea of such a thing, and it was a queer time to fall in love just when English was occupied with all kinds of princely and ministerial interviews, and when I had come all the way from San Francisco to show what I could do . . . For awhile we refused to believe our hearts . . . [then] English decided that the Russian Revolution was for the time being not the most important thing in the world!"[30] A day before his wedding, English summarized the sublime state of dependence he experienced in Anna's presence: "As for me I am simply her disciple in matters of the heart. She has the greatness and power to show me what our life can and must be . . . She is my environment, she is all around me. Her feeling and love and limitless hopes are what I desire most of everything in life. There is nothing, I feel nothing, that I need that she cannot give me."[31]

For Walling, the romantic identification that he experienced with Anna Strunsky in 1906 completed a revolution of personal sentiments that over the course of the previous decade had drawn him far from his roots in Louisville, Kentucky. Only ten years before, during his brief sojourn at Harvard Law School, he had complained to his father at having to dine alongside three "nigger" students.[32] Likewise, it appears that in earlier days his social tastes had been defined by genteel convention. His first recorded interest in female company at Harvard refers to meeting "several pleasant girls" including one who stood out, "a true southern type, unusually vivacious . . . the kind you would be taken with, Father, for besides these qualities she is a very pretty brunette and knows how to take and receive compliments in the old southern way."[33]

New political ideals coupled with the intense experience of living in an urban settlement house evidently changed Walling's view of both the ethnic and racial "other." On race relations it appears that Walling, like his settlement colleague Mary White Ovington, developed through settlement surveys of the black community a recognition of the environmental (as opposed to genetic) sources of black poverty.[34] Though the record is scanty regarding Walling's incremental yet dramatic shift in racial perceptions, his leadership in the mobilization against the 1908 Springfield race riot and subsequent organization of the NAACP suggests the projection of a sympathetic imagination connecting the plight of a downtrodden class (industrial workers), the persecution of an ethno-religious minority (East European Jews), and the systematic victimization of black Americans.[35] That Walling would put himself on the line for racial equality, moreover, attests not merely to political conviction but also to a willed rebellion against his own inherited instincts. Indeed, Walling was very self-conscious about his ongoing internal struggle, privately confessing, for example, to acute physical discomfort when W. E. B. Du Bois joined him for a swim at the Wallings' summer cottage.[36] Public reforms rested on private ones, and among the important examples of the latter was the romantic transcendence of difference effected in the settlement houses.[37]

For socialist men and ethnic women, appreciation of the other sometimes proved more than intellectual. New York's University Settlement, one of several serving the Lower East Side ghetto, seems in particular to have acted as a powerful catalyst between serious young male reformers of educated, Protestant backgrounds and women of the surrounding Jewish immigrant neighborhood. Like his friend and fellow settlement resident James Graham Phelps Stokes, Walling chose after a few years to leave the incremental daily neighborhood interaction of "social work" for more programmatically radical, socialist movement-building. Yet their encounters with "exotic" young women—if not the working girls themselves, then the intellectual New Women of ethnic backgrounds who populated the same circles—clearly left an impression on the male residents. How else to explain the fact that within the same few years two of Walling's closest settlement colleagues—J. G. Phelps Stokes and LeRoy Scott, like Walling "wealthy WASPs of impeccable social standing"—also married young Russian Jewish socialist women?[38]

In Walling's case, cross-ethnic sexual wanderlust only narrowly escaped scandalous consequences. As Anna Strunsky arrived in Paris from the United States to work with Walling, he was desperately trying to detach himself from an affair gone awry with *another* Russian Jewish Anna, this one Anna Berthe Grunspan, an eighteen-year-old French immigrant just out of boarding school and still living with her family in Paris. Berthe had traveled across Europe with Walling and had clearly fallen in love with him even as he made friends with her family—sharing a German hotel suite with Miss Grunspan in the company of her brothers and depositing a trunk of books in her family's Paris apartment. Yet after an initial dalliance, Walling evidently became alarmed as Berthe looked to him not only for a health cure for her frequent dizzy spells but to make good on his casual talk of commitment.[39] In vain, it appears, he tried to buy her off, offering monetary support both for medical or educational trips to Switzerland and England. But Berthe responded first with intimate reminders of passion ("dirty monkey, I am thirsty kissing you") and then with threats—"I implore you, dearest, have pity and write to your little friend if you wish to avoid terrible things . . . I am no longer the little girl whom you knew; I am a woman now, a woman with hardened features."[40] The final, bizarre meeting between Berthe Grunspan and Walling occurred in 1906 in an accidental encounter at the Place de l'Opéra with Walling in the company of his new wife and her sister Rose. In a later breach-of-promise suit that would go nowhere in American courts, Berthe claimed that even at that date, Walling declared his true love for her and whispered that he had only married Strunsky for her "socialistic ideas."[41] While the 1911 legal proceedings would cause Walling public embarrassment, the events as they happened (1905–1906) are perhaps more significant for the light they shed on Walling's experience of "true love" with Anna Strunsky. Just as Anna may have turned to Walling as a refuge from the emotional scars of the Jack London episode, so English may have been drawn to Anna as a savior from his own tawdry indiscretions.

Here, in any case, was a relationship unlike any he had known before. With only a touch of concealment, Walling struggled to tell his mother of the changes he had undergone:

You know I am not "easy" and never have been given in the least to illusions on this matter . . . I haven't been a fool about women at all. I've been as fond their company as [brother] Willoughby, Father, or

Uncle Will. But I've never let the romance obscure just plain friendship and common sense. That is why I have never dared to love before. Of course my relations have sometimes become quite intimate,
but I have always . . . left a good friend behind. More than one woman
has thought she loved me. I've always questioned even that and never
by word or deed given sign of any such height of feeling on my part.
The friendship may have become tender and stirring but I've never
forgot myself. I haven't done that now either but I feel I could just as
well. I've met a nature that I feel is quite larger than my own. That is
not a new experience for me with men or with older women. In a
young woman it is not to be resisted.[42]

In Anna Strunsky, Walling believed that he had found the perfect
complement to his own nature. In place of his own "temper, cold-
ness, [and] hardness," she was a "warm-hearted, high-minded character" who lacked only the practical, "earthy" virtues that would
surely come with everyday experience.[43]

The marriage formally united the ideals of socialism and free love.
The official ceremony was put off briefly while English secured a
still-grudging acceptance from his family, whose reservations included both political and religious scruples. Then, in a simple civil
ceremony in Paris before Anna's sister Rose and Karl Marx's grandson and French socialist activist Jean Longuet, the couple took their
vows on June 28, 1906. A religious service, Anna had explained to
Mrs. Walling, was out of the question. Neither she nor English belonged "to any creed" and, while English had won the hearts of her
parents, a Christian wedding "would literally kill my mother."[44] Yet,
even as she belittled the ceremony itself as "of no more importance
than getting a passport," Anna Strunsky interpreted her commitment to Walling as the ultimate manifestation of love unfettered by
convention. "Our love is as free as the soul. We hold each other and
will hold each other forever, by no force in the world except the
force of love."[45]

On an ideological plane, the harmony and mutual commitment
between a free woman and a free man celebrated by Anna Strunsky
and William English Walling served as the perfect socialist example
to set against the inevitable conflicts and compulsions of the capitalist order. In this respect, the most intimate decisions of two indi-

viduals were readily identified with the social struggle to change the world. Indeed, such political marriages were often christened with intimate, and occasionally even public, expression befitting the launching of great social experiments. A few years before Anna's marriage, for example, her friend Leonard Abbott found larger meaning in the wedding of Christian socialist George D. Herron to Carrie Rand, daughter of a famous abolitionist-cum-socialist family. At the end of the nuptial service, Abbott reported, the bride entertained her guests with a Beethoven sonata: "And as she played, the memory of a ghoulish press, of human vultures, of slave marriage, of cruel capitalism, was blotted out. We saw only the vision of the new life of socialism, when the love that made this union holy shall be the only basis of marriage, and when this love, stretching out, shall embrace the common life of the world."[46] It was in this same spirit that Rose Pastor Stokes readily referred to Walling as Anna's "comrade-lover," the same term she applied to her own husband.[47]

Among "new intellectual" circles in the prewar years, marriage thus beckoned as a private test of a larger romantic quest for individual fulfillment through democratic social relationships. Reinforced in the most intimate area of life with experiential proof for his beliefs, Walling strode with maximum confidence for the next few years as the leading socialist advocate of egalitarianism among all peoples. In addition to his better-known attack on race discrimination, his early years of marriage witnessed an endorsement of revolutionary principles of sexual equality and free sexual expression. Believing that men and women would find greater sexual fulfillment even as they were drawn into more "equal and co-ordinated" social and economic roles, Walling envisioned a day when "sports, heavy drinking, cynical talking and vile stories will no longer appeal to men, just as sentimental romance, mere prettiness, timidity and softness will no longer appeal to women."[48] Altogether, the Strunsky-Walling partnership began in unmitigated celebration of the intersecting orbits of American political and cultural radicalism.[49]

Putting ideals into practice, however, was something else again. Once married, Anna Strunsky and William English Walling returned to their work, determined to sustain a difficult and trying battle for a better world from the security of a warm and happy home. Yet, it was the home front itself that proved most vulnerable to unexpected events—so much so that the couple's public lives together would never be the same.

The forces of nature first interrupted the idylls of romance. The San Francisco earthquake and fire of 1906 occurred far from Anna's ongoing European travel and reportage with her new husband, but it wiped out all that her father had built. With house and home destroyed, Elias Strunsky, nearly sixty, was forced to return to New York City to find work with a distillery and wine importing business.[50] His new contacts, however, proved faulty; within five years, the victim of a corrupt business partner and bad real estate deals, he was deeply in debt. When he forfeited a $10,000 bond secured from English, shame gripped the Strunsky family and left Anna with a gnawing sense of dependency on the Walling fortune.[51]

Yet, if the earthquake took an extended toll on the Strunsky family, the pain that it inflicted on Anna and English was negligible compared to the loss of their first child in February 1908. Throughout Anna's pregnancy, the couple happily anticipated the joining of new family responsibilities to their ongoing political and professional work. Continuing their European travel, political journalism, and other writing, they arranged for Anna's brother Max to come to Paris for the birth and hired a British nurse to help Anna after the delivery. But the baby, whom they named Rosalind, born after a difficult day and a half of labor, died five days later under mysterious circumstances. Immediate blame focused on the nurse—with the family variously accusing her of mistreating jaundice with sugar water, shocking the baby with a hot water bottle, or, according to later family folklore, even intentionally leaving the newborn out on a hotel balcony.[52]

The event became a permanent marker in Anna Strunsky's life. As she would remind her husband in 1924, "Sixteen years ago today our First-born died. The greatest joy of my life was in five days' time succeeded by the greatest grief."[53] It must seem to English, she wrote just after the tragedy, that "very much of me died when she died." "Such dreams we had for her, such hopes!" Anna cried, adding that she had already informally christened the baby "my little International." English's mother, Rosalind (for whom the dead child had been named), had no easy answer for her daughter-in-law's distress. "Nature is very cruel to women," she told her son.[54]

As if this first distress were not enough, Anna suffered a miscarriage the following year. It was as if her own life had become a vanquished cause. "A loss and a defeat and tragedy," she called it, "another wound that can never be healed." While Anna's brother Hyman urged her to get on with her life—to think of little Rosalind "as something that you got, not something that you lost"—she could never consider the event with equanimity. Only Anna's female friends, it seemed, sensed the despair into which she had plunged. A second miscarriage, several years later, thus elicited the sympathy of her friend Mary E. Haskell: "You are living now without your second [sic] child but with this thing of having lost it . . . you have the key to me and other women."[55]

These losses, to be sure, did not alter Anna's basic political or philosophical beliefs, but they did subtly affect her behavior. One interpretation of the accused nurse's malign motives, for example, centered on Anna's outspoken feminism. The nurse, by this account, mistakenly assuming that Anna (who refused to wear a ring and kept her own name) was not the father's wife but a "harlot," had killed the child to spare the father certain shame.[56] Whether the story was true or not, it is clear that an important change came over the young bohemian feminist. "I shall never grieve you again," she promised her father-in-law two weeks after the death, "by using my maiden-name, for I want my daughter's name for whatever I write and do."[57] Symbolically, she thus renounced her autonomy. Formerly a determined "Lucy Stoner," Anna gave up her maiden name after Rosalind's death and proudly became Mrs. William English Walling. Moreover, it seems clear that the Wallings sought to bury their grief in a growing family. Bearing four children (Rosamund, Anna, Georgia, and Hayden) as well as suffering two miscarriages between 1909 and 1918, Anna Strunsky concentrated her strength on her own household.[58]

Anna's commitment to her children was uncompromising. "All the children and I have lived in the closest union," she would write her husband during one of his frequent leaves on political, journalistic, or family business, "as we always do in your absence . . . [and] I have eaten all their meals with them, slept with them on the

Anna Strunsky Walling with her daughter Georgia in New York City, January 1915. (Rose Pastor Stokes Papers, Manuscripts and Archives, Yale University Library)

porch, sung to them, told them stories and asked their advice on all kinds of subjects."[59] Her grown children recognized a dramatic split between their mother's professed political ideals (particularly as they related to women's emancipation) and her assumption of the role of "an old-fashioned Victorian wife and mother." "Until I was eleven years old," recalls Anna Walling Hamburger, "[my mother] never spent a night away from home." "We were raised being told one thing [i.e., 'full equality with men'] and seeing another thing." Emma Goldman, for one, was clearly dismayed at the loss of a favorite comrade-in-arms. "Forget your babies!" she chided Anna. "What a strange girl you are to have so many kiddies."[60]

Almost inevitably, Anna Strunsky's new responsibilities implied a pulling away not only from the public arena but also from the literary career she had long anticipated. Anna continued to write (as well as to speak at occasional political forums), but she experienced frustration and even periodic depression at never being able to finish a manuscript. As she once noted in good, but all too telling, humor to her husband, "Job's patience is a negligible thing besides which mine has been throughout the years of baby-mothering, for every day I have miscarried what to my brooding heart seemed an undying poem or essay! The blessed ones are causing another abortion—that of this letter—for they are clamoring at the door!"[61] Her daughters likewise remember her running around the house with notepad in hand, always writing and re-writing: "I'm scribbling," she would say.[62] Occasionally, Anna would self-consciously address her own lack of literary productivity. "At last I am organized," she exulted in one letter to her husband. In another, she vowed, "I am going to systematize my days and keep some hours sacred to myself (this is my personal version of next year in Jerusalem, my social version is next year in the cooperative commonwealth)."[63]

That Anna's struggles with such competing commitments were common to an entire circle of educated women is evident from her correspondence. Among "the million pent up things" her friend Louise Howe wished to confide to Anna Strunsky, for example, was an intermittent sense of feeling "stifled" and "suffocated": "You know exactly what I mean I am sure. Certain responsibilities of course one has and I, of all people, am in some ways over conscientious about responsibility to my family, but when there are so many vital things to do, and when one also sees certain talents and capabilities atrophying while one does other things it is rather maddening."[64]

Yet if Louise Howe suffered for staying home, another friend, Winifred Heath, agonized equally over the opposite arrangement. Compelled to "sell [her] whole day" in an office job to provide for her child, Heath wrote Anna, "I cannot tell you how I dread the daily separation from my one little link to life . . . It's a thing I had never taken into calculation in thinking of having a baby. So does life bring its totally unforeseen pains along with its deepest joys."[65] Even the incomparably freewheeling Emma Goldman did not escape the inner turmoil besetting female life choices. At the same time that she was berating Anna Strunsky for giving up politics for children, she expressed her own regret of "never . . . [getting] thoroughly acquainted with those one really cares for . . . My life is madness personified."[66]

Willingly taking on the management of a large house and family, Anna Strunsky accepted a life much more insulated and protected from the outside world than the one she had embraced as a young woman. In other respects, however—particularly in the exuberance, idealism, and sense of larger meanings in which she folded personal events alongside more public issues—she never let go of the democratic vision of her radical youth. Even with an infant child, for example, she joined her husband in the early meetings of the NAACP. Though no longer a public celebrity, she continued at least occasionally to speak out on public issues, and when she did, she seemed to select themes—or bring to them a twist—from her special vantage point. In 1914, for example, she registered her effusion for the Wobblies by calling them "the eugenic child . . . of all that is best and most robust and most developed . . . in all the revolutionary thinking that has gone before us today."[67] Endorsing divorce for women in 1917 while clinging to her romantic ideals, she told wives "to leave, if love goes."[68] And while offering a sympathetic account of the German practice of "twilight sleep" (the application of drugs in pregnancy) she publicly recalled her own experience of childbirth: "a memory of torture which my companion only knows by name—the torture of the heavy and the sorrowful hours of travail when the heart breaks with a kind of despair—when life calls with a thousand voices as never before, yet the doors of death stand wide open to receive. Only the prisoner who walks to execution can feel such inevitableness of misery."[69]

Overall, at least through the 1920s, Anna seemed content with her life, savoring the contrast between the balance of public and private commitments she had struck with what she considered the "mechanical and theoretical" feminism of family acquaintance and houseguest Charlotte Perkins Gilman.[70] Symbolic of both her adult choices and her continuing commitments was the seventieth birthday party dinner she organized for Harriet Stanton Blatch at the Women's City Club, an event that included among its honored guests Dr. and Mrs. W. E. B. Du Bois.[71] Combining preoccupation with family and political radicalism, she remained an "extraordinarily optimistic" soul.[72] A male friend and fellow militant pacifist, Jessie Wallace Hughan, still addressed her in the early 1940s as "Comrade Anna": "I like to use the old word 'Comrade', and I am glad that you do. We *are* comrades, are we not, and one of the things that has made us so for many years is that we both love our families as well as the Cause."[73]

Something of the inveterate optimism as well as the half-buried hopes of Anna's prewar sensibility is evident in her published novel of 1915, *Violette of Pere Lachaise.* Composed in the years following her child's death, the narrative—more a chain of associations about life, love, and death than a coherent story—touches the emotional chords of the author's psyche.[74] The adolescent Violette lives with her grandfather, a florist who makes funeral bouquets, on the edge of the famous Parisian cemetery. There, amidst the memories of the dead (including her immediate family, the circumstances of whose loss are never explained), the young girl meditates variously on the mysteries of nature, the innocence of children, the pain of unrequited first love, and the mission of Socialism: "Before her were unrolled movements, organizations, concepts like The People and Humanity, forces modern and all-embracing."[75] By a determined act of will, the lovely Violette draws strength even from her melancholic surroundings and vaguely "dares to be happy."

> She felt the subterranean sea which tossed beneath life and she wanted to go out into the world proclaiming, "Let us free youth! Let us free age." Her feeling was that life could be lived so much more fully—there was so much more to be had, to be felt, to be explored. She felt the loneliness of the eternal feminine.[76]

Perhaps not surprisingly, the greatest challenge for Violette arises in the tension between her "feminine" instinct towards total identification with her lover and her insistence on a sphere of independence defined by political acts and social responsibilities. Having once been hurt in love, the heroine determines that she will not disappear into her pain but will bounce back as "an adventurer toward the new and untried," ever the modern woman. Violette, in short, resolves to be a part of the larger struggles of her times, even as she anticipates an intimate family life.

> Her years would be shaped by the forces with which she was already allied, her whole life would take their stamp. Already she foresaw acts that carried her far, deeds that would be expressive of the struggle of the classes in which she would take a direct part. Dimly she foresaw that she would be called upon to play her part in this greatest of all dramas. She wished it to be so. But it would not mean abdication of her own personal existence; it must augment everything that had ever begun in her; it must always mean the full flowering of her whole personality. Out of it would be created her love and her motherhood.[77]

Barely veiled by its exotic setting and ethereal ruminations, the text reflects the author's struggle to reach beyond her own early losses and recapture the dreams of youth within a mature and loving marriage. "I have always believed," Anna confided to English in 1913, "in a long and passionate output of effort, and then, in a miraculous reward, an extraordinary fulfillment of everything the heart promises."[78] The intensity of Anna's quest for fulfillment was well known, and even the subject of a sly wink, among her Greenwich Village coterie. Norman Hapgood recalled the "inimitable imitation" of Anna offered by a mutual acquaintance, which focused on her "intense seriousness, unrelieved by any sense of humor. Her deep weeping voice, her lachrymose tones in pronouncing the name of 'English,' her husband, the profound emotional way in which she pronounced the word 'revolution' or 'socialism' (indeed, probably nobody in the world ever said 'socialism' with so much intensity, overflowing like a huge wave the infinite beach of life)."[79]

Yet the delicate balance that Anna Strunsky projected for her female protagonist in the novel proved more elusive in her own life. In the case of the Walling household, the twin pillars of Anna's modernized romantic ideal—public political commitments on the one hand and blissful private feelings on the other—collapsed with

equally destructive force. Indeed, in her case there seems an un-
canny correspondence between the dual public calamities of the
early century—a world war and later worldwide depression—and
the pressures brought to bear on two private lives.

Well before the Great War, certain tensions had already become
established within the relationship, as suggested by the impatience
and frustration that Walling often expressed. For English, these
were years of considerable influence and acclaim, at least on the
American left (see Chapter 4). But the demands of a political career
were also wearing. The predictable contentiousness of the public,
political sphere perhaps only augmented his need for peace and
quiet at home. Then, too, there was stress on the financial front.
Even a family inheritance did not easily cover a three-servant
household and frequent travel and hotel bills. As the intellectual of
his family, English had constantly to prove to his parents and patronizing brother that he in fact could manage his own affairs.
Finally, there were demands from aging parents. With his annual
pilgrimage to his parents in Florida coinciding with publication
deadlines for *The Masses* and *New Review* in 1914, Walling found it
hard to meet his obligations. His father, English wrote Anna, "demands a total of about six hours of my time everyday and perhaps
has that right as I'm supposed to be visiting him."[80]

Communication between Anna and English in the prewar years
generally remained affectionate and mutually supportive of two
busy, if differently focused, lives. Even then, however, there was a
contrast of sensibilities between the spontaneous and effusive wife
and the rational, often determinedly practical-minded husband. An
exuberant Anna thus openly "exulted" in her love, writing a traveling husband, "my English, I shall sleep by your side tonight" and
sending "a thousand kisses from your Girl the Wild Heart." English,
for his part, offered no such effusions and must have communicated
a preference for less sentimental prose. As early as 1911 or 1912,
Anna apologized for her gushy, unoriginal expressions and, recog-
nizing that English would prefer more discussion of "international
policies," promised as a good "radical and revolutionary" to try to
mend her ways.[81]

There is a hint in such communication of a larger issue that often
beset relationships between men and women intellectuals of the pe-

riod, a tension only exacerbated by ethnic differences. The very touch of the exotic that drew Protestant middle-class men to radical Jewish women also likely contained a division of emotional labor. As Mary Dearborn notes of the passionate but troubled relationship between philosopher John Dewey and immigrant writer Anzia Yezierska:

> The ethnic woman suffers considerably from the consequences of being associated with the erotic. Just as surely as emotionality becomes associated with sexuality—passion immediately assumed to be physical passion—so too do warmth and emotionality become related to excess. To be emotional is to run the risk of being considered overemotional, as Yezierska knew only too well. Time and again, her Deweyean heroes accuse their immigrant lovers of excessive emotion.[82]

With Dewey as with Walling, radical men appear at once attracted by and afraid of a woman-centered freedom of emotional expression. In Walling's case, it appears, he sought in marriage to contain the very exuberance that had attracted him in the first place, as the ferment of work and the demands of family life dulled his early sexual infatuation with his wife.

These early marital strains first developed into a full-fledged crisis by early 1917. The Great War, which bitterly split American socialist ranks, quickly became a civil war within the Walling household, where it only accentuated already swelling private hurts. As left-wing socialists, both Walling and Strunsky had initially condemned the European hostilities as a tragic distraction from class solidarities, a national-imperial conflict manipulated by the workers' class enemies. With her ties to radical peace activists—including such luminaries as Jane Addams, Elizabeth Gurley Flynn, Rose Pastor Stokes, and Emma Goldman—Anna Strunsky joined pacifist protest meetings (at least to the extent that pregnancy allowed her, with her fourth child, William Hayden English, born in December 1916) and publicly criticized President Wilson's mobilization plans in the fall of 1916. Unfortunately for the marriage, English was moving in the opposite direction. Thoroughly convinced of the necessity of rolling back German expansionism, Walling, along with other prowar socialists, sought new political allies. Already in 1916, for example, this formerly vituperative critic of the AFL hierarchy had reactivated his ties to Samuel Gompers, and his consultancy to the labor federation on international matters promised a financial reward to an increasingly strapped household.[83] While fretting privately over President Wilson's overly cautious response to the sinking of the *Lusitania*, by the spring of 1917 Walling was working feverishly for the President's efforts to keep Russia in the war.[84]

As Anna Walling Hamburger, then six years old, remembers it, the first "great difficulty" with her parents "was the First World War."[85] "When my father lost his temper, he raised his voice, and [there was] a lot of raised voice" at that time. A hint of the household tension is suggested in the correspondence of the period. A public antiwar statement with which Anna was associated in early 1917 stung English to write that "I think your proposal to attack in the back those who are giving up their lives for democracy, peace and anti-militarism is criminal to the last degree . . . Neither I nor mankind, nor the genuine idealists and revolutionaries of the world will forget or forgive what your kind has said and done in this great hour. If I fight it will be against the traitors to internationalism—I trust you will not be among them."[86] Walling had a word for antiwar socialists like his wife—"Quakers" he called them with contempt. At least once, Walling's temper went beyond words. In January 1917, while his wife was nursing their infant son, he became so agitated that he threw a metal cracker box at her feet. The resulting bruise required two days to heal.[87]

But it was clearly not the physical pain that most worried Anna. Keeping her head down during her husband's abusive outburst (and holding her silence at a subsequent doctor's visit), she reported that she experienced an inner "sinking sensation." The event shook her very image of her marriage. Remarkably, she continued for weeks to struggle with her husband as well as her own conscience on the subject of the war. She was no more a "Quaker" for opposing the war, she answered Walling, than he was a "militarist" for supporting it. Initially, she defended her position not in pacifist but in the revolutionary socialist terms to which they had together dedicated their lives.

> A revolutionist believes in the People and opposes the established order. My faith is in the People and is deep and integral with my whole

being. I am not a Quaker because I not only give my consent to the rioters in the streets of Petrograd . . . but had I not you and our children I would not have hesitated to join them . . . and fall by their side for a regenerated Russia. I, the most passionate lover of life ever born, may go out to meet death for my cause . . . but I will make sure that it is my cause and not the cause of my enemy.

Anna sought desperately to hang on at once to her principles and to her love for Walling. She pleaded with him to show her some mutual respect. "Some day you will understand me," she wrote, "as well as I understand you and then we will laugh together at our past sufferings. That is my day and night dream."[88] Underlying her sweet reason was an awful fear of rejection. Only a week before delivering another child, Anna announced that she had thrown away the kitchen cream and was embarking on a diet: "You must find me as I was when I came to you and to the Revolution in St. Petersburg, when I was only the potential mother of four daughters."[89]

Ultimately, the pressures at home, together with the increasingly complex news from the battlefront, combined to overcome Anna Strunsky's antiwar defenses. In March 1917, likely both physically and emotionally exhausted, she explicitly "capitulated" to her husband's position on the war and more generally withdrew from public political commitments of all kinds. Politically, she could see no other protection for her beloved Menshevik revolutionaries than the military defeat of the encroaching German armies. On the one hand such a position "freed" her from devoutly held antiwar principles. But on the other hand, both as pacifist and as mother, she told Walling, "it tortures me."

I have been weak and sick all day. To consent to war! I do finally "vote the money and the men," but I do not expect to survive it. In a sense I have already failed to survive it . . . Ever since Rosalind English was born I have seen everybody as a little baby shivering on a pillow or at a mother's breast; I have had a mother's tenderness towards the world of men and women; I could always see everybody as they were born to be, not as they were. I feel as if this, my motherhood, were slain this morning when . . . I vicariously flew to arms. I cannot mother when I have condemned to die, and those German troops on the Russian frontier must fall if the Revolution [is to survive].[90]

Had the war been the root cause of the Walling-Strunsky tensions, the closing of family ranks on the issue might have held out hope of a revival of the romantic dreams in which this partnership was conceived. Certainly Anna's "capitulation" (perhaps consciously) staved off the bitter rupture that afflicted their close friends Graham and Rose Pastor Stokes. Breaking with her husband and returning to the antiwar offensive following the Bolshevik Revolution, Rose Pastor Stokes earned a ten-year prison sentence on a felony conviction under the Espionage Act.[91] Although the charges were ultimately dropped on appeal, Rose's independence was never forgiven by Graham Pastor Stokes or his conservative family, and a permanent emotional scar led to bitter divorce. By contrast, Anna Strunsky's political about-face staved off any equivalent domestic explosion, although it did little to relieve the long-term stress on her marriage.[92]

The war was a watershed both in Walling's political career and in his evaluation of the problem of the "intellectuals." The left-wing activist turned from his earlier, revolutionary visions to what he now avowed as a democratic pragmatism, seeking new allies in high places even as he attacked his former comrades in the Socialist Party as dangerous and unpatriotic. Within this political metamorphosis, the intellectual enemy endured, if somewhat transposed in identity; no longer the bureaucratic state reformer blocking direct rule by the militant proletariat, the intellectual was now that very independent radical who substituted his own, power-hungry agenda for the more practical, down-to-earth needs of industrial workers. According to this "public" story of Walling's development, he takes his place as one more (if particularly dramatic) example of the disillusioning impact of the Great War on the optimism of the Progressive reform sensibility.

Yet perhaps there was more to the story. The "private" story—the history of the Strunsky-Walling marriage—suggests that politics was only the most visible of the influences that brought about the "taming" of William English Walling. From this perspective, public events, such as the war and the actions of the Socialist Party, seem rather to have collaborated with more intimate conflicts of family, household economy, and even the psychology of manhood in effecting a significant change in Walling's thought and action.

For example, apart from the tumultuous state of the world, what most preoccupied Walling in October and November of 1916 was his dream of owning a house and the delicate family negotiations that such a project entailed. The fact was that the comfortable life on which he and his wife both depended stretched his resources (drawn largely from his own family inheritance) to the limit. Purchasing a home, at least of the sort that fit their vision of beauty and comfort, involved additional revenues, and the inevitable complication of a loan from his parents. The Brookside Park house in Greenwich, Connecticut, that Anna and English had picked out was "a dream of comfort and beauty and charm." Anna additionally extolled it as being "built by Miss Chapman, one of the few famous women architects, and I am enough of a feminist to be pleased that a woman could have achieved this perfect house."[93] Yet, up to the moment that the parties closed the deal, uncertainty remained about the financial commitments from the Walling family. While English's mother seemed anxious from the beginning to see the couple established "where no disagreeable landlord could worry you," his father was pointedly less eager to loosen the family purse strings.[94]

Dr. Walling's relationship with his rebel son had long been strained by a disapproving condescension. Even when defending English in the Chicago newspapers amidst the Grunspan breach-of-promise case of 1911, for example, the father had revealed the tensions attached to the filial bond. It was simply "not in [English's] nature," the father had argued, to have "played fast and loose with a girl." His son, insisted the father, was "the last man in the world to become involved in such a matter." "He has the scholar's temperament and most of his life has been passed among books and the study of political problems."[95] While supporting English in a moment of crisis, Dr. Walling all but expressed doubt about his son's fitness to make his way independently in a tough world. The father—and after him, brother Willoughby—insisted on managing English's family finances down to the purchase of a used car.[96] The debility of old age, failing health, and real or imagined slights of attention only made father-son relations more difficult. Now, when it came to buying a house, the father took no chances. "If we are to negotiate for the purchase of this place," Dr. Walling informed his son in October 1916, "I must carry on all the negotiations without any aid from you except when I ask for it . . . Everybody will know that this father is buying his son a home and *there can be no pride involved.*"[97] At the end of the month, English received the gift of the house from his father. Yet, rather than delight in the moment, he was obliged to continue to eat humble pie: "I shall certainly do precisely as you say and see no reason why you should suppose I might do otherwise. You make a terrible and sad mistake when you say I try to dispose of you in a hurry. I write always with utmost care and with extreme anxiety to please you."[98] Within weeks of the closing on the house, Dr. Willoughby Walling collapsed and died.[99] The resolution of a complicated emotional relationship was now entirely in the son's hands.

It is impossible to judge just how prominently the need to "prove" himself to his father (or his father's memory) played in the subsequent behavior of William English Walling. There are abundant hints, however, that in the face of multiple pressures, Walling effectively responded by seeking to demonstrate his realism and toughness both in the public and private spheres. This may help to explain Walling's insistent attacks on "intellectuals" (as detailed in the previous chapter). The term itself seems to have been used in Walling's parents' household as a term of mild derision for one who was overly critical or excessively analytical.[100] And English's daughter, Anna Walling Hamburger, likewise remembers that her father "disliked the word 'intellectual' as a 'pretentious' word, a word that no one would use about themselves."[101] It is not too far-fetched, therefore, to suggest an underlying tension in Walling's career between the "pampered" radical scholar and the would-be man of will and action.

In the private sphere as well, Walling's need to define himself as a sensible and practical-minded man increasingly collided with the basic personality traits of the woman whom he had married. He had no patience, for example, with Anna's mystical-poetic nature: "I hear you are visiting the Gurdjieff thing again," he wrote in late 1916. "You wrote me that you had had your last to do with that idiocy."[102] This attitude quickly carried over to basic household management, where he worried that his wife did not command sufficient respect from the servants and generally lacked "system."[103] He insisted on being kept informed of all details concerning "anything that has gone wrong as to the house, servants, or school." In the end, such an administrative calculus likely left little room for the nourishing of the romantic compact that had once bound two young radical intellectuals to each other.

The postwar signs of estrangement emerged less in dramatic episodes than in the minutia of daily domestic life. As early as 1921, Anna referred obliquely in private correspondence to her mother-in-law of "dark and troubled hours which must come even to those as happily married as English and I." Years later, she would more openly refer to her husband's "frightful, self-destroying tantrums . . . always for an audience . . . How bad for the children, destructive for me and worse for himself." His ire apparently arose over the most petty and arbitrary of parental issues. "Since when is cheese cake a poison to a child? And why is R[osamund] *stealing* cake when she helps herself to cake in our house? What nonsense!"[104]

English's mood swings, however, were most often triggered by money worries. The purchase of a house apparently only left Walling in closer, continuing dependence on family resources, and repeated worry about getting "caught in a corner again."[105] It was a situation he deeply resented. Writing from London in 1922, for example, he first exploded at his brother Willoughby for not responding to repeated cables for funds. "Either he is interpreting my messages against me—e.g. I can't mean I want *more* money—or he thinks I *ought* not to want more . . . It's hell! And it's my money."[106] But when Anna responded with an immediate money order, English remained upset. "If I'd wanted it I would have asked you for it."[107] Disrespected by his parents in money management, English Walling seemed determined to be not only the king but the king's accountant in his own castle. Anna Strunsky, to be sure, was no penny-pincher. Her daughter remembers that she always ordered groceries over the phone and joked that "everyone should have three servants." Yet English's attempts to gain control over household expenditure took extreme form. From London, for example, he scolded Anna for buying his mother the wrong kind of purse ("Can you return it? I hate to waste money on useless gifts"),[108] selected the plants for the sun parlor, and assigned exact dollar amounts for Christmas gifts for the children.[109] As Anna later remembered, "The emphasis on money [was] a neurosis—so much talk of it! We had very little money, the Strunskys. There was never a tenth talk of it in our home."[110]

Then there was the fact of Walling's increasing absences. In 1923 alone, Walling was away on extended trips to New York, Chicago, Toronto, Havana, St. Augustine, and Oxford, England.[111] Nor, it became clear, was the separation particularly regretted on his part. On one occasion, for example, Walling urged his wife to stay longer on an extended trip to Paris with the children. "We must both keep ourselves free to make the most of those five or six months . . ."[112] By 1926, even Rosalind Walling was admonishing her son for neglecting his family.[113] Aside from trips connected to specific work assignments, English was then spending extended time at a New York City apartment. It is likely that he also commenced what would become a series of extramarital affairs in this period. If Anna knew of such relationships, however, she suffered the hurt of what she would later call his "wandering eye" in silence.[114]

The tremors affecting the Strunsky-Walling marriage characteristically kept pace with world events. If World War I marked the first crisis in the relationship, then 1929 equally signaled a cataclysmic crash and 1932 the final break and "great depression." It was no longer politics that divided the couple, moreover, but the combination of financial pressures and Walling's rediscovery of romance—with a new woman. Throughout the twenties, Walling had been beset by worsening financial circumstances. His income could simply not sustain the upkeep of a house in Connecticut, a cottage in Rhode Island, and a New York City apartment, in addition to extensive travel, but the family clearly found it difficult to curtail its refined expectations and elegant lifestyle. Thus, in the same period in which Walling was seeking multiple loans, he briefly joined the Nantucket Yacht Club and seriously debated whether to send two children to private school in Geneva, Switzerland.[115] The situation only exacerbated English's basic anxieties regarding autonomy and self-respect. He complained in particular of involuntary subordination to his brother. Willoughby, he wrote his mother in 1929, was taking a "wholly negative view of my affairs, . . . [treating me] financially as a minor or defective" on the basis of his own business success. "I am subject to all advice," Walling blustered, "but to no coercion."[116]

But it was on another front that Walling finally exercised his will and struck out against years of unhappiness. At the end of the summer of 1929—the first that the couple had ever spent entirely apart from each other—English announced his love for an interior decorator identified in the record only as "Mrs. Wertheim," with whom he apparently intended to cohabit in New York.[117] Walling no doubt hoped for a divorce, but Anna was adamantly opposed. The resulting impasse set off three years of most bitter recrimination between husband and wife.

For Anna Strunsky, the threat to her marriage undermined everything to which she had dedicated her life since 1905. She felt suddenly paralyzed, living "in terror and all the time like a drowning person grasping at a straw":

> I do not know from hour to hour what will happen. I cling to my role of passive waiting. I go about the business of life—ordering meals, seeing people, playing practice tennis under English's supervision, sunbathing, swimming, driving, all with English—and our nights together, as always. But this terrible thing that he has done to our lives, to my faith in his love!

She sought to weather the storm, stretching to understand her husband's behavior within the therapeutic framework of the midlife crisis. "He is at the dangerous age for men," she explained to her mother-in-law, "when he is trying to recapture his youth. He is looking for the full and free life, and he thinks a Mrs. Wertheim can give it to him!"[118] She took hope from her mother-in-law's view that the couple's tensions had an "economic cause" and that her son was ultimately a "one-woman man" who would never forsake his family. Anna seemed to acquiesce in her mother-in-law's suggested waiting game, tolerating her husband's weakness on condition that "all objectionable females should be kept at a distance [from the house] for all reasons—you have daughters to consider, as well as yourself."[119]

With English, Anna vacillated between a delicate negotiating posture and desperate outbursts of hurt and anger. She openly recognized a basic contradiction within herself between "principle" and "instinct," between the "modern woman" and the "primitive woman in me." "I speak of freedom who am bound to you more than any human being was ever bound to another!"[120] To her husband she now extended a refined and limited version of the "free love" doctrine they had both once embraced. "I cannot live without you—much less now than ever. But this lays no obligation on you. You are free."[121] Have your flings, she seemed to say, only don't give up on the marriage: "Enlarge your life, meet and know more and more and more—that which is mine will remain mine!"[122] In sober retrospection, Anna asked herself "how I, an intelligent modern woman" could have ended up at once so dependent upon and distant from her husband?

> Perhaps much of the fault lies in the fact that I am a woman and you a man—not a biological difference, of course, but one inbred by custom and environment and education. I had not dared uproot the children, fling them into a disruptive New York environment, do many things which had I been a man I would not have hesitated to do—and they came first in my life—their least need more important than all my undertakings—I left myself last until there was nothing left.[123]

Now, if they could just free themselves from debt, take pride in their "almost grown" children, she and English might yet enjoy a "new life." Lying alone under the "wild Nantucket winds," Anna clung to "long, long thoughts of youth . . . the great clarities, the eternal affirmations." "It was not little we expected when we first loved, but the best that life had to offer."[124]

Alas, it was not to be. When Walling rejected her entreaties and insisted on his right to "live my own life," Anna gave full vent to the accumulated frustrations of their years together. She recalled "night after night I dreamt over again in my sleep the scenes of the day—always the same nightmare—you with face distorted with anger, hands pointing at me, attacking reviling me for heaven knows what now, an opinion expressed, now, some trifle neglected." At worst, she accused English of allowing "no liberty of conscience . . . no liberty of action, of thought. All your liberality in private life a hollow sham. Every difference of opinion magnified and treated as high treason."[125]

The early years of the separation were undoubtedly the worst years of Anna's life. Living in a Madison Avenue hotel apartment with her ailing mother and two youngest children, she contended, mostly alone, with the side-effects of a broken family. She worried, for example, that their eldest daughter had fallen in among the "aimless and helpless young people of Greenwich Village and Provincetown."[126] An auto accident involving both her elder daughters in 1930 only increased Anna's parental anxieties.[127] Then, in 1932, daughter Anna, age twenty-one, announced that she was pregnant and planning to marry her forty-two-year-old suitor, a writer with uncertain prospects.[128] It was in this same year that English secured a Mexican divorce, a decree of legalized independence that Anna Strunsky never recognized as legitimate. Altogether, the extended travail of these years had clearly damaged a once-confident spirit. "I have failed miserably where I have most wanted to succeed, and failed in my work too, in everything a stupid, wasted life," Anna wrote English. "I am filled with overwhelming nausea."[129] At the end of 1932, Anna spoke of this "catastrophe that has befallen all of us through no fault of any of us."[130]

Between 1932 and Walling's death during his secret mission to Europe in 1936, Anna's contacts with the man she still recognized as her husband were infrequent and comparatively subdued. Ironically, just before the ill-fated trip, concern over their son Hayden's emotional problems appeared to reconnect their basic sympathies as had nothing else in years. Still, word of Walling's death touched Anna Strunsky to the core. Her writing in the period suggests an Ophelia-like delusion that her lover had returned:

> English darling, beloved, my love, my joy, my Only One, my husband English—English—English. Night is falling and I am alone. Come!
>
> You must sing: I love her! This is Anna, this is she. I met [her] in St. Petersburg . . . and who is the mother of the baby in Pere Lachaise. This she whom I believed good, talented, devoted to the common cause—beautiful, too, in her way, witty, gay, happier than any lady in the world because I love her![131]

Anna Strunsky survived William English Walling by almost three full decades. Yet, while he never fully left her thoughts, he was not the last love of her life. That distinction was won by her old friend, writer-anarchist Leonard Abbott. After the pain of what Anna called the "inferno of the last quarter of a century in Greenwich," her relationship with Abbott was gentle and soothing. As early as 1933, they took solace in each other, and they remained affectionate friends (although never physical lovers) for the next twenty years.[132] "Let's live a little . . . our own pattern, our own freedom," counseled Anna. "Everything ends. We survive much. Let us now survive on love . . . Hell, these cold words—so halting, finite, when what I want is to touch with my fingers the visible dearness of your face."[133] Abbott, she wrote, "led me back into the land of youth."[134] Until Abbott's death in 1953, the two shared what he called the unpredictable pattern of life's "beautiful surprises as well as its terrible miseries." As Anna continued to mix her preoccupation with her children with political interests and never-quite-complete manuscripts, Leonard Abbott commented sagely, "Our problem—your problem, my problem, everyone's problem!—are in a sense the same. We struggle for adequate expression (in our sense in our writing), for clarity, for effectiveness, for adjustment to our medium and to life."[135]

Anna's last years in many respects recalled the spirit of her more youthful days. As she prepared Walling's papers for archival preservation in 1962 (two years before her death at age eighty-four), she insisted for the record that "I never had a troubled life. There were sorrows, catastrophes, like the SF earthquake, [and a] hurricane, but I had always a happy life."[136] It was true enough that through her own effort she had maintained a remarkably steady, upbeat attitude towards the future. In the early 1960s, for example, nearly blind and unable to walk, Anna Strunsky asked her daughter Rosamund to provide a chair so that she could show support for a civil rights demonstration. This woman, who had assisted in the birth of the NAACP, was also likely the last of her circle to receive a Christmas card, many decades later, from the Rev. Jesse Jackson.[137] When, in 1962, the national secretary of the Socialist Party mistakenly issued condolences two years prematurely to Anna's family on the loss of "a life-long, dedicated socialist," it was in character for her to respond with appreciation and good humor. "I'll remain true as long as I live," wrote Anna. "You'll use [the tribute] again, but please don't hurry me!"[138]

Anna Strunsky Walling at the Women's Faculty Club, Bancroft Library benefit luncheon, New York City, February 4, 1961. Photo by George S. Hammond. (Anna Strunsky Walling Papers, Manuscripts and Archives, Yale University Library)

Anna Strunsky had survived more than three-quarters of a century with her democratic optimism and romantic imagination still largely intact. In her case, such continuity was less a product of a sheltered upper-class intellectual life than a resolute, if naive, act of will. Both her own and others' revolutions had threatened more than once to leave her own life in a state of anarchy. Yet from each shaking, she had always soldiered on with a smile. Late in life, she even renewed her friendship with her early suitor, Cameron King. In 1945 King, long since married and with a daughter serving in the WACs in the South Pacific, heartily "agreed" with Anna "that the human race is not hopeless."

> The great masses are disposed to be friendly and much of their meannesses and vices is just the result of the terrific pressures to survive. War, terrible and horrible as it is, discloses nevertheless a tremendous reservoir of devotion to ideals, a spirit of self-sacrifice and even in the most brutal situations kindliness and pity on the part of the "common man."[139]

IN A RECENT assessment of "independent intellectuals" in early-twentieth-century America, historian Steven Biel shrewdly takes note of the ways in which gendered identity helped to shape what was written and by whom. Despite their keen involvement in a myriad of associated reform activities, women were generally missing from the stable of published social critics. Issues of time and family responsibility were important impediments, Biel suggests, as was the lack of connections to literary magazines and socialist clubs nurtured at male-only Ivy League colleges. Moreover, even ostensibly feminist males did little to recruit female intellectuals. Concerned themselves to break out of a "feminine" literary culture in order to affect the "masculine" world of power and business, male writers, including political radicals, often displayed "a profound ambivalence about women's fight for equality."[140]

While the Walling-Strunsky case generally corroborates Biel's findings, it contains an extra historical dimension to consider. Like many talented women of her generation, Anna Strunsky produced neither the polished literary work nor the public record of accomplishment of which she perhaps was capable. Since she did not lack educational credentials or extended contacts with both socialist and literary outlets, Anna's failure to leave a more influential intellectual legacy is likely attributable to her domestic responsibilities. Still, it was in part Anna's own priorities that propelled her in another direction. Her political radicalism encompassed a romantic personal element; even as she endorsed revolution in the larger world, she sought the intimacy, fulfillment, and stability of marriage and family life at home. It was a valiant quest, one that perhaps echoes even more loudly in a day more explicitly anxious about the tradeoffs between public and private satisfactions. If little had turned out quite as she had planned, Anna Strunsky accepted the limits on her intellectual role as the price to be paid for active personal investment elsewhere. "I lost my life under a niggle of things," she reportedly explained without rancor.[141]

The private side of the intellectuals' world requires even more pointed (because comparatively neglected) emphasis in the case of the women's male partners. William English Walling presents a particularly intriguing and subtle example. Arguably one of the most open-minded men of his generation, he was committed in principle to the full participation of women on equal footing with men in public life. In private, as well, his radical sensibilities bent toward the demolition of the emotional walls between the sexes as well as the breaching of all other forms of social discrimination. Yet he carried the legacy of the late Victorian period as well. His reactions to the Great War, the black skin of his civil rights allies, his father's insults, the crisis of family income, and his wife's contrary opinions were all of a piece. When push came to shove, the radical idealist became the white male egoist, determined to protect his personal dignity, autonomy, and comfort with the earthy compromises (as opposed to intellectual abstractions) available to the self-styled pragmatist. If, in politics, youthful dreams of socialist democracy gave way to a more attainable liberal nationalism, so in matters of the heart radical romantic love yielded to the conventional expectations of gender roles associated with marriage. Resentful of those like his wife who did not so easily bend with the wind, Walling harbored fantasies that he could never realize of personal fulfillment beyond the compromises of everyday domestic life.[142]

For William English Walling as for Anna Strunsky, both public and private history was intimately interwoven in a historical text of thought and action. Here were two radical democrats determined to live their lives in keeping with their highest aspirations. How they struggled with dual commitments to political and personal revolution is at once the heritage of those years and a continuing challenge to those who would assume similar ambitions.

6 A Voice for the People

A. Philip Randolph and the Cult of Leadership

It is apparent that the Negro leaders, the hirelings of the Republican and Democratic bosses who are in turn the agents of anti-labor forces, are the worst enemies of the race.

—Chandler Owen and A. Philip Randolph,
The Messenger, July 1918

JUST THIRTY years old in 1919, Asa Philip Randolph was prepared to take on the world. Only eight years before, he had moved to Harlem, determined to escape the religious conservatism of his Florida hometown and anxious to develop his interests in drama and politics. In the course of doing odd jobs and taking social science and philosophy courses part-time at the City College of New York, Randolph had discovered Marxism and insinuated himself into the radical bohemian subculture of Harlem street corners. Marriage in 1914 to Lucille Campbell Greene, a financially secure businesswoman six years his senior, had permanently freed Randolph from menial work as a porter or waiter and allowed him to concentrate on political journalism and agitation. A second fortuitous alliance joined the austere and invariably proper Randolph to the more irreverent iconoclasm of Columbia University student Chandler Owen, a devotee of the reform Darwinist Lester Frank Ward. Together, the search for the passionate life led Randolph and Owen into the fold of the Socialist Party in 1916 and to a stint as co-editors of the *Hotel Messenger*, which lasted until they exposed corruption in the waiters' union that had hired them. Thereafter, it was Lucille's subsidy, derived from her ownership of a New York outlet of Madame C. J. Walker's cosmetics empire, that permitted them to publish an independent monthly, *The Messenger*, established in 1917.[1]

From the beginning, Randolph the journalist-activist sought to distinguish his relation to the black community from most of his intellectual predecessors. "Our aim," declared the editors of *The Messenger* in their second issue, "is to appeal to reason, to lift our pens above the cringing demagogy of the times and above the cheap, peanut politics of the old, reactionary Negro leaders." With supreme, cosmopolitan confidence, the young Harlem socialists adopted an emergent generational identity to distinguish themselves from established race leaders and organizations. "Yes, the Old Crowd is passing," exalted Randolph in 1919, "and with it, its false, corrupt and wicked institutions of oppression and cruelty; its ancient prejudices and beliefs and its pious, hypocritical and venerated idols." Linking Old Crowd institutions to reactionary white funds and white control—"a group which viciously opposes every demand made by organized labor for an opportunity to live a better life"—Randolph's Roll of Shame read like a Who's Who of Negro America.

> In the Negro schools and colleges the most typical reactionaries are Kelly, Miller, Moton, and William Pickens. In the press Du Bois, James Weldon Johnson, Fred R. Moore, T. Thomas Fortune, Roscoe Conkling Simmons and George Harris are compromising the case of the Negro. In politics Chas. W. Anderson, W. H. Lewis, Ralph Tyler, Emmet Scott, George E. Haynes and the entire old line palliating, me-[too]-boss gang of Negro politicians, are hopelessly ignorant and distressingly unwitting of their way.[2]

It was not long before Randolph himself would emerge as a prominent force in the black community. First, as president and general organizer of the Brotherhood of Sleeping Car Porters (1925–1968); second, as president of the National Negro Congress (1936–1940); and third, as architect of the March on Washington Movement (MOWM) (1941–1944), generally recognized as a key strategic forerunner to modern civil rights agitation, Randolph was a powerful presence in the struggle for black freedom in the twentieth century. It was in recognition of both his continuing advocacy within the councils of labor and his larger record of community activism that the Rev. Martin Luther King, Jr., christened him the "dean of Negro leaders" in 1958 and that he was selected as presiding officer over the 1963 March on Washington.

While Randolph's civic contributions have been well documented by recent biographers and by labor as well as civil rights historians, I want to focus on the character of leadership that Randolph reflected both in his opinions and personal example. The "leadership question" has stood for decades (and in some fashion still stands) as a distinct and peculiar feature of debate about and within the African-American community. It is not merely, I suspect, that invoking leaders' names has served the needs of whites for "representative colored men" (as was initially the case following Reconstruction) or, among blacks, as a convenient shorthand for invoking larger political questions.[3] Rather, in an oppressed community, the leader actually occupies a comparatively large social space, and charisma necessarily substitutes for missing organizational resources.[4] In African-American commentary and scholarship a focus on leadership has thus survived shifting historiographical fashion in favor of social historical or popular cultural subjects, while political divisions have continuously galvanized around the vision, strategy, and even personality of at least symbolically powerful individuals. The recent debate over film portrayals of Malcolm X, the bitter rift around the Reverend Ben Chavis and the NAACP, and controversy surrounding Nation of Islam leader Louis Farrakhan and the meaning of the Million Man March are only the latest manifestations of a longer discursive tradition.[5] A 1970 doctoral dissertation summarized a still-common wisdom: "Some of the most significant crises of democracy from the time of Booker T. Washington to the time of Martin Luther King, Jr., may be in part regarded as crises in Negro leadership. At every phase of our social and political system thousands of groups search among their members for leaders who can deal effectively with the critical issues of our time."[6]

The same assumptions help to drive the spirited cultural critique of contemporary scholar-activist Cornel West. A chief problem of the black community today, West contends, lies in the "crisis of black leadership." "There has not been a time in the history of black people in this country when the quantity of politicians and intellec-

tuals was so great, yet the quality of both groups has been so low
. . . How do we account for the absence of the Frederick Douglasses,
Sojourner Truths, Martin Luther King, Jrs., Malcolm X's, and
Fannie Lou Hamers in our time?"[7]

I want to position Randolph within the context of an earlier twentieth-century "black leadership crisis" and, at the same time, to illuminate an enduring tension in the role of any intellectual activist:
as a man (or woman) of the people, what is the intellectual's relationship with the movement's rank and file?

IN CONNECTING the destiny of the black community to the qualities of its leaders, Randolph and Owen were contributing to a discourse of leadership veneration and debunking already well established by 1917. The post-Reconstruction years in particular
witnessed a preoccupation with the subject on the part of the black
intelligentsia. The distinguished historian Nathan Irvin Huggins
noted the apotheosis of race leaders to larger-than-life status beginning with Frederick Douglass and continuing in turn with Booker
T. Washington and W. E. B. Du Bois. The classic period of black
leadership (1890–1930), Huggins argued, was dominated by a
"leadership of personality." Unconnected to specific, democratic
mandate, such leadership generally rested instead on exemplary
tutelage of the masses, what Huggins described as "the uplifting of
a downtrodden people . . . a leadership of aristocratic and elitist assumptions, not democratic ones. The black leader [by this unwrit-
ten formula] should not be one of his people; he should, alas, be better than his people."[8] To Huggins's largely secular explanation of
early leadership styles, historian Wilson Jeremiah Moses persua-
sively added the dimension of religious culture in stressing the
power of a messianic tradition within black politics. Booker T.
Washington, he notes, was frequently praised as the "Negro Moses,"
and he "was neither the first nor the last black American public
figure to be hailed with this title."[9]

When, in the pages of *The Messenger*, Randolph categorically lam-
basted the qualities of contemporary leaders, he was thus treading
on sacred ground (as well as sacred cows). For among respectable
black opinion by the turn of the century (as exemplified by *The Voice
of the Negro*, one of the literary staples in Randolph's Jacksonville

household) cultivation of the special responsibilities of the educated elite served as a sine qua non of race progress.[10] In a typical reflection from what Randolph would later call the Old Crowd, Wilberforce professor W. S. Scarborough insisted that "the future of the Negro people will largely depend upon the exceptions . . . It is to the far-sighted, the intelligent Negro that we must look to bring about the proper solution in time."[11] Such exceptions, Howard sociologist Kelly Miller concurred, would act as what latter-day sociologists would have called "role models": "It is essential that any isolated and proscribed class should honor its illustrious names. They serve not only as a measure of their possibilities, but they possess greater inspirational power by virtue of their close sympathetic and kindly touch."[12] In a collection of essays published in 1910, Miller added another critical function to the leader's portfolio: negotiation with the dominant social groups.

> If a beneficial and kindly contact between the races is denied on the lower plane of flesh and blood, it must be sought in the upper region of mental and moral kinship . . . The undeveloped races which, in modern times, have faded before the breath of civilization have probably perished because of their failure to produce commanding leaders to guide them wisely under the stress and strain which an encroaching civilization imposed. A single red Indian with the capacity and spirit of Booker T. Washington might have solved the red man's problems and averted his pending doom.[13]

In addition to political giants such as Douglass or Washington, writers credited collective entities such as "colored preachers" for "the great advances made in the acquisition of property, real and personal, since 1875" or invested hope in the "Negro teacher" as the leader "in all progress intellectual and economic." "He is so to do, or rather undo, the work of the ignorant parent."[14]

The African-American women's club movement partook of a similar idealism. The National Federation of Woman's Clubs, activist Fannie Barrier Williams argued, depended on the "effort of a few competent in behalf of the many incompetent." Following the model of the socially conscious Chicago Women's Club, the members of the black clubs, Williams hoped, would "become the civic mothers of the race by establishing a sort of special relationship between those who help and those who need help."[15] "Lifting as they climb," the motto of the national club movement, signified a combination of an individual success ethic with an attitude of noblesse oblige toward those left behind by economic progress.[16]

Altogether, such efforts added up to a philosophy of community self-help activated from above. In large measure, they resulted in a set of expectations friendly to the politically conservative politics of a Booker T. Washington. Washington's Tuskegee Institute, for example, presumed a gap between beneficent leaders and benighted followers, enlightened preachers and wayward flock, knowing teachers and ignorant pupils. Washington's secretary, Emmett J. Scott, described the annual Tuskegee Conferences, which were aimed at the southern rural population, as follows:

> How to stimulate this all too-inert mass, how to get at it, and quicken the necessary following without which leaders lead a forlorn hope— that were a question and a task. But these Conferences do it. They bring together annually men and women who are down and who know they are down, but desire to get up; also they bring together educated men and women, white and black interested in these first-named, and together they confer. The point of acutest need is developed and remedies suggested; how some man or woman has succeeded is the token by which others may succeed.[17]

The edifice of Washingtonian accommodationism first attracted a sustained critique from the Niagara movement intellectuals led by W. E. B. Du Bois. But on the question of the form and sources of leadership, it is noteworthy how much the famous Du Bois concept of the "talented tenth" overlapped with those of his political antagonists. As historian Evelyn Brooks Higginbotham has recently documented, the term and invocation of the "talented tenth" concept first emerged from the northern white leadership of the American Baptist Home Mission Society in the 1890s. Conceived with the same self-help intent as Washington's famous "Atlanta Compromise" speech of 1895, the term "talented tenth," as coined by ABHMS Executive Secretary Henry Morehouse in 1897, referred to the need for a group of "colored American Yankee[s]" who would serve in a "buffer" role to the black masses.[18] A kindred contemporary formulation was that of Episcopal minister Alexander Crummel, who preached at Du Bois's Wilberforce College in 1895 on the duty of the educated classes "to teach the common folk abstinence, monogamy, cleanliness and thrift."[19]

In the case of Du Bois, even before his re-creation of the concept in a 1903 essay, both political and intellectual interests had led him toward a functionalist view of community leadership. His Atlanta University studies, which he began publishing in 1899, led him to describe a "submerged tenth" of sharecroppers and an "Upper Ten" of landowners and renters.[20] A "talented tenth" of educated intellectual leadership was a logical outgrowth of such theorizing. The rudiments of the concept, moreover, were fully in keeping with contemporary opinion. To argue, for example, that "the Negro race . . . is going to be saved by its exceptional men" would have evoked no dissent from Du Bois's more conservative adversaries. Similarly, to Du Bois's rhetorical question "Was there ever a nation on God's fair earth civilized from the bottom upward?" a Kelly Miller, a Scarborough, or even a Washington might as easily have answered: "Never; it is, ever was and ever will be from the top downward that culture filters."[21] Indeed, Miller's condescending assumption that "the more ignorant and backward the masses, the more skilled and sagacious should the leaders be" may well have been borrowed from Du Bois's judgment "that the Negro people need social leadership more than most groups; that they have no traditions to fall back upon, no long established customs, no strong family ties, no well defined social classes."[22]

To be sure, against the Washingtonian emphasis on agricultural and manual training and individual assimilation into a white-dominated economy, the young Du Bois counterposed a vision of leadership for group liberation. His prescription of a "higher training" (i.e., liberal arts education) for the "brighter minds" was directed at the citizenship rights of the community: "the object of all true education is not to make men carpenters, it is to make carpenters men."[23] Moreover, Du Bois—who had grown up in an exceptional northern environment—complicated his rather conventional, hierarchical view of the black community with a romantic identification with the southern black masses. Beneath the outward air of "submission and subserviency" and the forced psychology of "patience, humility, and adroitness," he insisted, lay the "pent-up vigor of ten million souls." The expression of "the real Negro heart" needed only its "Awakening."[24]

A third vision of contemporary leadership was articulated by Marcus Garvey. Yet while organizing the only truly mass movement of African-Americans in the first half of the twentieth century, Garvey, like Washington and Du Bois, readily invoked the distinction between the visionary few and the "illiterate and shallow-minded Negro who can see no farther than the end of his nose." In an "appeal to the intelligentsia" enunciated around 1920, Garvey defined a kind of higher calling of leadership:

> Those of us who are better positioned intellectually must exercise forbearance with the illiterate and help them to see the right. If we happen to be members of the same organization, and the illiterate man tries to embarrass you, do not become disgusted, but remember that he does it because he does not know better, and it is your duty to forbear and forgive because the ends that we serve are not of self but for the higher development of the entire race. It is on this score, it is on this belief, that I make the sacrifice of self to help this downtrodden race of mine.[25]

Leadership, for Garvey, implied the substitution of the collective welfare for one's own personal fulfillment: "leadership means sacrifice, leadership means giving up one's personality, giving up of everything for the cause that is worthwhile." Upon arrest in 1922 for mail fraud in relation to the United Negro Improvement Association's Black Star Line, Garvey readily placed himself in the tradition of martyrdom: "There has never been a Movement where the Leader has not suffered for the Cause, and not received the ingratitude of the people."[26]

As self-styled evangels of a new "awakening" in the black community, Randolph and Owen separated themselves from Du Bois and Garvey even as they consigned Washington and his ilk to the scrapheap of history. Although they respected him as a "poet" of Negro radicalism, Randolph and Owen considered Du Bois ill-suited for the role of revolutionary liberator. Like the other "misleaders," he was indicted for his ignorance of political science (i.e., Marxism), his political opportunism (graphically symbolized in support for the

U.S. war effort), and his ultimate currying of bourgeois favor (i.e., white support of the NAACP).[27]

Against Garvey, to be sure, Randolph and Owen directed the more visceral reaction, seeing in his popularity the workings of a dangerous, false prophet. Indeed, once the leader of what Owen called the "Uninformed Negroes Infamous Association" announced his contacts in 1922 with the Ku Klux Klan, the *Messenger* editors (both through the newspaper and the anti-Garvey organization the Friends of Negro Freedom) called openly and contemptuously for his deportation. Attempting to deny Garvey all respect as a leader, the *Messenger* assailed him, among other insults, as "a blustering West Indian demagogue who preys upon the ignorant, unsuspecting poor West Indian working men and women who believe Garvey is some sort of Moses"[28]

To interrupt the pattern of leadership sellouts, Randolph unhesitatingly placed his hopes in a reconnection to "plain working people" by a youthful cohort dedicated to the principles of revolutionary socialism:

> The New Crowd must be composed of young men who are educated, radical and fearless. Young Negro radicals must control the press, church, schools, politics and labor. The condition for joining the New Crowd are: ability, radicalism, and sincerity. The New Crowd views with much expectancy the revolutions ushering in a New World . . . The New Crowd would have no armistice with lynch-law; no truce with jim crowism and disfranchisement; no peace until the Negro receives complete social, economic and political justice. To this end the New Crowd would form an alliance with white radicals such as the I.W.W., the Socialists and the Non-Partisan League, to build a new society—a society of equals, without class, race, caste or religious distinctions.[29]

Randolph thus gave a particular ideological twist to the sense of generational differences that was gathering in Harlem, a vague cluster of ideas immortalized in Alain Locke's collected commentaries from the "new Negro" in the mid-twenties.[30]

But just how new was Randolph's New Negro style of leadership? Like his predecessors, Randolph's relation to those he represented depended not only on sympathy with but also on a clear distinction between himself and the rank and file. To be sure, his distance from the Pullman Company (and thus the threat of dismissal) as well as his already established public reputation were prime considerations in the original appeal to Randolph from Ashley L. Totten and the initial nucleus of New York porters who founded the Brotherhood of Sleeping Car Porters (BSCP) in 1925.[31] Yet the distance was more than tactical. Randolph's lifelong epithet as "Chief" among the porters conveyed a relationship at once affectionate and awe-inspiring.

It was in part a matter of upbringing. As the namesake of an Old Testament king who, according to scripture, "took all the silver and the gold that were left in the treasures of the house of the Lord . . . and delivered them into the hand of his servants," Asa Philip Randolph believed from early on that he had talents worthy of cultivation. The son of an itinerant African Methodist Episcopal (AME) preacher and a mother who frequently managed the family's small tailoring shop, Randolph was raised in a household that greatly valued self-respect, ambition, and education.[32] Years later, Randolph would simultaneously recall his family standing up to the Klan with rifles and the relative opportunity afforded Negroes in Jacksonville, a city where a small black professional class (including the family of future writer and NAACP leader James Weldon Johnson) sustained a variety of educational institutions as well as a vigorous political life extending through the mid-1890s.[33] Together, young Asa Philip and his brother James grew up with a positive "feeling of the future."[34] A sense of leadership, of being trained to be "different," was apparently implanted by the boys' father:

> He said, "You have the ability to speak. Your brother has the ability to speak. You have books here that I've bought for you to read, in addition to your school work, and your school leaders and teachers, they love you and have faith in you, they believe you're unusually gifted chaps . . . You've got to make use of that, and this is what I'm trying to do for you, in order that you will not only be trying to make a dollar for yourself or become rich, but will create conditions that will help the people farther down who don't have your opportunities or don't have your gifts."[35]

As a child, Asa Philip Randolph was particularly impressed by local political leader and minister Joseph P. Lee: "He had the spirit

A. Philip Randolph, dapper New York socialist organizer and editor, circa 1912. (Library of Congress)

of an artist," Randolph would later recall, "and he spoke well"; he added, "He was collector of the port of Jacksonville, and his English was really beautiful, you know, and his manner was dignified, and the whites deferred to him."[36]

Although philosophically dedicated to the black working class, culturally Randolph had tried hard to escape it. Tellingly, at approximately the same time that he joined the Socialist Party, he reduced his Christian name to an initial in the style of other intellectuals like Fred R. Moore, T. Thomas Fortune, and W. E. B. Du Bois.[37] Moreover, historian Paula Pfeffer comments that Randolph "more nearly resembled a Shakespearian actor than a labor leader in diction and bearing." His speech, "a cultivated mating of the Bostonian and the West Indian" complete with references to the "mawsses" and "clawsses" as well as words like "verily" and "vouchsafe" developed, he said, from abolitionist oratory, his father's sermons, and, perhaps most decisively, from elocution and Shakespearian acting lessons pursued after his arrival in New York City.[38]

Randolph's early penchant for Shakespeare—an affinity he shared with another labor giant of the era, John. L. Lewis—seems to have derived less from the nineteenth-century plebeian common culture described by Lawrence Levine than from the thirst of a strictly raised, small-town, Deep South boy to share the forbidden fruits of the wider world.[39] Indeed, according to one of his biographers, Randolph turned to political science only because his other passion—the theater—was utterly proscribed by his parents.[40] As a symbol of high culture, moreover, Shakespeare provided his first link to his future wife, Lucille Campbell Greene, a Howard graduate and former schoolteacher whom he met through the amateur Harlem theater group Ye Friends of Shakespeare. A yearning for the cultivated life as well as the ethical principles of socialism helped to cement their alliance. Together, they regularly attended the lively New York City salon of heiress A'Lelia Walker, while Lucille became active in such staples of social respectability as the Debutantes Club, the Howard University alumni association, and the Fresh Air Fund for poor children.[41] Late in life, Randolph would refer to his and Lucille's joint reading of Shakespeare scenes and sonnets as "an avocation which has brought to our household profound enrichment of the spirit and the mind and a genuine sense of happiness."[42]

As a labor leader, Randolph maintained a reputation for upright, almost stolid, ways. His acquaintances marveled to the point of exasperation over the utter control he exercised over his public behavior. As Oakland, California, BSCP activist C. L. Dellums recalled, "Randolph learned to sit erect and walk erect. You almost never saw him leaning back reclining . . . He can't relax the way you and I do when we're sitting around talking." "In a tête à tête," one historian has written, "he tended to speak as if addressing a meeting." Randolph showed similar circumspection in regard to dress: "In the summer, he usually had on a blue serge suit, complete with a black vest—or a beige sweater buttoned down the front—or knitted black tie on white shirt, and a white handkerchief seeming sometimes to flower rakishly out of his breast pocket. At other times of the year, he showed a preference for heavy tweeds."[43]

Randolph's self-composed dignity and refinement were achievements that he knew did not come naturally or easily to those born in his station. His own view of the black masses he sought to lead thus mixed the fiercest of sympathy with a measure of condescension. It was not only that the union's journal, the *Black Worker* (successor to the *Messenger*), regularly preached the elementary virtues of temperance, thrift, reliability, and cleanliness.[44] There is the sense, as well, that without supreme effort the porters would succumb to the shambling subservience generally expected of blacks in society, behavior only enhanced by the "miles of smiles" expected of the Pullman porter.[45]

In upholding a standard of "manliness" above all other virtues, Randolph openly challenged the porters to transform themselves even as they sought to change their conditions of employment. Thus, over and over, in only slightly varying language, he would direct the porter "to hold your head erect and look all the world square in the face and say: *I am a man,* for I am doing the things red-blooded men do; namely, fighting for justice."[46] Fusing images of past suffering with those of future redemption, Randolph placed the unionizing project in the starkest of terms:

> Your forefathers whose bodies bowed, bent and bleeding under the lash of oppression, whose lives blighted, blasted and blinded for over

a thousand years, staggered across the stage of life in physical pain, in spiritual anguish and mental starvation, and finally stumbled into an unasked grave, the soon to be forgotten victims of a privileged plundering, heartless SLAVE-POWER, prayed that you, their sons, might have a better and brighter world than it was their lot to enjoy . . . Brothers, Be Men! Real Men! Sun-Crowned Men![47]

As if to underscore the rank and file response to their leader's challenge, BSCP vice-president Milton Webster would reminisce in 1956 that "the Pullman porter has done more to arouse Negro workers in this country up to their responsibility of doing something for themselves than any other group of people in this country."[48]

Perhaps more effectively than any labor leader of his time, Randolph stressed *self-control* as a key dimension of popular mobilization. At the individual level, he seemed to intuit that "respectable" bearing might serve as a symbolic repudiation of racial subordination, a kind of "bridge discourse" (in Evelyn Brooks Higginbotham's words) between the powerful and the powerless.[49] Of course, such appeal to the theme of respectability also paid strategic political dividends. Desperate for allies in the mid-twenties, Randolph won the endorsement from the influential (and previously anti-union) black fraternal organization the Improved and Benevolent Order of Elks in 1928.[50] Randolph's own behavior, matching his circumstances, was always a careful blend of assertiveness and forbearance. A telling example lay in his nonreaction to a potentially fatal snub from the AFL executive in 1934, placing porters and maids under the jurisdiction of the whites-only Sleeping Car Conductors union. Overruling angry subordinates who were prepared to quit the labor federation altogether in protest, Randolph quietly ignored the decision while pushing furiously, and ultimately successfully, for inclusion in representation elections under the Railway Labor Act.[51]

The issue of control, however, also took on expanded meaning for Randolph. In summoning the ranks of would-be unionists to a new standard of self-worth, Randolph did not limit himself to rational argument. A brief, early stint designing posters and handbills for an employment agency had apparently left him with an indelible impression of the power of consumer culture in shaping mass attitudes. The negative lessons of World War I propaganda and (for Randolph) the positive lessons of the Bolshevik Revolution likewise testified to the potential of "scientific" manipulation of mass emotion.[52] In his own way, Randolph sought to apply the principles of mass psychology to his own political work. Union organizing, Randolph assured his Chicago lieutenant Milton Webster, "follows the same principle of selling advertising or goods of any kind. Because a man doesn't buy an advertised article on the first day it is presented, is no reason for not continuing to present it to him, and with varying arguments, each one calculated to break down his resistance." Even the "role model" image of unruffled dignity that contemporaries marveled at was in part a matter of calculated contrivance. In advance of a scheduled Chicago address in 1926, he thus advised Webster to take "advantage of the psychology of personalities": "You will find that by playing up personalities, you will get much greater and better results than by playing up the name of the Organization . . . This is not a question of theory, but one of fact. I am now speaking as one who knows the advertising game from both study and experience."[53]

In addition to the arts of mass psychology, Randolph occasionally leaned on other mechanisms of social control in the pursuit of his beloved union. To counteract the elaborate system of espionage and intimidation that the Pullman Company had brought against the BSCP's organizing effort, Randolph in 1928 turned to the whites-only railway brotherhoods for help. In a letter to railroad trainmen's president W. G. Lee, Randolph requested that Lee order the trainmen "to actively speak to porters advising them to join the Brotherhood of Sleeping Car Porters . . . The porters have great respect for organized white workers on the railroads, so that I am sure that if a trainman told a porter that Mr. Lee feels that he ought to be in the Brotherhood, that he would be inclined to give it serious consideration."[54]

Beyond an individual quest for respectability and an instrumental use of power, Randolph elaborated what is not too far-fetched to call a "cult of leadership." Despite his earlier denunciations of the old Negro leaders, he had keenly imbibed the imperative for social revitalization from the top down as articulated from Washington through Du Bois and Garvey. His very effectiveness as both a labor and a civil rights figure stemmed in part from an internalization of the widespread community yearning for a messianic hero.

That Randolph was a charismatic figure there is no doubt. Historian William H. Harris carefully compares the profile of the BSCP's general organizer and president to the classic Weberian portrait of charismatic authority. A time of exceptional stress, an air of personal incorruptibility, an ignoring of formal rules of administration, and the ability to convince others to defy immediate logic and odds in favor of the leader's version of reality—all these qualities were part of Randolph's repertoire.[55] In the early 1930s, when the Brotherhood was reduced to a mere 600 members—nearly half in Chicago—Randolph still spoke confidently in the name of "12,000 porters and maids." Amazingly, he convinced both the federal government (which mandated a representation election under the Emergency Railway Transportation Act) as well as the Pullman workers that he did indeed represent a viable force.[56] As Harris concludes, "Little other than the intangible powers of charisma can explain why service employees of the Pullman Company, when given a chance to choose a bargaining agent under federal protection in 1935, chose the BSCP, whose tangible successes in the past had been negligible. In a real sense, they placed their faith not in the organization but in Randolph, who stood before them as a symbol of perseverance and courage." Similarly, in the March on Washington Movement in 1941, Randolph's threat to send tens of thousands into the streets was taken seriously despite the lack of any concrete mobilization plans. As effectively as any contemporary leader, Randolph had insinuated himself as the voice of the people.[57]

Beyond the fortuitous joining of exceptional personality with exceptional circumstances, Randolph's charisma was the result of painstaking effort. Randolph himself portrayed his BSCP position as a kind of Biblical covenant with the downtrodden. In a typical report to the members in 1926, he linked their welfare directly to his own moral character:

> Brethren, I have dedicated my whole heart, soul and body to the cause of your economic justice in particular and the race in general . . . May I say that when I enlisted in the cause, I knew that slander would attempt to blacken my character with infamy: I knew that among the

wicked, corrupt and unenlightened, my pleadings would be received with disdain and reproach; that persecution would assail me on every side; that the dagger of the assassin would gleam behind my back; that the arm of arrogant power would be raised to crush me to the earth; that I would be branded as a disturber of the peace, as a madman, fanatic, an incendiary, a Communist, Anarchist and whatnot; that the heel of friendship would be lifted against me, that love be turned into hatred, confidence into suspicion, respect into derision; that my world interest would be jeoparded [sic]. I knew that the base and servile would accuse me of being actuated with the hope of reward. But brethren, I am undaunted and unafraid.[58]

Similarly, when Randolph forced the *Chicago Defender* in 1927 to atone for its early opposition to the Brotherhood with an editorial retraction and about-face, he insisted that the copy refer to "the determined and lawful struggle of the Pullman porters, led by the brilliant and fearless A. Philip Randolph."[59]

Recurringly fashioning strength out of weakness, Randolph relied on the *appearance* of an undiluted, unchallenged sway over the rank and file. After a near-disastrous retreat from a strike threat against Pullman in 1928, Randolph in fact ceded much formal operational authority over the Brotherhood to a Policy Committee of experienced rank and file organizers led by Chicago vice-president Milton Webster (a move that William H. Harris credits with effectively saving the union).[60] Randolph, however, escaped this crisis with his formal titles and, more importantly, his *public* authority as the porters' leader intact.[61] The union newspaper (controlled by Randolph), for example, uninterruptedly portrayed him in all-powerful terms. In a typical entry, the *Black Worker* effused:

A picture presented itself. In the center of a vast field stands a man among men and women. From within him emerged basic qualities of courage, high intelligence, and honesty and love of humanity. These qualities which converge in the features are reflected in that poise and Buddha-like calm so characteristically Randolph.[62]

That Randolph believed in leadership as a quality, a skill, indeed a mission to be cultivated in its own right seems amply evidenced by his words and deeds. He even gave formal institutional expression to the concept. From his base at the A. Philip Randolph Institute, established in 1964 with support from the AFL-CIO, Randolph's last years were punctuated by various educational and worker-training efforts, including the Harlem-based scholarship program the A. Philip Randolph Leaders of Tomorrow. The project helped striving young students such as Arthur M. Powell, who at age thirteen in 1969 had been invited to give MLK's "Free at Last" speech at Randolph's eightieth birthday celebration, and then, with scholarship aid, graduated from a private prep school and entered Carleton College in Minnesota. As vice-president of his Black Pre-Law Club and participant in an international relations seminar in Geneva, Switzerland, Powell at age twenty-one "exchanged many letters" with Randolph and was still seeking the counsel of his eighty-eight-year-old mentor.[63]

IN IMPORTANT WAYS, a philosophy of social leadership helped to define Randolph's career. If Nathan Huggins was correct to see Randolph as an exception to earlier "emblematic" and "reform" modes of leadership—because he "would use black [mass] organization as an instrument of change"—in other respects one might stress the element of continuity, that Randolph was linked to an older pattern of community stewardship.[64] Even as he took aim at the "mental manikins and intellectual lilliputians" among his elders, this brash New Negro critic effectively mustered himself into the established role model of the intellectual-as-leader. Already powerfully articulated by Booker T. Washington and his allies and subsequently only mildly revised by Mary Church Terrell, W. E. B. Du Bois, Marcus Garvey, and others before Randolph, it was a tradition that might well be said to encompass figures from Frederick Douglass to Martin Luther King, Jr., Malcolm X, Jesse Jackson, and Louis Farrakhan. According to the canons of this tradition, the intellectual contributions of scholarship, criticism, interpretation, and even expert advice pale before the imperative of offering practical direction to the affairs of the community. For the African-American intellectual (defined broadly as a person exceptionally endowed with the resources of education or the capacities for discernment and communication), the leader figure beckons as both burden and blessing, an exacting yet exalted social role.[65]

A historical investigation of the sources of black leadership ideology lie beyond the scope of this chapter, but one influence immediately suggests itself. Although explicitly applying themselves to secular matters, Randolph and others certainly drew on a religious inspiration—what Wilson Moses has called the "Afro-American messianic myth"—for both the content and form of the leader ideal. In 1918 the influential black Presbyterian minister Francis J. Grimké powerfully invoked the contemporary belief in the redeemer-leader:

> The super-man of the future is not to be of the German type . . . but of the Christ type . . . The super-nation of the future is not to be the German nation, nor any of the existing nations, but the Commonwealth of Israel—the Church of the living God, purified, cleansed, Spirit-filled, God-centered, meek and lowly, girded with strength, and arrayed in beautiful garments of righteousness . . . And such a power or force we have in the personality of Jesus Christ.[66]

On earth, Christ's message was delivered by church leaders, the ministry, those whom AME Bishop Henry McNeal Turner—a man who commanded an awesome respect in Randolph's childhood home and struck young Asa as looking "like a tyrant"—called "God's Ambassadors," whose profession was "the most exalted occupation among men." According to one contemporary memoirist, Turner claimed that "the leadership of the race was in the Negro ministry . . . He taught, in all his Conferences and institutes among the men and women over whom he presided, that such a leadership, if it would maintain its place among men, must be fitted and prepared to do the world's work. And the race could hope to accomplish but little without this leadership."[67]

That such messages left a deep imprint upon the generally irreligious A. Philip Randolph seems clear. Years later, for example, he would extol another secular socialist revolutionary, Eugene Victor Debs, as "a spiritual type of revolutionist": "Just like the Bible preacher in the South, you know, [he] had the power of moving people."[68]

Randolph's rhetoric—so filled with images of suffering and redemption, personal trial and sacrifice, and contrasts of moral depravity and grandeur—frequently secularized an older spiritual message. But his very style of leadership may also have derived from cultural osmosis. As sociologist E. Franklin Frazier noted thirty years ago, "the Negro church has left its imprint upon practically every aspect of Negro life."

[It] has provided the pattern for the organization of mutual aid societies and insurance companies. It has provided the pattern of Negro fraternal organizations and Greek letter societies . . . Since . . . the pattern of control and organization of the Negro church has been authoritarian, with a strong man in a dominant position, the same pattern has characterized other Negro institutions.[69]

For this reason it is likely that Randolph's rendition of the intellectual-as-leader falls somewhat awkwardly on present-day democratic ears. The elevation of the leader in Randolph's day sometimes came at the expense of popular participation in decision-making as well as representative procedure. The election and deliberative process among BSCP delegates, for example, has been described by one historian as a "hollow ritual," and even some sympathizers of the March on Washington Movement complained of "an unhealthy degree of leader-worship of Mr. Randolph" in the National Office.[70] George S. Schuyler, longtime staffer for the *Messenger*, likewise allowed in 1942 that Randolph "has the messianic complex, considerable oratorical ability, and some understanding of the plight of the masses, but the leadership capacity and executive ability required for the task at hand simply is not there."[71]

Perhaps the greatest fault of the Randolph-style cult of leadership was its systematic undervaluation of women's roles in both the labor and civil rights movements. Among Randolph biographers, even the ever-admiring Jervis Anderson notes that Randolph was forgetful to the point of obliviousness of female associates, while Paula Pfeffer concludes pointedly that Randolph appeared "unable" to establish "mutually rewarding relationships" with women.[72] Willingly relying on the money-raising efforts of the Ladies' Auxiliaries of the BSCP and the underpaid female staff of civil rights organizations (not to mention his fundamental indebtedness to his wife's business earnings), Randolph, according to Pfeffer, never took women—including his wife—into serious, substantive counsel.[73] What is more, within the Brotherhood, Randolph not only maintained near-autocratic control over the affairs of the Colored Women's Economic Council (later called the Ladies' Auxiliary), but he consistently showed little interest in the specific concerns of as many as two hundred women actually employed by the Pullman corporation as maids.[74] A typical memo to Milton Webster in 1926, for instance, suggested that he "request the Ladies Auxiliary to supply a little refreshment for your anniversary meeting."

> Suppose you suggest to them having some punch without a kick in it and some little cakes . . . I would request that the Auxiliary donate the refreshments to the occasion and handle the serving . . . May I suggest also that you get together a musical program—something you don't have to pay for—perhaps the Ladies Auxiliary can handle this . . . Have the Auxiliary to organize a committee . . . and you may advise with them. I would not let them spend a whole lot of money on it.[75]

One legacy of the 1960s has been a severe questioning of both the motives and the behavior of officially sanctioned leaders. Randolph's "great man" approach to leadership did not come under explicit criticism during his active career, either with the BSCP or the MOWM. Yet the model he embodied has indeed come under fire since the creation of the Student Non-Violent Coordinating Committee (SNCC) in 1960 and the subsequent development of the New Left and new social movements. Explaining her own largely unheralded role in the civil rights movement, SNCC founder Ella Baker would later explain, "I have always felt it was a handicap for oppressed peoples to depend so largely upon a leader, because unfortunately in our culture, the charismatic leader usually becomes a leader because he has found a spot in the public limelight." In particular, Baker recognized "that as a woman, an older woman, in a group of ministers who are accustomed to having women largely as supporters, there was no place for me to have come into a leadership role."[76] SNCC's emphasis on building "community movements, not organizations" reflected an early attempt to break down hierarchies between leaders and rank and file.[77]

In place of the professionalized, charismatic, or messianic leader, younger radicals, black and white, turned increasingly to "group-centered" or "facilitative" leadership and "participatory" or "direct" democracy.[78] In African-American historical scholarship, Evelyn

Brook Higginbotham has emphasized the activism of lay women within the Baptist Church as a kind of countertradition to better known male roles, while Hazel V. Carby has discovered a female literary vision of "racial uplift . . . defined not as individual gestures by an educated hero and heroine but within the development of a community of intellectuals."[79]

In addition to a strong sensitivity to gender bias, the new social movements have generally shared a concern that entrenched organizational leaders inevitably retard mass mobilization and stifle creative initiative from below.[80] In history and the social sciences, moreover, "progressive" scholars have similarly ignored leaders in favor of searching for the "movement culture" or "mentality" of the masses. At least since Watergate, leadership—whether applied to labor and other popular movements, to government and politics, or even to civil institutions—rouses a spirit of exposure rather than reverence.[81]

The legacy of A. Philip Randolph does not require that we abandon such skepticism, but it may ultimately suggest a more complicated social dynamic behind the figure of the leader than is commonly supposed. In particular, focus on a leader's words and deeds does not in itself fully explain that leader's relationship to public or rank and file.

The story of Randolph and the "blank check" is illustrative. In 1978, public folklorist Jack Santino found among the oral culture of retired Pullman porters a mythic tale about the Pullman's Company's effort to bribe Randolph by offering him a blank check. Santino discovered many variations of the story. According to one:

> They went to him twice and offered him some money. I don't know how much money they offered him, but he told them that the Brotherhood wasn't for sale. And the third time they sent an instructor out of New York over to his office with a check. Blank. And told him to put his figures on it. And Mr. Randolph took the check and had it photostated, and he sent the check back, and he kept the photostat and framed it and put it in his office.

In another version, Randolph referred to slavery as he refused the check, saying, "You could buy my parents but you can't buy me." A third rendition reports Randolph's words to the Pullman emissary as "I don't want nothing but the porters." Among those closest to Randolph and his office at the time, no one remembers seeing either the check or a photostat of it. The story, it seems, functioned not only to ennoble Randolph as leader but to empower the porters. As Mrs. Rosina Tucker, a Ladies' Auxiliary officer who in the Brotherhood's early days had organized secret meetings and disseminated literature, explained: "He wouldn't be bought. And that's one thing that made us so successful."[82]

From this angle, perhaps, we may see Randolph less as a self-created figure than as a joint production that combined his own ingenuity with popular projections of him. Like the mythical John Henry or the legendary Jack Johnson, his heroism, however exaggerated, served as a collective sword of defiance within the African-American community.

Is the cult of leadership, then, merely a substitute for a more democratic and popular politics? Or is the personage and image of the leader regularly reshaped to meet popular needs? Rosina Tucker, for one, had an answer:

> It got to the point where sometimes I was a little discouraged. But I'd call Mr. Randolph and say to him, "Mr. Randolph, how are things coming along?" "Mrs. Tucker, they are progressing nicely." I found out that I was having faith in his faith. That's where my faith derived, from his faith.[83]

A similar, if indirect, reply is also recorded in the description by the St. Paul, Minnesota, *Recorder* in 1939 of the organized Pullman porter who regularly "dressed impeccably in the height of fashion, with mirrored polished shoes, his razor-edged pressed pants, his high silk hat setting at exact angle" and "walked with an air of authority . . . with the walk of a Lord Chesterfield."[84]

The leader who is larger than life likely draws that life in part from those he or she is leading. Two additional examples will serve as illustrations of the point. In the mining wars of southern Illinois in the 1890s—ultimately presided over by United Mine Workers President John Mitchell—there developed a legend around a certain Alexander "General" Bradley. For weeks Bradley, an outspoken, versifying, mining mule-driver, closed mine after mine in a great campaign against armed opposition. One day, according to oral sources, Bradley's army "was camping in a ball park, when they missed the general."

> The commissary was low, one or two mines had not come out, and there were ugly rumors from town that Bradley had been seen drinking with some St. Louis operators. A committee started out to find the lost leader when a wagon was seen approaching the camp with a high-hatted, frock-coated man on the seat waving a beribboned umbrella. It was General Bradley all right, but where had he got those fancy duds? The general would explain. When the army assembled, the general reared up in his full sartorial glory and told how he had been secretly sent for to meet with the St. Louis mine owners. He met them in a downtown saloon, and there, after many drinks they gave him $200 as bribe money.
>
> "I figured your general needed some clothes that was befitting your leader," said Bradley, "so I got me these duds, secondhand. But here is all the rest of the money," he went on, bringing from his back pocket a roll of bills and flinging it out to the crowd with a free-handed gesture, "go get yourself eats, boys, the goddam operators is paying for it."[85]

The use of clothes to make a social impression (as Randolph did) perhaps deserves particular scrutiny. In a study of the leadership of Sun Yat-sen, historian David Strand, adopting a metaphor from sociologist Georg Simmel, notes that Sun "had great personal prestige but lacked the authority that comes from being clothed in institutions and law. The relative nakedness of his position in this regard made him extremely attentive to the way he looked and acted." The charismatic leader, typically drawn from the margins of society like Randolph, necessarily harnessed a politics of personal prestige, complete with the projection of signs of glamour and power, to offset what Strand calls an "[un]stable institutional structure."[86]

The second example deals with a better-known strongman, Argentinian populist Juan Domingo Perón. In October 1945 what proved later to be only the first phase of Perónism appeared to be the last. The military government over which Perón had presided since 1943 in coalition with militant meat-packers faced overwhelming domestic as well as external opposition with the dawn of a postwar liberal order. Perón himself, according to historian

Charles Bergquist, "accepted his defeat after October 9" and even accepted nominal arrest in a Buenos Aires military hospital. Yet even as the "indecisive, pajama-clad Perón" privately succumbed to a realistic political calculus, his working-class followers took a different route, engaging in mass action to free their leader. What Bergquist calls "the major turning point in twentieth-century Argentine history" occurred on October 17, 1945, when tens of thousands of workers "walked off the job and headed for the city," effectively pulling off a massive general strike:

> As night fell the power and resolve of the workers seemed to grow. In the flickering yellow light of thousands of makeshift newspaper torches the chanting of perhaps a quarter of a million men and women reverberated through the city, literally shaking the walls of the main government buildings. Finally, just before midnight, workers achieved their purpose. Perón was freed and addressed the multitude. A new and powerful force had made its debut in Argentine politics.[87]

These two incidents reveal the delicate interplay of call and response in the elevation of the individual to folk-leader status. Political theorist Richard J. Bernstein insists on a relational understanding of leadership character: "Because power is not an individual property but an intersubjective capacity which," he argues, quoting Hannah Arendt, "'springs up between men when they act together and vanishes the moment they disperse,' leadership is always *of* a public and never *over* it."[88] Sociologist Georg Simmel put the same point more simply: "All leaders are also led."[89]

Bound in both a behavioral and a discursive relationship to those who follow them, the leader figure remains a mysterious historical subject. Preoccupied for years now with the collective values of "movement culture," students of labor and other social movements might usefully orient themselves as well to the singular, and sometimes ironic, impact of individuals on human events. In Randolph's case, at least, the hauteur and even outright arrogance of one man seems paradoxically to have inspired democratic resistance among an oppressed class.

The preoccupation with the problem of social leadership in African-American history perhaps raises a special question. We might well wonder whether the arc of stewardship from Frederick

Douglass through Randolph to Martin Luther King, Jr., et al. taps a peculiarly African-American, or even African, cultural wellspring. Do these men derive from a strong-leader culture, and were their perceptions of the role of leadership influenced by ideas (not to mention circumstances) distinct from Euro-American influences? Any answer must rely on mere fragments of evidence, both because the system of slavery so limited autonomous expressions of authority and because the subject itself has largely escaped serious historical inquiry. Yet it is conceivable that leadership traditions—like music, dance, and religious traditions that Africans had "buried in their heads and hearts"—might have been retained within a larger cultural repertoire.[90] Was there, for example, a running connection between early-eighteenth-century inductions of African-American "kings" and "queens" in New England towns and the heroics of "King Dick" in Dartmoor prison with the twentieth-century model of the leader as community deliverer?[91]

If so, one connecting rod was surely to be found in the paternal authority commonly exercised by nineteenth-century Black Baptist or AME ministers. Religious historian Edward L. Wheeler has emphasized the paradox of preachers at once representing and standing apart from their communities. The sense of a special calling, he argues, and the confirmation of that calling by the community placed the minister in a high place of influence that had consequences for his activity in "uplifting the race."[92] One of the quintessential role models from this tradition—and a man with direct personal influence on the Randolph family—was the AME preacher Bishop Henry McNeil Turner. Yet even he perhaps bequeathed a mixed legacy. On the one hand, Turner was memorialized by W. E. B. Du Bois as "the last of his clan: mighty men, physically and mentally, men who started at the bottom and hammered their way to the top by sheer brute strength; they were the spiritual progeny of ancient African chieftains."[93] On the other hand, a modern-day, and generally admiring, biographer notes Turner's tendency to be "quite rigid in his opinions" and inclined to "refuse to back down even when an overwhelming majority of his closest associates disagreed with him."[94] As one African-American religious feminist recently generalized, "The preacher in the black church *is* more directive, authoritarian, and singular in his administration."[95] Randolph, an outwardly secular, even Marxist social thinker, nevertheless likely owed much to the tradition of black male church leadership. From a distance, Randolph's relation to BSCP members resembles that of the African-American preacher to his flock.

A related image, at once religious and secular, is the power of the "Negro Moses" figure. Like other great leaders of the African-American community, Randolph cultivated both a personal distance from and an emotional intimacy with the sufferings of the mass public. As one later-day interpreter of the Exodus story notes, Moses "is separate from the people in his growing up, and later on he separates himself again." This template of western liberation stories, so central to African-American religious culture, establishes the leader as an outsider—as one who does not so much identify with his followers as uphold a standard to which they should aspire.[96]

Finally, elements of Randolph's operating procedure—in particular, his use of deception and bravado to cover a weak negotiating position, as in his securing of a union representation election in 1937 and President Roosevelt's executive order banning discrimination in the military and war industries in 1941—recall the folkloric figure of the Afro-Caribbean slave trickster. The harnessing of wit, bluster, and the power of positive thinking to moments of liberation holds a venerated place in black history, from Nat Turner's clandestine organizing to the uniforms of Garvey's UNIA to the rise of the Jamaican labor leader Alexander Bustamante in the 1930s, another outsider to the masses, whom one historian likens to the image of Anancy the spiderman-trickster of African folktales.[97] As a wielder of mass psychology on friend and foe alike and as a strategist with a masterful sense of timing, Randolph appeared to draw on his own deep bag of tricks.

But surely the logic of such ethno-cultural explanations carries only so far. Whatever residual indigenous material turn-of-the-century African-Americans might have drawn on to fashion a hierarchy of social-political organization must be balanced against the abundant stock of signals about the role of the leader within the larger contemporary Euro-American culture. The heroic rendering of political leaders, for example, occupied a prominent niche within nineteenth-century romantic thought. Like many of his Caucasian contemporaries, for example, Du Bois first found political inspiration in the heroizing writings of Thomas Carlyle, an influence notably manifest in Du Bois's celebration of the life of Bismarck in his Fisk commencement speech of 1888.[98]

In the culture of the day Du Bois's—and later Randolph's—reach for the heroic was the rule rather than the exception. Perhaps there was no better model for the cult of leadership than that most learned of modern American presidents, Woodrow Wilson. In 1896 the distinguished Democrat and political scientist completed his biography of George Washington with this Carlylian invocation of the "happy warrior": "The country knew him when he was dead: knew the majesty, the nobility, the unsullied greatness of the man who was gone, and knew not whether to mourn or to give praise. He could not serve them any more; but they saw his light shine already upon the future as upon the past, and were glad."[99] The most influential Progressive tract of the period—Herbert Croly's *The Promise of American Life* (1909)—was cut from the same cloth. Croly's new nationalism depended on a publicly engaged intellectual elite united by a great leader as a saving counterpart to the narrow businessmindedness of the larger society.[100]

Alongside the apotheosis of the patriot-hero and the engaged intellectual, moreover, lay perhaps the even more apposite Anglo-American tradition of the gentleman leader or "tribune of the people." Associated in the early nineteenth century with radical English writer-agitators such as William Cobbett, Henry Hunt, and Feargus O'Connor, the ranks of middle- and upper-class politicians who earned a special plebeian fealty included such varied figures as Andrew Jackson and Abraham Lincoln (and later Franklin Roosevelt) in the United States as well as Giuseppe Garibaldi in Italy and the "People's William" Gladstone in mid-Victorian England.[101] Whatever the gentleman leader's social origins, notes British historian James Vernon, the people customarily preferred to venerate him in his gentlemanly appearance. Cobbett, for example, had been born into a poor agricultural family but was posthumously evoked through a description of his clothes: "There he stands as we were wont to see him in his life, at his lectures, with his blue coat and gilt buttons, white neck cloth, light linen waistcoat, and drab pantaloons, white hair, dead eyes and pudding face."[102] In his own venue, Randolph too—raised in poverty, striving for refinement, attaining a measure of respect and respectability, yet always passionately fighting for his people—offers a later-day version of a familiar historical model. All told, then, creation of the American intellectual-as-leader figure may best be seen as a multicultural enterprise.

Randolph, in short, appears to have drawn selectively and pragmatically from a medley of possible leadership styles. Images of the gentleman leader, the messianic religious and race leader, the trade union leader, the populist leader—all may well have beckoned to the young African-American intellectual as ways he might turn radical ideas into reality.

Projection of A. Philip Randolph as a prototype of the intellectual as political leader raises one final question. What is the normative relationship between the democratic intellectual and those he or she seeks to represent? In this regard it may be worth considering the Randolph case within the concept of the "organic intellectual" as conceived by the Italian social philosopher Antonio Gramsci. Briefly, Gramsci distinguished between "traditional" intellectuals (scholars and scientists who see themselves as autonomous, free-floating agents of knowledge) and "organic" intellectuals (ecclesiastics, administrators, journalists, etc.), who work consciously for their own social group or class.[103] Among the latter, Gramsci was particularly concerned with the leadership or hegemonic functions of those who might be drawn from or won over to the workers' and peasants' cause. "Every organic development of the peasant masses, up to a certain point," noted Gramsci, "is linked to and depends upon movements among the intellectuals."[104]

To be effective, however, intellectuals "of the masses" needed at once to understand and to uplift the common people. On the one hand lay the danger of cultural condescension, knowledge without understanding or passion, of relationships between the intellectual leader and the people that remained "formal," "bureaucratic," and "caste-like." Gramsci illustrated such "lack" of "organic quality" with a historical example: "It was all rather like the first contacts of English merchants and the negroes of Africa: trashy baubles were handed out in exchange for nuggets of gold. In any case one could not have had cultural stability and an organic quality of thought if there had [not] existed the same unity between the intellectuals and the simple as there should be between theory and practice."[105]

On the other hand, mere sympathy with and understanding of

the common folk on the part of the intellectual elite did not make for hegemonic leadership. Rather, the intellectuals must also engage in a form of internal critique, at once identifying with ordinary people's needs yet, as Richard Bellamy has summarized, "challenging the traditional nostrums of 'common sense' ways of thinking."[106] For Gramsci the "philosophy of praxis" (his only slightly disguised term for revolutionary Marxism) depended on this intimate connection of "intellectuals" to the "simple" (or working classes). As he put it, only when "feeling-passion becomes understanding and thence knowledge (not mechanically but in a way that is alive), then and only then is the relationship one of representation."[107]

To a remarkable degree, the concerns of A. Philip Randolph about the relationship of intellectual leaders and the masses mirrored those of Antonio Gramsci. Randolph, like Gramsci, insisted on an intellectualism that made its social and political loyalties clear. He equally savaged those (like Du Bois) who claimed to speak for a neutral, academic science and those (like Washington or Garvey) who openly served what he considered reactionary social forces within the larger community. Also like Gramsci, Randolph demanded a probing, critical intelligentsia, not a fawning populist obeisance to mass tastes. For Gramsci, the new, counter-hegemonic leadership of the "Modern Prince" would be delivered by a "progressive" Communist Party; Randolph, it could be said, sought the first step of emancipation for the black masses through a politicized trade unionism. The chief internal difficulty of the Gramscian scheme lay in the vagueness of a vision that simultaneously promised democracy and revolutionary rationalism.[108] Randolph's leadership likewise vacillated between encouragement of a creative, militant rank and file and paternal manipulation from the top down.

If Randolph did not solve the problem of the intellectual as democratic leader, he nevertheless offers one of the more robust examples of efforts to join the instincts and interests of what Christopher Lasch has called the "thinking classes" with common laborers.[109] Of course, Randolph did not venture forth in isolation but rather in step with an enduring strain of African-American intellectual activists.[110] How appropriate that the most vital source of "organic" intellectuals in the New World should derive from the children of Gramsci's "simple" natives of Africa.

7 The People's Strategist

W. Jett Lauck and the Panacea of Plenty

B Y THE BEGINNING of the twentieth century the American labor movement was already moving to adopt rising living standards as its chief objective and raison d'être. In place of a direct contest over the control of the agents of production or the political order (as signaled in nineteenth-century calls for "workingmen's democracy" and an end to "wage slavery"), the ensuing decades witnessed an ever stronger focus on the goal that American Federation of Labor (AFL) president Samuel Gompers defined in 1912 as "the best possible conditions obtainable for the workers."[1] As exemplified in the "living wage" standard of the National War Labor Board (1917) in World War I, the industrial codes of the National Industrial Recovery Act (1933), the preamble to the National Labor Relations Act (1935), and the minimum wage of the Fair Labor Standards Act (1938), public policy substantively reinforced organized labor's demands for workers' inclusion in a consumer economy. The common sense nature of such progress (for who was not concerned with material improvements?), however, at once belied the strategic genius required to turn a consensual affirmation of values into an effective organizational and political program and masked the inherent limits of that very same enterprise. With lengthening hindsight, we can begin to identify the key building blocks in the development of both an industrially and politically powerful labor movement and the sources of the movement's frailty, which is so manifest today.

One critical brace of twentieth-century labor strategy lay in the assimilation of a new economic science (and its accompanying discourse) by labor leaders and a cadre of skilled professional advisors.

The creative heart of this enterprise was located in the dynamic paths of the men's clothing workers union on the one hand and the mine workers' union on the other. Initially developing separately and then joining forces in 1936, these twin pillars of the Congress of Industrial Organizations (CIO) had independently discovered the secret trinity to union survival under consumer-capitalist culture: (1) industrywide organizing; (2) political mobilization and active use of state regulatory powers; and (3) recruitment of representatives of the liberal intelligentsia as part of a larger campaign for public support.

While John L. Lewis, longtime leader of the United Mine Workers of America (UMWA) and father of the CIO, remains one of the best-known, even legendary, architects of the American labor movement, his influential policy advisor W. Jett Lauck, never much of a public figure, is unknown to all but a few specialists in labor history.[2] Contemporaries were more observant. Looking back on the explosive achievements of the previous few years, labor journalists of the mid-thirties and early forties credited Lauck with having a major influence on labor's political agenda, including at least contributing authorship to the pathbreaking Section 7A of the National Industrial Recovery Act (NIRA), which recognized workers' rights to "organize unions of their own choosing" and engage in collective bargaining.[3] Indeed, a 1936 commentary in the *Christian Science Monitor* called him the CIO's "one-man brain trust" and the "Sydney [Webb], Beatrice [Webb] and [Harold] Laski" of the American Labor Party."[4] While this chapter does not claim quite so glorious or potent a portfolio for its subject, it does suggest that Lauck's deeds and public writings, supplemented by a considerable private correspondence and the several-year notations of a daily diary, offer an important window on the world of twentieth-century labor leadership and decision-making.[5] Here I concentrate on the evolution of Lauck's strategic vision for the labor movement and the ways that his own special role and circumstances contributed to the peculiar historical legacy of his chief client.

IT WAS LAUCK'S service on the seminal Commission on Industrial Relations (CIR) of 1913–1915 (see Chapter 3) that seems to have first sparked the reform instincts of this young professional, who had previously been preoccupied with establishing himself as a neutral expert in the sprouting world of applied economics. Born in Keyser, West Virginia, in 1879 into a family headed by hardworking railway stationmaster William Blackford Lauck—a descendant of German-Protestant refugees from the Thirty Years War who had first come to America in 1750 (and who boasted a soldier under the command of Benedict Arnold at the Battle of Quebec)—Jett, the second of eight children, was the only child of this struggling middle-class family to earn a college degree. A graduate of Washington and Lee University in 1903, Lauck briefly pursued graduate work in political economy at the University of Chicago before returning to Lexington, Virginia, to teach at his alma mater and marry his college sweetheart, Eleanor Moore Dunlap, herself the product of an old-stock Scots-Irish farm family.[6] Lauck's prize-winning graduate school thesis, "The Causes of the Panic of 1893," was published in 1905 and professionally accepted as a convincing application of the "orthodox view that fear of unsettling the gold standard upsets markets."[7]

Despite an academic appointment, Lauck quickly gravitated to the opportunities available in the world of applied research and policy analysis. His early assignments included work as director of industrial investigations for the U.S. Immigration Commission (1907–1910), chief examiner for the Tariff Board in Washington, D.C. (1910–1911), and secretary of the National Citizens League for Promotion of a Sound Banking System (1911–1912). His work in these years betrayed little sign of social or political unorthodoxy; within a few years Lauck would distance himself from his early writings, considering them the conventionally conservative reflections of an economist interested mostly "in money and banking."[8] Yet once exposed to the influences of the labor reform community around the CIR (Lauck was first hired as consulting statistician, then promoted to managing expert of research until Charles McCarthy joined up with chairman Frank Walsh), Lauck made a permanent career shift. Despite occasional bouts of college teaching, Lauck became a full-time labor expert—as union representative to the railway labor boards (1912–1919), secretary to the Walsh-led National War Labor Board (1918–1919), and then primarily as consulting economist for John L. Lewis and the United Mine Workers (1919–1939).

One of the earliest themes to which Lauck would apply his professional talents was workers' standard of living. His reports to the Industrial Commission, for example, justified a conventionally restrictionist policy stance on grounds that "the extensive employment of recent immigrants has brought about living conditions and a standard of living with which the older employees have been unable or have found it extremely difficult to compete."[9] Indeed, it was a sign of how deeply the concept had already penetrated the larger political culture that Lauck could write offhandedly in his initial application letter to CIR chairman Walsh, "I am trying to develop work as an independent economist and statistician . . . So far, [it has] just about yielded a *living wage* but I am hoping to do better" (italics added).[10] While this was not the last time that the economic problems he was investigating at work corresponded to issues in Lauck's own life, his framing of the problem undoubtedly derived from well-established practice in contemporary economic and public policy circles.

By the eve of World War I, a generation of middle-class social scientists and social reformers, backed by the agitation of the labor unions, had placed the problem of workers' purchasing power squarely on the public agenda. Already by the 1880s labor agitation had begun to turn from a total rejection of the "wage system" to a concentration on greater earnings, spelled out variously in demands for a "living wage," a "minimum wage," or, as in AFL president Samuel Gompers's famous expression, "more."[11] Carroll Wright, head of the Massachusetts Bureau of Labor Statistics and later U.S. Commissioner of Labor, first invoked the notion of a minimum wage in a 1875 report, in which he demonstrated that the traditional male breadwinner could no longer support a family of wife and children on a typical industrial income.[12] The issue had subsequently been pressed through the Roman Catholic Church, as expressed in the call for "just payment" by Pope Leo XIII's *Rerum Novarum* (1891) and the more explicit appeal by Father John Ryan in his book *A Living Wage* (1906).[13] The concept gathered momentum over the next fifteen years, as signaled by passage in Massachusetts of the first state minimum wage law in 1912 and the adoption of some version of the measure in party platforms by the Progressives and Socialists in 1912, Democrats in 1916, and even the Republicans by 1920.[14]

From a more academic perspective, economists Simon Nelson Patten and George Gunton had also helped to transform social science discourse from a focus on scarcity to the problem of distribution of a growing economic surplus. As Gunton argued as early as 1887, in his work *Wealth and Progress*, escalating consumer desires would prop up a higher standard of living, which in turn would be the basis of a higher civilization. The early years of the twentieth century witnessed a series of applied studies, including Robert C. Chapin's *The Standard of Living among Workingmen's Families in New York* (1909), that demonstrated the desperate need for higher and/or minimum industrial wages.[15] The demand for a "living wage," articulated in the Walsh Report to the CIR as a prerequisite for the national welfare, was thus only the extension of a growing consensus within the labor reform community.

But it was the wartime mobilization and coordination of labor by the government that first demonstrated the practical weight of the new discourse of wages and living standards. When the National War Labor Board (NWLB), jointly led by Frank Walsh and ex-President William Howard Taft, adopted the "living wage" as an immediate objective, a once-vague principle suddenly became significant. As enunciated in a precedent-setting packinghouse decision by Chicago judge Samuel Alschuler in 1918, wartime arbitration addressed fairness and need as well as market principles in establishing wage standards. Overall, notes one recent historian, NWLB actions, based on "continuous reappraisals of the cost of living" conducted by an entire division of trained examiners overseen by Board secretary Lauck, "significantly raised the standard of living for countless workers," in effect setting a minimum wage for common laborers.[16] Lauck's direct appropriation of the cost-of-living argument was apparent in his 1920 arbitration testimony on behalf of New York State Street Car Employees, an argument he pithily summarized in the phrase "Cheap men make cheap citizens."[17]

If the wartime pattern of significant governmental intervention in the marketplace provided a preview of Lauck's later labor reform strategy, so did one other aspect of NWLB procedures. Lauck's chief conflict during the short tenure of the Board was with women's rights advocate Marie Obenauer, who sought greater autonomy for her Division of Women Administrative Examiners in pursuing the

Board's stated goal of "equal pay for equal work." Lauck resisted any challenge to his notion of a "integrated, cohesive staff directed by the chiefs of existing divisions," who happened to be all men. Indeed, when Obenauer persisted in her complaints of inadequate staff and authority, Lauck abolished her division entirely. Both in his top-down administrative style and in his inclination—demonstrated previously in his attitude toward the new immigrants—to accept traditional social hierarchies (in this case perceiving women as "mother[s] of the race . . . [who] can not be dealt with on the same terms as men workers"), Lauck showed the qualities that would define the limits of his democratic commitments in future years.[18]

The war years convinced Lauck that a marriage of economic science with responsible labor leadership offered a formula that would guarantee American social progress. His ideas, moreover, seemed in accord with those of such national luminaries as Secretary of Labor William B. Wilson, philanthropist Julius Rosenwald, and Food Administrator Herbert Hoover, all of whom endorsed the living wage as the keystone of postwar economic recovery at President Wilson's Second Industrial Conference in 1920. Just how the economist might function as social-political mediator Lauck demonstrated in a characteristic presentation to the Railway Labor Board on behalf of the Maintenance of Way Employees union in 1922:

> The approximate amount of a living wage—i.e. the annual income necessary to support a family in mere health and decency—is no longer a matter of conjecture. Scientific studies of the subject have been made by authorities of such undoubted competence that no question can be raised as to the substantial accuracy of the results . . . For a family to attempt to support itself on a lesser amount does not mean a mere inconvenience, a doing without certain comforts . . . Except when other conditions are extremely favorable, it easily becomes the breeder of disease, unrest, immorality, and crime. In all of these ways, it saps the strength of the nation itself, and undermines the vitality of democratic institutions.[19]

Lauck's simultaneous appeal to moral sentiment and expert authority, exercised as it was before a quasi-political body, captured the optimistic spirit of the Progressive labor reformer in one of his last institutional redoubts. But, as the devastating defeat of the railway shop crafts strike of the same year would demonstrate, time had largely run out on labor agreements based on consensual principles among all the parties. In a memo prepared for the Railroad Labor Board by one of his assistants, Lauck acknowledged that "now, in the name of 'readjustment' America's employers have carried on a propaganda and concerted effort toward wage reduction such as never before was equaled or approached."[20]

It was during the fading twilight of the Progressive reform era that Jett Lauck first made his connection to the UMWA and their new leader, John L. Lewis. Like Lauck, the young Lewis, who had scratched his way up the union leadership pole from his Illinois base, had initially lent his political allegiance to Woodrow Wilson and a spate of government-sanctioned labor reforms. He continued to back the President, at least until federal troops and a declaration of martial law forced him to accept a compromise settlement ending the 1919 wartime strike and as late as 1921 remained on record supporting government credits to the unemployed, compulsory employer-financed unemployment insurance, and nationalization or at least stringent governmental regulation of the mining industry.[21] But as well as anyone in the labor movement, Lewis read the handwriting on the postwar wall. The government had evaporated as a potential ally and protector, while soft-coal operators targeted union power and high wages as a source of their chronic instability. A nationwide showdown in the bituminous fields in 1922 brought home to Lewis just how stacked the odds were against union power. Faced with expanding nonunion fields and all-out mobilization against the strike by the Harding administration, the UMWA achieved at best a temporary reprieve from the powers determined to roll back union influence in the industry.[22]

It was time, determined Lewis, to cut a deal. The new Lewis emerged in a full-blown Republican era. Driving his left-wing opposition out of the union, the autocratic UMWA president tried for the rest of the decade to find a common ground of self-interest with both the Republican administration and the big soft-coal operators. For Lewis the connection was both personal and organizational. A frustrated entrepreneur himself, he enjoyed the company of men of wealth; his biographers note that his passport through the twenties read "executive," not "labor leader," and his interest in banking (initially cultivated through his friend Jacob Harriman) ultimately led to the creation of the union-financed United Labor Bank and Trust Company of Indianapolis with Lewis as president.[23]

Organizationally, the essence of the union's strategy lay in the self-regulation of coal markets (which would affect both price and wage structures) as achieved through areawide collective bargaining agreements. Taking a cue from the "new capitalism" rhetoric of Secretary of Commerce Herbert Hoover (himself a former mining engineer) and other corporate leaders, Lewis appealed to business to move beyond the law of the jungle and into an age of managed competition. With the help of Hoover and utilities magnate George G. Moore, the resulting Jacksonville Agreement of 1924 locked into place for three years the relatively high wage ($7.50 per day) of the Central Field, which stretched from Illinois to Central Pennsylvania. The Jacksonville Agreement was the capstone of this era of UMWA voluntarism.[24]

The public and ideological justification for Lewis's move toward business principles was provided by a document drafted by Lauck and other UMWA advisers under Lewis's name in 1925. Essentially an adaptation of the law of supply and demand, *The Miners' Fight for American Standards* took as its premise an American system built on wages high enough to sustain an expanding home market. "Trade unionism," it argued, "is an integral part of the existing system" happily called "capitalism." "Trade unionism is a phenomenon of capitalism quite similar to the corporation. One is essentially a pooling of labor for purposes of common action in production and in sales. The other is a pooling of capital for exactly the same purposes. The economic aims of both are identical—gain." When things worked right, there was indeed no reason for workers to look beyond their own resources in meeting their material needs: "The American workingman, no more than the American businessman, wants to be babied by any paternalistic agencies, governmental or private." But all was not right, for the self-adjusting market equilibrium had come undone. The problem that had regularly disrupted the industry—causing pain to both workers and operators—was overproduction: simply put, "too many mines and too many min-

W. Jett Lauck examining a report on the meatpacking industry in his
Washington, D.C., office, circa 1925. (W. Jett Lauck Papers, #4742, Special
Collections Department, University of Virginia Library)

ers." In the natural scheme of a healthy capitalism, argued the mineworkers' scribes, unsound sectors of the industry would be shut down to allow the healthy, technically advanced sectors to flourish. The cancer of nonunion competition—centered in the new pits of Kentucky and West Virginia and the so-called captive mines of the steel companies in Pennsylvania—however, disrupted this system, for "lowering wages and breaking unions would serve only to prolong the maladies of the industry, while sacrificing the rights of the miners." Only the maintenance of an "American wage standard" could save the industry by forcing a "reorganization . . . upon scientific and efficient lines."[25]

While the guiding hand of Jett Lauck as UMWA economist is written all over *The Miners' Fight*, it is nevertheless interesting that he chose not to complement the union-as-capitalist-partner theme in that work with ideas evoked in a work of his own the following year. In *Political and Industrial Democracy, 1775–1926*, Lauck gave voice to an older idealism of the Progressive past that played little role in the UMWA's history or immediate future. Harnessing the findings of the 1920 Industrial Conference to a roster of similar expressions from religious leaders, Lauck's work focused on the "aspirations towards participation by workers to exert a larger and more organic influence upon the processes of industrial life." Lauding individual examples of cooperation and industrial self-management initiated in the prewar period, Lauck seemed at once to recognize that time was running out on such idealistic models and to regret their passing. In Lauck's extensive corpus of public and private writing, the book stands as an uncommon projection of his hopes for the active enfranchisement of ordinary working people.[26]

As it happened, the 1920s' mining industry was not kind to either the industrial democracy or the capitalist collaboration fantasies of their labor union creators. Even while professing common interests with the mine owners, *The Miners' Fight* was in fact an attempt to stem an already rapid seepage of operators away from the Jacksonville Agreement. But neither the appeal to business logic nor to the good offices of Secretary of Commerce Hoover to stem the tide paid any tangible dividend.[27] Expanding southern production combined with competing fuels, including natural gas, petroleum, and electricity, weakened the demand for coal and depressed both prices and profits. Even the Mellon-owned Pittsburgh Coal Company, union operated for thirty-five years, shut down and reopened nonunion in 1925.[28] Throughout the decade the number of miners employed dropped, as did their hours of work. As for the union, Melvyn Dubofsky and Warren Van Tine describe the UMWA by 1928 as "in a headlong race for oblivion." From a peak of 500,000-plus bituminous members in 1921, a bare 80,000 (two-thirds from Lewis's Illinois home district) survived on the rolls, and employers were regularly paying 30 to 50 percent below union scale. Altogether bloodied and broke, the organization faced its most desperate hours.[29]

For reasons only partly connected to the union's slide, economist Jett Lauck's fortunes also worsened appreciably during the nation's "prosperous twenties." It certainly was not foreordained that a union professional, let alone a union leader, should suffer according to the vicissitudes of the union's organizational health. President Lewis, for example, survived the decade navigating between three houses in his private Cadillac and supporting a large extended family with a combination of union and bank salaries as well as successful stock market investments.[30] Lauck was not quite so lucky. Supporting a wife and three children on a large Chevy Chase estate with three servants, Lauck clearly aspired to a level of professional middle-class respectability that was not easily accommodated by union consulting work.[31] While regularly retained by a few union patrons, Lauck depended, sometimes to the point of desperation, on the UMWA for his bread and butter.[32] As early as July 1923, for example, he beseeched Lewis for a spot in the upcoming anthracite negotiations "because I have done nothing practically since the close of the [1922] coal strike but to accumulate liabilities."[33] Then, a few months later, Lauck took a fateful gamble, borrowing nearly $10,000 from the Harriman Bank against the signatures of Lewis and UMWA vice president Philip Murray to help purchase an office building in Washington, D.C. He had jumped into a pit from which he never fully escaped. Through the end of the decade and beyond, his relations with his boss (and others with whom he was professionally involved) would become complicated by personal debts. The building proved an albatross: in 1926 he was again seeking "temporary financial help" (this time while awaiting completion of a cotton deal he had arranged for a southern cooperative marketing association), hoping to sell the building, which had never proven credit-worthy, and determined as he told Lewis "to be a free man once more." "You know my interests and inclinations are not towards the accumulation of property or an oppressive amount of wealth," Lauck explained. But escape from this "recent financial jam"—and refusal to declare personal bankruptcy—had become "a matter of honor."[34] With the Harriman Bank pressing in on him in a "quite hard-boiled" manner, Lauck, self-confessedly at his "lowest ebb" by the end of the decade, was forced to sell his beloved Chevy Chase home and relocate to Fredericksburg to an older house overlooking the Rappahannock River.[35] Against the background of such private discomforts, one passage from Lauck et al.'s *Miners' Fight* may have rung with special meaning for its ghostwriter: "[The American workingman] may submit when he has to, to a feudal overlord in industry. He may even for a time, accept philanthropic largesse dispensed in that manner, but he will never like it. He will never become spiritually reconciled to such conditions."[36]

Whatever toll they may have taken emotionally, Lauck's private troubles seemed only to stimulate his intellectual contributions to labor's organizational rebirth in the 1930s. Overall, it is noteworthy that the two liveliest centers of New Deal–era labor strategy derived from "sick" industries of the pre-Depression era—namely Lewis's mineworkers and Sidney Hillman's clothing trades. In both cases adversity led to broadly inventive strategies for industrial planning and regulation, efforts designed to restore economic stability on the back of an American living standard for an organized labor force.[37]

The first step, as Lauck had recognized and pressed on a reluctant boss since the official expiration of the Jacksonville Agreement in 1927, was to get the federal government involved in the control of runaway free markets. John L. Lewis's official break with his prior commitments to "voluntarism" came in 1928 when he threw the union's remaining leverage behind the proposal of Indiana Republican senator James Watson to use the interstate regulatory authority of Congress to establish a coal commission, which would in turn regulate wages, prices, and profits and guarantee collective bargaining.[38] Updated as the Davis-Kelly bill of 1932, such initiatives, while doomed to failure under President Hoover (whom Lewis had mistakenly expected to come to the union's aid in 1928 and still backed in the election of 1932) formed the intellectual and political crucible for the pathbreaking NIRA of 1933.[39]

Once Lauck had gotten Lewis to reject what he called Hoover's "old rugged individualism," an array of possibilities opened for the imaginative union strategist. As the stock market crash of 1929 began dragging the entire domestic economy into the ditch already long occupied by the soft-coal industry, Lauck produced a steady drumbeat of advice in President Lewis's ear. Hoover's "big-man theory" of economic progress—the idea that the way to "help the underdog is to first help the man on top with the assumption that the big man . . . will drag the lower levels up with him"—had come to naught.[40] The times demanded a leader and a plan, insisted Lauck, and no one was better positioned than Lewis to provide both. "In this period of depression," Lauck wrote Lewis in July 1930, "it is necessary for you above all other considerations to take advantage of the psychology of the business world and the great mass of people outside of the organized labor movement . . . The fundamental consideration . . . is for you to be the first to give voice to a plan of real constructive industrial statesmanship to lead the country out of the Wilderness."[41] To clinch the issue, Lauck appealed to his patron's artistic soul as well as his vanity: "You are a Shakespearean scholar and you know that 'there is a tide in the affairs of men which taken at its ebb leads to victory' or words to that effect." Seated as he was as but one constituent within the leadership council of the larger American Federation of Labor, Lewis initially demurred, responding that he could not "with propriety" act as a spokesman for industries beyond coal, yet allowing that "one or two" of Lauck's ideas demanded further thought.[42]

Over the course of the new decade Lauck would lay out before Lewis an almost mind-boggling set of reform ideas, an agenda that, accepted as it was even in part, helped to transform the political discourse of the New Deal era. That Lewis had seized the political moment was first apparent with the National Recovery Administration (NRA), established by the NIRA. Negotiated through a variety of advisory committees to President Roosevelt (in one of which Lauck toiled tirelessly under the supervision of Senator Robert Wagner), the basic licensure authority of the resulting industry boards, together with the commitment to collective bargaining, drew heavily on the Watson and Davis-Kelly coal stabilization bills as well as Lewis's testimony to the Senate Finance Committee in February 1933.[43] Lewis, in short, knew what he was doing when he immediately trumpeted the Blue Eagle, symbol of NRA code compliance, as the equivalent to the Emancipation Proclamation in the coal fields. Temporarily freed from the downward pressure on wages and the iron hand of employer resistance, the men in the pits responded en masse. Virtually every miner in the state of West Virginia had joined the union by the end of the first week of the new regime, and an industrywide campaign begun on June 1 was all but complete (except for the captive mines) two months later.[44] Not surprisingly, it was precisely the two outposts of organized labor that had intellectually prepared for the government's new role in the economy—the mine and the garment workers—that alone were able to take advantage of the NRA regime.

Yet even as the first stage of the New Deal program took hold, Jett Lauck was already dreaming bigger thoughts involving drastic changes in the American economy. "Socialization," he wrote in 1934 notes intended for John L. Lewis, "had ceased to be an academic question." He added, "We know that a continuance of the capitalistic system as we have had it, is impossible. Profit motive and profit system must be eliminated. Otherwise there is no hope for humanity or democracy."[45] The stabilization of industry needed for recovery and reform required, in Lauck's view, either nationalization ("state socialism") or strict regulation on a "public utility basis." For political reasons, Lauck proposed the second alternative, a kind of super-NRA for the nation's fifteen or twenty basic industries, including explicit profit limitations, shorter hours, higher wages, and control of credit facilities by the government.[46] As if to underscore the direction of his own proposals, Lauck carefully copied into his notes the following words from a 1936 New Republic editorial: "The real question is not whether we go back to laissez-faire . . . also not whether we shall go forward to economic planning. This is inevitable under either private or public auspices . . . But what about planning to increase production, to raise the material and cultural standards of life? What about planning under a government expressing the interest of the masses, rather than those of a profit-seeking business? Would that not be democracy of a high order?"[47]

Soon Lauck had even the old voluntarist Lewis singing out of his liberal-statist hymnbook. Perhaps the most convincing public unveiling of the "new Lewis" came in a feature entitled "What I Expect of Roosevelt" in *The Nation* just after the 1936 election. Starting with the premise that the goal of public policy was "a life of plenty" for all groups of people, Lewis argued (in a script obviously written by Lauck) that the nation's experience since 1933 "conclusively demonstrated that our financial and industrial leaders are unable of themselves to govern our economic life in the public interest." The necessary role of the federal government for the future was thus to guarantee "economic freedom and democracy to wage and salary workers, accompanied by a high degree of economic planning and regulation for both industry and agriculture."[48] By 1937 Lauck was openly taking pride and partial credit for the "evolution" of Lewis "from a reactionary labor leader to a liberal constructive statesman."[49]

Although his interactions with President Lewis only occasionally strayed from issues of public policy to matters of direct union administration, it is clear that Lauck himself projected his long-held "living wage" commitments into a full-scale battle plan for the emergent CIO. Only two months after Lewis had socked Carpenters' leader William Hutcheson in the jaw at the October 1935 AFL convention, Lauck, responding to a direct request for advice, pressed his boss to turn the fledgling Committee for Industrial Organization into a practical reality. What was needed, Lauck suggested, were "mass meetings" like the crusade that had swept the coal fields in 1933, this time beginning in the steel towns. The touchstone for such organizing should be the "living wage idea," which he believed would offer "a terrific impetus for success somewhat akin to the Townsend old age movement."[50] Lauck followed up such thoughts with a more elaborate statement of the "objectives of labor," a list that indicated the neat intersection of workplace, political, and broad economic themes in its author's mind:

1. Organize the unorganized, develop economic-political strength.
2. Organizing campaign itself requires political action, right to organize and bargain collectively.

3. Formulate constructive policy for . . .
   a. industrial freedom and liberty, free America from judicial oligarchy, from financial oligarchy.
   b. industrial policy—stability, abundance, leisure, security.[51]

Through the CIO and the New Deal, it seemed, Lauck had found the perfect vehicle to pursue the question of living standards that had inspired his work since the prewar days.

In many respects, Lauck's connection of economic recovery with the strengthening of the labor movement resonated with the most far-reaching of New Deal measures. In the case of the newly enacted National Labor Relations Act on which Lauck consulted with Senator Wagner, robust economic growth served in the legislation's preamble ("inequality of bargaining power . . . substantially burdens and affects the flow of commerce, and tends to aggravate recurrent business depressions") as the justification for the whole enumerated set of labor rights.[52] Likewise, Lauck's expressed fear of "judicial oligarchy" linked long-standing labor concerns over injunctions and annulment of hours legislation with the administration's alarm at the Supreme Court's evisceration of its farm relief and industrial recovery acts. While President Roosevelt proposed only to dilute the Court's conservative bloc with the power of additional appointments, Lauck and the CIO leadership pushed strongly for a constitutional amendment to eliminate the power of judicial review.[53] Although neither idea bore legislative fruit, the Court's own switch (beginning with acceptance of the Wagner Act in 1937) towards a more pliant respect for federal economic initiative was well understood at the time as a response to a shifting political climate.[54]

But in other respects—as hinted at in his rhetorical determination to free the nation from "financial oligarchy"—Lauck clearly wanted to go much further than most of his contemporaries in either government or the labor movement toward a social democratic state.[55] His focus on the banks was not a new theme. Ever since the breakdown of the Jacksonville Agreement in the coal fields, Lauck and Lewis had regularly identified the "Morgan interests" (or a broader Morgan–Mellon–Du Pont–Rockefeller nexus) as the ultimate source of reactionary politics in the country.[56] The captive mines controversy regularly added fuel to the fire until it was tentatively resolved in 1933. Then, with the newly created CIO gearing up to take on the mass-production industries, Lewis & Co. again addressed the evil power behind the employers' throne. As early as his preparations for a July 1936 radio broadcast scheduled to open the steelworkers' organizing drive, Lauck urged Lewis "not [to] leave Morgan & Co. out of speech but should attack this banking house as the seat of economic dictatorship of the country."[57] He further sent Lewis a memo "reiterating" and "emphasizing this point," urging his boss to connect the steel drive to talk of "finance-capitalism, the living wage, and economic planning."[58] Uncharacteristically, Lauck threw himself into the center of a radical attack on the financial sector. Suggesting that Lewis appoint Lauck himself to draw up a plan to replace private investment banking with an agency modeled on the Reconstruction Finance Corporation, Lauck explained, "Let the resolution recite further that Morgan & Co . . . dictate the reactionary labor policies of steel, motors, rubber, and other basic industries . . . and that under a public fiscal institution such industries will have enlightened labor policies and function in the public interest."[59]

And this was just the beginning. When FDR momentarily shifted his own rhetoric leftward in 1938, promising to investigate monopoly enterprises, Lauck positively exulted. Such an investigation, Lauck counseled Lewis, "could be utilized to show that there was no hope for the Labor Movement until the Morgan or Investment Banking Control were eliminated from industrial and other corporations."[60] Indeed, in the same period, Lauck advised a *New York Times* reporter that the financial problems of the nation's railroads also derived from the same investment bankers "who rooked the railroads in times of prosperity and threw them back upon the government . . . for increased freight rates or upon wage reduction of employees in times of adversity."[61]

Why such a sustained rhetorical assault upon the banks when there was little realistic expectation of major political reform in this area? One answer may be that it served immediate tactical as well as long-term strategic ends. Thus, after outlining his proposed CIO initiative for a new finance system, Lauck added the justification to Lewis that "if you take the above action in the Committee [CIO] and you give it out to the press, the big banking interests will be so alarmed over the threat to the continuance of their power that they will agree to the unionization of steel, motors, rubber, etc."[62] Indeed, when U.S. Steel's Myron Taylor stunned the country with his willingness to recognize the Steel Workers Organizing Committee, Lauck rationalized the decision as the culmination of exactly the pressure he had helped bring to bear, a matter of the corporation finally seeing "the handwriting on the wall" and taking the only "realistic course" available.[63] From one angle, therefore, Lauck's "bank war" strategy toward the steel companies appears to have anticipated the later-day "corporate campaign" approach to union organizing, whereby pressure is brought to bear on stockholders or banks to bring an offending employer to heel.[64]

Still, tactical advantage in the steel campaign alone cannot explain Lauck's continuing preoccupation with restructuring of the banking system. His hopes were most clearly revealed in the program of the American Association of Economic Freedom (AAEF), a tripartite organization of church leaders, academics, and independent "public" representatives, which Lauck formed and presided over (with substantive help from the UMWA treasury) as "acting chairman" from 1938 to 1940.[65] Acting as a political battering ram on economic policy, the AAEF officially spoke through a National Policy Board that included such liberal luminaries as Monsignor John Ryan, Rabbi Stephen S. Wise, journalist William Allen White, and university president Frank Porter Graham. But its message reflected vintage Lauckian craftsmanship. "Late at night," his diary entry of January 26, 1938 read, "I began the preparation of an outline of a Bill for democratizing our investment banking system . . . to be used in connection with [a] Bill for expansion of recovery on basis of planned economy of abundance."[66] As Lauck stressed in a letter to President Roosevelt urging him to include the AAEF in a 1940 recovery conference, the organization "has devoted a great deal of time to the preparation of a concrete plan to bring about reemployment and general well-being under governmental controls."[67]

At the core of the AAEF reconstruction plan stood a prescription for "an economy of plenty" based on public control of investment capital. Private investment banks would give way to a "capital-issues banking system" charged with maintaining "purchasing power . . .

in approximate balance with increasing production." An "Industrial Reconstruction Commission" appointed by the President would preside over a vast network of planning boards, industry councils, an assurance and marketing corporation, and banks, which alone would underwrite all securities affecting interstate commerce. To guarantee a rising floor under wages and workplace practices, the plan stipulated that "no articles, commodities or goods produced in the major industries shall be shipped, transported or delivered in interstate commerce, if produced, manufactured, processed or distributed by any business which has not been licensed by the Industrial Reconstruction Commission."[68] Lest there be any mistake about the animus of the financial reform plan, Lauck chastised so-called bank reformers within the administration and Congress for climbing "on all fours towards Big Business."[69] The AAEF's preferred bill, which he hoped to make a "fundamental issue of the New Deal," sought no less than to "tax private bankers out of business."[70]

It does no disservice to Lauck's political commitments (which of course could not have been advanced without at least tacit support from John L. Lewis) to note that his own public financial radicalism likely derived at least in part from his unhappy private economy. The same day in 1938, for example, that he vowed to abolish investment banking, a survey of his own finances revealed that while his expenses averaged $3,000 per month, his income barely reached $1,300 per month.[71] Indeed, the formation of the visionary AAEF corresponded to a second act of downward mobility in the Lauck family. Following a devastating 1938 flood, Lauck was forced to put his Fredericksburg "Island" home on the auction block and move again, this time to a modest farmhouse in Port Royal.[72] Although ostensibly aimed at working people who lived on far more meager incomes than did he, Lauck's recurrent emphasis on "plenty," "abundance," and "security" surely possessed a personal meaning as well.

There is no doubt that Lauck pictured himself as a radical democrat, helping to "meet the challenge of Fascist and Communist dictatorships" with "the idea of industrial democracy and economic planning."[73] In the context of his times (or our times for that matter) the institutional enfranchisement of working people that the CIO and the New Deal effected in both industry and government did indeed constitute a massive shift toward social power-sharing. But it is also worth taking stock of the limits of the message of democratic abundance promulgated by Lauck, Lewis, and the CIO. Both in theory and practice, the message betrayed a characteristically circumscribed sense of democratic process and popular self-government.

To begin with, of course, no one ever accused John L. Lewis, to whom Lauck was inescapably linked, of an overzealous concern for democratic procedure. From the bruising leadership wars of the UMWA in the teens to his ouster of the left opposition in the twenties, Lewis had made clear his insistence on undivided power within his organization. Even as he reached out to respond to the aspirations of mass production workers in the 1930s, the same top-down organizational instincts prevailed. The Steel Workers' Organizing Committee (SWOC), for example, the most direct extension of the Lewis-centered organizing mission, was notoriously autocratic in internal structure, a virtual political machine controlled by Lewis's hand-picked adjutant general, Philip Murray.[74]

The evidence suggests, however, that Jett Lauck was no mere conduit of his master's will when it came to matters of union decision-making. Rather, as advisor and strategist he actively aided and abetted Lewis's tendencies to achieve desirable ends by the most efficient means possible. It was to Lauck, for example, that John L. Lewis's younger brother, Dennie, repaired for advice on how "to obtain closer contact and control over districts" in the often unruly UMWA.[75] Similarly, at the dawn of the CIO, it was Lauck who helped design a plan "on [the] precipitation [of] organization of Industrial Unionism by having mine workers convention direct him [Lewis] to take up steel," a mandate that quickly allowed a hefty $500,000 in UMWA funds to be pumped into the SWOC drive.[76] Moreover, as his own AAEF first took shape, and as he was recruiting some 150 leading church and academicians in a campaign for economic democracy, Lauck advised Lewis, "It is very important for me to control the program and the organization in its initial stages."[77]

Perhaps the clearest signals of Lauck's taste for hierarchy emerged in his 1937–1938 consultancy to United Auto Workers (UAW) president Homer Martin, who, in the aftermath of the astounding sitdown victory over General Motors at Flint, Michigan, was contending at once with recalcitrant GM bargainers and a growing rank and file opposition movement led by, among others, the Reuther brothers.[78] Lauck, undoubtedly with Lewis's blessing, judged the erratic but charismatic Martin the "best man" available for UAW leadership, agreed to help him "write a strong centralized constitution for the Union—like the United Mine Workers," and favored quick accommodation with GM.[79] In the face of recurrent wildcat sitdown threats, Lauck even sketched a plan to move Martin and other UAW officers from Detroit to Washington, D.C., "to remove them from constant direct contact and interference by local person and committee[s]."[80] Despite such basic sympathies, Lauck also readily perceived the weaknesses of the erratic Martin and his ideologically overzealous strategist, Jay Lovestone. The factional threat from UAW "reds," Lauck advised Lewis, had been greatly exaggerated by the Martin-Lovestone forces; and, fearing disruptive internal bloodletting, Lauck counseled against impending purges of middle-level union staff.[81] By January 1939, Martin had left the UAW in shambles, having greeted union opponents with a pistol, accepted an utterly concessionary contract with GM, secretly drafted another sweetheart deal with the Ford Motor Company, and then fired most of the union's executive board members. Lauck, for his part, had officially severed his ties with the Martin faction a year before, alienated at once by Martin's political incompetence and his managerial irresponsibility in delaying Lauck's salary checks.[82]

A clue to the underlying ideological assumptions upheld by Lauck and other left progressives in the late 1930s is revealed in the work of business writer and reformer Ordway Tead. An Amherst College graduate (1912) who spent three years at Boston's South End settlement house before entering a career as social worker, industrial relations consultant, writer-editor, and educational administrator, Tead collected his reform-minded wisdom in a 1939 volume entitled *New Adventures in Democracy: Practical Applications of the Democratic Idea.* Attracted to the book by a newspaper review, Jett Lauck was so taken with its message that he corresponded with the author and invited him to testify for the AAEF in public hearings.[83] Combining a general sympathy for the union shop with an economic focus on rising levels of consumption for all, Tead provided a fitting theoretical complement to Lauck's policy priorities. The emphases within Tead's schema are especially suggestive. The first principle of democracy in Tead's accounting was "representation of interests" such that "every group which has a clearly identifiable set of interests is safeguarded in its dealings with other groups." By its very presence, the all-inclusive industrial union constituted a "democratizing agency"; further tests of the "maturity" of the industrial system, Tead argued, were demonstrated by such practices as uniform wage rates for newcomers, seniority rights, safeguards against arbitrary discharge, quality of output, medical care, vacation pay, a safe workplace, and limitations on overtime. Tead made clear, in ways that both Lauck and John L. Lewis would surely have approved, that democratic results combined with a procedure of group representation defined the significant measures of democratic practice. "What is a democratic approach to economic problems?" Tead asked rhetorically. The answer was simple. "A democratic approach . . . is that approach which puts the welfare of the great majority of people above the welfare of any small group in the community."[84] By such logic, rising living standards and the closed shop were the surest and safest tests of democratic progress. Government of the people and for the people, by all means, Tead and Lauck might have said, whereas government *by* the people was a luxury that might have to wait.

Unfortunately for Jett Lauck, just as his vehicle of economic democracy began to take on a refined and ever more concrete shape, his designated driver deserted him. Throughout the thirties, from Lauck's point of view, no one was more crucially situated to effect historic social change than John L. Lewis. As both the New Deal and CIO gained in staying power, offering the opportunity for ever more intense cooperation between labor and the state, Lauck had taken it upon himself to turn Lewis into the perfect prod to steer the diffuse forces behind the New Deal coalition toward institutionalized social democracy. With Lauck's help, ever since the NRA, Lewis had operated as both crucial supporter and critical goad to President Roosevelt, ensuring that issues of union rights and worker welfare were constantly present on the nation's political table. Yet all too soon the approach of a second world war raised the stakes on labor's delicate political balancing act. As FDR turned away from domestic reform plans in deference to both foreign policy and a rapprochement with business leaders, so Lewis the Welshman determined not to allow "British imperialists" and the "Morgan interests" to sidetrack the nation into a new military conflict. By 1940 Lewis's attacks on administration policy (including labor's governmental liaison, Sidney Hillman) grew ever more harsh even as the President called for reconciliation of domestic conflicts (including a vain attempt at reunification of the AFL and the CIO).[85] Lauck was caught in the middle. In rapidly changing political circumstances, his strategic antennae proved at once keen and useless.

Anticipating the inevitable expansion of governmental regulatory powers in wartime, Lauck attempted at once to grab Roosevelt's ear on behalf of labor-friendly measures and to corral the irrepressible Lewis into a more patient posture that would serve his (as well as his members') long-term interests. In early October 1940, for example, Lauck confided to his diary that he had

> had a confidential talk with Lewis today relative to my proposal for a National Defense Labor Board and about Labor policies for the future. He approved the proposal, thought highly of it as a constructive measure, but did not believe the President would approve it . . . Said that Big Business had been practically allowed to write there [sic] own ticket for the Defense Program. . . . Then talked briefly with him as what should be the role of leaders of organized labor during the next 4 years and left memorandum with him on this subject, stating that English labor was going to take a dominant position after [the] War, and should a leader like himself advocate a program of fundamental reform in principle here in America he would attain great prestige and possibly high political preferment, because [of the] present lack of such leadership.[86]

Once again playing Machiavelli to his would-be Prince, Lauck tried to turn Lewis's justifiable frustration with FDR labor policies into an extended war for political position.

Just how little patience Lewis had for progressive strategy of any kind was revealed just two weeks before the presidential election, when to Lauck's chagrin the CIO chieftain publicly endorsed Wendell Willkie for president and promised to resign as CIO president if Roosevelt was reelected. "I did not approve of the speech,"

Lauck noted privately, "principally on account of [the] bad effect it would have on Lewis' future career and usefulness because of his deal with [the] Wilkie [sic] Democrats—representing the most reactionary banking groups . . . [I] decided to continue to support and vote for Roosevelt."

In an instant, the whole social-democratic project to which Lauck had dedicated himself came crashing down. Inseparably attached to Lewis professionally, he could not and did not openly break with his patron.[87] Yet Lauck knew that in his willing detachment from the Democratic Party masses of the CIO, Lewis had rendered himself—and thereby Lauck as well—a political nullity. Lauck would have preferred to offer critical support to the Roosevelt administration. "This attitude," he believed, "would have retained progressive groups in support of CIO and laid the way open to Lewis becoming a progressive leader—and possibly obtaining high public office in the future. [I] considered his action tragic from this perspective."[88] Several days later, after again playing back to himself his unsuccessful efforts to reach and dissuade Lewis from a suicidal course, Lauck confided simply, "Result broke my heart."[89]

Just as Lauck feared, the war years were not happy times for policymakers who stuck with John L. Lewis. Consumed at first with internal union fights leading first to resignation from the presidency, then total withdrawal from the CIO that he had created, a resentful Lewis retreated behind the bulwark of the UMWA. But it was his direct defiance of presidential orders as well as AFL and CIO no-strike policy that caused Lewis to change from mere maverick to outcast in much of the public's mind. His running confrontation with the War Labor Board over the government's right to set wage ceilings—climaxed by extended walkouts in 1943—effectively cut Lewis off from the larger left-liberal coalition he had cultivated since the beginning of the Depression. While he had permanently consolidated the loyalty of his own UMWA base (a constituency that would rapidly shrink in the postwar decades with the declining use of coal), Lewis, for all practical purposes, had surrendered his claim to national economic policy or political influence. Len De Caux, one of several left-wingers Lewis had recruited onto his CIO organizing train, recalled the pathos of these years: "I saw and felt how alone Lewis was, most of all in 1940, when others fled from him—in ways he recognized, if not formally. In his period of wartime defiances, Lewis must have felt all the more alone."[90]

While dutifully maintaining his UMWA consultancy, Lauck's own portfolio of operations grew increasingly constricted throughout the 1940s. Intellectually, to be sure, he remained as ambitious as ever. As early as 1943, for example, Lauck seized with a passion on plans for a postwar World Government, reading everything he could get his hands on about possible replacements for the discredited League of Nations. His own "preamble for a Constitution for a World Federation" tellingly extended the pronouncements of the Atlantic Charter and Allied summits to "prevent imperialism and the causes of war by permitting international cartels under governmental control"—a kind of worldwide NRA.[91] Even regarding domestic affairs, he did not entirely abandon hope for a progressive resurgence. FDR's "Economic Bill of Rights," enunciated in the President's Annual Message to Congress in January 1944, Lauck hailed as a modern-day equivalent to "Jefferson's Bill of Rights" and immediately began lobbying to incorporate the new charter as amendments to the Wagner Act.[92] Such moments of bubbling enthusiasm, however, were inevitably quieted with doses of political reality. At a luncheon in December 1943, for example, Lauck ventured the thought that "Pres. Roosevelt's reelection and post-war success in establishing a new World Order was dependent on a unified labor support under Pres. Lewis. [Consulting economist Hugh] Hanna agreed with me, but with me also, could not think of any successful way of bringing this about at the present time."[93] Most of Lauck's business time was now devoted to comparatively mundane advice on union contracts and energy industry developments; the reform ideals that had once sparked endless rounds of active engagement had become matters of idle speculation.

Moreover, at a personal as well as programmatic level, Lauck was experiencing hard times. His son Peter recalls an emotional "rift" in the household over his father's loyalty to Lewis while his mother remained a "big fan" of FDR. The tensions were likely exacerbated by Lauck's long absences from home. Since the thirties, in fact, the pressures and passions of his public role often made Lauck a near stranger to his own children. As son Peter remembers, "All he did was work."[94] Lauck's diary entries confirm the stress of a typical day, which might begin with a bus ride from Port Royal to Fredericksburg, Virginia, then a crowded train to Washington, D.C., where he would spend the "rest of day catching up on accumulated articles and miscellaneous matters at offices," "taking data home at night to go over," then "reading to midnight in evening."[95] Nor had Lauck ever escaped the burdens of debt under which he had labored for many years. Of the three Lauck children, only the oldest son, William (who became an architect), was given the advantage of a professional education. The youngest child, Eleanor, who never attended college, suffered particularly during the family's Depression-era privation and (according to her brother Peter) bore emotional scars that led to her later institutional confinement.[96]

In the face of mounting obstacles Lauck soldiered on. A day after Roosevelt's electoral victory in November 1944, Lauck was still strategizing, anticipating "the final constructive policies" of the President's agenda, including "an assured program of industrial expansion, full employment and plenty."[97] But constantly borrowing new money and covering old loans, Lauck himself was pressed financially to the wall. In 1944 he spent a frantic week vainly preparing his entry for a Budweiser Beer Company contest on the "best plan of post-war revival."[98] By the end of the year he realized that he did "not have resources sufficient to pay apartment and office rents."[99] In desperate straits, in 1947 he joined with John L. Lewis in a speculative scheme for oil exploration in Wyoming.[100] But Lauck had no time to wait for the ripening of investments. Unbeknownst to his family and friends, he had been diagnosed several years before with arteriosclerosis of the brain. Only when they noticed a sudden falloff in his work routine did his loved ones learn of his condition. Nursed at home by his family in his final months, he died at age sixty-nine on June 18, 1949.

IN ONE SENSE Lauck departed at an appropriate moment. For not only the people he relied on but basic assumptions he had subscribed to since the Progressive Era had been dramatically displaced from the center of American public life. As historian Alan Brinkley makes clear in a penetrating treatment of the denouement of New Deal liberalism, the structural tinkering with capitalism envisioned by earlier twentieth-century reformers—linked variously with antimonopoly initiatives, the associative or regulatory state, and direct state planning—had all but disappeared from pragmatic political discourse by the end of World War II. What had taken its place (beginning in the aftermath of the 1937–1938 "Roosevelt recession" and then consolidated through de facto wartime pump-priming and after) was Keynesian fiscal policy. Economists and political reformers alike changed their focus from controlling Big Business to guaranteeing a continually expanding economy.[101] Social welfare, by postwar liberal standards, became less a matter of balancing power at the point of production than ensuring higher living standards on the principle later enunciated by President Kennedy that "a rising tide lifts all boats."[102]

Even the labor movement—the century-long champion of capitalist restructuring—was in no position, and for the most part in little mood, to buck the tide. UAW president Walter Reuther's 1945 proposal for a guaranteed annual wage for auto workers, like AFL president William Green's call "for the maintenance of a high national income . . . [and] equilibrium between producing and consuming power," accepted the new orthodoxy of high consumption divorced from structural economic reforms.[103] Even James Matles of the left-wing United Electrical Workers of America defined his union's aim by 1944 in "one proposition—more money." "Bring home the gravy to your people," declared Matles; "that's all you have to worry about."[104] All in all, the world of liberal fiscal policy and even postwar collective bargaining was far removed from the crusades for "economic democracy" or "public utility capitalism" conducted by W. Jett Lauck and an entire generation of Progressive intellectual reformers.

And yet, as Lauck's career neatly illustrates, there was at least one important point of continuity, a theme that postwar liberals owed their interwar and even Progressive Era forebears. Consumerism—the preoccupation with mass consumption and rising living standards as the chief test of social progress—was hardly the brainchild of those fiscal reductionists Brinkley calls the New Liberals.[105] Rather, decades before the Roosevelt recession and its aftermath, strategists of Lauck's generation had already fashioned the brilliant synthesis between a democratic social movement like organized labor and the rise of a corporate-centered consumer capitalism in America. The chief difference in reform projects, in pre- and post-

Keynesian synthesis, was that Lauck and company were convinced that an Economy of Plenty required "democratic planning" or tight restrictions on capitalist institutions, while the extended post–World War II boom lent dramatic credence to an opposite conclusion: the less internal meddling the better. No doubt Lauck's much-belabored AAEF plans for recovery would have appeared irrelevant five years after their creation and utterly unrecognizable antiques of social thought ten years later. By Lauck's calculus, the sustained recovery, rising living standards, and heightened consumer power of the post-war years must have seemed like the right answer to the wrong question. The Angel of Plenty, whose arrival he had so ardently anticipated and championed, proved a most ungrateful guest.

Now, nearly a half-century after Lauck's death, the tables have turned again. Stretching far into the once-affluent middle classes, American living standards regularly stumble and fall. A fiercely competitive international economy, accompanied by neoliberal principles, has largely consigned Keynesian liberalism —and with it much of organized labor's accumulated strength—to the historical scrapheap. And just as the Great Depression only temporarily opened a window for a labor-state alliance, so the postwar boom's socially conciliatory politics has met its temporal end. Indeed, the moment may have arrived for a reexamination of the social-democratic project built in a time of economic pain and scarcity. In an era when capital investment regularly crosses borders in search of cheaper labor markets, when downsizing and concession bargaining define a downward spiral of income and benefits for employees, might not Lauck's call for minimum living standards, controls on investment capital, and even an "economic United Nations" carry renewed relevance? Might social-economic stagnation combined with the "death of Communism" reinvigorate international left-liberal alternatives? If so, an alliance of popular forces and reform-minded intellectuals may again play a vital role in public affairs. Yet if such far-flung changes are to carry any realistic potential, they will have to rely on another change to which Lauck gave relatively little thought. Democratic ends must be supported by democratic institution-building. After all, when abundance finally arrived for the great mass of the American people, it proved a frail reed upon which to perch a democratic culture. Will it be different next time?

8 Teaching the People

Wil Lou Gray and the Siren of Educational Opportunity

They wish to make cheap the business of *learning to read*, if that business be performed in their schools; and thus inveigle the children of poor men into those schools; and there to teach those children, along with reading, all those notions which *calculated to make them content in a state of slavery.*

—William Cobbett

Enlighten the people generally, and tyranny and oppressions of body and mind will vanish like spirits at the dawn of the day.

—Thomas Jefferson

O NE MIGHT think that two women spearheaded the movement for literacy among textile workers and other adult poor in early-twentieth-century South Carolina. The first was an agent of upper-class paternalism, in league with mill owners, who attempted at once to tame the wild and unruly lower classes and provide for a more efficient labor force. A representative of the cultural wing of scientific management, she feared a vulgar democracy and sought to develop a middle-class morality among her lower-class "children" with a regimen that combined school attendance, teeth-brushing, a daily change of underwear, and good work habits.

The other reformer drew inspiration from much more radical democratic sources. Comparing her own initiatives with those of the Danish Folk School movement and even the labor-centered Bryn

Mawr Summer School, she drew on yearnings for an active citizenry fostered by her Columbia University professor, James Harvey Robinson, in translating scientific knowledge to a lay public. Challenging the regressive laissez-faire policies of race-baiting southern politicians, she crusaded for a strong government role in economic and social welfare, anticipating (and later endorsing) the interventionist state of the New Deal. Working within tight budgetary and political limits, this closet revolutionary determined to free working-class women in particular from the shackles of domestic as well as economic and religious tyranny. Operating within a Jim Crow social order, she went to great lengths to establish schools for the black as well as the white working poor. Among her disciples was one of the state's pioneer civil rights organizers.

The challenge for the historian is that both reformers inhabited the same character, Wil Lou Gray (1883–1984). The same person— the same practice—seems to have been simultaneously an agent of liberation on the one hand and control on the other. The analytical puzzle offered in this single case, moreover, reflects a larger analytical tension affecting historians' treatment of American progressive reform in general and education issues in particular: Can professionals be accountable to democratic ideals? Is schooling (as Thomas Jefferson believed) a basic agent of popular liberty, or is it more often designed (as William Cobbett feared) to make its working-class students "content in a state of slavery"? The case of one southern literacy reformer thus treads on ever-uncertain relations between the intentions of reformers and intellectuals on the one hand and the aspirations and experience of those to be educated on the other.

IN SEVERAL respects Wil Lou Gray, born in 1883 in Laurens, South Carolina, fits the profile of the Progressive Era female reformer. Intelligent and quick-witted, of upper-class means and devoutly Protestant background, strongly influenced by her father (her mother died when she was ten years old) and unmarried, she dedicated herself from early on to a social vocation.[1] Broadly speaking, the issues to which Gray responded fall under the category of what some historians have labeled social Progressivism, a "configuration of humanitarian causes" relating to public health, family welfare, and education, issues "long identified with the sphere of women."[2] A 1903 graduate of Methodist-endowed Columbia College, she first prepared for a teaching career with summer school courses from Winthrop College, the state's normal school for women, before undertaking an assignment in a one-room country school. This demanding and somewhat frustrating experience led her back to graduate school, first as a student of English literature for one year at Vanderbilt University and then at Columbia University in New York, where she earned a master's degree in political economy, taking courses in European history with James Harvey Robinson, Victorian literature with Ashley Horace Thorndike, and American political history with William A. Dunning, under whom she wrote an admiring thesis on political philosopher J. C. Hurd, a northern defender of southern states rights theories.[3] Something of the stimulus of her graduate education was evident a full half-century later when, after a lecture by a visiting historian, she commented, "I haven't had such a thrill since I left Vanderbilt and Columbia Universities. It was a big view of history and a plea that we recognize we were a part of the world and that change was inevitable."[4]

Exactly when Wil Lou Gray adopted her own crusade for social change is unclear. Initially she returned from New York intending to teach history in a college setting. Family expectations of a woman's proper role, however, prevailed upon her to accept an appointment as supervisor of Laurens County rural schools. As she later remembered it, her uncle appealed to her, asking, "Why not *make* history? You can do that here in Laurens County."[5] In recounting the sources of her educational commitments, Gray variously cited an employee of her father who was unable to sign his name, an English professor at Vanderbilt who challenged her by asking how many poor people lived in each student's home town, and an inspiring, standing-room-only lecture in Nashville by the leading African-American educator of the period, Booker T. Washington.[6] It was sometime during her Columbia University studies that Gray most likely had first learned about the Danish residential "folk schools" for adult learners (most likely from one of her instructors, educational reformer James Harvey Robinson)—a concept that she would also list as an influence on her own later projects.[7]

Whatever her initial impetus, basic adult education soon became Wil Lou Gray's lifelong cause and career. Her characteristic approach to the field was established early on. Among her responsibilities in Laurens County was direction of a night school in Young's Township, which served a largely illiterate population of white tenant farmers and small landowners. From the beginning, Gray brought enthusiasm and a thirst for both professional respectability and cultural uplift to her task. In her first class, for example, she showed stereopticon pictures of Yellowstone Park. At the county fair she led her students in a rendition of a song she had taught them: "Day school, day school / Take a back seat! / Night school, night school / Got them far beat!" In addition, Gray arranged for all county teachers to attend National Education Association meetings in Washington, D.C., and effectively made NEA membership a requirement for employment in the county.[8] Dwindling state expenditures for education drew Gray briefly back to Columbia University, then to an appointment as superintendent of rural schools in Montgomery County, Maryland.[9] By this time, however, she had already established herself as one of the busy spirits of reform in a state that was about to undergo a brief springtime of progressive reform fervor.

Just how progressive (or genuinely democratic and broadly empowering) were the type of reforms to which Wil Lou Gray contributed remains in dispute. Even at a national level, social progressivism (particularly as contrasted with earlier Populist and antimonopoly movements) is generally portrayed as a set of moderate, middle-class initiatives that did not seriously rearrange political and economic power.[10] But southern historians have tended to go even further in their suspicion of Progressive reformers' self-avowed democratic claims. In the South, perhaps more than anywhere else in the country, progressive reforms, including expanded schooling, appear to have eased the transition of an agrarian to an industrial society without seriously challenging conservative propertied interests or white supremacy.[11] In particular, according to this theory, an urban-industrial elite initiated what changes did come over not only the objections of parsimonious rural legislators but also the indifference if not outright hostility of the masses for whom the programs were aimed.[12] According to now conventional wisdom, an abiding paternalism—deriving in part from the moralism of evangelical Protestantism, from plantation tradition, from extraordinary gaps in means and education even among the region's white population—effectively divided reformers from the "alien folkways" of the region's mass public. In public health, education, and child labor reform crusades alike, social reformers shared an "impulse to uplift and a certainty of the inadequacy of the uplifted."[13]

The adult schools that began to dot the region after the turn of the century (and in which we shall rediscover Wil Lou Gray) have been easily assimilated into this model of coerced modernization. The phenomenon was most noticeable in the southern Appalachians, where a mixture of missions and social settlements began to spring up in the 1890s. The timing was tied to the "discovery" of the region by an interlocking set of developers on the one hand and philanthropic missionary-educators on the other. The latter, who included recent veterans of post–Civil War freedmen's schools, approached their new poor-white charges with the same missionary zeal once bestowed on ex-slaves. Just as had occurred among the freed people, moreover, the women schoolteachers satisfied themselves with the thought that they were exercising a generally positive, if vague, "influence" rather than solving the immediate social, economic, and political problems of their students.[14]

If education of the common folk of the mountains was in the hands of a patronizing gentility, the process applied to the piedmont millworkers, according to recent revisionist historians, was no less condescending but perhaps even more directly exploitative. As the new scholarship documents, the mill owners supported such schools as an agent for improvement and discipline over their operatives, even as the schools encountered a fiercely resistant traditional culture. The native southern white working class, argues historian I. A. Newby, typically "didn't believe in education." Drawing on early anthropological contrasts between primitive and modern peoples, Newby distinguishes between the plain folk's desire to transmit traditional knowledge to their children and the modernist educators' to create something new. The sensibility of the modern educator, Newby approvingly quotes Margaret Mead, was inspired by "the will to teach, convert, colonize, or assimilate out-groups"; in such circumstances schooling "involves a sort of deliberate violence to other people's developed personalities."[15] Where education was experienced as a kind of cultural assault upon its subjects, it is no wonder that the subjects themselves did not fare well in the eyes of the educated. Truancy, for example, was rife in the mill villages of South Carolina, and school performance was so poor that standardized tests administered in the 1920s found an overwhelming majority of mill children either "feeble-minded" or "dull," "below average" in basic intelligence.[16]

In South Carolina, issues of education and development came dramatically to a head during the first two decades of the twentieth century. The first serious educational initiatives coincided with a significant socioeconomic transformation centered on the rise of the textile industry. From a mere 2,000 employees in 1880, the mill population grew to nearly 50,000 operatives by 1920, with nearly a sixth of the state workforce situated in concentrated mill villages.[17] The creation of mill districts within larger cities of the state especially attracted attention, drawing a population from a previously remote and scattered hinterland into direct contact with the commercial centers. Within the capital city of Columbia alone, four mills sprang up by 1900. That the new workforce was young (a majority under twenty-five) and more than one-third female added to the exoticism and unsettling quality of the industrializing moment. Popular impression had it that the mills formed a catch basin for an economically displaced and socially disorderly white population—a mixture of failed yeomen farmers, anarchic mountaineers, and congenitally poor "white trash."[18] In short, South Carolina offered plenty of raw material for those intent on cultural modernization. In 1910, over one-quarter of the population aged ten and older was listed as illiterate by census takers, the second worst percentage in the nation next to Louisiana. Over the course of the following two decades, despite some material improvement, the state actually fell further, into the lowest position in the union.[19]

Initially the institutional responses to the crisis were local and private. As early as the mid-1890s, Winthrop College teachers volunteered their time to instruct millworkers at Rock Hill; more than a decade later, with support from the Winthrop faculty, the city school superintendent, and an availing mill owner, a well-function-ing Rock Hill Night School was in place. An even more elaborate effort was that led by Julia Selden, an independently wealthy schoolteacher from Spartanburg, who set up evening instruction for millworkers in fifteen schools across the county beginning in 1910.[20] Another step was the Textile Industrial Institute, also in Spartanburg, which allowed alternation of schoolwork and work in a "model" mill setting.[21] Established in 1911 by David English Camak, a young Methodist minister, the Textile Institute attempted to save what Camak believed was a noble race of Anglo-Saxon mountaineers from the threat of barbarism. As he would later explain, "The human society, for whose well-being I lived and worked, seemed slipping into the sea, and I was sick with the slush of it."[22] The most ambitious private educational effort in the state, however, did not take root until the mid-1920s, when Greenville industrialist Thomas Fleming Parker, combining Deweyite rhetoric of child-centered learning and the efficiency-mindedness of scientific management, laid out plans for both youth and adult instruction among millworkers through high school in what would become the Parker School District.[23]

It was not mere cultural embarrassment, however, that caused the state's polite society to begin to focus attention on its untutored masses. Fear of social disorder also surfaced, especially in the wake of the political success of Cole L. Blease, two-term governor (1911–1915) and U.S. senator (1924–1930), who for many epitomized the threat of ignorance and envy combined into uncontrollable social rage. A disciple of "Pitchfork" Ben Tillman's 1890s populist—and racist—attacks against the state's old low-country aristocracy, Blease gave voice to the feelings of alienation among the expanding white millworker constituency toward the state's urban commercial elite. Inveighing against urbanites who sneered at the plain people of the state, educators and child labor reformers who would "interfere" with the rights of parents to manage their own children, and "uppity niggers," Blease ran on a platform of lower taxes and the right to be "left alone."[24] In practice, the combination of his "negative" government (he regularly vetoed levies or regulatory authority for compulsory school attendance, universities, factory inspections, and public health examinations), generous pardons of convicts, and fiery attacks on black civil rights (including open condonation of lynching) utterly polarized state politics and made "Bleasism" a code word in genteel circles for mob rule.[25] The atmosphere surrounding national mobilization for the Great War only enhanced sectional alarms, as fears about new weapons of mass propaganda together with appalling statistics regarding the illiteracy of U.S. conscripts invigorated calls for state action. William Davis Melton, state chairman of the wartime Four-Minute Men and future president of the University of South Carolina, thus identified the illiteracy problem in 1921 as "appalling and fraught with the gravest dangers . . . No taxation levied for educational purposes is too high . . . The masses must be educated."[26]

As a middle-class response to both social and political crises of industrialism, state-centered educational initiatives first blossomed in South Carolina under the progressive governorship of Richard I. Manning (1915–1919). Compulsory school attendance (1915), a limited hours bill for child labor (1916), a minimum age of fourteen for factory work (1916), and the first state appropriations for night schools (two-fifths of which went to mill villages) established an agenda for an active governmental role in the state's industrial and social development.[27] Governor Manning also placed the state imprimatur on adult educational efforts. The governor's appointment of a state illiteracy commission further united university educators with a host of men and women drawn from philanthropy, church work, and women's clubs.

Among these shock troops of South Carolina progressivism was Wil Lou Gray. Already established as an articulate exponent of the educational crusade, she was undoubtedly well versed in the Bleasite threat; indeed her uncle, Nathaniel Barksdale Dial, challenged and defeated Blease for the U.S. Senate nomination (and sure election in the one-party state) in 1918, the same year she was recruited as field secretary to the illiteracy commission.[28] Quickly her appointment was elevated to that of State Supervisor of Adult Schools, a position she would hold until 1946.[29]

Gray would preside over a jerry-built structure of four related programs: "lay-by" schools set up in rural districts while crops were maturing in July or August; "continuation schools," evening classes taught as a supplement by day school teachers for teenage mill operatives; special "all-time schools" endowed by joint state-

Wil Lou Gray (fourth from left) and the South Carolina Illiteracy Commission, 1918. (South Carolina Archives)

millowner arrangements to support a full-time adult educator / social worker with a curriculum ranging from literacy to cleanliness and budget-making; and Gray's self-created summer boarding sessions or "opportunity schools," geared to adults seventeen and older with no more than a fifth grade education.[30] Vast in ambition, Gray's projects were carried out on a shoestring budget; state funding for literacy programs as a whole grew from $5,000 to $50,000 across the commission's first decade of operations.[31]

From the beginning, South Carolina's literacy campaign was incorporated into the larger goals of the state's progressive reformers for economic productivity on the one hand and social cooperation on the other. Adult school classes thus taught the three R's in a context of broader socialization in utilitarian virtues and religious piety, with emphasis on health habits and work habits, church attendance and Bible reading, civics, domestic science, and arts and crafts. Students in a men's advanced arithmetic class, for example, studied the application of figures to textile calculations in carding, spinning, and weaving, and were introduced to taxes, savings accounts, and insurance. Women computed domestic purchases, kept household accounts, and learned the rules of a balanced diet, proper table settings, and the like. At a typical commencement, the female graduate would cross the stage in a dress that she had made herself while the teacher announced its cost and materials.[32]

Appealing to the heart as well as the head, Gray's curricula regularly set aside time for organized play and outdoor singing, including familiar songs typically rearranged to address school themes. For example, to the tune of "Keep the Home Fires Burning" were sung the following lyrics:

> Keep the night oil burning
> Keep the pages turning
> Keep the adults yearning
> Thinking for knowledge rules . . .

The following would be sung to the tune of "Battle Hymn of the Republic":

> We've all attended Adult School
> We've learned to read and write
> We have overcome the darkness
> And the new way seems so bright
> We want to help our fellowman
> To do the thing that's right—
> To join the Adult School.[33]

In 1927, Gray summarized the larger social messages communicated in the adult school curriculum in a compendium of her writings entitled *Elementary Studies in Civics*. Self-discipline, thrift, hard work, and conscientious citizenship, she made clear, were her developmental goals; proper manners, or responsible deportment in every area of life, the first means to get there. "Just as we have laws about driving," she wrote, "we have customs about how to treat people and to act in company . . . A well bred people follow these customs . . . A person who considers the feelings of others is a gentleman. A person who won't learn, who giggles at church, who wears too loud clothes, who talks too loud on the street is just common. That is why he is called a *Nobody*. Be a *Somebody*."[34] Manners, in Wil Lou Gray's gentle but carefully catalogued world, applied equally at the table, in the home, at public gatherings, at work, and in the schools.[35]

Gray's curriculum, moreover, intended to support established authority both in the state and in civil society. A citizenship quiz, for example, included the questions "Do I work regularly and loyally?" "Do I pay or do I borrow?" "Do I pay my taxes gladly and honestly?"[36] The fact that students depended on scholarships, loans, or at least release time from their employers to attend Opportunity Schools clearly handed their bosses considerable discretionary power over their workers' deportment, both on the job and outside it.[37] One cooperating owner promised "everybody in his mill half [in scholarship money] of what they will save."[38] The superintendent of the Riverside Mills in Anderson endorsed the schools on the basis that "of the young men we sent to these schools, three have risen to the position of section men in their respective rooms while one has been made night overseer since his return."[39] The routine of the Opportunity School itself was geared to socialization of students into a world of effort, self-control, study, and supervised play. Every waking hour was carefully accounted for, with no fewer than nine bells dividing each day.[40]

Manners equipped Wil Lou Gray's students to reach out to a larger world, literally as well as figuratively.[41] Drawing inspiration from her own European travel in 1913, Gray quickly grafted an annual group "pilgrimage" to the state capitol in Columbia or the historic sites of Charleston (and occasionally Washington, D.C., or New York City) to the curriculum of the Opportunity Schools.[42] Appealing for cooperation from the military head of Charleston's Fort Moultrie, for example, Gray explained that her students "have never seen the ocean, ridden on it, or have any idea what a fort is like."[43] Such trips openly aimed to instill respect for the traditions of the state and its great men—from early colonial fathers through Revolutionary heroes such as Francis Marion and Charles Pinckney to southern statesmen such as John C. Calhoun. The trips also served to put on public display the lessons of literacy, understanding, and behavior that had been practiced for weeks. In preparation for the Charleston excursion of 1928, for example, lessons were devoted to How to Get Money for Trip (including "cutting out nonessentials and getting extra work"), What to Wear and Take (including "the suitcase question—sharing it with friends"), and Hotel Conduct (where students acted out in advance such issues as "registering," "eating politely," and "toothpicks and chewing gum").[44]

As a behavioral prescription, South Carolina's literacy crusade shared fundamental assumptions with the "Americanization" campaign adopted toward immigrant workers in northern cities during World War I. War fever had raised alarm bells across the nation about a culturally underequipped, ill-educated, and potentially disloyal population. A massive English-language literacy campaign sponsored by the Bureau of Naturalization, for example, aimed at nothing less than remaking the adult student immigrant into a 100 percent American. As in South Carolina, the lessons of citizenship for the immigrant, according to historian John F. McClymer, involved not only the "meaning of the ballot" but "an American way to brush his teeth, an American way to clean his fingernails, and an American way to air out his bedding."[45]

By some measures, Wil Lou Gray was a perfect exemplar of the bourgeois modernizer. She willingly aligned herself with the progressive, anti-Bleasite section of the Democratic Party, boasting in 1922 that "27,000 ignorant, prejudiced creatures have been transformed into enlightened, thinking men and women" and anticipating the end of a time "when political demagogues swayed men and women too ignorant to form their own opinions."[46] To support her schools, Gray appealed instinctively to the state's commercial classes, soliciting scholarship funds for needy students from bankers, industrialists, and storeowners on the one hand and the American Legion, United Daughters of the Confederacy, and the state's Baptist and Methodist churches and conferences on the other. Her Opportunity School was initially supported by a $1,000 donation from sympathetic millowner J. P. Gossett, matching the state appropriation for the project.[47]

Not surprisingly, the South Carolina literacy campaign was also racially coded. While the state generally lagged far behind the rest of the country in education and social welfare expenditure, it had all but neglected public provisions for its African-American citizenry, who made up 51 percent of the state's population in 1920. The first legislative contribution to black schools did not come until 1919. And if state pensions to Civil War veterans had proved a major, if primitive, source of social insurance since the latter decades of the nineteenth century, the first state pensions for blacks in South Carolina, awarded in 1923, went only to faithful ex-slaves who had rendered special service to the Confederacy.[48] Colored institutions received only one-tenth of the state night school budget in 1928, while enrolling nearly one-quarter of all night school students.[49] In short, it fit the dominant political temper of the state that Wil Lou Gray's first Opportunity School was established at the blue-blooded Daughters of American Revolution school in Tamassee, that no blacks were invited to attend in its first decade of operation (and after that only in occasional, segregated sessions), and, perhaps most tellingly, that the selected slogan for the groundbreaking 1920 campaign was "Let South Carolina Secede from Illiteracy!"[50]

But racial exclusion was not the only conservative aspect of the state's adult education campaign. Like earlier moral crusades against drinking, the campaigns of the South Carolina Illiteracy Commission sought support from the substantial burghers of the state by openly invoking the specter of social breakdown, a threat to the security of stable republican homes, families, and communities. The wartime atmosphere of national mobilization against powerful enemies and the accompanying Red Scare undoubtedly accentuated a martial spirit exemplified in a 1918 recruiting speech for the commission, which declared that America "in her battle for universal love, liberty, and light is waging a war against barbarism, brutality, and blackness."[51] The implicit racial hierarchy in such rhetorical injunctions did not impede literacy reformers from declaring war on the "backwardness" of their own nearby *white* social hinterland. The superintendent of the Spartanburg city schools thus reported to Wil Lou Gray a conversation with the wife of a soldier stationed at nearby Camp Wadsworth: "She says that last night her husband was late getting into camp. He was challenged by a sentinel—a Dago— who could not read his pass. The sentinel submitted it to two white American soldiers, neither of whom could read it. Then he called in a Negro soldier who read the pass for them."[52] While personally condemning anti-Red riots, Wil Lou Gray warned in 1920 that "the state now faces the question of either providing sufficient funds for the education of the illiterate . . . or run the risk of having doctrines similar to the IWW [Industrial Workers of the World] permeate a large percent of our people. Is it not expedient to prevent an evil rather than to permit it to develop?"[53]

In the eyes of reformers, illiteracy implied not only a want of specific intellectual skills but more general backwardness. A teacher whom Wil Lou Gray had recruited to conduct an adult school in Hampton wrote discouragingly in 1922,

> I remember your illustrations . . . on illiteracy . . . Here is another for you—giving babies nine woodlice in a teaspoon-ful of honey for yellow jaundice and gun powder out of shells for whooping cough. It is done right here among my neighbors, two miles from the county seat—a few hours ride from our state capitol . . . There is not a single club or charitable organization in this community. All the people being Primitive Baptist, and absolutely opposed to anything of the kind. Does that give you an inkling of what I struggle against?[54]

At worst, impatience with the conduct of the lower classes degenerated into the crudest social engineering. One night school teacher, appalled by such students as the mother of ten who carried a sixteen-month-old baby to school and worried about a further pregnancy, believed that "a Birth-Control Act or Sterilization Law as well as Compulsory School Attendance law for this class would not be too much. I often think of Dr. Morse's statement—'they know nothing to do, and have nothing to do, and have nothing to think of, except to breed like rabbits'—true that is in many cases. Sadly true too for they are *liabilities* to any community rather than *assets.*"[55] In general, both benevolence and embarrassment were registered by reformers in their determination to stamp out the saying "As illiterate as South Carolina."[56]

It would be a mistake, however, to treat Wil Lou Gray's literacy campaigns simply as an ideological defense of southern industrial capitalism, the preparation of a new labor force, or a kind of forced march from peasant communalism to possessive individualism. Notwithstanding the paternalist gloss of all Progressive Era "protectionist" measures, and the particular political constraints in the South respecting both employer power and white supremacy, Gray's initiatives should also be seen as part of a more democratic reform tradition linking her to other contemporary intellectuals and educators. That she and her associates were self-conscious "modernizers" is indisputable but insufficient as an analytical framework on at least two counts. First, the term suggests a singular pathway toward an industrial- consumerist society, and neglects the inner conflicts of political-institutional development. Second, this conventional formulation assumes a sharp dichotomy between a passive (if not openly resistant) public and the enlightened (if not utterly arrogant and even imperialistic) reformer. Both assumptions deserve critical scrutiny.[57]

In her own mind Wil Lou Gray's literacy programs were linked early on to a vision of an activist state quite out of step with the politics of South Carolina's powers that be. The political lesson to be drawn from such a perspective was evident in the First Southeastern Conference on Adult Education, sponsored by the Illiteracy Committee of the National Education Association and hosted by Gray at the Columbia, South Carolina, YMCA in 1919. The conference closed with a resolution backing the Smith-Towner Bill, which authorized a federal department of education and aid to public school systems as a matter of "simple justice to every American."[58] It need hardly be said that such a message ran counter not only to the demagogic anti-establishment appeals of a Cole Blease but also to the parsimony of much of the state elite toward general welfare expenditures.

The most immediate conflict concerned money for expanded adult education programs. Gray fought recurrent battles with legislators and recalcitrant employers over the rights and access of poor people to basic educational opportunity. She complained to an out-of-state friend in 1922 about state legislators "entertaining themselves by cutting out many of our appropriations for public schools . . . I don't feel that our State will ever progress very much until as a State we value education, are willing to pay for it and thus give our children a chance."[59] Her reliance on mill owners to finance adult programs, moreover, led her to running arguments with individual industrialists as well as the Cotton Manufacturers' Association, who complained by the mid-twenties that "the corporations are being taxed too much for philanthropy" and by 1930 that "progressive programs, unwarranted by the business outlook" were bleeding the productive citizenry dry.[60] In short, common commitment to the modernization of the South hid significant differences between the intentions of regional elites and those of intellectual reformers. Perhaps Gray herself did not recognize the chasm of region or class interest that historians have clearly demarcated between "moral reformers" on the one hand and "social justice" or "social welfare" Progressives on the other.[61]

Gray's vision of expansive democratic government was perhaps best exemplified in the adult education curriculum itself. Her civics text, for example, went to great lengths to identify ongoing and potential uses of state authority. Following a list of activities that included factory inspection, public health supervision, police protection, water conservation, and bank and securities regulation, Gray asked her students rhetorically, "How many of these things could you have if you had to arrange and pay for them by yourself? Could you: Build your own colleges? Examine your own drinking water? Build your own highways? . . . Examine merchants' scales to see if they were honest?"[62] Even more distant subject matter was suffused with the same social lessons. "Arithmetic," Gray explained, "is socialized for opportunity students in problems of family and personal budgeting, . . . health studies are related to community sanitation as well as to personal hygiene. And so throughout the school program, whether the subject taught be history or cooking or sewing, or carpentering—it is all to one purpose, the making of better citizens, more useful to themselves and to their State, and happier in their homes and private lives."[63] A lesson plan Gray commissioned entitled "Lessons in Democracy," while stressing the "mutual interest" of labor and capital, openly endorsed labor organization and social legislation as corrective measures.[64] Altogether, the adult education paradigm had likely imbibed something of what Gray's own teacher James Harvey Robinson in 1921 called "education for citizenship," an end he contrasted to "personal worldly success or personal culture."[65] Although Gray was less openly confrontational with business-centered power and culture than her teacher, who had gravitated to the radical New School for Social Research, she, like him, was helping to set the terms for the legitimation of the progressive state.

And indeed, Gray proved an enthusiastic supporter of expansive social welfare initiatives at both the state and federal level. As early as 1934 she was encouraging a favorite student to enter an essay-writing contest with the theme the "accomplishments of the New Deal."[66] Nor was the attachment merely abstract; her Opportunity School programs depended in the thirties on scholarship monies funneled through the Federal Emergency Relief Administration.[67] By the late thirties, she was openly calling on the state's women's clubs and parent-teacher school associations to take the lead in convening public discussion meetings on "education, health, social and economic conditions, and government." But, she warned, "Merely sponsoring a meeting to arouse public sentiment will mean little unless plans be so carefully laid that community study and action will follow."[68] Perhaps most significant in this respect, Gray formed both a strategic and a personal friendship with Olin D. Johnston—himself an ex-millworker educated by Rev. Camak's Textile Industrial Institute—who beat Cole Blease for the governorship in 1934. In addition to open support of labor unions and New Deal worker rights measures, Johnston (with help from the moderately progressive young legislator and former school superintendent Strom Thurmond, whom Wil Lou Gray had earlier befriended) signed notable education measures, including an expansion of the school term, a raise in teacher salaries, and a textbook rental bill.[69]

From the 1930s on, in fact, Wil Lou Gray judged her compatriots by the standards of a New Deal Democrat in the mold of a Frances Perkins.[70] Late in life she looked back and deplored the desertion of many conservative South Carolinians from the Democratic Party standard, beginning with Thurmond and the Dixiecrats in 1948. In 1960 she wrote to a friend, "It pleases me to note that you have not deserted the Democratic Party and that, after all, you are Americans. I cannot understand the rush to the Republican Party for if I have observed affairs correctly in South Carolina we made little progress in the state until Roosevelt came to office and gave us a new social philosophy which embraced not just the top level of our society but made an effort to raise all levels. I can't see how anyone can call that socialism."[71] In correspondence with her family in the same era, Gray made clear the passion of her own continuing commitments. "When I receive my social security and retirement checks, I feel I must do some service for I am so grateful for these programs and I am always realizing that many who worked just as diligently as I were not under covered employment. I hope to live to see the day where all [will] be under some type of covered work. It seems wrong that only we [who] have had the best advantages or are naturally endowed with many talents which make us strong get the breaks." As state director of the Senior Citizens of America at age seventy-nine in 1962, Wil Lou Gray remained an activist, this time for Medicare, for which she even appeared on television to debate an American Medical Association opponent.[72]

In addition to social welfare issues, Wil Lou Gray broke with her more conventional contemporaries in two other areas worthy of mention. First, the cause of women's rights and uplift of women's general social standing was part and parcel of her literacy crusade. While she may have adopted a deferential tone obligatory for a southern woman in political spaces, her correspondence suggests that she was acutely aware of the limitations that gender imposed on her. In one of her yearly battles with the legislature for the funding of her programs, she complained, "You see I am just a woman and regardless of training, twelve months active work and long hours running into the night I am not worth what men are to the State. Twenty years from now that will not be the case but that is the penalty I must pay for being born in the early eighties."[73] Ample evidence suggests that Gray recognized her own striving for self-respect as a woman in the efforts of many of those in the adult schools. Though demand from male family members in the mill villages quickly convinced her to include men in the Opportunity Schools, she nevertheless maintained a special connection to her original subjects, whom she labeled "my girls."[74] Indeed, Gray's devotion to women's empowerment as well as social welfare was evident in her 1937 appeal to Eleanor Roosevelt to run for President in 1940.[75]

Second, Wil Lou Gray betrayed little personal sign of prejudice or racial double standard. On the contrary, even while operating under the strict segregation of a Jim Crow culture, she eagerly embraced contacts with black educators. Gray complained, for example, in 1925 that state educational efforts among Negroes were being "forced out" due to demands from whites for the same resources. With help from the Jeanes Fund, the Rosenwald Foundation, and a battery of volunteer black teachers, Gray helped to coordinate separate black night school classes beginning in the late twenties. The result was astounding. Representing only 24 percent of total state night school enrollment as late as 1928, a black enrollment of 37,800 students accounted for over two-thirds the entire state enrollment in 1930.[76] One black community even proposed to name their school after Wil Lou Gray.[77]

A breakthrough of another kind for black education was the Carnegie Study conducted at Clemson College and the nearby Seneca Institute, a Negro Baptist Junior College (the first formal Opportunity School for blacks) in the summer of 1931. A Carnegie Corporation grant brought noted reading scholar William S. Gray, "father of the basal reader," from the University of Chicago and Yale psychologist J. W. Tilton together with Wil Lou Gray to test the learning ability of a selected group of black and white adults under the unique circumstances of the Opportunity School.[78] Although the overall literacy gains of the test group, both black and white, were only moderate (for beginners progress at the four-week-long adult session was the equivalent of three to four months of primary grade school children), the differences between the races were minimal (3.9 months' progress for whites; 3.4 months' gain for blacks), "statistically not significant," according to the coauthored study.[79] That the black students, who on average were twenty years older than their white counterparts and who were judged "seriously handicapped at the beginning of the term by eyestrain or poorly adjusted glasses," achieved nearly equal educational gains openly impressed the researchers as "a credit to their zeal, to their teachers, and to the unprejudiced effort made by . . . Miss Wil Lou Gray."[80] Further evidence suggests that Wil Lou Gray's own interest in black educational achievement was more than coldly clinical. The official chronicle of Columbia's venerable Washington Square Methodist Church, for example, cites Gray's personal invitation (over considerable protest) of black educator and church leader Mary McLeod Bethune to address a Sunday evening service.[81]

Perhaps the most significant, if symbolic, message to the state's black adult students was sent by their inclusion in the 1930s in Wil Lou Gray's famous pilgrimage tours. In one such venture on an April Sunday in 1935, some 4,000 black South Carolinians gathered on the steps of the Capitol in Columbia. Outwardly the proceedings were tame enough; following the itinerary of their white counterparts on the previous weekend, the students visited the gravesites of a few of the state's great white men (including that of "Redeemer Governor" Wade Hampton), then paused on the steps of the Capitol before entering to sign the statehouse register as a symbolic act of literacy. Although the black visitors, unlike the whites before them, were not personally received by the governor, they were greeted by the state superintendent of education and Wil Lou Gray herself before attending a special group pageant under the theme "Vanguards of Our Race," which depicted notable black contributions to poetry, science, literature, and music. In this secular gathering, which was probably larger than any before the civil rights demonstrations of the 1960s, one wonders what silent as well as public lessons participants drew about their own rights of citizenship. The very assemblage of this well-dressed, well-disciplined black crowd on the Capitol steps as they prepared for a name-signing ritual, which for

An estimated 5,000 African-American Opportunity School students on the steps of the State House in Columbia, South Carolina, in 1937, before they signed their names on the register inside. (South Carolina Archives)

whites signaled political enfranchisement, must surely have triggered powerful emotions. Pilgrimage guest speaker Dr. C. H. Tobias,
an African-American representative from the YMCA executive
council in New York, commented to the 1935 Columbia assemblage
that he was aware of "no record of a similar occasion anywhere."[82]

On balance, Gray's actions with regard to racial issues must be regarded as progressive but not crusading. Her actions in the changing and contentious climate of the 1940s are perhaps most revealing. Initially proposing two all-year Opportunity Schools, one white
and one black, she acceded to the priorities of state legislators when
only a Caucasian school was funded (a decision that prompted a
legal remonstrance from the state NAACP). She weakly defended
such discrimination on grounds that most black students could better afford night school than the residential Opportunity program. At
the same time, however, Gray disassociated herself from the dead-
end segregationists in South Carolina politics, urging acceptance of
a 1947 ruling that blacks be admitted to the Democratic Party primary. As she wrote to a friend, "We have fought one war and lost;
why attempt to fight another? . . . I am sure that there are many of
us who are tired of trying to justify the situation in our state."[83] Like
other southern white liberals, Wil Lou Gray sought to dispatch with
the race issue—out of fatigue and embarrassment as well as principle—in order to attend to the rest of her agenda.

The mixed message embodied in Wil Lou Gray's educational practice—on the one hand emphasizing social control and discipline, on
the other implying social criticism and transformation—reflects
what many have seen as a classic ambivalence at the heart of
American progressivism. The assumptions built into progressive
measures, especially those geared to the uplift or education of the
lower classes, make it difficult, if not impossible, to separate the
wheat of enlightenment from the chaff of paternalism in the policies of early-twentieth-century liberal reformers. The unblinking
optimism of such an outlook, particularly the refusal to admit difference of interests along class lines, is well recognized as a corner-
stone of "American exceptionalism," an enduring feature of popular as well as social science thought.[84] In the case of adult education
reform, the ambivalent trajectory of American exceptionalism ran
through Denmark.

Wil Lou Gray was only one of many adult education and literacy leaders in the 1920s and early 1930s who looked to the Danish folk school as a successful model for reviving the poor and illiterate regions of the American South. Even in very free translation, the Danish model was a peculiar blend of innovative and traditional elements. Rejecting the prevailing system of elitist, Latin formal schooling, the liberal Lutheran theologian, educator, and nationalist poet Bishop Nikolai Grundtvig (1783–1872) inspired the folk high schools *(folkhochschulen)* as short-term adult institutions with both a religious and secular-nationalist mission. Spreading out across the countryside, Grundtvig's disciples extolled nature, the simple life, the inner light, and spiritual harmony—a pietistic emphasis enhanced by a homelike atmosphere established by the wives of the Danish male teachers. Not surprisingly, contemporary American observers took less interest in the sectarian aspects of the schools than in a pedagogy conducted in "pure Danish," steeped in Nordic myths, and emphasizing oral communication, especially singing, which was said to have a "democratic empowering effect on the peasants."[85] Government-financed but administered by local boards of trustees, the folk school fit into a spreading pattern of twentieth-century Danish community welfare institutions that included pensions, health and unemployment insurance, and producer cooperatives. Some early American adherents clearly struggled to make this "Danish socialism" as palatable as possible to a trans-Atlantic audience. University of North Carolina education professor Edgar Wallace Knight, for example, summed up Danish social arrangements as a perfect example of "protection through self-help."[86] Olive Dame Campbell, who followed the wishes of her late husband in establishing the John C. Campbell Folk School in the North Carolina Blue Ridge directly on the Danish model in 1925 similarly took pains to contrast the Danish vision—"a socialism not incompatible with private ownership and with a state church or at least with recognition of Christianity"—with "the Marxian philosophy imported from Germany."[87]

Although the South Carolina Opportunity Schools, like the Campbell School, eschewed the ambitious linkage between education and a worker-peasant political alliance common to latter-day developments in Denmark, the elements of Wil Lou Gray's schools did match the original Grundtvig formula to a remarkable degree. While extending the target population from the depressed country-side to the industrial enclaves of the textile mills, Gray followed the Danish script in offering varied programs of informal training and instruction that provided at once for the social, moral, and personal needs of the students. Like the Danish schools, moreover, the Opportunity Schools in their teachings combined religious inspiration with national and community pride. A female staff and her own maternal nurturing similarly stressed a homelike atmosphere, and the emphasis on demonstration (borrowed from contemporary home economics curricula) as well as group singing and other morale-boosting exercises reproduced many of the distinct features of the classic Danish folk school model.[88]

It is true, however, that the Danish model of adult education had far more radical interpreters than Wil Lou Gray, and these other exponents of the folk school pedagogy provide a position from which the Opportunity School model can be severely criticized. Indeed, we can still identify today a strain of working-class education that offers a different spin on the Danish folk school model. Drawing on the "cultural oasis" of his parents' homeland, social worker and labor education activist Eduard Lindeman identified two streams of adult education: an "organic," nonvocational approach that drew on working people's native wisdom and experience versus a "mechanistic" approach where the educators "bestowed their intellectual gifts on a disadvantaged but eternally grateful population."[89]

Like Lindeman, Joseph K. Hart (professor of education at Reed College, editor of *Survey Graphic,* and instructor at the New School for Social Research) made a voyage of discovery to Denmark in the 1920s. Taking Danish education as an ideal training ground for democracy, Hart posited the folk school as a kind of humanistic counterinstitution to the mass social control he associated with the standardized tests and formulas of educational psychologist Edward Thorndike. In particular, the symbiotic relationship between Danish intellectuals and rural folk contrasted sharply to what Hart saw as contemporary cultural conflicts at home:

> I talked with a village pastor about the Scopes case . . . "Such a thing could not happen with us," said this religious leader of the country-

side. "Why are you so sure of that?" I asked with some irritation. "Because we believe in ideas . . . We do not fight ideas, just as we do not fight machines: we welcome them both; we use them both; and we would just as soon think of fighting an eclipse of the sun by means of the police as we would think of fighting ideas by police power."[90]

If Hart and Lindeman set the terms for a radical-democratic interpretation of the folk school, Myles Horton's Highlander Folk School, originally established at Monteagle, Tennessee, in 1931, first realized its promise. To the emphasis on community and personal development championed by the other theorists, Horton—who had studied at the Union Theological Seminary and the University of Chicago before making his own personal pilgrimage to Denmark in 1931—added a tincture of class conflict. The result, as Horton self-consciously departed from the letter of the Danish institutions, which he felt had lost their original moral impetus, was an uncommon laboratory for social action. Indeed, once the folk school students were identified less as a primitive and disadvantaged population in need of exposure to the advantages of civilization (à la Wil Lou Gray), and less even as a community needing revitalization (Lindeman and Hart), but rather as an exploited or oppressed class for whom education would foster group awareness and empowerment, then the institution assumed a very special (as well as sometimes very precarious) place in society.[91] Beginning in the late 1950s, Highlander transferred its commitment to education as community self-awakening to the emergent black civil rights movement. Soon the "citizenship school" became an institutional fulcrum of voting rights campaigns, especially as organized by the Southern Christian Leadership Conference throughout the South.[92] By 1970, according to one estimate, "perhaps one hundred thousand blacks had become literate through Citizenship Schools," a southern adult education model that led back to Highlander in the first instance, but indirectly bore the imprint of the nineteenth-century Danish folk schools.[93]

Finally, it is worth noting that in contemporary Third World contexts, the Grundtvig-Lindeman-Horton legacy receives its most openly political expression in the "pedagogy of the oppressed" championed by Brazilian theorist Paulo Freire. In circumstances even more sharply polarized than in the civil rights South, Freire, directly drawing on his experience in the impoverished Brazilian northeast, fashioned peasant-centered literacy as communal resistance to autocratic, often dictatorial, authority.[94] "Education," according to Freireian theory, "either functions as an instrument which is used to facilitate the integration of the younger generation into the logic of the present system and bring about conformity to it, *or* it becomes 'the practice of freedom,' the means by which men and women deal critically and creatively with reality and discover how to participate in the transformation of their world."[95] In this scheme very different approaches distinguish truly "liberating" education (for example, "dialogic" and "group-centered" methods) from "oppressive" practices (for example, the "banking model" where the teacher "deposits" learning on "mere objects") that sustain the "dominant" order.[96]

Freire and his disciples find inspiration for their methods in the reactions of the students:

> When an illiterate peasant participates in this sort of educational experience, he comes to a new awareness of self, has a new sense of dignity, and is stirred by a new hope. Time and again, peasants have expressed these discoveries in striking ways after a few hours of class:
>
> - "When I started I couldn't read, but I soon realized that I needed to read and write. You can't imagine what it was like to go to Santiago to buy parts. I couldn't get orientated. I was afraid of everything . . . Now it's all different.
> - "I now realize I am a man, an educated man."
> - "Before, letters seemed like little puppets. Today they say something to me, and I can make them talk."
> - "We're so tired our heads ache, but we don't want to leave here without learning to read and write."[97]

Compare the commentaries above, noted by Freire from a self-consciously radical pedagogical framework influenced by liberation theology, to the following examples:

- "I never thought a man at thirty five years could be taught anything but I see nawr that [it] can be done."[98]
- "The young men say that the school is a Godsend to them . . .

> One man 40 years old comes about six miles at night to get the benefit of the school."[99]

- "The young wife was so pleased with her education and the improvements in her life that when her daughter, Betty Jean Elizabeth, was born, she declared that the baby 'will begin going to night school at the age of one month . . . provided she is quiet and doesn't misbehave.'"[100]

- "I learned so much that it amazes me, not from books but just common sense about living. Something about that month has inspired me to live better, work harder, and to use this head of mine for something more than just a hatrack."[101]

That this second group of expressions—so similar to Freire's collection both in its witness to educational yearning and to an accompanying sense of self-worth—derives from the South Carolina Opportunity Schools should temper our judgment of educational reformers and their projects. Is there truly an identifiable "dominant / hegemonic" pedagogy on the one hand and a "radical / democratic" formula on the other, a clear-cut conflict, in Freire's terms, between "education for domestication" and "education for liberation?"[102] If so, how shall we interpret the siren of educational opportunity—to know when it raises utterly false expectations and when it truly empowers those who heed its message? Historical assessments of educational reformers typically depend for their evidence on a formal evaluation of the *reformers'* motives and methods. What is crucially missing—whether because of inattention to or lack of evidence—are the motives and methods of the *students.* "People use literacy," Katherine F. Tinsley and Carl F. Kaestle remind us in a recent commentary, "not only for information and entertainment but also in shaping their cultural and political beliefs . . . They do so within constraints of cultural inheritance and class relationships, but individual responses to those constraints are unpredictable."[103]

South Carolina adult learners appear to have interpreted educational opportunity in diverse, if not conflicting, ways. There is ample testimony, for example, to indicate that economic mobility was both a functional stimulus and a result of literacy training. For many male workers, schooling resulted in tangible economic benefits within the mills. Of the letters of appreciation Wil Lou Gray received in 1931, for example, one read, "I have increased my wages from $8.00 to $13.00 a week" and another, "I have just been promoted to Superintendent at the number one plant at Jutson mill . . . I can never forget the benefits that I have derived from night class."[104] For others, literacy training was merely the beginning of an extended upward economic and social path. A. C. Floyd, an Opportunity School student at Erskine College in 1929, ultimately became an accountant in Alabama but never forgot the early break that allowed him to gain "cash and prestige and respect in the community."[105]

Among Gray's most distinguished alumni was James F. Miles, who became a professor of agriculture economics at Clemson University and an expert on the dairy and broiler chicken industries. Miles's story suggests the mixture of individual, familial, and outside stimuli that can account for one's receptivity to educational opportunity. James's mother, Fannie, had already learned to read and write and to value learning when her father moved the family to the Darlington mills and she became a spinner. Married at age twenty to a millhand who gambled and drank his way to death, Fannie was left with three children: her first son, who died in an auto accident at age eighteen; her daughter, who was abandoned by a husband who turned out to be already married; and a second son, James, who, Fannie wrote in a Works Progress Administration narrative in 1938, "is the one we're proud of."[106] Having dropped out of school to enter the mills at age thirteen in 1926, James rediscovered his educational interests beginning in 1929 at both night school and Opportunity School summer sessions. With direct financial help from Wil Lou Gray, he continued his schooling, first with vocational education credits at the Olympia Public School attached to the Olympia Mills in Columbia, then at C. A. Camak's Textile Industrial Institute in Spartanburg. Miles ultimately earned his bachelor's degree from the University of South Carolina and a doctorate from Cornell University.[107]

If schooling served as a necessary precondition to James Miles's economic success, it nevertheless meant more to him than a rise in occupational status. While still contemplating his own recent achievements and continuing ambitions at age twenty, he wrote Wil Lou Gray:

The Night and Opportunity Schools have certainly instilled that inspiring motive in me. It was at the first night school . . . that I learned that I did not know anything, and I would never be as big and as good as God had made it possible for me to be, unless I prepared myself . . . My reminiscence of the plesant and delightful days that I spent on the [fragrant], tree covered campus of Erskine College recalls the efforts of our devoted teachers who taught us to stand for and admire all that is high and honorable in life . . . If it be my lot not to attend school this year, I pass the flaming torch on to others. May it not flicker into darkness, but may its light guide others out of darkness as it did me [sic].[108]

Education, for Miles, meant not only a rise out of the working class but also self-discovery, or what might be called the "cultural capital needed to succeed by mainstream standards."[109]

In the case of female students, this yearning for personal improvement or social respectability was equally fervent, indeed perhaps more so for being unattached to any likely prospect for economic advance within or beyond the mill village. Teacher Verna Humphries reported from Clifton night school on her "most interesting pupil," thirty-two-year-old Bertha Wyatt, who had begun mill work at age seven, had "never gone to school a day in her life" and "didn't know one letter from another," yet now "never missed a lesson" and "refused to work unless she could keep up with her lessons."[110] On a visit to a Pickens night school in 1919, Gray took personal note of an elderly lady and her daughter: "The husband said he would whip her [the daughter] if she went, but she was there and enjoying it immensely."[111] Similarly, a Greenville alumnus of the Opportunity School wrote Gray that returning to the Anderson College campus "has been my only plans since I came home last year . . . I have worked hard all winter and have saved fifty cents each week and I am going to pay my own expenses this year . . . Mr. Gossett was real nice to us girls last year and I hope he will be the same to send some back this year."[112] Following her trip to Charleston in 1938, Annie Holcombe testified, "I enjoyed the things we saw in the museum and to tell the truth I enjoyed everything from the time I left home till I got back, for we went one way and came back another, and everything was new. I never get to go anywhere for I have to work. I have been left a widow twice so you see I have no chance to go."[113] It was likely from such encounters that Wil Lou Gray had identified the passion for schooling among the adult women of the villages as an attempt "to escape the alternatives: the mill and her home."[114]

Did such escape constitute a formula for liberation or domestication? To ask the question is to evaluate the literacy project against a gradient of class power. Much of the critical literature on the history of popular literacy and education supports the view that education is "a vehicle for social mobility," a way in which workers are "incorporated into the dominant cultural values, norms and lifestyles of the bourgeoisie . . . the seduction rather than the liberation of the working classes."[115] Little of the evidence from South Carolina openly challenges this view. To the extent that literacy changed the lives of millworkers and the rural poor, it did tend to incorporate them into a world of property, consumerism, government, and manners that respected the authority of the first three. On balance, there may well have been a conservative influence to the identities developed through state-sponsored literacy programs. A measure of cultural shame, for example, clearly figured in the motivation of the Tamassee widow who, embarrassed by the schooled accents of her own children, determined to learn "to talk proper."[116] Jewish immigrant department store owner Morris Rosenfeld of Florence, South Carolina, likewise thanked his adult education classes for acquainting him with "a true and pure Americanism": "next to my religion," he wrote Gray in 1920, "I worship our George Washington."[117] James Smith, a millworker in Anderson County, learned for the first time that he could decorate his house for Christmas even without "lots of money." With bells and crepe paper, Smith learned to transform a drab setting into one in which he could proudly invite his teachers.[118]

Yet the process of education does not fall neatly on one side or the other of the balance of class power. The report of a mill school caught in the general textile strike of 1934 is instructive. The teacher at the South Greenwood mill school wrote Wil Lou Gray that although she "could not approve of the strike," she was continuing her lessons, going from home to home and including union and nonunion members and even the overseer in her routine. All told, she reported, "I enrolled the regular number for regular time—simply because they wish to be taught."[119]

What does it tell us that notwithstanding their own teacher's prejudices, and locked out of their proper classroom, striking millworkers (as well as nonstrikers) determined to continue their education? If education was entirely an imposition from outside, who exactly was doing the imposing, and who was resisting? In the end, perhaps, the attitudes toward education among the southern working classes remain too much assumed and too little explored; the subordinated classes may have incorporated schooling into their own calculations as a good in itself, a necessity of life like food and shelter. Such, at least, is the message from one Paul Bumgarner of Lyman, South Carolina, who wrote Gray to protest a threatened legislative cutback on adult school appropriations: "That man that wanted to cut out the night school money ought to be in a padded cell instead of Legislature[;] that isn't gentlemanly but you cannot be a gentleman all the time."[120]

By such reckoning an education reformer like Wil Lou Gray could rest assured that in teaching the people, she was offering a service for which there was a broad and sure (if not unanimous) demand. Yet, just as assuredly, she could never be certain what would be learned from the lessons she taught. At an official celebration of Gray's eighty-sixth birthday in 1969, former student Glenn Wesley Turner pledged a whopping $1 million to sustain the educational institution (by then officially known as the South Carolina Opportunity School, permanently housed in a former Army air base outside Columbia) that had first helped to steer him to the pinnacle of worldly success. Turner, the harelipped son of a poor sharecropper from Marion, South Carolina, had dropped out of school in the ninth grade to join the Air Force and had returned to adult school in 1953 under the G.I. Bill. Undoubtedly the most economically successful of all Opportunity School graduates, Turner credited his year and a half under Wil Lou Gray's tutelage (including service as her personal chauffeur in meetings around the state and lip surgery at her initiative) with the quantum of self-confidence he needed to tap his native talents.[121] Beginning in 1966, after a decade knocking around as a low-level salesman, Turner's prospects changed dramatically when he combined a toiletries and cosmetic business called Koscot with salesmanship motivation courses marketed under the title "Dare to Be Great" into a $300 million empire.[122] The Turner sales formula—depending as it did on the personal growth, drive, and self-discipline of the individual participant—resembled the basic themes of the Opportunity School itself. More explicitly, licenses to sell Koscot products were distributed at "Golden Opportunity" meetings.[123] A Koscot recruiting session similarly imitated the school's use of songs in its motivation sessions. According to one observer, "To the melody of 'I'm Gonna Let It Shine' I sang: 'In my new El Dorado, I'm gonna let it shine; In my new Mark IV, I'm gonna let it shine.' And to the school children's song that usually goes 'If you're happy and you know it, clap your hands (CLAP, CLAP),' I sang: 'If you wanna make lots of money, clap your hands (CLAP, CLAP).'"[124]

Unfortunately, Turner's creation proved a perverse application of the opportunity themes. Within three months of Turner's "gift" to the school, the scandal of fraud broke around the G. W. Turner enterprises. Turner's enterprise, it was alleged, was no more than a giant pyramid scheme.[125] A wave of unhappy investors followed in the wake of each Turner sales crusade. By 1973 he faced indictment on consumer fraud or tax evasion in forty-two states and Britain and France as well as penalties from the Federal Trade Commission and the Securities Exchange Commission. Soon Dare to Be Great had been shut down, and Koscot began trying to pay off creditors. More serious still, the federal government prosecuted Turner on federal mail fraud charges. Following an initial trial that ended in a hung jury and a prolonged second trial, Turner finally agreed to a plea bargain, a felony securities violation reduced by the judge to a misdemeanor in 1975.[126]

An inveterate publicity hound, Turner made two unsuccessful runs for the Florida Democratic Senate nomination (in his 1974 race he predicted that George Wallace would win the presidency in 1976 "and I'm going to be his legs") and involved himself in new motivation courses even in the midst of a legal nightmare that saw him ultimately enter bankruptcy proceedings in the face of $700 million in debts and $182 million in potential extended liabilities. Needless to say, the Opportunity School never saw its million-dollar prize.[127]

If Glenn W. Turner represented the most unsavory application of the methods of educational opportunity, perhaps the most benign was reflected in the work of teacher Septima Poinsette Clark. Clark grew up on Johns Island and was educated at Charleston's Avery Institute before moving to Columbia in 1929 for an eighteen-year stint that included public school teaching, active membership in the NAACP, and ultimately matriculation at Benedict College. Her autobiography records her first encounter with Wil Lou Gray in 1935 while Clark was instructing illiterate black soldiers at Fort Jackson on how to sign their name, write their company numbers, and read the names of buses going to the fort. Here Clark first put to use what she described as Gray's "kinesthetic" method—or memorized physical tracing of words—in teaching the earliest steps toward literacy. For Clark, the method would have later application as well, most notably in the Citizenship Schools aimed at black voting rights, which she pioneered at Johns Island with support from the Highlander Folk School in 1957. For the soldiers at Fort Jackson, she wrote, "signing their names . . . made them *feel* different. And in the same way our Johns Island folk would learn things that would be of much help to them . . . Knowing how to sign their names, many of those men and women told me after they had learned, made them *feel* different. Suddenly they had become a part of the community; they were on their way toward first-class citizenship.[128] In addition, the citizenship book Clark devised for her would-be voters—complete with discussion of state election laws and descriptions of local and state government, social security, and taxes—drew directly from Gray's older civics text.[129] In subsequent oral reminiscences, Clark willingly heaped credit on "Miss Wil Lou Gray": "Although we had segregation, I think when she came over to the place where we were, I think she had just as much of a good feeling about the blacks as she did about the whites . . . she had a big influence on me in teaching me to have enough patience to work with people who could not read or write."[130]

If the ideas of the Progressive educational reformer ultimately informed the most powerful social movement in twentieth-century America, they nevertheless required some further democratic adulterations. In 1963 Septima Clark became supervisor of teacher training for Martin Luther King, Jr.'s Southern Christian Leadership Conference, reaching an estimated 100,000 people through far-flung citizenship education programs. In Clark's case, the path from individual education for its own sake to the Highlander-SCLC approach clearly challenged some of her earlier instincts. Reflecting back on her experience, Clark believed that the very process of educating people for action had forced her and other SCLC teachers to change their pedagogical approach. "Sometimes my own growth embarrasses me," Clark noted in 1986. "I don't like to admit, even to myself, that I was once ill at ease with white people or so middle-class in my attitudes that I had a hard time teaching poor people." Esau Jenkins, another South Carolina civil rights activist, described a similar democratizing conversion from lecturing to dialogue with those he hoped to mobilize. "My ideas of community leadership have changed in many ways since my stay at Highlander last year," he wrote Myles Horton in 1955.[131]

WIL LOU GRAY was no more directly responsible for the voting rights crusade of the 1960s than she was for the abuses of sales-motivation schemes in the 1970s. That leading practitioners in both of these expressions of modern-day American culture traced their roots to the lessons of the same teacher only underscores the fact that is at once the ever-present dilemma and the saving grace of the intellectual instructor: you can lead a horse to water but you can't make it drink. Those who take advantage of the pedagogy of literacy manage that gift for their own ends—more or less in synchrony with the intentions of their teachers. That lesson might serve at once to temper premature judgments about pedagogical styles and renew respect for those who offer the opportunity of self-transformation to others.

Epilogue

The Once and Future Career of the Public Intellectual

IT IS NO WONDER that people today find it difficult to connect the projects of Progressive intellectuals with present-day concerns and no surprise either that today's rediscovered public intellectual bears little resemblance to the original. The world has changed. The twentieth century has proven unkind to democratic ideals. If by World War I the depredations of national chauvinism, mass psychology, and lethal technology disabused many erstwhile reformers of the efficacy of a democratic public sphere, then surely subsequent events—most notably the rise of fascism, communism, and the national security state combined with ever more sophisticated forms of consumer manipulation—only raised the odds further against the development of what John Dewey had called the Great Community. Disenchantment with the deliberative capacity of the masses settled thickly on American intellectuals in the post–World War II world and established a barrier that in important ways has still not been breached between today's would-be democratic intellectuals and those of an earlier generation.

Many left-wing intellectuals who flocked to the banner of postwar humanism tended to withdraw from democratic affirmations altogether in favor of a defense of the lonely voice of critical reason. Perhaps best represented in the United States through the exiles from the Frankfurt Institute for Social Research (Theodor Adorno, Max Horkheimer, Herbert Marcuse, Walter Benjamin, Leo Lowenthal, Erich Fromm), this disillusioned radicalism looked not to the community of the political act but to the solitary work of the intellectual to uphold human freedom. As Adorno would summarize in *Negative Dialectics* (1966), "In this age of universal social repression, the picture of freedom against society lives in the crushed, abused individual's features alone."[1] For the critical theorist—disabused of instrumentalism as played out in politics, the mass media, and the commercial marketplace—art and aesthetic vision beckoned as the only authentic alternative to a fraudulent environment.[2] Ironically, in formulating his Critical Theory in the late 1930s, Horkheimer had borrowed approvingly from John Dewey—not the Dewey of the socialized individual or the Great Community, however, but the Dewey of *Art as Experience* (1934). In extolling art as imaginative, unscripted communication, Dewey had explained, "Indifference to response of the immediate audience is a necessary trait of all artists that have something new to say." Horkheimer took hope from Dewey's artists, who "are animated by a deep conviction that since they can only say what they have to say, the trouble is not with their work but those who, having eyes, see not, and having ears, hear not."[3] The flight of the heroic intellectual had thus come full circle. Ushering in the century on the imperative of breaking down walls between the study and the workplace, thought and experience, and the individual and society, the radical thinker now sought above all to protect the moral and creative conscience from the assaults of the multitude.

If Hitler's *Volk* could inspire the aestheticism of the critical theorist, revulsion at America's own mass culture provoked a similar reaction among others. The so-called New Critics (most notably John Crowe Ransom, Cleanth Brooks, and Allen Tate) who dominated American literary criticism in the 1940s and 1950s sought to identify, and indeed to classify in positivistic, scientific fashion, the saving aesthetic impulses of great literature.[4] The careful cultivation of literary irony, Cleanth Brooks elaborated in a famous essay, helped the poet to overcome the "depletion and corruption of the very language itself, by advertising and by the mass-produced arts of radio, the moving picture, and pulp fiction." Unlike Emerson's appeal to the reader as a rough equal, the modern American scholar self-consciously assumed the "special burden" of addressing "a public corrupted by Hollywood and the Book of the Month Club."[5] Against such drivel, the New Critics held up the work of art—isolated from context and studied as an autonomous verbal structure—as a digestible alternative for popular cultivation.[6]

Art + the New Criticism

Although he disassociated himself from the New Critics for their lack of historical sensitivity and aversion to ideological combat, literary critic Lionel Trilling, the humanist with the perhaps the widest following among postwar social scientists, also accepted literature as a conservative brace against popular passions. Rejecting the cultural mood of the 1930s Popular Front as a new form of philistinism, Trilling openly suspected the moral certainty of the committed intellectual and even momentarily praised the "strange virtue of weariness."[7] His dominant tone, according to literary biographer William M. Chace, was one of caution and control, appropriate for the intellectual critic who was to exercise a kind of "supervisory" role in the larger culture.[8]

Trilling's influential colleague at Columbia, historian Richard Hofstadter, offered a further variation on the dominant theme of disenchantment. Still drawing on a Marxian skepticism toward political pieties and moralistic reform thought (he had resigned from a Communist Party unit at Columbia in 1939), Hofstadter introduced his collection of famous essays, *The American Political Tradition* (1948), with the admonition that "American traditions . . . show a strong bias in favor of equalitarian democracy, but it has been a democracy in cupidity rather than a democracy of fraternity."[9] By the 1950s, however—and particularly after the chilling crusade of Senator Joseph McCarthy—this acerbic radicalism aimed at the culture as a whole had narrowed to a focus on the quality and preservation of *intellectual* culture. As Hofstadter himself would later describe it, "The outburst of McCarthyism, instead of provoking a radical response, aroused in some intellectuals more distaste than they had ever thought they would feel for popular passions and anti-establishment demagogy."[10] It was thus that Hofstadter, in his "most personal piece of work," settled on "anti-intellectualism" as a seminal force in American life.[11] In Hofstadter's evolving view, the democratic values inherent in the "Populistic" element in American culture were regularly undone by underlying envy and vulgar materialism at the roots of popular motivation.[12] Since the Whig Party of the 1840s, argued Hofstadter, even the "Gentlemen's Party" had assimilated and effectively manipulated the egalitarianism of the Populist creed to the ends of narrow power politics. This same stale anti-intellectual synthesis had lasted, in Hofstadter's opinion, until the advent of Progressivism.[13] Most comfortably identifying with the New Deal (and reading New Deal intellectual principles first backward to the Progressives, then forward to Adlai Stevenson and John F. Kennedy), Hofstadter's America reached its highest potential only through the aegis of the intellectual "as expert." "In the interests of democracy itself," Hofstadter suggested of the Progressive Era, "the old Jacksonian suspicion of experts must be abated. The tension between democracy and the educated man now seemed to be disappearing—because the type of man who had always valued expertise was now learning to value democracy and because democracy was learning to value experts."[14] Not the quality of popular culture itself, but the tolerance if not veneration of that culture for "a combination of intellect and character"—seemingly represented in the campaign of 1960 by John F. Kennedy—was now the chief critical criterion to be applied to American democracy.[15]

Faith in expertise linked the liberal humanism of a Trilling or a Hofstadter to the dominant temperament of postwar social science. Overall, the carnage of twentieth-century politics—on the one hand associated with antidemocratic fascist or communist dictatorship, on the other hand linked to excessive democracy in Weimar Germany or outbreaks of popular paranoia as in McCarthyism—led postwar political scientists toward a new and tamer model of democratic culture. Mass participation in politics, previously a given in democratic theory, was increasingly hedged in by considerations of order, outcome, and efficiency. The people—too ignorant, too suggestible, or simply too busy—were now officially recognized as poor candidates for conducting the day-to-day affairs of democracy themselves. In the first and perhaps most influential expression of the new process-oriented paradigm, the émigré economist Joseph Schumpeter in *Capitalism, Socialism, and Democracy* (1942) postulated democracy as a means rather than an end in itself. Given the practical impossibility of "the people" defining the common good, the democratic method depended less on popular visions of governance than the fact of "institutional arrangements for arriving at political decisions . . . [involving] a competitive struggle for the people's vote."[16] In this view, continuity in the system of selection rather than the nature or degree of participation from below sustained the democratic

Schumpeter

process. To Schumpeter's basic economic model American political scientist Anthony Downs in 1957 added the concept of "rational abstention": since many voters will not be materially affected by an election one way or another, their apathy is a logical and defensible aspect of a functional democracy. It was a period, as Robert Dahl would later recall without apology, when political theory naturally focused more on "the conditions of democratic 'stability'" than the "conditions of democratic change."[17]

Confronting contradictions between the democratic creed and the workings of mass society, liberal intellectuals of the post–World War II era faced an enduring enigma. Given contemporary circumstances, should social scientists accept the deceptions involved in the control of public opinion as a necessary part of a stable social order? Were the people—ignorant, uneducated, and uncultured as they appeared for the most part—really capable of much better? Were not the developing deep divisions in society between mental and manual labor, intellectuals and workers, an inevitable part of the modern world? Had not the radical sideshow of the thirties with "the literature of a party disguised as a literature of a class" proved that oil and water don't mix?[18] As political scientist Sheldon Wolin emphasized in 1960, "the concept of the masses haunts modern political and social theory." Instead of Marx's "highly self-conscious proletariat" proudly designing a brighter future, history, it seemed, had "disgorged a 'glob of humanity'" who required shaping, one way or another, by their social superiors.[19]

Just how far the masses had fallen was scientifically charted by social scientists, such as those at the University of Michigan's Survey Research Center. Examining the results of the Center's voluminous survey data in an influential article in 1964, for example, Philip E. Converse was struck by the "differences in the nature of belief systems" between those variously labeled "elite political actors," "college educated," "sophisticated observers," and "ideologues" on the one hand and the "mass public," "the majority," and the "poorly educated" on the other. "First," noted Converse, "the contextual grasp of 'standard' political belief systems fades out very rapidly, almost before one has passed beyond the 10 percent of the American population that in the 1950s had completed standard college training. Increasingly, simpler forms of information about 'what goes with what' (or even information about the simple identity of objects) turns up missing." In the end, a kind of cognitive "continental shelf" appeared to divide the "history of ideas" upon which elite decisions were erected from the relative innocence of popular understandings. Given their lack of socially coherent belief systems, the masses, it appeared, had best stick to the intellectual equivalent of a subsistence diet. "These people have a clear image of politics as an arena of group interests and, provided that they have been properly advised on where their own group interests lie, they are relatively likely to follow such advice."[20]

With some agony and internal division, then, American social scientists and liberal reformers generally accommodated themselves to the "process democracy" of elite rule and a passive public.[21] In doing so, they effectively closed a door on the Progressive legacy of democratic intellectual engagement, finding it hopelessly sentimental and naive. Replicating Walter Lippmann's skepticism toward popular participation, the liberal intellectual heirs to America's progressive tradition opted at midcentury either for a reliance on technical and institutional powers of command or an aesthetic retreat into high culture.

Yet the early yearnings for a partnership between intellectual tutelage and democratic activism were never entirely snuffed out. More than they realized, the student activists of the 1960s drew significantly on a legacy of democratic thought dating to the pre–World War I years. At their founding convention in June 1962 at Port Huron, Michigan, the Students for a Democratic Society (SDS) formally deplored the idea that man is "a thing to be manipulated, and that he is inherently incapable of directing his own affairs." In contrast, this harbinger of a "new left" sought "the establishment of a democracy of individual participation, governed by two central aims: that the individual share in those social decisions determining the quality and direction of his life; that society be organized to encourage independence in men and provide the media for their common participation."[22] Drawing inspiration from the civil rights movement (especially the close community of the Student Non-Violent Coordinating Committee, SNCC), these advocates of direct experience paid no official homage to their theoretical mentors.[23] And yet the ghosts of Dewey, Cooley, et al. walked

SDS didn't recognize its own intell. debts to pre WWI soc dems.

freely amidst the social experimentalism of the early New Left. The concepts contained in the Port Huron Statement not only dovetailed with the twin emphasis on individual growth and democracy common to pragmatic Progressive rhetoric, but the authors openly deplored the post-Progressive instrumentalism of social science thought. "Theoretic chaos has replaced the idealistic thinking of old . . . To be idealistic is to be considered apocalyptic, deluded. To have no serious aspirations, on the contrary, is to be 'tough-minded'." Calling for a return of democratic idealism, the pragmatists reborn counseled, "We have no sure formulas, no closed theories—but that does mean values are beyond discussion and tentative determination."[24]

The similarity of rhetoric between Progressives and New Leftists was not entirely coincidence. As James Miller has documented, iconoclastic sociologist C. Wright Mills, whom Tom Hayden had identified as "the one scholar with something to say to the student left," was perhaps the key intellectual mediator between generations. Mills, whose highest accolade was "That guy's a real Wobbly," had rebelled against his Catholic, Texas A&M upbringing and gravitated, in a sociology dissertation at the University of Wisconsin, to the writings of C. S. Pierce, Thorstein Veblen, and John Dewey.[25] A recurrent theme of Mills, as for his philosopher-heroes, was the unhappy divorce between the intellectual and a "potential public." While initially celebrating the organic intellectual within the labor movement, by 1960, in his "Letter to the New Left," Mills looked to independent intellectuals themselves "as a possible immediate, radical agency of change."[26] This was the Mills who electrified the young ranks of the New Left. As chief drafter of the Port Huron Statement, Hayden (who had already started a graduate thesis on Mills) identified his central concern as "the complete absence of an active and creative set of publics."[27]

For their part social scientists who hearkened to the promise of the new social movements reckoned uncomfortably with the accumulated "disenchanted" literature of their predecessors. The democratic theorist, said Peter Bachrach in 1967, faced a Hobson's choice: "a theory which is normatively sound but unrealistic, or a theory which is realistic but heavily skewed toward elitism."[28] The ensuing confrontation produced a critique of the assumptions of "democratic elitism" underlying most postwar behavioralist scholarship. Reasserting his faith in "the major tenet of classical democratic theory—belief and confidence in the public"—Bachrach offered a theoretical justification for the claims of a participatory decision-making that would reach beyond election day into the operation of "the factory, the office, the enterprise."[29]

Swept away by the action of their times, the new radicals of the 1960s largely missed the chance to build on scholarly foundations that honored their basic commitments. With political ends taking precedence over interpretive ones, the rhetoric of reform, symbolized in the term "participatory democracy," soon became a catchword rather than an opening to sustained, critical analysis. In attempting to hide a particular philosophical-intellectual construction within an appeal to traditional American values, the early New Left tended, in Miller's words, "to thicken rather than dispel the fog of rhetoric surrounding democracy."[30] In particular, the challenge of democratic communication, originally highlighted by Dewey and reformulated in the Millsian-SDS formula of "participatory process," not only lost out to other political ends but was itself saddled with two conceptual dilemmas.

In the first place, the critique of "liberal" (i.e., electoral or parliamentary) democracy cultivated by the New Left threw into doubt any practical means of building a legitimate democratic consensus on a large scale. Indeed, without acknowledgment, participatory radicals drew on venerable themes of twentieth-century disenchantment. Mills's arguments against the rituals of electoral politics as the "images of a fairytale" and Herbert Marcuse's critique of the "rule-of-the-game" in effect extended Lippmannesque analysis in the service of allegedly revolutionary ends.[31] Liberal democracy, by this light, represented more a mechanism of control than a barometer of popular will. The official public sphere could therefore not be trusted as the true voice of the people: "Free elections of the master by the slaves doesn't eliminate the masters or the slaves."[32] Besotted by media manipulation, Marcuse argued, "the majority of the people is the majority of their masters."[33] In short, the same disillusionment with the mass public that had led mainstream social scientists to sanction the instruments of elite control led the new radicals to demands for systemic transformation.

Marcuse

Yet, in the circumstances, how was Dewey's Great Community to reassemble itself? The problem was less acute in the early 1960s when the movement focus was on local organizing projects of small, decentralized communities like the Newark Community Union Project with its slogan "Let the people decide!"[34] But it was something else again when the center of action was national policy, as in stopping the Vietnam War. The New Left never busied itself with a serious answer to the question.

Aside from the question of *how* democratic change would come about was the problem of agency: *who* would make the revolution? As with the issue of process, the long decade of the 1960s also divided on the list of potential agents. In the early half of the decade, movement efforts centered on organizing *outside* constituencies: variously, the poor, black people, or the working class. If none of these entities, practically speaking, were ever likely to add up to a majoritarian movement, at least they suggested the theoretical necessity of a diverse coalition-building process. By the mid-sixties, however, the combination of Black Power rage (and more generally Third World anticolonialism à la Frantz Fanon) and the war in Vietnam added a moral imperative to New Left politics that transcended considerations of even theoretical majorities. The fear of fascism, as historian Nigel Young has documented, was palpable in the writings of Mills, Marcuse, Hayden, and Staughton Lynd.[35] In the circumstances, resistance and ultimately liberation took precedence over democracy. A movement that had begun self-consciously as marginalized critics seeking to engage a larger "potential public" had in the end identified *themselves* either as the people or the people's stewards—either way rendering unnecessary any further discussion of, or experiment with, deliberative process.[36] Theoretically, the New Left had reached a dead end long before political cooptation, repression, or the long arm of academe stilled its fervor.

The search by American scholars for a more democratic culture did not die with the movements of the 1960s. Indeed, the recent rediscovery of the thinkers of the Progressive Era and a renewed search for a more democratic engagement among scholars across diverse academic fields are promising signs. John Dewey is the "one American *philosophical* thinker," argues philosopher of religion

Cornel West, who "has put forward a conception of the meaning and significance of democracy."[37] For West, the Deweyan example opens the way to a vision of the social role of the intellectual "as a critical organic catalyst, one who brings the most subtle and sophisticated tools to bear to explain and illuminate how structures of domination and effects of individual choices in language and in nondiscursive institutions operate."[38]

Yet it must be said that each wave of intellectual engagement carries its own specific gravity, which is sometimes to say its own peculiar comedy. In this regard, if the Deweyans of the 1960s in the end sacrificed their democratic idealism on the altar of their own activism, the current resurrection (including some of the same characters three decades later) tends to invert both the promise and the pitfalls of the prior model. Here I am referring to the search for the public intellectual and, more generally, the stance of the postmodern academic theorist.

Among modern-day critics, for example, who powerfully assert the role of the public intellectual via the pragmatist tradition is philosopher Richard Rorty. According to Rorty (just as for Dewey et al. before him), the ultimate hope for a renewed social science is obliteration of the distance (perhaps hubris is the better word) separating the researchers from their objects of study:

> If we get rid of traditional notions of "objectivity" and "scientific method" we shall be able to see the social sciences as continuous with literature—as interpreting other people to us, and thus enlarging and deepening our sense of community. We shall see the anthropologists and historians as having made it possible for us—educated, leisured policy-makers of the West—to see any exotic specimen of humanity as "one of us." We shall see the sociologists as having done the same for the poor (and various other sorts of nearby outsiders), and the psychologists as having done the same for the eccentric and the insane.[39]

Unfortunately, emulation is not the same as reincarnation. A discursive summons of the spirit of John Dewey does not, in itself, reestablish a democratic intellectual practice. At times, what we might call today's postmodern democrats appear to mistake the word for the deed. Erasure of the boundaries between intellectual and nonacademic lives takes a surprising turn, for example, when Rorty willingly inducts coal miners into the imagined fraternity (or in his parlance, sorority) of the Lost Generation:

> Complaints about the social irresponsibility of the intellectuals typically concern the intellectual's tendency to marginalize herself, to move out from one community by interior identification of herself with some other community—for example, another country or historical period, an invisible college, or some alienated subgroup within the larger community. Such marginalization is, however, common to intellectuals and to miners. In the early days of the United Mine Workers its members rightly put no faith in the surrounding legal and political institutions and were loyal only to each other. In this respect they resembled the literary and artistic avant-garde between the wars.[40]

The awkwardness of Rorty's construction (miners, unlike writers, were not choosing their marginalization) exposes the dilemmas facing any serious democratic move by today's academic elite. First, on a critical-intellectual level, few of the new democrats have dealt seriously with the questions of popular "capacity" long raised against progressive dreams.[41] The rush to reinvigorate the Deweyan example will likely be remembered as simply another click in the romance-disenchantment cycle of American intellectual life unless this latest movement comes to grips with the immediate holes in the body politic as well as longer-term weaknesses pinpointed over the years by skeptical American social scientists.

But there is a deeper structural problem as well. The social distance is now so great between intellectuals and public that intellectuals' attempts to connect positively to working people or the poor are likely to sound forced or even hollow. On a more practical level, even the most well-intentioned and sensitive intellectuals have trouble dislodging themselves from their own sheltered perches to make honest, let alone efficacious, contact with the world of ordinary citizens. The lack of specific historical and political context is especially troubling among those very scholars (associated with the work of Jurgen Habermas) most determined to resuscitate a vital public sphere. To take but one example, there is a breathtaking abstraction to the claims of feminist political scientist Nancy Fraser, who writes that she is "committed to theorizing the limits of democracy in late-capitalist societies." What comfort may we take from her assertion "All told, then, there do not seem to be any conceptual (as opposed to empirical) barriers to the possibility of a socially egalitarian, multicultural society that is also a participatory democracy"?[42] All told, we might worry, today's democratic intellectual renaissance appears richer in words than in deeds. It is as if we had donned the clothes of a John Dewey or a Jane Addams but forgotten their walking shoes.

The issue, to be sure, goes beyond perspective or individual intention. Critic John McGowan has starkly defined the manner in which "the institutional sites that intellectuals now inhabit (the universities and the media, primarily) conspire to insulate their work from political discussion":

> Absolution from the political means not only that the intellectuals' hypothetical models never take up social existence but also that the intellectual himself achieves an identity by negation. The point here is not primarily hypocrisy (the charge that self-proclaimed radicals never live their radical views or do much politically to bring them about), but that the very form in which intellectual thought proposes its alternatives to current social life reinforces the image of freedom as distance and the belief that one's true identity is achieved in isolation from the restrictions of everyday concerns, relationships, and contingencies. Thought is separated from practice as a matter of both principle and institutional arrangement, and then we intellectuals agonize over why we are so politically ineffective.[43]

Academics who regularly bewail the state of contemporary American culture, who effectively condemn both the powerlessness and the ignorance of the mass public, have themselves precious little contact with the people upon whom they pass judgment. If this is an ironic commentary on contemporary commentary itself, it is not necessarily fatal to the purposes of that commentary. But it is a warning. The very advantages (education, time, financial security) that accrue to intellectuals may benefit a project of moral and political reawakening only if accompanied by an awareness of the *limits* that those same advantages impose on social understanding.

Theoretical critique, in fact, may not prove the best avenue by which to pursue the problem of the intellectual as would-be democrat. A serious reckoning with past such efforts may better orient today's American scholars to the pitfalls as well as the possibilities imminent in their aspirations. Certainly the record of the early twentieth century provides due warning of the internal contradictions and bitter disappointments facing the idealist determined at once to serve and uplift the People. A Sisyphian heroism may well be the lot of the intellectual activist caught in a web of institutional and cultural frustrations that is beyond individual remedy. And yet historical hindsight offers ample example of generous and passionate intellectuals who expanded the very meaning of American democracy by their practical visions. May we learn from their deeds as well as their dilemmas.

Notes

Abbreviations

ASWP	Anna Strunsky Walling Papers, Yale University Library
BCSPP	A. Philip Randolph personal papers, Brotherhood of Sleeping Car Porters Chicago Division Papers, Chicago Historical Society
CIR, RG 174, NA	Commission on Industrial Relations, Record Group 174, National Archives
CMP	Charles McCarthy Papers, State Historical Society of Wisconsin, Madison
FWP	Frank Walsh Papers, New York Public Library
ISR	*International Socialist Review*
JFMP	James Franklin Miles Papers, South Caroliniana Library, Columbia, South Carolina
OSP	Opportunity School Papers, Student Correspondence, South Carolina Department of Archives and History, Columbia, South Carolina
SHSW	State Historical Society of Wisconsin, Madison
SPAP	Socialist Party of America Papers, William E. Perkins Library, Duke University
WEWP	William English Walling Papers, State Historical Society of Wisconsin, Madison
WJLP	W. Jett Lauck Papers (#4742), Special Collections Department, Alderman Library, University of Virginia
WLGP	Wil Lou Gray Papers, South Caroliniana Library, Columbia, South Carolina

Introduction

1. Russell Jacoby, *The Last Intellectuals: American Culture in the Age of Academe* (New York: Basic Books, 1987), 5. Jacoby confirms that he invented the term "public intellectual" or at least was "unaware of any previous usage." Telephone conversation with the author, May 17, 1995; e-mail, May 16, 1995.

2. Nexus/Lexus search conducted April 1995; see, e.g., Janny Scott, "Thinking Out Loud: The Public Intellectual Is Reborn," *New York Times,* Aug. 9, 1994.

3. See, e.g., James Farr, "Citizen Education and Post-Behavioral Political

Science," paper delivered to Past and Present of the Social Disciplines Conference, University of North Carolina at Chapel Hill, Dec. 12, 1992.

4. For a thoughtful view of how to reconnect both roles, see Stanley Aronowitz and Henry A. Giroux, *Postmodern Education: Politics, Culture, and Social Criticism* (Minneapolis: University of Minnesota Press, 1991), 87–135.

5. Neil Jumonville, *Critical Crossings: The New York Intellectuals in Postwar America* (Berkeley: University of California Press, 1991), 236. *Chicago Tribune*, April 7, 1996, review of Stephen L. Carter, *Integrity; Lakeland (Florida) Ledger*, May 12, 1996, review of Gates and West's *The Future of the Race.*

6. See, e.g., Adolph Reed, "The Current Crisis of the Black Intellectual," *Village Voice* 40 (April 11, 1995), 31–36; and Sean Wilentz, "Race, Celebrity, and the Intellectuals," *Dissent* 42 (Summer 1995), 293–299.

7. Jacoby, 237.

8. Emerson's lecture "The American Scholar" was delivered to the Phi Beta Kappa Society at Harvard University in 1837. For Emerson's notion of the intellectual's calling, I draw heavily from Mary Kupiec Cayton, *Emerson's Emergence: Self and Society in the Transformation of New England, 1800–1845* (Chapel Hill: University of North Carolina Press, 1989), 137–160.

9. Emerson quoted in Cornel West, *The American Evasion of Philosophy: A Genealogy of Pragmatism* (Madison: University of Wisconsin Press, 1989), 24.

10. Walt Whitman, *Democratic Vistas* (New York: Liberal Arts Press, 1949 [1871]). On Whitman's artifice and self-conscious distance from his subjects, see, e.g., Gregory W. Bush, *Lord of Attention: Gerald Stanley Lee and the Crowd Metaphor in Industrializing America* (Amherst: University of Massachusetts Press, 1991), 24–25; and Richard Poirier, review of *Walt Whitman's America: A Cultural Biography* by David S. Reynolds in *The New Republic* 212 (June 19, 1995), 33–39.

11. *Democratic Vistas*, 17–20.

12. A contemporary editor's description of Phillips's lectures, as quoted in James Brewer Stewart, *Wendell Phillips: Liberty's Hero* (Baton Rouge: Louisiana State University Press, 1986), 323.

13. Phillips as quoted in Stewart, *Wendell Phillips*, 326–327; cf. Whitman, *Democratic Vistas*, 20.

14. See, e.g., Ellen C. Dubois, "Making Women's History: Activist Historians of Women's Rights, 1880–1940," in Leon Fink, Stephen T. Leonard, and Donald M. Reid, eds., *Intellectuals and Public Life: Between Radicalism and Reform* (Ithaca: Cornell University Press, 1996), 214–235.

15. See, e.g., John L. Thomas, *Alternative America: Henry George, Edward Bellamy, and Henry Demarest Lloyd and the Adversary Tradition* (Cambridge, Mass.: The Belknap Press of Harvard University Press, 1983); Ruth Birgitta Bordin, *Francis Willard: A Biography* (Chapel Hill: University of North Carolina Press, 1986); and Kathryn Kish Sklar, *Florence Kelley and the Nation's Work* (New Haven: Yale University Press, 1995).

16. Leon Fink, *Workingmen's Democracy: The Knights of Labor and American Politics* (Urbana: University of Illinois Press, 1983), 219–233, and *In Search of the Working Class: Essays in American Labor History and Political Culture* (Urbana:

University of Illinois Press, 1994), 89–143. With its strong and expanding labor movement, Chicago, however, largely defied the generalization just made. See Georg Leidenberger, "Working-Class Progressivism and the Politics of Transportation in Chicago, 1895–1907" (Ph.D. diss., University of North Carolina at Chapel Hill, 1995). On the logic of labor education, see Chap. 1 in this volume.

17. See Robert H. Wiebe's classic, *The Search for Order, 1877–1920* (New York: Hill and Wang, 1967) and *Self-Rule: A Cultural History of American Democracy* (Chicago: University of Chicago Press, 1995), esp. Chap. 6, "Raising Hierarchies," 138–161. See also Richard Sennett, *Families against the City: Middle Class Homes of Industrial Chicago, 1872–1890* (Cambridge, Mass.: Harvard University Press, 1970).

18. On the breakdown of nineteenth-century institutions, cf. Wiebe, *Self-Rule,* 113–180.

19. Alexander Keyssar, *Out of Work: The First Century of Unemployment in Massachusetts* (New York: Cambridge University Press, 1986), 225–237, quotation 225.

20. George Cotkin, *William James, Public Philosopher* (Baltimore: Johns Hopkins University Press, 1990), 124; Ross Posnock, "The Politics of Pragmatism and the Fortunes of the Public Intellectual," *American Literary History* 3 (1991), 566–587; Raymond Williams, *Keywords: A Vocabulary of Culture and Society* (New York: Oxford University Press, 1983), p. 169–171.

21. Posnock, "Politics of Pragmatism," 567.

22. Cotkin, *William James,* 90–94.

23. Ibid., 172–173.

24. On the Young Americans, see Casey Nelson Blake, *Beloved Community: The Cultural Criticism of Randolph Bourne, Van Wyck Brooks, Waldo Frank, and Lewis Mumford* (Chapel Hill: University of North Carolina Press, 1990), quotation 4.

25. Edward Shils, *The Intellectuals and the Powers and Other Essays* (Chicago: University of Chicago Press, 1972), 155.

26. Among works that have emphasized the social engineering and social control strands of Progressive thought, see Arthur S. Link and Richard L. McCormick, *Progressivism* (Arlington Heights, Ill.: Harlan Davidson, 1983); David J. Rothman, *Conscience and Convenience: The Asylum and Its Alternatives in Progressive America* (Boston: Little, Brown, 1980); and John R. Diggins, *The Promise of Progressivism: Modernism and the Crisis of Knowledge and Authority* (Chicago: University of Chicago Press, 1994).

27. Bob Herbert, "A Nation of Nitwits," *New York Times,* March 1, 1995; Paul Fussell, *Bad or, the Dumbing of America* (New York: Summit Books, 1991). See also Michael Kinsley, "The Intellectual Free Lunch," *The New Yorker* 70 (February 6, 1995), 4–5; and Neil Postman, *Amusing Ourselves to Death: Public Discourse in the Age of Show Business* (New York: Viking, 1985).

28. Lewis Lapham, "Seen but Not Heard: The Message of the Oklahoma Bombing," *Harper's* 291 (July 1995), 29–36, quotation 36.

29. Lasch, *The Revolt of the Elites and the Betrayal of Democracy* (New York: Norton, 1995), 20.

1. Progressive Reformers, Social Scientists, and the Search for a Democratic Public

1. See, e.g., Robert M. Crunden, *Ministers of Reform: The Progressives' Achievement in American Civilization, 1889–1920* (New York: Basic Books, 1982), 3–15; Andrew Feffer, *The Chicago Pragmatists and American Progressivism* (Ithaca: Cornell University Press, 1993).

2. Horace M. Kallen, *Education, the Machine, and the Worker: An Essay in the Psychology of Educaton in Industrial Society* (New York: New Republic, 1925), 3.

3. "Intellectual," *Encyclopedia of the Social Sciences*, vol. 8 (New York: Macmillan, 1944), 118–126.

4. "The Social Value of the College-Bred," in William James, *Essays, Comments, and Reviews* (Cambridge, Mass.: Harvard University Press, 1987), 106–112, quotations 109–110.

5. E. F. Andrews, "The Monopoly of Intellect," *International Socialist Review* 1 (June 1901), 765–768.

6. Bentham quoted in *Oxford English Dictionary*, 2nd ed., vol. 12 (Oxford: Oxford University Press, 1989), entry "Publicity."

7. Ward, as quoted in Henry Steele Commager, *The American Mind: An Interpretation of American Thought and Character since the 1880s* (New Haven: Yale University Press, 1950), 213; Lester Frank Ward, *Applied Sociology: A Treatise on the Conscious Improvement of Societ by Society* (Boston: Ginn and Co., 1906), 95–110, quotation 96; on gender, see 231–232; on race, see 107–110. On Ward's connections to workers' and women's education initiatives, see Clifford H. Scott, *Lester Frank Ward* (Boston: Twayne Publishers, 1976), 59–60. Ward's egalitarianism may have stemmed from his upbringing. The last of ten children born to a rural Illinois family of modest means (he called himself a "true Pleb"), Lester Frank Ward's political convictions were actually a paler version of those of his lesser-known older brother Cyrenus Osborne Ward, with whom he briefly collaborated in an unsuccessful wagon-wheel business. As a machinist and labor advocate at the Brooklyn Navy Yard, Osborne Ward developed connections to the international socialist movement in the 1870s (he met Marx during European travels) and published numerous pamphlets and labor journals. In 1887 he set up his own print shop from which issued two years later his "most noted" work, *A History of the Ancient Working People*, later entitled more simply *The Ancient Lowly*. In *A Labor Catechism of Political Economy: A Study for the People* (Washington, D.C.: Osborne Ward, 1877–1892), Osborne Ward anticipated much of the thrust of the confident rationalism championed by his brother and other reform-minded social scientists. "How much do men know?" he began. "How much are they capable of knowing? Can men take mutual care of themselves? . . . It is the belief of the author of these pages, that it is as possible for any enlightened people, who possess such facilitating instruments of research, and of Industrial Economy . . . to govern their economic methods of labor, as it is to govern their political methods of law-giving" (1, 6–7).

8. Julius Weinberg, *Edward Alsworth Ross and the Sociology of Progressivism*

(Madison: State Historical Society of Wisconsin, 1972), 29–31. Ross named his first son Lester and his third child Ward.

9. At Stanford, Ross's defense of Eugene Debs and the Pullman strikers, his advocacy of free silver during the populist campaigns, and his extreme opposition to Japanese immigration set him on a collision course with Jane Lathrop Stanford, activist widow of the university founder, who effected his dismissal in 1900, despite widespread protests in the academic community. Weinberg, *Edward Alsworth Ross*, 42–55. For conflicting evaluations of Ross's "social control" theories, cf. ibid., 39–55, 80–81, 206–210, and Christopher Lasch, *The New Radicalism in America, 1889–1963: The Intellectual as a Social Type* (New York: Knopf, 1965), 168–177.

10. Robert M. Crunden, *Ministers of Reform: The Progressives' Achievement in American Civilization, 1889–1920* (New York: Basic Books, 1982), ix.

11. Crunden, *Ministers of Reform*, 16–89, quotation 63. On Dewey's early Christian idealism as well as his substitution, by the turn of the century, of a nonteleological democratic process for divine faith, see Robert B. Westbrook, *John Dewey and American Democracy* (Ithaca: Cornell University Press, 1991), 13–113.

12. James Kloppenberg, "Democracy and Disenchantment: From Weber and Dewey to Habermas and Rorty," in Dorothy Ross, ed., *Modernist Impulses in the Human Sciences, 1870–1930* (Baltimore: Johns Hopkins University Press, 1994), 69–90. To be sure, a call to action might take many forms, and James sometimes invoked a kind of moral elitism in upholding the resistance of the heroic few against the "herd of nullities" in the common culture. William James, *Will to Believe*, as quoted in Joshua Miller, "William James and Democratic Action" (unpublished ms., 1995, courtesy of author); see also Ross Posnock, "The Politics of Pragmatism and the Fortunes of the Public Intellectual," *American Literary History* 3 (1991), 566–587.

13. In his very criticism of Dewey, historian John Diggins re-emphasizes this point. In Diggins's eyes, Dewey's solution "merely socializes the concept of virtue while subverting its moral content." Rejecting in turn a religious (God-centered), classical republican (state-centered), or utilitarian (self-centered) calculus of morality, "[Dewey's] liberal man is asked to adopt the common norms of society." John Patrick Diggins, *The Lost Soul of American Politics: Virtue, Self-Interest, and the Foundations of Liberalism* (New York: Basic Books, 1984), 343.

14. John Dewey, "The School and Social Progress," in *The School and Society* (Chicago: University of Chicago Press, 1960 [1900], 28–29.

15. Dewey, *The Public and Its Problems* (New York: Henry Holt, 1927), 168.

16. Ibid., 159–160.

17. Ibid., 162–163.

18. Westbrook, *John Dewey*, 51–58; James Harvey Robinson, *The Mind in the Making: The Relation of Intelligence to Social Reform* (New York: Harper and Brothers, 1921).

19. See John Patrick Diggins, *The Promise of Pragmatism: Modernism and the Crisis of Knowledge and Authority* (Chicago: University of Chicago Press, 1994),

299–305; and Bernard Crick, *The American Science of Politics* (Berkeley: University of California Press, 1964), 74.

20. Crick, *The American Science*, 75, 84–85. It was likely in this sense that the Progressive political scientist J. Allen Smith said of his generation, "We were all Deweyites before we read Dewey." Quoted in Charles Forcey, *Crossroads of Liberalism* (New York: Oxford University Press, 1961), 21.

21. "Charles Horton Cooley," *Encyclopedia of the Social Sciences*, vol. 3 (New York: Macmillan, 1937), 355–356.

22. Among classic writings to which Cooley was likely responding were those of John Stuart Mill, Alexis de Tocqueville, and Gustav Le Bon. For a synthesis of such criticism of public opinion, see Jurgen Habermas, *The Structural Transformation of the Public Sphere: An Inquiry into a Category of Bourgeois Society* (Cambridge, Mass.: MIT Press, 1991), 129–140; Charles Horton Cooley, *Social Organization: A Study of the Larger Mind* (New York: Charles Scribner's Sons, 1909), 118, 121–123, 149, 152–153; David E. Price, "Community and Control: Critical Democratic Theory in the Progressive Period," *American Political Science Review* 68 (1974), 1663–1678, Cooley quoted on 1666; See also Marshall J. Cohen, *Charles Horton Cooley and the Social Self in American Thought* (New York: Garland Publishing, 1982), esp. 197–239; and Dorothy Ross, *The Origins of American Social Science* (New York: Cambridge University Press, 1991), 246–247; on the Progressive intellectuals' construction of the concept of public opinion, see Eldon J. Eisenach, *The Lost Promise of Progressivism* (Lawrence: University Press of Kansas, 1994), 74–103.

23. Croly quoted in Forcey, *Crossroads of Liberalism*, 19–20, 156–158.

24. Ibid., 77, 79, 82.

25. Lippmann quoted in ibid., 114.

26. Ibid., 118.

27. "A Toast to John Dewey," in Christopher Lasch, ed., *The Social Thought of Jane Addams* (Indianapolis: Bobbs Merrill, 1965).

28. John Dewey, "Introduction," in Jane Addams, *Peace and Bread in Time of War* (Boston: G. K. Hall, 1945), xix–xx.

29. Jane Addams, *Twenty Years at Hull House* (New York: Signet Classics, 1960 [1910]), 94, 98.

30. Jane Addams, *Democracy and Social Ethics* (Cambridge, Mass.: Harvard University Press, 1964), 206.

31. Addams, as quoted in Anne Firor Scott, "Introduction," in ibid., xliv–xlv.

32. Dorothy Ross, "Gendered Social Knowledge: Domestic Discourse, Jane Addams, and the Possibilities of Social Science," in Helene Silverberg, ed., *Gender and American Social Science: The Formative Years* (Princeton: Princeton University Press, forthcoming); see also Kathryn Kish Sklar, "Hull-House Maps and Papers: Social Science as Women's Work in the 1890s," in Martin Bulmer, Kevin Bales, and Sklar, eds., *The Social Survey in Historical Perspective, 1880–1940* (New York: Cambridge University Press, 1991), 111–147.

33. Jane Addams, *Newer Ideals of Peace* (New York: Macmillan, 1907), 17–18.

34. Ibid., 18.

35. Addams, *Democracy and Social Ethics*, 178–180, 199–200.

36. Scott, in ibid., xxxviii.
37. *Jane Addams: A Centennial Reader* (New York: Macmillan, 1960), 181–182.
38. Vida D. Scudder, *A Listener in Babel* (Boston: Houghton Mifflin, 1903), 316–319; "Vida D. Scudder," *Notable American Women: The Modern Period* (Cambridge, Mass.: Harvard University Press, 1980), 636–638 (reference courtesy Sarah Deutsch).
39. Ellen Fitzpatrick, *Endless Crusade: Women Social Scientists and Progressive Reform* (New York: Oxford University Press, 1990), 79, 81–82. On the distinctive characterisics of the world of the female professional reformer, see Robyn Muncy, *Creating a Female Dominion in American Reform, 1890–1935* (New York: Oxford University Press, 1991), esp. 3–37.
40. Fitzpatrick, *Endless Crusade*, 197.
41. Ibid. 144.
42. Ibid. 191.
43. See, e.g., Eileen Janes Yeo, *The Contests for Social Science: Relations and Representations of Gender and Class* (London: Rivers Oram Press, 1996), 254–256; and Martha Vicinus, *Independent Women: Work and Community for Single Women, 1850–1920* (Chicago: University of Chicago Press, 1985), 211–246. On class tensions within the benevolence of female professionalism, see Muncy, *Creating a Female Dominion*, esp. xv, 21–22.
44. For closer examination of Lewis's work, including the philosophical crudeness of his appropriations of great works, see Mark Pittenger, *American Socialists and Evolutionary Thought, 1870–1920* (Madison: University of Wisconsin Press, 1993), 139–145.
45. Miss E. F. Andrews, "The Monopoly of Intellect," *International Socialist Review* 1 (June 1901), 765, 768. E. F. Andrews "of Montgomery, Alabama" also contributed occasionally to the *ISR*. See, e.g., Andrews, "Socialism and the Negro," *International Socialist Review* 5 (March 1905), 524–526.
46. Taylor as quoted in Georg Leidenberger, "Working-Class Progressivism and the Politics of Transportation in Chicago, 1895–1907" (Ph.D. diss., University of North Carolina at Chapel Hill, 1995), 153–154; see also 45, 83.
47. Hutchins Hapgood, *The Spirit of Labor* (New York: Duffield & Co., 1907), 210–211.
48. Weinberg, *Edward Alsworth Ross*, 152–159.
49. For the problem of periodization in progressive thought generally, see Henry May, *The End of American Innocence: A Study of the First Years of Our Own Time, 1912–1917* (New York: Columbia University Press, 1992 [1959]).
50. Jackson Lears, *The Fables of Abundance: A Cultural History of Advertising in America* (New York: Basic Books, 1994), 223–224.
51. On the structural setting for Progressive politics, see Richard L. McCormick, *The Party Period and Public Policy: American Politics from the Age of Jackson to the Progressive Era* (New York: Oxford University Press, 1986), 263–288; and Michael E. McGerr, *The Decline of Popular Politics: The American North 1865–1928* (New York: Oxford University Press, 1986).
52. Frank Parsons, for example, a chief proponent of direct democracy, argued that professional politicians had become an "elective aristocracy" selling the

fruits of popular sovereignty to economic "monopolists." Stow Persons, *American Minds: A History of Ideas* (New York: Henry Holt, 1958), 363–367.

53. George Kibbe Turner, "Manufacturing Public Opinion: The New Art of Making Presidents by Press Bureau," *McClure's Magazine* 39 (July 1912), 322.

54. Ibid.; see also William Irwin, "Publicity, Public Opinion, and the Wily Press Agent," *Literary Digest* 67 (Oct. 2, 1920), 58–62. On the rise of public relations, see Gregory W. Bush, *Lord of Attention: Gerald Stanley Lee and the Crowd Metaphor in Industrializing America* (Amherst: University of Massachusetts Press, 1991), esp. 132–134.

55. Turner, "Manufacturing Public Opinion," 327.

56. For elaboration on this theme, see Chapter 3.

57. References here are to Burke's *Reflections on the Revolution in France*, Bagehot's *Physics and Politics*, and Maine's *Popular Government;* Martin J. Wiener, *Between Two Worlds: The Political Thought of Graham Wallas* (Oxford: Clarendon Press, 1971), 61–97 passim; see also Patrick Brantlinger, *Bread and Circuses: Theories of Mass Culture as Social Decay* (Ithaca: Cornell University Press, 1983), 53–81.

58. H. Stuart Hughes, *Consciousness and Society: The Reorientation of European Social Thought, 1890–1930* (New York, Knopf, 1958), 65.

59. Alexis de Tocqueville, *Democracy in America*, 2 vols., ed. Phillips Bradley (New York: Random House, 1954 [1835, 1840]) and James Bryce, *The American Commonwealth* (New York: Macmillan, 1924 [1888]; see also Edmund Ions, *James Bryce and American Democracy, 1870–1922* (London: Macmillan, 1968).

60. E. L. Godkin, *Problems of Democracy* (New York: 1896); Moisei Ostrogorski, *Democracy and the Organization of Political Parties*, 2 vols. (New York: Quadrangle Books, 1964 [1902]). Ostrogorski's close descriptions of English and American institutions set the stage for the subsequent, even more sober theoretical masterworks of Max Weber and Robert Michels. Seymour Martin Lipset, "Ostrogorskii, Moisei Ia," in *International Encyclopedia of the Social Sciences*, 11 (New York: Macmillan, 1968), 347–351; Wiener, *Between Two Worlds*, 63, 81.

61. Wiener, *Between Two Worlds*, 81.

62. Lowell, *Public Opinion and Public Government* (1913) as quoted in Terence Ball, "An Ambivalent Alliance: Political Science and American Democracy," in James Farr, John S. Dryzek, and Stephen T. Leonard, eds., *Political Science in History: Research Programs and Political Traditions* (New York: Cambridge University Press, 1995), 51–52.

63. As quoted in Wiener, *Between Two Worlds*, 45. Despite his doubts, Wallas himself remained committed to the principles of industrial democracy.

64. As quoted in ibid., 65.

65. Ronald Steel, *Walter Lippmann and the American Century* (New York: Vintage, 1980), 42–43; Walter Lippmann, *A Preface to Politics* (Ann Arbor: University of Michigan Press, 1962 [1914]), 49. On modernism see Morton Gabriel White, *Social Thought in America: The Revolt against Formalism* (Boston: Beacon Press, 1957).

66. Steel, *Walter Lippmann*, 155–170; see also Randolph S. Bourne, *War and the*

Intellectuals: Collected Essays, 1915–1919, ed. Carl Resek (New York: Harper and Row, 1964).

67. John Dewey, review of Lippmann's *Public Opinion* (originally published in *New Republic,* 1922) in *John Dewey: The Middle Works, 1899–1924* (Carbondale: Southern Illinois University Press, 1983), 337–344, quotation on 337.

68. Walter Lippmann, *Public Opinion* (New York: Free Press, 1922), 13–14; on Lippmann, cf. Robert H. Wiebe, *Self-Rule: A Cultural History of American Democracy* (Chicago: University of Chicago Press, 1995), 173–176.

69. For a sample of postwar progressive disillusionment, see "Where Are the Pre-War Radicals?" *Survey* 55 (Feb. l, 1926), 556–565. This symposium suggested opposite pathways, either a tendency (like Lippmann's) toward political re-treat (e.g., George W. Alger, William Allen White, Norman Hapgood, Ida Tarbell, Fremont Older) or a hardening of leftism toward open affiliation with socialist or workers' movements (e.g., Frederic Howe, Roger N. Baldwin, Norman Thomas). See also John A. Thompson, *Reformers and War: American Progressive Publicists and the First World War* (New York: Cambridge University Press, 1987), 234–286.

70. Creel as quoted in Thompson, *Reformers and War,* 280.

71. On the developing critique of mass culture, see Patrick Brantlinger, *Bread and Circuses: Theories of Mass Culture as Social Decay* (Ithaca: Cornell University Press, 1983). The word "ballyhoo" as a term for sensational advertising first entered American discourse in 1901. Its use may derive from an 1880s ref-erence to a "ballyhoo bird," a creature reportedly with four wings and two heads that could whistle through one bill while singing through the other. *American Heritage Dictionary of the English Language* (Boston: Houghton Mifflin, 1992), 142; Lee W. Heubner, "The Discovery of Propaganda: Changing Attitudes toward Public Communication in America, 1900–1930" (Ph.D. diss., Harvard University, 1968), 200, 274.

72. Bernays quoted in Henry F. Pringle, "Mass Psychologist," *American Mercury* 19 (February 1930), 160.

73. Edward L. Bernays, *Biography of an Idea: Memoirs of Public Relations Counsel Edward L. Bernays* (New York: Simon and Schuster, 1965), 292.

74. *Progaganda* (New York: Horace Liveright, 1928 [1920]), 92.

75. For elaboration of this theme, see T. J. Jackson Lears, "From Salvation to Self-Realization: Advertising and the Therapeutic Roots of the Consumer Culture, 1880–1930," 1–38, and Robert Westbrook, "Politics as Consumption: Managing the Modern American Election," 143–174, in Richard Wightman Fox and T. J. Jackson Lears, eds., *The Culture of Consumption: Critical Essays in American History, 1880–1980* (New York: Pantheon, 1983).

76. Lears, "From Salvation to Self-Realization," 31–33.

77. Ralph Volney Harlow, *Samuel Adams: Promoter of the American Revolution* (New York: Henry Holt and Co., 1923), 25.

78. George Creel, *Rebel at Large: Recollections of Fifty Crowded Years* (New York: G. P. Putnam's Sons, 1947), 359; Bernays as quoted in Lears, "From Salvation to Self-Realization," 20.

79. Review of Lippmann, *Public Opinion,* 337–344.

80. Review of *The Phantom Public* (originally published in *New Republic* in 1925), in Jo Ann Boydston, ed., *The Later Works of John Dewey, 1925–53*, vol. 2 (Carbondale: Southern Illinois Press, 1984), 213–220.
81. John Dewey, *The Public and Its Problems* (New York: Henry Holt, 1927), 123.
82. Ibid., 124–125.
83. 110–142.
84. Ibid., 158.
85. Ibid., 163.
86. Ibid., 167–181. Indeed, for a few postwar social democrats, education in "scientific thinking" became a grand reclamation project. James Harvey Robinson, who quit his position in the Columbia University history department to take up residence at the New School, believed that from "the slaying or maiming of fifteen million of our young men, resulting in incalculable loss, continued disorder, and bewilderment," the first priority and "remaining hope is Intelligence." The challenge was to take advantage of the "great stock of scientific knowledge unknown to our grandfathers" and somehow apply it to human affairs. Moral and economic regeneration of the world required a new, "unprecedented attitude of mind," for until now, society had just been "muddling through." *The Mind in the Making*, 4–5, 13, 23–24.
87. *The Public and Its Problems*, 181.
88. Ibid., 184; see also George Dykhuizen, *The Life and Mind of John Dewey* (Carbondale: Southern Illinois University Press, 1973), 226–227. In more recent years, the work of Jurgen Habermas has posed a similar, if equally elusive, vision of democracy as "communicative rationality." See, e.g., Dieter Misgeld, "Education and Cultural Invasion: Critical Social Theory, Education as Instruction, and the 'Pedagogy of the Oppressed,'" in John Forester, ed., *Critical Theory and Public Life* (Cambridge, Mass.: MIT Press, 1985), 77–118.
89. Dewey as quoted in Richard Wightman Fox, "Epitaph for Middletown: Robert S. Lynd and the Analysis of Consumer Culture," in Fox and Lears, *The Culture of Consumption*, 127.
90. In the last chapter of *The Public and Its Problems* Dewey himself acknowledges that "perhaps to most, probably to many, the conclusions which have been stated as to the conditions upon which depends the emergence of the Public from its eclipse will seem close to denial of the possibility of realizing the idea of a democratic public" (185). For a more sympathetic reading of Dewey's defense vs. Lippmann, see Thomas Bender, *New York Intellect: A History of Intellectual Life in New York City from 1750 to the Beginnings of Our Own Time* (New York: Knopf, 1987), 312–316; see also Westbrook, *John Dewey*, 300–318, and Wiebe, *Self-Rule*, 176–177.
91. Dewey as quoted in Fox, "Epitaph for Middletown," 127.
92. *The Public and Its Problems*, 215, 184.
93. See Arthur E. Murphy, "Philosophical Scholarship" in Merle Curti, ed., *American Scholarship in the Twentieth Century* (New York: Russell & Russell, 1953), 185–186; on Dewey's response to Lippmann, cf. Westbrook, *John Dewey*, 300–318.

94. Dorothy Ross, *The Origins of American Social Science* (New York: Cambridge University Press, 1991), 158.

95. Ibid., 311.

96. Fred H. Matthews, *Quest for an American Sociology: Robert E. Park and the Chicago School* (Montreal: McGill-Queens University Press, 1977), 95–97.

97. Martin Bulmer, *The Chicago School of Sociology: Institutionalization, Diversity, and the Rise of Sociological Research* (Chicago: University of Chicago Press, 1984), 47.

98. Dorothy Ross, *American Social Science*, 352–356.

99. William I. Thomas and Florian Znaniecki, *The Polish Peasant in Europe and America*, vol. 2 (New York: Alfred A. Knopf, 1927), 1462–63.

100. Ibid., 1472.

101. Ibid., 2240–44.

102. Donald Fleming, "Attitude: The History of a Concept," *Perspectives in American History* 1 (1967), 329, 333–334, 344–347, 358–359.

103. C. S. Yoakum as quoted in Sarah Lyons Watts, *Order against Chaos: Business Culture and Labor Ideology in America, 1880–1915* (New York: Greenwood Press, 1991), 127–128.

104. Robert E. Park and Herbert A. Miller, *Old World Traits Transplanted* (New York: Harper and Brothers, 1921), 262. William I. Thomas apparently wrote most of this volume, although his contemporary notoriety forced him to remain anonymous, as documented by Winifred Rauschenbush, *Robert E. Park: Biography of a Sociologist* (Durham: Duke University Press, 1979), 93.

105. Lumley quoted in Weinberg, *Edward Alsworth Ross*, 93–94.

106. From *Introduction to the Science of Sociology* (1921), as quoted in Robert E. Park, *On Social Control and Collective Behavior* (Chicago: University of Chicago Press, 1967), xiii. The unseen hand of economic development, Park believed, would eventually generate "a vast unconscious cooperation of races and peoples." Cf. Gary Gerstle, "The Protean Character of American Liberalism," *American Historical Review* 99 (October 1994), 1043–73.

107. Matthews, *American Sociology*, 57–84, quotation 82.

108. Merriam as quoted in Raymond Seidelman, *Disenchanted Realists: Political Science and the American Crisis, 1884–1984* (Albany: State University of New York Press, 1985), 125, 135; Charles Merriam, *New Aspects of Politics* (Chicago: University of Chicago Press, 1925), 7, 18–19. On Merriam see also Dorothy Ross, *American Social Science*, 452–453; and Barry D. Karl, *Charles E. Merriam and the Study of Politics* (Chicago: University of Chicago Press, 1974), esp. 90, 105–107.

109. *The Making of Citizens* (New York: Teachers College Press, 1966 [1931]), 60.

110. Mark C. Smith, *Social Science in the Crucible: The American Debate over Objectivity and Purpose, 1918–1941* (Durham: Duke University Press, 1994), 218–219.

111. Harold Lasswell, *Propaganda Technique in the World War* (New York: Alfred A. Knopf, 1927), 216, 222.

112. Lawrence R. Veysey, *The Emergence of the American University* (Chicago: University of Chicago Press, 1965), 180–251. Cornell's Andrew Dickson White recalled his reaction to his first view of Oxford and Cambridge: "My heart sank within me. Every feature of the little American college seemed all

the more sordid. But gradually I began consoling myself by building air-castles." *Autobiography* (New York: The Century Co., 1905), 288 (reference courtesy of Scott de Marchi).

113. Gerald Graff, *Professing Literature: An Institutional History* (Chicago: University of Chicago Press, 1987), 59–60.

114. Santayana quoted in Veysey, *American University*, 214.

115. Bruce Clayton, *Forgotten Prophet: The Life of Randolph Bourne* (Baton Rouge: Louisiana State University Press, 1984), 212.

116. Luther V. Hendricks, "James Harvey Robinson and the New School for Social Research," *Journal of Higher Education* 20 (January 1949), 1–11, 58, quotation 5. On the New School leaders, see also Thomas Bender, *Intellect and Public Life: Essays on the Social History of Academic Intellectuals in the United States* (Baltimore: Johns Hopkins University Press, 1993), 67–70.

117. Richard Hofstadter, *The Progressive Historians: Turner, Beard, Parrington* (New York: Alfred A. Knopf, 1968), 174–175.

118. Robert J. Schaefer, "Educational Activities of the Garment Unions, 1890–1948: A Study in Workers' Education in the International Ladies Garment Workers' Union and the Amalgamated Clothing Workers in New York City" (Ph.D. diss., Columbia University, 1951), 53–71.

119. On worker education initiatives in the early twentieth century, see Richard J. Altenbaugh, *Education for Struggle: The American Labor Colleges of the 1920s and 1930s* (Philadelphia: Temple University Press, 1990), 19–55. On the independent worker colleges, see Altenbaugh, *Education for Struggle*, passim; for the Southern Summer School, see Mary F. Frederickson, *A Place to Speak Our Minds: The Southern Summer School for Women Workers in Industry, 1927–1950* (Bloomington: Indiana University Press, forthcoming).

120. Altenbaugh, *Education for Struggle*, 72–75.

121. Ibid., 106.

122. Ibid., 285, n. 43, 76–77; Gloria Garrett Samson, "Toward a New Social Order—The American Fund for Public Service: Clearinghouse for Radicalism in the 1920s," (Ph.D. diss., University of Rochester, 1987), 359.

123. Herbert Ellsworth Cory, *The Intellectuals and the Wage Workers: A Study in Educational Psychoanalysis* (New York: Sunwise Turn, 1919), 58–59, 270. The case of a jailed Seattle Wobbly who had ordered a copy of Kant's *Critique of Pure Reason* helped convinced Cory that "most socialists" had moved "beyond economic determinism" to "a more complex point of view" (72–73).

124. Ibid., 245–248, 241–243.

125. Ibid., 272–273.

126. "Labor's Challenge to Education," *The New Republic* 2 (March 1921), 16; Peter Dodge, ed., *A Documentary Study of Hendrik de Man, Socialist Critic of Marxism* (Princeton: Princeton University Press, 1979), "Introduction," 3–17.

127. Horace M. Kallen, *Education, the Machine, and the Workers: An Essay in the Psychology of Education in Industrial Society* (New York: New Republic, 1925), vii–viii, 34–35.

128. Ibid., 52–58, quotation 58.

129. Ibid., 184–194.

130. For a carefully nuanced treatment of organized labor strategies in the 1920s, see Dana Frank, *Purchasing Power: Consumer Organizing, Gender, and the Seattle Labor Movement, 1919–1929* (New York: Cambridge University Press, 1994), esp. 212–246.

131. Schaefer, "Educational Activities of the Garment Unions," 91–96, 124–137.

132. Charles Sweeney, "Labour's Need for Educational Equipment to Effectively Exercise the Newly Secured Right of Collective Bargaining," n.d.; Felix Frankfurter to Grosvenor Clarkson, Sept. 11, 1918; Matthew Woll to Clarkson, Oct. 24, 1918. Although Sweeney's proposal failed to interest the AFL, it did intrigue Secretary of Labor William B. Wilson, who dispatched Sweeney on his projected tour as a special agent of the Bureau of Labor Statistics. In sending Sweeney, the ex–trade unionist Wilson tried to mollify Woll by agreeing with him that Sweeney had underestimated the native intelligence of American working men: "Personally," he wrote, "I have come in contact with college professors, clergymen, sociologists, lawyers, capitalists, . . . and I have no hesitancy in saying that I have found a larger percentage of . . . workers who are familiar with the principles of Voltaire, Rousseau, Adam Smith, Malthus, Ricardo, James Mill, John Stewart Mill [sic], Herbert Spencer, Owen, Marx, Engle [sic], George, and even the lesser lights in the firmament of political economy than I have amongst any of the other other groups." William B. Wilson to Mathew Woll, Oct. 28, 1918, William B. Wilson Papers, Historical Society of Pennsylvania (references courtesy of Daniel Ernst).

133. For elaboration on AFL attitudes towards intellectuals, see Chaps. 2 and 4.

134. David Saposs, "Role of [the] Intellectual in the U.S." (unpublished ms., April 1932), David J. Saposs Papers, State Historical Society of Wisconsin, Madison (hereafter SHSW).

135. Cory, *The Emancipation of a Freethinker* (Milwaukee: Bruce Publishing Co., 1943), 35, 59, 62.

136. Henry [sic] de Man, *The Psychology of Socialism* (London: George Allen & Unwin), 36, 268–269.

137. Still fashioning private dreams of a future socialism within a united Europe, de Man escaped to Switzerland after the war, but was ultimately convicted in absentia of treason by a Belgian military court. He died in an automobile accident in 1953. Dodge, *A Documentary Study of Hendrik de Man*, 16–17.

138. Robert B. Reich, *The Work of Nations: Preparing Ourselves for 21st Century Capitalism* (New York: Knopf, 1991).

2. Defining the People: The Wisconsin School of Labor History

1. Mark Perlman, *Labor Union Theories in America: Background and Development* (Evanston, Ill.: Row, Peterson, 1958), 1.

2. From 1870 to 1910, the number of university and college students rose four times as fast as the country's population. The change was especially dramatic at the postgraduate level. The number of graduate students had increased from

fewer than 50 in 1870 to nearly 6,000 by 1900, with 90 percent of Ph.D.s awarded by fourteen institutions, and a full 55 percent from a "big five": California, Chicago, Columbia, Harvard, and Johns Hopkins. The social sciences formed a part of this wave, with history, economics, anthropology, and political science creating graduate departments and journals in the 1880s and sociology following in the 1890s. Within economics, or political economy as it was then called, 3 Ph.D.s were awarded in the 1870s, 11 in the 1880s, and a further 95 in the 1890s. A total of 228 American women received doctoral degrees prior to 1900: of these, 66 were in the social sciences and only 5 in economics. A. W. Coats, "The Educational Revolution and the Professionalization of American Economics," in William J. Barber, ed., *Breaking the Academic Mould: Economists and American Higher Learning in the Nineteenth Century* (Middletown, Conn.: Wesleyan University Press, 1988), 344–345; Alexandra Oleson and John Voss, "Introduction," xii and Dorothy Ross, "The Development of the Social Sciences," 108, in Oleson and Voss, eds., *The Organization of Knowledge in Modern America, 1860–1920* (Baltimore: Johns Hopkins University Press, 1979); Walter Crosby Eells, "Earned Doctorates for Women in the Nineteenth Century," AAUP Bulletin 42 (Washington, D.C.: American Association of University Professors, 1956), 646, 648. For the best elaboration on women's distinct experience in the emerging world of social science research see Ellen Fitzpatrick, *Endless Crusade: Women Social Scientists and Progressive Reform* (New York: Oxford University Press, 1990).

3. Four of the most prominent young scholars to engage the labor question in the late 1880s—Richard T. Ely, Edmund J. James, Simon Nelson Patten, and Henry Carter Adams—had each been influenced by evangelical religious backgrounds as well as graduate work in Germany. The German graduate education model was already being adapted to American circumstances, beginning with Johns Hopkins University, by the late 1870s. Mary O. Furner, *Advocacy and Objectivity: A Crisis in the Professionalization of American Social Science, 1865–1905* (Lexington, Ky.: University Press of Kentucky, 1975), 35–58; Paul J. McNulty, *The Origins and Development of Labor Economics: A Chapter in the History of Social Thought* (Cambridge, Mass.: MIT Press, 1980), 127–140.

4. *John L. Thomas, Alternative America: Henry George, Edward Bellamy, Henry Demarest Lloyd, and the Adversary Tradition* (Cambridge, Mass.: Belknap Press of Harvard University Press, 1983).

5. Bruno Cartosio, "Strikes and Economics: Working-Class Inurgency and the Birth of Labor Historiography in the 1880s," in Dirk Hoerder, ed., *American Labor and Immigration History, 1870–1920: Recent European Research* (Urbana: University of Illinois Press, 1983), 23–25, 27. By 1886 fifteen states, following Massachusetts' lead in 1869, had organized bureaus of labor statistics.

6. Benjamin G. Rader, *The Academic Mind and Reform: The Influence of Richard T. Ely in American Life* (Lexington: University of Kentucky Press, 1966), 2–27, 54, 56.

7. Richard T. Ely, *The Labor Movement in America* (New York: T. Y. Crowell and Co., 1886), 5–6.

8. Quoted in Rader, *The Academic Mind,* 83.

9. Quoted in George M. Fredrickson, "Intellectuals and the Labor Question in Late Nineteenth-Century America," paper presented to the AHA Annual Meeting, New York City, December 1985.

10. Ely, *Labor Movement,* 75; Rader, *The Academic Mind,* 82.

11. Rader, *The Academic Mind,* 82; Ely, *Labor Movement,* ix, xi; Powderly to Ely, June 6, 1885, and Dec. 22, 1886, Richard T. Ely Papers, State Historical Society of Wisconsin, Madison (hereafter cited as SHSW).

12. Joseph Dorfman, *The Economic Mind in American Civilization,* vol. 3 (New York: Viking Press, 1949), 164–174.

13. Cornell trustees were skeptical enough of evolving currents in professional economics that they "balanced" Adams's appointment with that of a non-professional high-tariff advocate, a humiliating arrangement that the *Nation* called the "Duplex Professorship." Furner, *Advocacy and Objectivity,* 130.

14. Henry Carter Adams, "The Labor Problem," *Scientific American Supplement* 22 (Aug. 21, 1886), 8861–63.

15. Dorfman, *The Economic Mind,* 188–205, quotation 188; see also Franek Rozwadowski, "From Recitation Room to Research Seminar: Political Economy at Columbia University," in Barber, *Breaking the Academic Mould,* 199–200. On the political significance of Clark's marginalism, see James Livingston, "The Social Analysis of Economic History and Theory: Conjectures on Late Nineteenth-century American Development," *American Historical Review* 92 (February 1987), 69–95.

16. John B. Clark, *The Philosophy of Wealth: Economic Principles Newly Formulated* (Boston: Ginn & Co., 1894), 126–148, 174–202.

17. Rozwadowski, "From Recitation Room," 196–197; Furner, *Advocacy and Objectivity,* 98–99.

18. *Journal of Social Science* 27 (October 1890), 44, 84–85, 87–88; cf. Rhoda Hellman, *Henry George Reconsidered* (New York: Carlton Press, 1987), 70–73, and Thomas Bender, *Intellect and Public Life: Essays on the Social History of Academic Intellectuals in the United States* (Baltimore: Johns Hopkins University Press, 1993), 53–66.

19. Dorfman, *The Economic Mind,* 160–61.

20. For contrasting treatments of the AEA, see Furner, *Advocacy and Objectivity,* and Thomas L. Haskell, *The Emergence of Professional Social Science: The American Social Science Association and the Nineteenth-Century Crisis of Authority* (Urbana: University of Illinois Press, 1977); on the centrality of the labor problem to the early professional economists, see McNulty, *The Origins and Development of Labor Economics,* 142–151.

21. *Labor: Its Rights and Wrongs* (Westport, Conn.: Hyperion Press, 1975 [1886]), 30. Of fifty chartering members of the AEA, twenty-three were ministers or ex-ministers. A. W. Coats, "The Educational Revolution and the Professionalization of American Economics," in Barber, *Breaking the Academic Mould,* 358.

22. Roger D. Horne, "John R. Commons and the Climate of Progressivism" (Ph.D. diss., University of Oklahoma, 1989), 57.

23. Lafayette G. Harter, Jr., *John R. Commons: His Assault on Laissez-Faire* (Corvallis: Oregon State University Press, 1962), 13–19. Commons was attracted to Johns Hopkins precisely by the radical notoriety of Ely, choosing his college after reading a nasty review in *The Nation* of Ely's *Studies in the Evolution of Industrial Society.* Ely to Robert Hunter, Oct. 21, 1903, Richard T. Ely Papers, SHSW. A baseball aficionado (and pretty fair pitcher in his Oberlin college days), Commons dated his conversion to economic scepticism to his personal refutation in 1885–86 of Herbert Spencer's casual claim that a curve ball defied the laws of physics: "He knew not the seams on the ball and forgot the friction of the air." Commons, *Myself: The Autobiography of John R. Commons* (Madison: University of Wisconsin Press, 1963 [1934]), 28.

24. Dorfman, *The Economic Mind,* 285.

25. Arthur T. Hadley, "Economic Theory and Political Morality," and "Comment" by John R. Commons in *Publications of the AEA, Papers and Proceedings of the Twelfth Annual Meeting* (New York: Macmillan, 1900), 45–88, quotations 61, 65, 69, 77, 79; cf. Furner, *Advocacy and Objectivity,* 273–277.

26. Dorfman, *The Economic Mind,* 101–110.

27. *Publications of the AEA* 3 (New York: Macmillan, 1889), 162.

28. Richard Hofstadter and Walter P. Metzger, *The Development of Academic Freedom in the United States* (New York: Columbia University Press, 1955), 31.

29. Furner, *Advocacy and Objectivity,* 271–272.

30. On the problem of contemporary intellectual authority, see Furner, *Advocacy and Objectivity,* 81–106; Richard Hofstadter and Walter P. Metzger, *Development,* 401–402; and Haskell, *The Emergence of Professional Social Science,* 190–210. Having dislodged natural law, the radical economists faced the problem of what authority to turn to, other than arbitrary moral claims or public opinion, neither of which was satisfactory to academics as a basis for expertise. Academic professionalism, reigning in its political judgments and public interventions, proved one enduring solution.

31. James Livingston, "The Social Analysis of Economic History and Theory: Conjectures on Late Nineteenth-Century American Development," *American Historical Review* 92 (February 1987), 69–95.

32. Related cases of political discrimination involved economist E. Benjamin Andrews at Brown and sociologist E. A. Ross at Stanford. Dorfman, *The Economic Mind,* 240; Hofstadter and Metzger, *Academic Freedom,* 420–423. While Hofstadter and Metzger's long view of free speech conflicts in American academe remains a most valuable basic work, it is flawed by their own ideological blinders. So concerned were they in the early 1950s to ward off totalitarianism (and intellectual intolerance) from the extremes of left and right that they were inclined to miss the debilitating effects of bureaucratically imposed norms of academic behavior by the "liberal" center. By identifying the philosophical "empiricist" and "commonsense" traditions of American thought as the chief source of the relative political "neutrality" of American academics, the authors underestimated their own evidence for the political limits imposed on university faculty by the turn of the century. See esp. 400–403, 450–451, 506.

33. Adams, "The Labor Problem," 8863, 8877–78; A. W. Coats, "Henry Carter Adams: A Case Study in the Emergence of the Social Sciences in the United States, 1850–1900," *American Studies* 2 (October 1968), 189.

34. Furner, *Advocacy and Objectivity*, 115–124, 139–142, 277; Coats, "Henry Carter Adams," 195; Dorfman, *The Economic Mind*, 171–172; Coats, "Professionalization," 365; Haskell, *The Emergence of Professional Social Science*, 187.

35. Furner, *Advocacy and Objectivity*, 147–158; Rader, *The Academic Mind*, 152–154. Excusing his apparent hypocrisy, Ely explained to the associate editor of the *Outlook*, "Suppose if you should become known as a radical you would lose your position on the 'Outlook,' and on account of alleged radicalism you could never secure any other position. Would you not under these circumstances feel a little sensitive about the epithet 'radical'? You see what it can do in the case of Professor Bemis"; Rader, *The Academic Mind*, 153.

36. Rader, *The Academic Mind*, 152–154.

37. Ibid., 192–222, 224–227, 236.

38. Hofstadter and Metzger, *Academic Freedom*, 427–428; Furner, *Advocacy and Objectivity*, 168–198. For a careful assessment of the Bemis case, see Harold E. Bergquist, Jr., "The Edward W. Bemis Controversy at the University of Chicago," *AAUP Bulletin* 58 (Winter 1972), 384–393; Furner, *Advocacy and Objectivity*, 196–198.

39. Commons, *Myself*, 52; Furner, *Advocacy and Objectivity*, 202; Ely to Robert Hunter, April 26, 1903, reel 25, Richard T. Ely Papers, SHSW; *Myself*, 95.

40. Commons, *Myself*, 58–59.

41. On Commons's four phases of trade union analysis, see Mark Perlman, *Labor Union Theories*, 176–190, esp. 180, 182.

42. Pressed by reporters to explain his departure from Syracuse, Commons kept mum. "He [the Chancellor] gave me a rousing send-off. Speaking to a general University convocation, he bewailed the loss of one of their ablest and most popular professors . . . And there I was sitting on the platform beside him. So I learned the virtue of silence. It makes eulogists instead of avengers." *Myself*, 60–61; T. N. Carver to Richard T. Ely, Dec. 20, 1903, Richard T. Ely Papers, SHSW. As early as Ely's problems with the Board of Regents, Commons had expressed sympathy towards Ely's fears about the "timeliness of expressions of advanced views." With a touch of wishful thinking, Commons wrote Ely in 1895, "I believe I am getting more cautious." Bari Jane Watkins, "The Professors and the Unions: American Academic Social Theory and Labor Reform, 1893–1915" (Ph.D. diss., Yale University, 1976), 17.

43. Harter, *John R. Commons*, 89–129.

44. Furner, *Advocacy and Objectivity*, 271–272. This is not to say that respectable reformist intentions assured academic immunity from outside pressures. In 1910, for example, a visit by Emma Goldman to Madison triggered charges and a Board of Visitors investigation of "socialist teaching" on campus, which centered on Edward A. Ross and the Economics Department, of which both Ross and Commons were members. Among graduate students called to tes-

tify, Selig Perlman was asked, "Do you think Sociology and Socialism are identical?" Perlman, who had sworn to his mentor Commons, "Brother, they will not fire you on my testimony," would take pride in the official exoneration of the faculty, especially the reference to "striking instances of foreigners who have come to the university as students believing in anarchism and violence, who have been led to discard such beliefs through the instruction given in the university." Merle Curti and Vernon Carstensen, *The University of Wisconsin: A History, 1848–1925*, vol. 2 (Madison: University of Wisconsin Press, 1949), 63–67; Selig Perlman interview, SHSW, April 13, 1950.

45. Commons, *Labor and Administration* (New York: Macmillan, 1913), 72, 78–79, 83. These comments were first published in the *American Journal of Sociology* based on remarks before a 1906 meeting of the American Sociological Society.

46. Commons, *Myself*, 88.

47. John R. Commons to Lloyd, June 5, 1903, Henry D. Lloyd Papers, SHSW (reference courtesy of Steven Sapolsky).

48. U.S. Senate Committe on Education and Labor, *Report upon the Relations between Labor and Capital and Testimony*, vol. 1 (Washington, D.C.: Government Printing Office, 1885), 460; Gompers, quoted by Commons, *Myself*, 87; AFL, *Proceedings of the 18th Annual Convention*, 1898, 5.

49. Matthew Woll, "Labor Will Lead," *American Federationist* (June 1919), 513; see also Lyle Cooper, "The AFL and the Intellectuals," *Political Science Quarterly* 43 (1928), 388–407.

50. John Frey to W. A. Appleton, Dec. 21, 1928, Frey Papers, Library of Congress.

51. For elaboration on some of the intellectual and political differences between Gompers and Commons, see Chapter 3, "The People's Expert."

52. Commons et al., *History of Labour in the United States* (New York: Macmillan, 1918), vol. 1, 18–19. On comparable intellectual-labor relations in Europe during the same period, see David Beetham, "Reformism and the 'Bourgeoisification' of the Labour Movement," in Carl Levy, ed., *Socialism and the Intelligentsia, 1880–1914* (London: Routledge and Kegan Paul, 1987), 106–134.

53. Commons, "Labor Movement," in Edwin R. A. Seligman, *Encyclopaedia of the Social Sciences*, vol. 8 (New York: Macmillan, 1932), 685–686.

54. Commons, *Myself*, 87. Commons traced his first encounter with a destructive intellectual to T. A. Schaffer, the "unsuccessful or dismissed minister" whose apparent misguided militancy led the steelworkers to disaster in 1902.

55. Commons et al., *History of Labour*, vol. 1, 19.

56. Commons et al., *History of Labour*, vol. 2, p. 438. The theme is reiterated in Selig Perlman and Philip Taft, eds., *History of Labor*, vol. 4 (New York: Macmillan, 1935), 4–5. Perlman's emphasis on the worker's psychology of job scarcity would soon lead him to abandon Commons's term "wage-consciousness," in favor of "job consciousness." Harter, *John R. Commons*, 196.

57. Selig Perlman, *A Theory of the Labor Movement* (New York: Macmillan, 1928), 5–6.

58. *Theory*, 13–23. In his classic essay "Why Is There No Socialism in the United

States?" (1906) German sociologist Werner Sombart found the answer "on the reefs of roast beef and apple pie." Sombart quoted in Daniel Bell, *The End of Ideology* (Glencoe, Ill.: Free Press, 1960), 267.

59. Selig Perlman to Leiserson, Jan. 28, 1928, William M. Leiserson Papers, SHSW.

60. Robert Park and Herbert E. Miller, *Old World Traits Transplanted* (New York: Harper, 1921), 104 (reference courtesy of John Higham).

61. Stuart A. Rice, "Motives in Radicalism and Social Reform," *American Journal of Sociology* 28 (March 1923), 577–585. Rice's critical scrutiny of social movements apparently developed after his own unhappy immersion in third-party poltitics (most likely the Non-Partisan movement) in 1920. See David L. Sills, ed., *International Encyclopedia of the Social Sciences*, vol. 13 (New York: Macmillan, 1968), entry "Stuart Arthur Rice," 512–513.

62. "When a [workers'] movement is still naive and inchoate," suggested Michels, "the intellectual who offers his services appears as a savior and as such worthy of confidence and admiration . . . [Later, however] labor leaders of proletarian origin tend to discipline severely, to displace and even to mistreat colleagues of upper class origin from a sort of feeling of class struggle." "Intellectuals," in Seligman, ed., *Encyclopaedia*, vol. 8, 122.

63. Perlman, *Theory*, 281. On Deweyan pragmatism and its relation to reform thought, see Andrew Feffer, *The Chicago Pragmatists and American Progressivism* (Ithaca: Cornell University Press, 1993), 1–17, 91–116.

64. Perlman, *Selig Perlman's Lectures on Capitalism and Socialism*, ed. by A. L. Riesch Owen (Madison: University of Wisconsin Press, 1976), 127. On the pragmatists' educational philosophy, see Frank C. Wegener, *The Organic Philosophy of Education* (Dubuque: W. C. Brown, 1957), 26–48, 209–222; and Feffer, *Chicago Pragmatists*, 113–171, 267–316. For Commons's version of this dualism, see "Utilitarian Idealism" and "Horace Greeley and the Working Class Origins of the Republican Party" in Commons, *Labor and Administration*, 1–6, 33, 49–50.

65. Selig Perlman left no papers, and remarkably little biographical information about him survives in published form. Most of the following portrait is drawn from an interview with his son, Mark Perlman, conducted by the author, Jan. 19, 1989, in Pittsburgh. Although the father-son relationship was marked by a classical, European-style formality, Mark Perlman recalls that his father talked to him for a few hours each day about many matters, including the elder's work. That Mark Perlman followed his father into labor economics seems to have sharpened both his understanding and his recollection of his father's words. See Fink, "A Memoir of Selig Perlman and His Life at the University of Wisconsin: Based on an Interview of Mark Perlman," *Labor History* 32 (Fall 1991), 503–525.

66. *New York Times*, March 30, 1908; Selig Perlman to Walling, March 31, 1908, Anna Strunsky Walling Papers, Yale University Library (hereafter cited as ASWP). In this correspondence from New York, Selig spells his family name "Perelman." On Gershuni and the "SRs" see J. L. H. Keep, *The Rise of Social Democracy in Russia* (Oxford: Clarendon Press, 1963), 74; and Oliver H.

Radkey, *The Agrarian Foes of Bolshevism* (New York: Columbia University Press, 1958), 47–87. The SRs, Radkey notes, picked up considerable financial support from Russian immigrant Jews in the United States who were "bitterly hostile to tsarism" (62).

67. Selig Perlman to Walling, March 31, 1908, ASWP.
68. Reminiscence of Selig Perlman, recorded April 13, 1950, SHSW.
69. Selig Perlman, "History of Socialism in Milwaukee, 1893–1910," unpublished ms., University of Wisconsin, 1910, copy in author's possession courtesy of Mark Perlman.
70. Selig Perlman to Walling, Dec. 12, 1910, ASWP.
71. Selig Perlman to Anna Strunsky Walling, Dec. 12, 1910, SHSW.
72. Reminiscence of Selig Perlman, recorded April 13, 1950, SHSW.
73. Mark Perlman interview. For evidence of Commons's stereotypes of Jews, typical for his time, see his *Races and Immigrants in America* (New York: Macmillan, 1920), 88–95, 132, 152–153. The extensive nature of anti-semitism in American academe is amply documented in Peter Novick, *That Noble Dream: The "Objectivity Question" and the American Historical Profession* (New York: Cambridge University Press, 1988), 172–174. For elaboration on the personal relationship between Perlman and Commons, see Leon Fink, "'Intellectuals' versus 'Workers': Academic Requirements and the Creation of Labor History," *American Historical Review* 96 (April 1991), 395–421.
74. Commons, *Myself,* 81; Mark Perlman interview.
75. Mark Perlman recalls the break with Commons as lasting for several years, but this recollection appears contradicted by the timing of reconciliation, after the suicide of Commons's daughter, Rachel, in the early 1930s. Mark Perlman remembers answering a distressful call from Commons, with Commons pleading, "I want Selig," "I must have Selig." Selig Perlman spent the evening trying to comfort his former teacher, who had already been doubly wounded by the death of his devoted wife, Ella (Nel), in 1928 and the disappearance of his son Jack (after abandoning his wife and child, Jack was found fourteen years later driving a milk truck in Hartford, Connecticut, the apparent victim of a combination of mental illness and amnesia).
76. Selig Perlman to Walling, July 27, 1957, ASWP. Perlman died two years later.
77. His only professionally connected government service was his early work for the Commission on Industrial Relations in 1913–14, arranged by Commons, and later consultancy on a history of the World War II War Labor Board; in addition, he had one unsatisfying experience as a labor arbitrator. Mark Perlman, "The Jewish Contribution as Distinct from the Contribution of Jews to Economics," Selig Perlman Memorial Lecture presented April 14, 1981, SHSW (copy in possession of author); Edwin Witte, "Selig Perlman," *Industrial and Labor Relations Review* 13 (April 1960), 335–337.
78. Nor was the lack of contact a mere matter of physical distance from the leading labor figures. Samuel Gompers's official correspondence, a voluminous exchange with thousands of contemporaries inside and outside the labor movement, contains not a single letter to or from Selig Perlman (*AFL Records: The Gompers Era,* SHSW and University of Maryland and Pace University,

microfilm edition, reel 58 correspondence index). Outside Wisconsin, the one labor leader whose company Perlman did enjoy was David Dubinsky; the two spoke Yiddish together. Telephone interview with Mark Perlman, Feb. 14, 1989; Selig Perlman's Lectures, 47–51.

79. Perlman reported to his research supervisor that had it not been for an envelope addressed to William English Walling found on his person, a group of suspicious Wobblies in Lawrence, Massachusetts, might well have thrown him out a window. Perlman to Basil M. Manly, Dec. 4, 1913, U.S. Department of Labor, Commission on Industrial Relations, Administrative file, Record Group 174, National Archives (courtesy of Philip Scranton) (hereafter CIR, RG 174, NA).

80. Selig Perlman, "Preliminary Report of an Investigation of the Relations between Labor and Capital in the Textile Industry in New England," July 24, 1914, CIR, RG 174, NA.

81. Selig Perlman, "Preliminary Report on the Relation of the Immigrant to the Trade Agreement in the Anthracite Region" [1913–14], CIR materials, Box 241, W. Jett Lauck Papers, Special Collections, Alderman Library, University of Virginia.

82. Beginning in the late 1920s, Perlman did have regular contact with trade unionists as one of the directors of the Wisconsin School for Workers. The interaction was very much on his terms, however; Perlman enjoyed a reputation as a "spell-binding lecturer . . . [who] looked at the ceiling all the time." Mark Perlman interview; telephone interview with Robert W. Ozanne, Jan. 4, 1991. For a simplistic political-psychological profile of Perlman, see Benjamin Stolberg, "An Intellectual Afraid," *The Nation* 128 (June 26, 1929), 769–770.

83. Leon Fink, "Labor, Liberty, and the Law: Trade Unionism and the Problem of the American Constitutional Order," *Journal of American History* 74 (December 1987), 904–925.

84. Leiserson quoted in Christopher L. Tomlins, *The State and the Unions: Labor Relations, Law, and the Organized Labor Movement in America, 1880–1960* (New York: Cambridge University Press, 1985), xi–xii, 79–80. Leiserson's thoughts were later codified in *Right and Wrong in Labor Relations* (Berkeley: University of California Press, 1938), 7–12.

85. J. Michael Eisner, *William Morris Leiserson: A Biography* (Madison: University of Wisconsin Press, 1967), 41.

86. James A. Gross, *The Reshaping of the National Labor Relations Board* (Albany: State University of New York Press, 1981), 113.

87. Philip Taft, "Reflections on Selig Perlman as a Teacher and Writer," *Industrial and Labor Relations Review* 29 (January 1976), 250. Taft's rather grudging praise for Perlman may have dated to their argument over the authorship of volume 4 of the *History of Labor in the United States*. Taft wanted it to read Taft and Perlman, but Perlman (perhaps reflecting a continuing sense of slight for his own omission from authorship of volume 1) insisted on "Perlman and Taft." Mark Perlman interview; on Taft, see David Brody, "Philip Taft: Labor Scholar," *Labor History* 19 (Winter 1978), 9–22.

88. Tomlins, *The State and the Unions*, 80–82, 241–243; Gross, *National Labor Relations Board*, 112–130, 239.

3. The People's Expert: Charles McCarthy

1. Graham Adams, Jr., *Age of Industrial Violence, 1910–15: The Activities and Findings of the United States Commission on Industrial Relations* (New York: Columbia University Press, 1966), 48, 50.

2. Charles McCarthy to W. Jett Lauck, Jan. 10, 1914, Charles McCarthy Papers, State Historical Society of Wisconsin, Madison (hereafter cited as CMP).

3. To be sure, many were inspired by the commission's message, especially the so-called Manly report backed by Chairman Walsh. The "most remarkable official document ever published in this country," the *Masses* exulted, "the beginning of an indigenous American revolutionary movement." Adams, *Age of Industrial Violence*, 220–223.

4. Eugene M. Tobin, *Organize or Perish: America's Independent Progressives, 1913–1933* (New York: Greenwood, 1986), 58.

5. Samuel Gompers's narrow public relations approach to the commission's work is best revealed in his quibbling response to the overwhelmingly pro-labor final report authored by Gerald Manly. In a section on the law and trade union rights, the Manly report recorded the "grave doubts" of "eminent legal authorities" that the Clayton Act (which Gompers had prematurely hailed as "labor's Magna Charta") would effectively outlaw the labor injunction: shrewdly, the report predicted that "it does not seem to remove the root of the existing injustice." In a fit of private bombast directed to Walsh, Gompers railed that the "doubters" were all "well-known enemies of the labor movement," and that labor's true friends "must resist every attempt to foster the impression that the labor provisions of Clayton Antitrust Act will not accomplish everything the legislators intended." Gompers to Frank Walsh, Sept. 15, 1915, Samuel Gompers Papers, University of Maryland, College Park.

6. Barry D. Karl, *The Uneasy State: The United States from 1915 to 1945* (Chicago: University of Chicago Press, 1983), 46–49.

7. Marie L. Obenauer to Charles McCarthy, March 3, 1915, and John A. Fitch to Charles McCarthy, March 22, 1915, CMP; Adams, *Age of Industrial Violence*, 219–223; Valerie Jean Conner, *The National War Labor Board: Stability, Social Justice, and the Voluntary State in World War I* (Chapel Hill: University of North Carolina Press, 1983), 14. The contemporary impact of the CIR is suggested in the observation that the commission's conflicting final reports confirmed young economist Wesley Clair Mitchell's faith that quantitative facts of hard science were the only means to reduce differences of opinion. Dorothy Ross, *The Origins of American Social Science* (New York: Cambridge University Press, 1991), 321.

8. On the CIR, cf. Adams's rather whiggish *Age of Industrial Violence*, esp. 223–228, with James Weinstein, *The Corporate Ideal in the Liberal State*

(Boston: Beacon Press, 1968), 172–213, which subordinates often revealing detail about commission conflicts to a broader thesis of corporate liberal reform and interprets the aegis of the National Civic Federation as an insidious buffer against more radical and socialist claims. See also Mark Perlman, *Labor Union Theories in America: Background and Development* (Evanston, Ill.: Row, Peterson, 1958), 279–301. On McCarthy and the CIR see Edward A. Fitzpatrick, *McCarthy of Wisconsin* (New York: Columbia University Press, 1944), 189–206, and Marion Casey, *Charles McCarthy: Librarianship and Reform* (Chicago: American Library Association, 1981), 102–260.

9. The best survey of prior investigations of the labor question is Clarence E. Wunderlin, Jr., *Visions of a New Industrial Order: Social Science and Labor Theory in America's Progressive Era* (New York: Columbia University Press, 1992). Adams, *Age of Industrial Violence*, 73. See also William Leiserson's advice to the CIR on learning from the mistakes of the 1902 federal labor commission. U.S. Commission on Industrial Relations, *Final Report and Testimony*, 11 vols. (Washington D.C., 1916), vol. 1, 344–357.

10. The nine commission members included as public representatives Walsh, Commons, and Florence Hurst "Daisy" (Mrs. J. Borden) Harriman, a Democratic party stalwart who also had ties to the social work community; as labor representatives president of the Order of Railway Conductors Austin B. Garretson, AFL vice-president and director of the Metal Trades Department James O'Connell, and AFL treasurer John B. Lennon; and as business representatives railroad owner Frederic A. Delano, liberal California department store and real estate owner Harris Weinstock, and Kentucky liquor baron S. Thruston Ballard.

11. Gompers quoted in Adams, *Age of Industrial Violence*, 48.

12. George Creel, *Rebel at Large: Recollections of Fifty Crowded Years* (New York: G. P. Putnam's Sons, 1947), 48.

13. Boyd Fisher to Walsh, Sept. 13, 1913, Frank Walsh Papers, New York Public Library (herafter FWP).

14. George Creel to Walsh, May 27, 1915, FWP.

15. Creel, *Rebel at Large*, 48. Beginning in 1890, councilman James Pendergast organized a family-based political machine that ruled Kansas City until 1939.

16. Adams, *Age of Industrial Violence*, 69–72. The young James was reportedly so impressed with his counsel's performance that he himself became a lawyer and "clean-government insurgent" (70).

17. A. Theodore Brown and Lyle W. Dorsett, *K.C.:A History of Kansas City, Missouri* (Boulder, Colo.: Pruett Publishing Co., 1978), 156–157.

18. Creel, *Rebel at Large*, 48.

19. Adams, *Age of Industrial Violence*, 57, 62. Walsh's only hesitation about working with labor representatives on the CIR was that railway conductor leader Austin B. Garretson represented "the most conservative labor organization of the country." Walsh to George Creel, Sept. 3, 1913, FWP (reference courtesy of Steven Sapolsky).

20. Weinstein, *The Corporate Ideal*, 186.

21. L. A. Herbert to Walsh [June or July 1913], FWP.

22. Walsh to George Creel, Sept. 3, 1913, FWP.
23. Commons clearly shared the general enthusiasm for Walsh apparent in the progressive community. The professor's college-aged son, for example, chose to feature a portrait of Walsh for a magazine-writing class based on "what I've read and heard from Dad and others." John Alvin Commons to Walsh, March 10, 1914, FWP. For more on "Jack" Commons, see Chap. 2, n. 75.
24. Adams, *Age of Industrial Violence*, 56; John P. Henderson, "Political Economy and the Service of the State: The University of Wisconsin," in William J. Barber, ed., *Breaking the Academic Mould: Economists and American Higher Learning in the Nineteenth Century* (Middletown, Conn.: Wesleyan University Press, 1988), 318–339; Wunderlin, *Visions of a New Industrial Order;* John F. McClymer, "The Pittsburgh Survey, 1907–1914: Forging an Ideology in the Steel District," *Pennsylvania History* 41 (1974), 168–186; Adams, *Age of Industrial Violence*, 46, 52, 58.
25. Adams, *Age of Industrial Violence*, 73; Commons, *Myself: The Autobiography of John R. Commons* (Madison: University of Wisconsin Press, 1963 [1934]), 166–167. Besides Charles McCarthy, Wisconsin students associated with the commission included F. H. Bird, Carl Hookstadt, William L. Leiserson, Selig Perlman, David J. Saposs, Sumner Slichter, Helen Sumner, and G. L. Sprague. In addition, Clara Richards and two other librarians from the Wisconsin Legislative Reference Library would assume similar duties for the federal commission.
26. Adams, *Age of Industrial Violence*, 205–206.
27. McCarthy to Sir Horace Plunkett, Feb. 27, 1913, CMP. McCarthy, *The Wisconsin Idea* (New York: Macmillan, 1912).
28. McCarthy to Walsh, March 3, 1914, CMP.
29. McCarthy to Horace Plunkett, Feb. 27, 1913, CMP; Casey, *Charles McCarthy*, 10.
30. Jameson had recommended that McCarthy work with Turner; the connection to Ely may have been planted by Brown's social gospel president, E. Benjamin Andrews. McCarthy won the Justin-Winsor Prize of the American Historical Association in 1902 for the best dissertation in American history. Fitzpatrick, *McCarthy of Wisconsin*, 23–25.
31. Casey, *Charles McCarthy*, 21–23.
32. Quoted in ibid., 18–19.
33. Quoted in Fitzpatrick, *McCarthy of Wisconsin*, 7.
34. Casey, *Charles McCarthy*, 29, 90–95. One contemporary account estimated that more 90 percent of Wisconsin state legislative acts from 1901 to 1921 were composed in McCarthy's "bill factory" (ibid., 38). The host of measures that McCarthy christened "the Wisconsin Idea" included direct primaries for all state offices, establishment of state railroad and civil service commissions, creation of an extension division of the university, and, in a tide of legislation in 1911, passage of workmen's compensation, an industrial commission pioneering in health and safety regulation, child and female labor regulations, continuation schools for workers on the European model, and finally a creation of a state board of public affairs with a planning capacity for a con-

tinuing reform agenda. Robert S. Maxwell, *La Follette and the Rise of the Progressives in Wisconsin* (Madison: State Historical Society of Wisconsin, 1956), 74–86, 153–172.

35. McCarthy, *The Wisconsin Idea,* 1–4.

36. As McCarthy perceived it, Ely "saw an empire being fashioned by men regarded in his own country as merely theorists; he realized that these Germans were more than mere theorists; that they were laying the foundations for a great insurance system; that they foresaw the commercial prosperity of the country built upon the happiness, education and well-being of the human units of the empire; that order, intelligence, care and thought could be exercised by the state" (ibid., 27–28). See also David P. Thelen, *The New Citizenship: Origins of Progressivism in Wisconsin, 1885–1900* (Columbia: University of Missouri Press, 1972). On the "free translation" of German social science ideas to American shores, see Jurgen Herbst, *The German Historical School in American Scholarship: A Study in the Transfer of Culture* (Ithaca: Cornell University Press, 1965), esp. 129–159. On the discrepancies between actual developments in German academic culture and American perceptions of the same, see Konrad Jarausch, "The Universities: An American View," in Jack R. Dukes and Joachim Remak, eds., *Another Germany: A Reconsideration of the Imperial Era* (Boulder: Westview Press, 1988), 181–206.

37. McCarthy's idolization of Prussian developments rested on a combination of Bismarck's three-pronged social legislation of the 1880s (sickness insurance, accident insurance, and old-age pensions) and the fact that such measures appeared to defer in part to the agitation of the academic *Kathedersozialisten* ("socialists of the chair") around Gustav Schmoller and the Verein fur Sozialpolitik. For a more skeptical view of German social welfare legislation, see J. Tampke, "Bismarck's Social Legislation: A Genuine Breakthrough?" in W. J. Mommsen, ed., *The Emergence of the Welfare State in Britain and Germany, 1850–1950* (London: Croom Helm, 1981), 71–83.

38. McCarthy, *Wisconsin Idea,* 174; cf. the remarkable similarity of McCarthy's reasoning with that of Ann Shola Orloff and Theda Skocpol, "Why Not Equal Protection? Explaining the Politics of Public Social Spending in Britain, 1900–1911, and the United States, 1880s–1920," *American Sociological Review* 49 (December 1984), 726–750. See also Edwin Amenta, Elisabeth S. Clemens, Jefren Olsen, Sunita Parikh, and Theda Skocpol, "The Political Origins of Unemployment Insurance in the Five American States," *Studies in American Political Development* 2 (1987), 137–182.

39. McCarthy, *Wisconsin Idea,* 2–4.

40. Ibid., 174; McCarthy to Milton A. Miller, Feb. 19, 1914, CMP. David J. Saposs, who also worked on the CIR as a young graduate student, later argued that Commons served government "not only as a technician. His conception of the tri-partite bodies, like the Wisconsin Industrial Commission, introduced a revolutionary means of administering laws concerned with intricate social and economic problems." "The Wisconsin Heritage and the Study of Labor: Works and Deeds of John R. Commons" (unpublished ms., 1960), David J. Saposs Papers, SHSW.

41. McCarthy, *Wisconsin Idea,* 172.
42. Ibid., 190–193.
43. Ibid., 298, 300; see also James T. Kloppenberg, *Uncertain Victory: Social Democracy and Progressivism in European and American Thought, 1870–1920* (New York: Oxford University Press, 1986), 145–286.
44. CIR, *Final Report and Testimony,* vol. 1, 379–380, 382.
45. See Commons's essays "Utilitarian Idealism" (1909) and "Constructive Research" (1907) reprinted in his *Labor and Administration* (New York: Macmillan, 1913), 1–13.
46. See, e.g., Helen L. Sumner to Commons, May 20, 1914, and Jan. 19, 1905, John R. Commons Papers, SHSW.
47. J. Michael Eisner, *William Morris Leiserson: A Biography* (Madison: University of Wisconsin Press, 1967), 9–10; David J. Saposs to Leiserson, Oct. 17, 1915, Carl D. Thompson to Leiserson, Dec. 28, 1912, William M. Leiserson Papers, SHSW.
48. CIR, *Final Report and Testimony,* vol. 1, 345–347.
49. McCarthy to William M. Leiserson, Dec. 16, 1914, CMP.
50. McCarthy to Walsh, "Suggestions for the Federal Industrial Relations Commission," January 1914 and Feb. 14, 1914; McCarthy to Judson King, June 8, 1914, all CMP; Selig Perlman proposal, n.d., in U.S. Department of Labor, CIR, Administrative file, RG 174, Box 2.
51. Walsh to McCarthy, June 5, 1914; McCarthy to Walsh, August 11, 1914; Walsh to McCarthy, August 20, 1914; McCarthy to Walsh, August 11, 1914; Walsh to McCarthy, July 13, 1914; McCarthy to John S. Murdock, Jan. 14, 1915, all in CMP.
52. On the commission's financial woes, see Adams, *Age of Industrial Violence,* 206–209; Casey, *Charles McCarthy,* 112; Fitzpatrick, *McCarthy of Wisconsin,* 195–196. An initial CIR appropriation for $100,000 first became available in October 1913 for the fiscal year ending in July 1914. An additional "deficiency" appropriation of $50,000 was secured in March 1914. With only $200,000 appropriated for 1914–15 ($50,000 less than McCarthy calculated as minimally necessary), by February 1915 the commission was literally running out of money. In March Congress again appropriated an additional and final $100,000. In a March 1, 1915, letter to Commons, McCarthy recounted his experience of the budget nightmare: "When I came on last July, I could get no budget until October and then did not get a budget rightly itemized or an account of the expenditures rightly itemized. I was told repeatedly by Walsh not to worry about the money and Mr. L. K. Brown told me that Walsh did not want to let me have the budget. Finally, when I got the budget or some idea of it, I found we were going in the hole completely." Fitzpatrick, *McCarthy of Wisconsin,* 195–196.
53. Almost from the day of his arrival at the commission, McCarthy called (in vain) for suspension of the hearings on grounds of inefficiency and financial exigency: "Cannot the Commissioners themselves be of more service working at some specific work than to be sitting up there all day listening to these speeches?" McCarthy to Walsh, June 22, 1914, CMP.

54. Walsh to McCarthy, Dec. 23, 1914, CMP; Adams, *Age of Industrial Violence,* 208.
55. Adams, *Age of Industrial Violence,* 209; minutes of CIR meeting, Feb. 28, 1915, CMP.
56. Adams, *Age of Industrial Violence,* 146–161.
57. Ibid., 146; see also Creel, *Rebel at Large,* 128.
58. Adams, *Age of Industrial Violence,* 175.
59. Peter Collier and David Horowitz, *The Rockefellers: An American Dynasty* (New York: Holt, Rinehart, and Winston, 1976), 122–123. Rockefeller, who received expert guidance from Canadian labor reformer Mackenzie King before his appearance, disarmed many listeners with a declaration of good intentions: he accepted unions in principle, he said, and allowed that "combinations of capital are sometimes conducted in an unworthy manner, contrary to law and in disregard of the interest both of labor and the public." In short, according to Rockefeller, if things had gone wrong in Colorado, the problem lay in administration farther down the corporate ladder. To correspondent Walter Lippmann, Rockefeller thus emerged in his testimony as a "weak despot governed by a private bureaucracy which he is unable to lead . . . I should not believe that the inhumanity of Colorado is something he had conceived . . . there seemed to be nothing but a young man having a lot of trouble, very much harassed and very well-meaning." "Mr. Rockefeller on the Stand," *New Republic* 1 (Jan. 30, 1915), 12–13. Even Mother Jones was inclined to look kindly on Rockefeller after his testimony. H. M. Gitelman, *Legacy of the Ludlow Massacre: A Chapter in American Industrial Relations* (Philadelphia: University of Pennsylvania Press, 1988), 75–77. In contrast, Carl Sandburg offered the orthodox left-labor view of Rockefeller in "The Two Mr. Rockefellers—and Mr. Walsh," *Internatonal Socialist Review* 16 (July 1915), 18–24.
60. For the case of Professor James H. Brewster of the University of Colorado, see Walter P. Metzger, ed., *Professors on Guard: The First AAUP Investigations* (New York: Arno Press, 1977), 47–120. On Rockefeller money ties to the state's universities, see Collier and Horowitz, *The Rockefellers,* 125.
61. On corporate subversion of democratic government, see CIR, *Final Report and Testimony,* vol. 1, 58, 78–79, 84; Collier and Horowitz, *The Rockefellers,* 119. For Lee's CIR testimony, see CIR, *Final Report and Testimony,* vol. 8, 7897–7916; vol. 9, 8715–30, 8849–63. Lee transcended his temporary notoriety to build a whirlwind career, counting not only Standard Oil but also American Tobacco and General Mills as clients, creating for the latter the immortal Betty Crocker persona and the "Breakfast of Champions" slogan for Wheaties cereal. The life of this millionaire consultant ended in infamy, however, when in 1934, already afflicted with brain cancer, he was exposed before the Special House Committee on Un-American Activities for his alleged role in protecting the image of the German petrochemical firm I. G. Farben (which had entered into a cartel with Standard Oil of New Jersey) and the Third Reich. Collier and Horowitz, *The Rockefellers,* 118, 225–226. For Lee and the general development of the field of public relations, see Richard S.

Tedlow, *Keeping the Corporate Image: Public Relations and Business, 1900–1950* (Greenwich, Conn.: JAI Press, 1979), 36–39.

62. CIR, *Final Report and Testimony,* vol. 9, 8784–85.
63. On King's recruitment to the foundation and subsequent influence on John D., Jr., see Gitelman, *Ludlow Massacre.*
64. Walsh to McCarthy, Oct. 7, 1914; McCarthy to W. H. Allen, Oct. l, 1914; McCarthy to Walsh, Oct. 8, 1914; William Leiserson to McCarthy, Jan. 11, 1915, all in CMP.
65. Boyd Fisher to Walsh, June 20, 1913; Walsh to Fisher, June 24, 1913, both in FWP. CIR, *Final Report and Testimony,* vol. 8, 7427.
66. Frank Walsh, "The Great Foundation" (1915), FWP.
67. *Survey* 33 (Oct. 10, 1914), 54–55. While still hopeful with regard to the work of the CIR, *Survey* complained, "It is an open secret that for ten months following the commission's appointment it floundered badly, without a clear-cut program of work, without clear-cut division of responsibility, and with great areas of the field before it practically untouched." For *Survey's* close coverage of the CIR, see *Survey* 27 (Dec. 30, 1911), 1419–29; 29 (Dec. 28, 1912), 385–386; 31 (Nov. 8, 1913), 152–153; 30 (July 5, 1913), 452–453; and 30 (August 2, 1913), 571–588.
68. *Survey* 33 (Nov. 14, 1914), 177. Creel's article appeared in the March 1915 issue of *Pearson's Magazine* (289–297). Paul Kellogg to Walsh, FWP. Adams, *Age of Industrial Violence,* 26.
69. Richard T. Ely to John R. Commons, Dec. 16, 1903, reel 27, Richard T. Ely Papers, SHSW.
70. Gitelman, *Ludlow Massacre,* 20–21, 58; Walsh to McCarthy, Oct. 8, 1914; Walsh to McCarthy, Oct. 10, 1914; McCarthy to Walsh, Dec. 21, 1914; McCarthy to Walsh, Dec. 14, 1914; all in CMP.
71. The Rockefeller-McCarthy "old school" network included attorney John S. Murdock (Brown, class of 1896); Everett Colby (class of '97), the Progressive chairman of the New Jersey Commission on Old Age Insurance; and Lefferts M. Dashiell (class of '97), assistant treasurer of the Rockefeller Foundation. Colby was Rockefeller's undergraduate roommate as well as captain of the football team. McCarthy actually received his degree in 1897 but always listed his class as 1896.
72. John D. Rockefeller, Jr., to McCarthy, March 16, 1914. After talking with Rockefeller only days after the Ludlow Massacre, Everett Colby wrote McCarthy, "The trouble with John is he thinks that controversies of this kind can be stripped to a naked principle . . . which you know is not the case." Disappointed, McCarthy yet insisted that it was "of the utmost importance to this country that a powerful man like J.D.R. will broaden out his life and his concepts as he grows older. Somebody must get near to him and counteract the forces which are making his life stiff . . . He problably thinks I am an idealist and I would have very little influence along that line with him." Colby to McCarthy, April 27, 1914; McCarthy to Colby, April 29, 1914, CMP.
73. Still, McCarthy was not about to browbeat his old friend. "Understand," he dissimulated, "that I have nothing to do with the hearings or the findings of

the commission. I am a radical, at least I am called radical, and you are naturally a conservative, but whatever comes up in this world, there shall be nothing but personal friendship between us." McCarthy to Rockefeller, Aug. 7, 1914, CMP.

74. McCarthy to John Murdock, Oct. 10, 1914, and Jan. 14, 1915; Rockefeller to McCarthy, Oct. 20, 1914. By the end of October, McCarthy betrayed a sudden impatience with his conversion mission: "Your viewpoint and your attitude is so absolutely different from mine that I cannot hope to explain my attitude to you in this letter . . . Your institution will not do the great work which you planned for it unless it is done upon a different basis entirely . . . The years have gone by and I never had a chance to see you or talk with you to an great extent upon the gerat economic queston with which we have been struggling." McCarthy to Rockefeller, Oct. 29, 1914; all in CMP.

75. McCarthy to Jerome Greene, Oct. 8, 1914; McCarthy to John D. Rockefeller, Jr., Oct. 17, 1914; both in CMP.

76. McCarthy to John S. Murdock, Jan. 14, 1915; McCarthy to Lefferts M. Dashiell, Jan. 15, 1915; Dashiell to McCarthy, Jan. 18, 1915 (telegram); Murdock to McCarthy, March 18, 1915; Walsh to McCarthy, Jan. 15, 16, 18, 1915; all in CMP.

77. See CIR, *Final Report and Testimony,* vol. 8, 7763–7897. Only a few vague questions were directed to Rockefeller about the industrial investigation, and these not by Walsh but by Commissioner James O'Connell (7892–95).

78. William M. Leiserson to McCarthy, March 4, 1915, CMP.

79. Leiserson to McCarthy, March 4, 1915, and John Fitch to McCarthy, March 22, 1915; both in CMP. In vain, Commons offered a counterplan to the commissioners that would reinstate McCarthy and his research priorities, while abandoning future hearings. McCarthy received numerous expressions of support from those who had worked with the CIR. "If you lose out we shall all resign in a body," wrote researcher Carl Hookstadt. But McCarthy himself counseled against anything destructive to the work of the commission. While Leiserson and "one or two others" resigned in protest (others, including Perlman, had already been terminated for budgetary reasons), most of McCarthy's friends stayed on to complete their work. Particularly after an additional congressional appropriation came through, Chairman Walsh, ironically enough—though with the exception of his famous second grilling of Rockefeller in Washington, D.C., in May 1915—basically returned to the priority on research and writing that McCarthy had counseled. See Carl Hookstadt to McCarthy, March 5, 1915; W. Jett Lauck to McCarthy, Jan. 30, 1915; McCarthy to Lauck, April 3, 1915; McCarthy to R. H. Hoxie, April 10, 1915; Leiserson to McCarthy, March 12, 1915; all in CMP. Walsh to William Marion Reedy, April 17, 1915, FWP.

80. Casey, *Charles McCarthy,* 116.

81. Walsh to Reedy, April 17, 1915, FWP.

82. Letter to the *New Republic* 2 (March 27, 1915), 209–210.

83. Leiserson to McCarthy, March 2, 1915; McCarthy to Leiserson, March 3, 1915; CMP.

84. Clara Richards to McCarthy, Feb. 2, 1916, CMP. McCarthy privately compared Walsh to Travelyan's treatment of Ferdinand of Naples: "While you are with him he will put his arm around you and say caressing things to you . . . Go five minutes away from him and he becomes fearful and suspicious. At once vague terrors seize him and he issues an order for your destruction." McCarthy to W. Jett Lauck, April 3, 1915, CMP.

85. The three employer commissioners also felt compelled to offer a separate report attacking the commission staff for its "manifestly partisan" attitude and balancing the critique of management practices with a bill of particulars against union violence.

86. CIR, *Final Report and Testimony*, vol. 1, 19, 35, 38, 91, 123–124, 156–165, 265–266, 171–230, 156–157.

87. Ibid., 81–86, 269. Though the Walsh-led offensive against the corporations failed in its ultimate aims, it did affect the future style of corporate support for social research. Instead of direct foundation sponsorship, "in the 1920s academic holding companies rooted in the discipline associations—for example, the American Council of Learned Societies (ACLS) and the Social Science Research Council (SSRC)—emerged to mediate the direct contact between wealth and knowledge exposed and denounced by the [CIR]." Edward T. Silva and Sheila A. Slaughter, *Serving Power: The Making of the Academic Social Science Expert* (Westport, Conn.: Greenwood, 1984), 263.

88. One recurrence of basic CIR divisions is seen in the split that later developed on the National Labor Relations Board in 1939 between Leiserson and the left-wing "adversarial" approach of Edwin Smith and Joseph Madden. See Christopher L. Tomlins, *The State and the Unions: Labor Relations, Law, and the Organized Labor Movement in America, 1880–1960* (New York, Cambridge University Press, 1985), 199–213.

89. Leiserson to Commons, August 14, 1915, Wiliam M. Leiserson Papers, SHSW.

90. Julie Greene, "Negotiating the State: Frank Walsh and the Transformation of Working Class Political Culture in Progressive America," in Kevin Boyle, ed., *Organized Labor and American Politics, 1894–1996* (New York: New York University Press, forthcoming).

91. David Montgomery, *The Fall of the House of Labor: The Workplace, The State, and American Labor Activism, 1865–1925* (New York: Cambridge University Press, 1987), 361.

92. Indeed, frustrated by employer resistance to dispute settlement during the war, Walsh was so drawn into the administrative orbit as to recommend that the Board be reconstituted to impress the largest employers—including John D. Rockefeller, Jr.!—into service (Weinstein, *The Corporate Ideal*, 248). On the nature of WLB machinery and its indebtedness to CIR proposals, see Valerie Jean Conner, *The National War Labor Board: Stability, Soical Justice, and the Voluntary State in World War I* (Chapel Hill: University of North Carolina Press, 1983), 15, 18–34. Walsh in general seems less a man of fine distinctions than of broad commitments. Unlike his more restrained academic colleagues on the CIR, he led with his heart, not his head. For more on his personal impetuousness and flights of passion, see Leila J. Rupp, "Feminism and the

Sexual Revolution in the Early Twentieth Century: The Case of Doris Stevens," *Feminist Studies* 15 (Summer 1989), 294.

93. In the years after World War I, Creel continued to mix journalism and reform advocacy with use of the state apparatus of social control. Though his autobiography of 1947 lambastes Mexican president Lazaro Cardenas for his socialist excesses, Creel's papers show him to have been a consultant to Cardenas in establishing a Mexican Ministry of Public Information and Propaganda in 1940. Creel, *Rebel at Large*, 81–85; index of George Creel Papers, Library of Congress.

94. Mark Sullivan quoted in John A. Thompson, *Reformers and War: American Progressive Publicists and the First World War* (New York: Cambridge University Press, 1987), 17. See also Cletus E. Daniel's characterization of Creel's role as "patron-savior" and "authoritarian progressive" in his role as NRA regional administrator in the early 1930s. *Bitter Harvest: A History of California Farmworkers, 1870–1941* (Ithaca: Cornell University Press, 1981), 174–217, (reference courtesy of Cindy Hahamovitch).

95. Interview with Selig Perlman, April 13, 1950, SHSW; Commons, *Myself*, 182, 185; Fitzpatrick, *McCarthy of Wisconsin*, 213–214, 217. McCarthy even tried to organize a company of famous football players and other athletes for wartime service, offering himself among 236 volunteers, before the plan fell through.

96. Stephen Skowronek, *Building a New American State: The Expansion of National Administrative Capacities, 1877–1920* (Cambridge: Cambridge University Press, 1982), esp. 12–14, 121–176.

97. The intellectuals' own self-consciousness of the limits of their public role was more evident after the war in the spate of disillusioned commentary on the problem of "public opinion" in a modern democracy. As is evident in the writing of Walter Lippmann, a prime concern was the difficulty of introducing experts and expertise into the consideration of public issues. In this sense the CIR might be considered a skirmish in intellectual disillusionment before the onset of the Great War. See Lippmann, *Public Opinion* (New York: Free Press, 1965 [1922]), esp. 250–257; see also Thompson, *Reformers and War*, 279–286.

98. On the social-psychological complexity of gift giving see Marcel Mauss, *The Gift: The Form and Reason for Exchange in Archaic Society* (New York: Norton, 1990). McCarthy to Rockefeller, February [n.d.], May 24, 1899, and March 16, 1900, CMP. The first letter refers to repayment of an earlier loan (presumably during their college years) "under similar circumstances," while the second mentions a $9 interest payment for loans of $100 (compared to $200 requested) in March and $50 (compared to $100 requested) in May.

99. McCarthy to Rockefeller, Feb.28, 1901; March 6, 1901; Oct 6, 1901; Jan. 10, 1903; Lucile McCarthy to Rockefeller, Feb. 14, 1903; all in CMP. While discountenancing any further aid for himself, McCarthy continued to suggest to Rockefeller other worthy outlets for his largesse. See, e.g., McCarthy to Rockefeller, April 8, 1904, and Oct 2, 1905; McCarthy to Rockefeller, March 5, 1914; all in CMP.

100. McCarthy's $4,500 state salary afforded him little personal security. The difficulty of his situation was at times quite painful. Amid his CIR labors in

1914, for example, an old friend of McCarthy's literally begged him on separate occasions for a loan: "You have become a national, even an international figure, while I have gone down," wrote Fred Read. In fending Read off, McCarthy gave vent to his own frustrations. Insisting he had done the "best I could" for his friend, McCarthy noted that he himself was "deeply in debt" and "cannot lay hands on $50 . . . I do not know where I can get money to carry out the simple things in my own life." Fitzpatrick, *McCarthy of Wisconsin*, 75; Fred N. Read to McCarthy, Feb. 12, 1914; March 19, 1914; June 30, 1914; McCarthy to Read, March 27, 1914; all CMP. During World War I, when McCarthy went to Washington to serve under Herbert Hoover in the Food Administration, a friend was shocked to find him living "in a basement room on the edge of a Negro quarter" for which he paid $2.00 a week. Fitzpatrick, *McCarthy of Wisconsin*, 213.

101. McCarthy to Rockefeller, May 25, 1915, Feb. 19, 1916; Rockefeller to McCarthy, Feb. 24, 1916; CMP.

102. Casey, *Charles McCarthy*, 13.

103. Max Weber, "Politics as a Vocation," as quoted in James T. Kloppenburg, *Uncertain Victory: Social Democracy and Progressivism in European and American Thought, 1870–1920* (New York: Oxford University Press, 1986), 342.

104. Fitzpatrick, *McCarthy of Wisconsin*, 14; McCarthy to Charles F. McCarthy, Dec. 15, 1915, CMP.

105. See also, e.g., Herbert Hoover's rhetoric during the presidential campaign of 1928: "It is as if we set a race. We, through free and universal education provide the training of the runners; we give to them an equal start; we provide in the government the umpire of fairness in the race. The winner is he who shows the most conscientious training, the greatest ability, and the greatest character." Quoted in Richard Hofstadter, *The American Political Tradition* (Kingsport, Conn.: Kingsport Press, 1948), 294.

106. George Creel, "How 'Tainted' Money Taints," 293–294.

107. McCarthy to William H. Edwards, April 11, 1916, CMP; Fitzpatrick, *McCarthy of Wisconsin*, 12. On the early world of American football, see Tom Perrin, *Football: A College History* (Jefferson, N.C.: McFarland, 1987), and Allison Danzig, *The History of American Football: Its Great Teams, Players, and Coaches* (Englewood Cliffs, N.J.: Prentice-Hall, 1956).

108. Casey, *Charles McCarthy*, 122–123.

4. Joining the People: William English Walling

1. Richard Hofstadter, *Anti-Intellectualism in American Life* (New York: Knopf, 1962), 4; Lewis D. Eigen and Johathan P. Siegel, eds., *Macmillan Dictionary of Political Quotations* (New York: Macmillan, 1993), 70; *Bergen City [N.J.] Record*, Oct. 7, 1992.

2. Hofstadter, *Anti-Intellectualism*, 6, 19, 55–80. For Hofstadter on the anti-intellectualism and irrationalism of the Populists, see *The Age of Reform: From Bryan to F.D.R.* (New York: Knopf, 1956), 60–93.

3. Hofstadter, *Anti-Intellectualism,* 50.
4. Ibid., 3–9, quotations 7–8.
5. Walling had authored *Russia's Message* (1908), *Socialism As It Is* (1912), *Larger Aspects of Socialism* (1913), *Progressivism—and After* (1914), and *Whitman and Traubel* (1916). In addition, he had coedited several documentary collections, including *Socialists and the War* (1915), *Socialism of Today* (1916), and *State Socialism, Pro and Con* (1917).
6. For more extended Walling biography, see Jack Meyer Stuart, "William English Walling: A Study in Politics and Ideas," (Ph.D. diss., Columbia University, 1968) and Anna Strunsky Walling reminiscence in Anna Strunsky Walling, ed., *William English Walling: A Symposium* (New York: Stackpole Sons, 1938), 7–20.
7. Donald D. Egbert, *Socialism and American Life,* vol. 2 (Princeton: Princeton University Press, 1952), 217–219.
8. Lassalle quoted in Arthur M. Lewis, *Ten Blind Leaders of the Blind* (Chicago: Kerr, 1909), 5–6.
9. John Spargo, *Karl Marx: His Life and Work* (New York: B. W. Huebsch, 1910), 96, 300, 303; *Sidelights on Contemporary Socialism* (New York: B. W. Huebsch, 1911), 92–93, 100–101; Howard H. Quint, *The Forging of American Socialism: Origins of the Modern Movement* (Columbia: University of South Carolina Press, 1953), 3.
10. This treatment and quotations from Bakunin are derived from Richard B. Saltman, *The Social and Political Thought of Michael Bakunin* (Westport, Conn.: Greenwood Press, 1983), 151–155, 161; and Noam Chomsky, *Intellectuals and the State* (Baarn, Netherlands: Wereldvenster, 1978), 4.
11. Marx quoted in Hubert Lagardelle, "The Intellectuals and Working Class Socialism," Part 2, *International Socialist Review* (hereafter *ISR*) 8 (July 1907), 33–41; cf. Tony Judt, *Past Imperfect: French Intellectuals, 1944–1956* (Berkeley: University of California Press, 1992), 205–206.
12. Karl Kautsky, *The Class Struggle (Erfurt Program)* (Chicago: Charles Kerr, 1910), 163–164, 156–157.
13. John H. Kautsky, "Karl Kautsky's Conception of History," in John H. Kautsky, *Karl Kautsky and the Social Science of Classical Marxism* (Leiden: E. J. Brill, 1989), 89.
14. Max Adler, *Der Sozialismus und die Intellecktuellen* (Vienna: Ignaz Brand, 1910).
15. A. M. McBriar, *Fabian Socialism and English Politics, 1884–1918* (Cambridge: Cambridge University Press, 1962), 1–28, quotation 67.
16. The phrase is from American socialist editor A. M. Simons, as quoted in Mark Pittenger, *Socialism Inevitable: American Socialists and Evolutionary Thought, 1870–1920* (Madison: University of Wisconsin Press, 1993), 209.
17. Ibid., 2–11.
18. George Cotkin, "'They All Talk Like Goddam Bourgeois': Scientism and the Socialist Discourse of Arthur M. Lewis," *Et Cetera* 38 (Fall 1981), 272–284.
19. Arthur M. Lewis, *An Introduction to Sociology* (Chicago: Kerr, 1913), preface; *Vital Problems in Social Evolution* (Chicago: Kerr, 1909), 31–32; cf. Kautsky, *Class Struggle,* 156: "One of the most remarkable phenomena in modern so-

ciety is the thirst for knowledge displayed by the proletariat. While all other classes kill their time with the most unintellectual diversions, the proletarian displays a passion for intellectual culture."

20. Anna Strunsky Walling, *William English Walling*, 7–9.
21. Stuart, "William English Walling," 32–33; John R. Commons, *Myself: The Autobiography of John R. Commons* (Madison: University of Wisconsin Press, 1963), 83.
22. Stuart, "William English Walling," 30–33. In late 1860s Russia, the Narodniki envisioned a revolutionary socialist alliance between peasants and intelligentsia.
23. Ernest Poole, *The Bridge: My Own Story* (New York: Macmillan, 1940), 71.
24. James Gilbert, *Designing the Industrial State: The Intellectual Pursuit of Collectivism in America, 1880–1940* (Chicago: Quadrangle Books, 1972), 202–203.
25. In a letter from Russia in 1906, Walling wrote his parents that "the Revolutionaries tell me what they will tell no one else . . . [There is] no single man to whom Russia is so open." Letter to Walling Willoughby and Rosalind Walling, Jan. 29, 1906, William English Walling Papers, State Historical Society of Wisconsin, Madison (hereafter cited as WEWP).
26. Stuart, "William English Walling," 44; "The Real Russian People," *New York Independent* 63 (Sept. 26, 1907), 728–735, quotation 730.
27. *Russia's Message: The True World Import of the Revolution* (New York: Doubleday, 1908), 342. On Walling's treatment of Marxist attitudes towards the peasantry, see ibid., 370, 435.
28. Ibid., 342, 161–162.
29. Ibid., 436. Walling came away from an interview with Lenin shocked at the "very deep distrust" that this "most popular leader in Russia" expressed toward the great peasant majority of his own country (369–370). Walling's fear of state manipulation (whether by Bolsheviks or Fabians) reflected his own lingering antistatist, liberal radicalism, which he saw epitomized in the Russian revolt against czarism. "The political problem [in Russia]," he summarized, "is to do away, not with the violence of individuals, but with that of the State" (163).
30. Ibid., xiii.
31. Robert A. Nye, *The Anti-Democratic Sources of Elite Theory: Pareto, Mosca, Michels* (London: Sage Publications, 1977), 26.
32. Decades later a Georgia attorney general would revile the NAACP as a "subversive" and "sinister" organization founded by a "southern scalawag journalist and Russian trained revolutionary named William E. Walling." Quoted in William Jones, "Identity, Militancy, and Organization: The Robert Williams Case and the NAACP in North Carolina, 1949–1959" (unpublished ms., 1995).
33. Walling wrote, "We have closed our eyes to the whole awful and menacing truth—that a large part of the white population of Lincoln's home, supported largely by the farmers and miners of the neighboring towns, have initiated a permanent warfare with the negro race . . . I do not speak of the leading citizens but of the masses of the people, of workingmen in the shops, the store-

keepers in the stores, the drivers, the men on the street." William English Walling, "The Race War in the North," *New York Independent* 65 (Sept. 3, 1908), 529–534.

34. For Walling's penetrating, and scathing, denunciation of Socialist Party trimming on the race question, see *Progressivism—and After* (New York: Macmillan, 1914), 377–389. The inner deliberations of the NAACP founders are carefully catalogued in Charles Flint Kellogg, *NAACP: A History of the National Association for the Advancement of Colored People* (Baltimore: Johns Hopkins University Press, 1967), 10–12, 35; see also B. Joyce Ross, *J. E. Spingarn and the Rise of the NAACP, 1911–1939* (New York: Atheneum, 1972), 18–19.

35. On Michels' syndicalist phase, see Arthur Mitzman, *Sociology and Estrangement: Three Sociologists of Imperial Germany* (New Brunswick, N.J.: Transaction Books, 1987), 282–309.

36. Jeremy Jennings, *Syndicalism in France: A Study of Ideas* (New York: St. Martin's Press, 1990), 7.

37. Michels quoted in Mitzman, *Sociology and Estrangement*, 308.

38. Lagardelle, "The Intellectuals," Part 1, *ISR* 7 (June 1907), 721–730, quotations 721, 730. Lagardelle's writings were translated by prominent left-wing publisher Charles H. Kerr. On anti-intellectualism within French syndicalist circles, see Jennings, *Syndicalism in France*, 1–10.

39. Sorel (1900, 1898) quoted in Jennings, *Syndicalism in France*, 59.

40. H. G. Wells, *The New Machiavelli* (New York: Duffield and Co., 1910), 135.

41. Though partisans in 1908 had predicted as many as 2 million presidential votes for the SPA following a spirited campaign capped by Debs's whistle-stop campaign across the West aboard the *Red Special*, the final tally of some 420,000 votes was little more than the party had garnered four years before. Kent Kreuter and Gretchen Kreuter, *An American Dissenter: The Life of Algie Martin Simons, 1870–1950* (Lexington: University of Kentucky Press, 1969), 106–111.

42. Former Idaho governor Frank Steunenberg, who had been elected a decade earlier with labor support but had turned against the miners in the Coeur d'Alene strike of 1899, was killed by a bomb explosion outside his house in 1905. In an atmosphere polarized by violence, Haywood was one of three miners' leaders charged with complicity for murder. Weighing the charges of the confessed perpetrator (a former police informer who had been promised clemency by a Pinkerton agent) against the integrity of a union man represented by Clarence S. Darrow, the jury found Haywood not guilty.

43. James Weinstein, *The Decline of Socialism in America, 1912–1925* (New York: Monthly Review Press, 1967), 82. On the interaction of workers and intellectuals in these events, see Steve Golin, *The Fragile Bridge: Paterson Silk Strike, 1913* (Philadelphia: Temple University Press, 1988).

44. Theodore Draper, *The Roots of American Communism* (New York: Viking, 1957), 47–48.

45. Paul M. Buhle, *A Dreamer's Paradise Lost: Louis C. Fraina / Lewis Corey (1892–1953) and the Decline of Radicalism in the United States* (Atlantic Highlands,

N.J.: Humanities Press, 1995), 104–107; John P. Diggins, *The Amerian Left in the Twentieth Century* (New York: Harcourt Brace, 1973), 73–88; Draper, *Roots of American Communism*, 48–49. *ISR* publisher Charles Kerr dismissed editor A. M. Simons for his lack of support for Haywood and the Wobblies. Elliott Shore, *Talkin' Socialism: J. A. Wayland and the Role of the Press in American Radicalism, 1890–1912* (Topeka: University Press of Kansas, 1988), 200.

46. *New York Independent* 75 (Sept. 4, 1913), 576. On the New Intellectuals, see Buhle, *A Dreamer's Paradise Lost*, 107–108. The *New Review* (1913–1916), edited by Louis Fraina, is most closely identified with the New Intellectuals.

47. Walling to Hyndman, Nov. 18, 1909, WEWP; Walling, "Laborism versus Socialism," *ISR* 9 (March 1909), 689. Another measure of Walling's hostility to the AFL was reflected in an exchange with Debs in the same year: the Socialist Party leader wrote Walling on Dec. 7 that "I *am with you* thoroughly [on the matter] . . . The Socialist Party has already *catered far too much* to the American Federation of Labor, and there is no doubt that *a halt will have to be called.*" Jean Y. Tussey, *Eugene V. Debs Speaks* (New York: Pathfinder, 1970), 170; See also Gilbert, *Designing the Industrial State*, 200–239.

48. Appendix F, "American Socialists and the Race Problem," *Progressivism—and After*, 383–384.

49. Walling to Hyndman, Feb. 19, 1910, WEWP.

50. For interpretations of Wallings's work, see Stuart, "William English Walling,", 89–97; Buhle, *A Dreamer's Paradise Lost*, 107–108; and Pittenger, *Socialism Inevitable*, 396–405.

51. William English Walling, "State Socialism and the Individual," *New Review* 1 (May 1913), 507–515.

52. Walling to George H. Shibley, March 9, 1910; Walling to Fred Warren, Feb. 26, 1910; both in WEWP.

53. *Progressivism—and After*, 366–377. For Walling's difficulties in clearly defining a revolutionary-socialist alternative, see Christopher Lasch, *The True and Only Heaven: Progress and Its Critics* (New York: Norton, 1991), 330–336.

54. *Proceedings of the First Convention of the IWW* (New York: Merit News, 1969 [1905]), 65–70. After being scolded as a "parasite" and as a man whose "pocket [must be] tainted with the blood of workingmen in some way or other," Boudin was ultimately seated as a "fraternal" (i.e., nonvoting) delegate.

55. Boudin, *The Theoretical System of Karl Marx* (Chicago: Kerr, 1907), 189–190, 209. In the pages of the *ISR* Charles H. Kerr supplemented Boudin's argument with translations from the French syndicalist Lagardelle.

56. Spargo, *Sidelights on Contemporary Socialism* (New York: B. W. Huebsch, 1911), 68–69; cf. Chris Waters, *British Socialists and the Politics of Popular Culture, 1884–1914* (Stanford: Stanford University Press, 1990).

57. Ghent letter to the *New York Call*, Dec. 4, 1909, quoted in Buhle, *A Dreamer's Paradise Lost*, 111.

58. Lagardelle, "The Intellectuals," 730.

59. *ISR* 9 (February 1909), 589–593.

60. *ISR* 8 (March 1908), 533–537.

61. Mass-produced letter from Walling to friends, Nov. 26, 1909; A. M. Simons to Walling, Dec. 1, 1909; John Spargo to J. G. Phelps Stokes, Dec. 3, 1909, Socialist Party of America Papers, William E. Perkins Library, Duke University (hereafter SPAP); Kreuter and Kreuter, *An American Dissenter*, 110–113.

62. Spargo to H. G. Phelps Stokes, Dec. 3, 1909; Spargo to Simons, Nov. 29, 1909, both in SPAP.

63. Walling's comments first appeared in "The New Fabianism," *Intercollegiate Socialist* 12 (December–January 1913–1914), then were reproduced in *Progressivism—and After*, 243–244.

64. Lippmann, "Walling's *Progressivism—and After*," *New Review* 2 (June 1914), 346–347, 349. Cf. Walling's weak response, "Why a Socialist Party?" in 2 (July 1914), 400–403.

65. Traubel was also a Whitman biographer and one of three, selected executors of the Whitman's literary estate. *Whitman and Traubel* (New York: Albert and Charles Boni, 1916), 137, 140–141.

66. Mitzman, *Sociology and Estrangement*, 339.

67. Walling, "The Defense of German Socialists," *ISR* 15 (January 1915), 418–422; Walling, "Karl Kautsky—Nationalist," *ISR* 15 (February 1915), 470–471.

68. Walling, review of Louis Boudin, *Socialism and the War*, in *Intercollegiate Socialist* (April–May 1916), 28–29.

69. The ranks of prowar socialists included John Spargo, Charles Edward Russell, Robert Hunter, Upton Sinclair, W. J. Ghent, George D. Herron, and Winfield Gaylord from the party's right; and Walling, Charles Edward Russell, and James Graham Phelps Stokes from the left wing. Walling himself tended to characterize the wartime divisions on ethnic grounds, predicting in 1916 that "Russian Jews" and "Germans" would remain in the party, while "American socialists" would withdraw. Draper, *Roots of American Communism*, 80–96; Stuart, "William English Walling," 140, 159.

70. Stuart, "William English Walling," 141.

71. John A. Thompson, *Reformers and War: American Progressive Publicists and the First World War* (New York: Cambridge University Press, 1987), 180.

72. Walling to Gompers, May 16, 21, June 14, Oct. 6, Oct. 26, 1917, Samuel Gompers Papers, University of Maryland, College Park. The Walling-Gompers duo not only posted the President on the politics of international anti-Bolshevism, they actually lobbied the Council of Workingmen's delegates in Moscow as late as October 6, 1917.

73. With unprecedented access to Washington policy circles, Walling personally lobbied President Wilson against recognition of the Soviet Union, blamed Creel's Committee on Public Information for being insufficiently vigilant against Soviet interests, and even opposed food aid to the new regime. The once-sympathetic interpreter of the Russian masses concluded in 1919: "There are some matters that take precedence even to the prevention of starvation of innocent millions." Stuart, "William English Walling," 177–178, 182.

74. Stuart, "William English Walling," 187, 189–191.

75. Ibid., 191–196; William English Walling, *The Mexican Question* (New York: Robins Press, 1927), 194.

76. *American Labor and American Democracy* (New York: Harper and Bros., 1926), 171–174. In the early 1920s, Walling wrote regularly for the AFL's official publication, *The American Federationist.*

77. In the period 1917–1923, Gompers and Walling exchanged some sixty letters or telegrams. As was Gompers's style, his pieces kept strictly to the immediate end in view, and Walling's never deviated from a tone of utter respect and unswerving agreement with the aims of the labor leader. General correspondence, Samuel Gompers Papers.

78. Frey quoted in Stuart, "William English Walling," 239.

79. Quoted in Stuart, "William English Walling," 240.

80. William English Walling, *Sovietism: The ABC of Russian Bolshevism—According to the Bolshevists* (New York: E. P. Dutton, 1920), 94.

81. Ibid., 95.

82. Also see Chap. 2.

83. *American Labor and American Democracy,* 22.

84. Walling, "American Labor Leads the Way," *American Federationist* 31 (September 1924), 738–739.

85. Editor's introduction, *American Labor and American Democracy,* xi.

86. Anna Strunsky Walling, *William English Walling* 90.

87. Undated ms., WEWP.

88. Anna Strunsky Walling, *William English Walling,* 18–19.

89. Fraina (1918), quoted in Diggins, *The American Left,* 86. On Fraina's own strange and fascinating career, see Buhle, *A Dreamer's Paradise Lost.*

90. Draper, *Roots of American Communism,* 66, 232–233, 408.

91. S. J. Rutgers, "The Intellectuals and the Russian Revolution," in N. Lenin, N. Bukharin, and S. J. Rutgers, eds., *The New Policies of Soviet Russia* (Chicago: Charles Kerr, n.d.), 70–71.

92. Ibid., 127.

93. Arthur Koestler, *The Invisible Writing: An Autobiography* (New York: Macmillan, 1954), 31, 33.

94. W. J. Ghent, *The Reds Bring Reaction* (New York: Arno Press, 1977 [1923]), 75–76, 80, 81, 85, vii, xvii.

95. John Spargo, *The Psychology of Bolshevism* (New York: Harper and Bros., 1919), 21–23, 32–33.

96. On the the gender-typing of political reformers, see Hofstadter, *Anti-Intellectualism,* 190–191; Spargo, *Psychology of Bolshevism,* 35.

97. Spargo, *Psychology of Bolshevism,* 86–87.

98. "John Spargo," *Encyclopedia of the American Left* (New York: Garland Publishing, 1990), 747.

99. On Benda's career, see Ray Nichols, *Treason, Tradition, and the Intellectual* (Lawrence, Kans.: Regents Press, 1978); Machajski, *The Evolution of Social Democracy* (1898), as presented by Max Nomad, *Aspects of Revolt* (New York: Bookman, 1959), 98–101.

100. "Cultural elite" entered the 1992 presidential campaign by way of Vice-President Dan Quayle's attack on a *Murphy Brown* television episode for its purported substitution of the perverted values of the "cultural elite" for right-

thinking "family values." The cultural (vs. structural) attributes of new-class theory are forcefully presented in Daniel Bell, *The Cultural Contradictions of Capitalism* (New York: Basic, 1975), and Norman Podhoretz, "The Adversary Culture and the New Class," in B. Bruce-Briggs, ed., *The New Class?* (New Brunswick, N.J.: Transaction Books, 1979), 19–31. Podhoretz himself draws on Lionel Trilling, *Beyond Culture: Essays on Literature and Learning* (New York: Viking, 1965). Quayle most likely picked up on the issue through his special assistant, William Kristol, son of neo-conservative intellectual leaders Gertrude Himmelfarb and Irving Kristol. On the historical elaboration of new-class theory, see B. Bruce-Briggs, *The New Class?*, esp. introduction by Bruce-Briggs, 1–18; Christopher Lasch, *The True and Only Heaven: Progress and Its Critics* (New York: Norton, 1991), 509–532; Jean-Christophe Agnew, "A Touch of Class," *democracy* 3 (Spring 1983), 59–72.

101. Alexis de Toqueville, *Democracy in America*, vol. 2, bk. 1, chap. 1 (New York: Vintage, 1945 [1835]), 4.

5. A Love for the People: Anna Strunsky Walling

1. Christopher Lasch, *The New Radicalism in America, 1889–1963: The Intellectual as a Social Type* (New York: Vintage, 1965), 90.

2. In keeping with the documentary sources of their personal lives, I will frequently refer to the two main characters as they and their friends called them, "Anna" and "English."

3. Like Anna, Rose also drew attention both for her beauty and for her sharp intellect, numbering Sinclair Lewis among her early admirers. Mark Schorer, *Sinclair Lewis: An American Life* (New York: McGraw-Hill, 1961), 204–205.

4. Introduction to Anna Strunsky Walling Papers, Yale University Library (hereafter cited as ASWP).

5. Interview with daughter Anna Walling Hamburger, Dec. 14, 1991, New York City.

6. On the uncommonly permissive style of the Strunsky household, see Richard O'Conner, *Jack London: A Biography* (Boston: Little, Brown, 1984), 135; and Emma Goldman, *Living My Life* (New York: New American Library, 1977 [1931]), 227. Although the evidence suggests that Anna's early relationships stopped short of physical intimacy, her generation of Bay-area college students was clearly testing the borders of sexual as well as political convention. According to one recollection of Berkeley in this period, "In order to be modern . . . you had to say 'syphilis' at least once a day." Joyce Antler, *Lucy Sprague Mitchell: The Making of a Modern Woman* (New Haven: Yale University Press, 1987), 116.

7. Hal Waters, "Anna Strunsky and Jack London," *American Book Collector* 17 (November 1966), 28–30.

8. Jack London to Anna Strunsky, Dec. 29, 1899; March 22, 1900; Nov. 27, 1900; Dec. 26, 1900; all ASWP.

9. Anna Strunsky to Charmian Kittredge, Jan. 17, 1919, ASWP.

10. Rose Wilder Lane, "Life and Jack London," *Sunset, the Pacific Monthly* [1918], 27–30 (clipping in ASWP). London was particularly unsparing in his criticism of Strunsky's often airy prose style: "You understand: yet you have not so expressed your understanding as to make the reader understand . . . [I] would make this same criticism of all your short stories." Jack London to Anna Strunsky Walling, Oct. 13, 1904, ASWP.

11. Jack London to Anna Strunsky, Dec. 26, Dec. 29, 1899, ASWP.

12. Jack London defended himself against a reproach from Anna that "not all Jews haggle and bargain," Jack London to Anna Strunsky, Dec. 12, 1899, ASWP. The economist Phillip Kaiser recalls that during a 1955 meeting with Anna Strunsky Walling she quoted Jack London to the effect that marriage between them was out of the question because "I don't believe in race mixing." Telephone interview with Kaiser, 1991. On London's theories of Nordic supremacy, see O'Conner, *Jack London*, 148; general racial Darwinism, see Mark Pittenger, *American Socialists and Evolutionary Thought, 1870–1920* (Madison: University of Wisconsin Press, 1993), 169, 172, 174, 202.

13. O'Conner, *Jack London*, 143.

14. *The Kempton-Wace Letters* (New York: Haskell House, 1903). Reviewed in the *New York Times Book Review*, June 27, 1903, p. 446.

15. *Kempton-Wace Letters*, 42.

16. Ibid., 222–223.

17. Ibid., 206–207, 64.

18. Ibid., 87, 90.

19. Ibid., 50, 157, 104–105.

20. Ibid., 160–161, 256.

21. O'Conner, *Jack London*, 191–192, 198–200, 225.

22. Waters, "Anna Strunsky and Jack London," 30.

23. Cameron King to Anna Strunsky, Jan. 1 [1906], ASWP.

24. Ibid., March 15, 1906.

25. Ibid., March 24, 1906. In words that Anna neither acknowledged nor heeded at the time, but that in retrospect carry a haunting foreboding, King urged her to contain her own independent-mindedness for the sake of her marriage: "Look for possible points of disagreement and let him assert his beliefs into your love-submissive consciousness. That will be an insurance against future troubles." King to Anna Strunsky, April 4, 1906, ASWP.

26. William English Walling to Willoughby and Rosalind Walling, Jan. 29, 1906, William English Walling Papers, State Historical Society of Wisconsin, Madison (hereafter cited as WEWP).

27. William English Walling to Anna Strunsky [1905], ASWP; William English Walling to Willoughby and Rosalind Walling, Jan. 29, 1906, WEWP.

28. Capt. William E. English to Willoughby Walling, Jan. 19, 1906, WEWP; *Chicago American, New York Times*, Oct. 21, 1907. Anna later recalled the circumstances of the couple's arrest for alleged revolutionary activity in St. Petersburg in October 1907 and the frenzied response by the Walling family back home: "The news reached this country during a telegraph strike. English's Uncle Will, Captain William Easton English, drove in the middle of

the night from his home in Lexington, Kentucky, to Indianapolis, where he tried to get his messages through to [President] Theodore Roosevelt and members of the State Department. There was no one who would operate the telegraph keys. Somewhere toward morning Uncle Will found a committtee of the strikers. He told them that his nephew and his wife, with her sister, were imprisoned in Russia, where martial law prevailed, and that every hour counted. He reminded them that the arrested Americans were friends of labor, and that their predicament was due precisely to that fact. The point struck home; the telegrams and cables were sent." Anna Strunsky Walling, ed., *William English Walling: A Symposium* (New York: Stackpole Sons, 1938), 11.

29. Anna Strunsky to William English [1906], ASWP.
30. Anna Strunsky to Rosalind Walling, Feb. 24, 1906, ASWP.
31. William English Walling to Willoughby and Rosalind Walling, June 27, 1906, WEWP.
32. Ibid., Oct. 22, 1897, WEWP.
33. Ibid. [1897], WEWP.
34. On Ovington as an exception to the general moral turpitude of the settlement movement on the race issue, see Elizabeth Lasch-Quinn, *Black Neighbors: Race and the Limits of Reform in the American Settlement House Movement, 1890–1945* (Chapel Hill: University of North Carolina Press, 1993), esp. 42–46.
35. On Walling's tendency to find in the immigrant Jew the prototype for all industrial workers and ethno-racial prejudice, see James Gilbert, *Designing the Industrial State: The Intellectual Pursuit of Collectivism in America, 1880–1940* (Chicago: Quadrangle Books, 1972), 209–211.
36. In notes that she assembled for the archival collection of the William English Walling Papers in 1962, Anna wrote: "How wonderful that a typical Southern aristocratic boy with ingrained prejudices can develop and found an NAACP! . . . [But] he did not change viscerally when Dr. Dubois [sic], that great man, did us the honor of spending two or three weekends with us on Caritas Island, and he went in swimming with English and me, English confessed to me that he felt he was 'swimming with a monkey.' I did not reproach him. I was silent. He could not help it . . . Mom's son! But we had Negro visitors. Weldon Johnson for one whom English honored and loved to be with and Walter White as well [but] both these men were white . . . impossible to [tell] a difference [between them and a white man]." WEWP.
37. Allen F. Davis, *Spearheads for Reform: The Social Settlements and the Progressive Movement, 1890–1914* (New York: Oxford University Press, 1967), 84–102.
38. *New York Independent* [1906], clipping in WEWP. Indeed, the three couples clearly felt a common bond, all establishing summer cottages on Caritas Island, Connecticut. Arthur Zipser and Pearl Zipser, *Fire and Grace: The Life of Rose Pastor Stokes* (Athens: University of Georgia Press, 1989), 51.
39. Walling's only veiled reference to his parents of his adventures came in his report that he had been "as intimate as the law allows" yet "indifferent . . . as far as love is concerned." William English Walling to Rosalind Walling [1906], WEWP.

40. Berthe Grunspan to William English Walling, July 24, 1905; [n.d., 1906], breach of promise suit file, WEWP. Documents from Grunspan are in original French, but translations were made for the legal record. For this son of middle-class Victorians, the monkey image (which Berthe suggests was the couple's favorite term of endearment), surfacing at once within illicit sexual adventure as well as interracial contact (n. 36), may have embodied the world beyond propriety for Walling—a world at once attractive and repulsive.

41. Testimony from Berthe Grunspan, breach of promise suit file, 1911, WEWP. The Walling attorneys invited international legal experts from France, Germany, and Russia to testify to the inadmissibility of the charges under whichever national laws were considered relevant. Bronislaw Kulakowsky, an attorney for the court of appeals of Russian Poland, for example, testified in Chicago that "only in America" could a person even dream of recovering monetary damages under breach of promise law for "missing out on promised opportunities." This would not be an issue, in any case, in his homeland, he declared, where a Jewess was prohibited by law from marrying a Gentile.

42. William English Walling to Rosalind Walling [1906], WEWP.

43. See Karen Lystra, *Searching the Heart: Women, Men, and Romantic Love in Nineteenth-Century America* (New York: Oxford University Press, 1989), 42–46, on romantic love as "a process of individual development."

44. Anna Strunsky to Rosalind Walling, Feb. 24, 1906, ASWP. Anna's daughter, Anna Walling Hamburger, recalls that each of her parents thought of themselves as "freethinkers" and disdained organized religion. Anna Strunsky Walling, granddaughter of a rabbi, ridiculed Jewish tradition, even teasing her mother with the invitation to "have a little bacon." The Walling children grew up in a home without formal religious instruction and were raised with no religion, although there was always a Christmas tree. Interview with Anna Walling Hamburger, Dec. 14, 1991, New York City. The religious imbalance of the Strunsky-Walling match was not untypical. Graham Stokes, for example, described his fiancée, Rose Pastor, to his parents as "as Christlike a Christian as I ever knew"; later, at their wedding, the bride wore a cross. Zipser and Zipser, *Fire and Grace*, 34, 44.

45. Anna Strunsky to Mr. and Mrs. Elias Strunsky, July l, 1906, ASWP.

46. Leonard D. Abbott, "A Socialist Wedding," *International Socialist Review* 2 (July 1901), 14–20.

47. Rose Paster Stokes to Anna Strunsky, Jan. 21, 1911, ASWP.

48. William English Walling, "Man, Woman, and Socialism" in *The Larger Aspects of Socialism* (New York: Macmillan, 1913), 321–372, quotations pp. 338, 371–372. On Walling's debates with other contemporary feminists, see Pittenger, *American Socialists*, 79–81, 178–179, 183, 240.

49. Indeed, the desire openly articulated by Walling to consecrate sexual union with interpersonal intimacy within marriage anticipated broader trends in sexual radicalism, which historian Ellen Kay Trimberger discovered among Greenwich Village intellectuals in the 1920s. See her "Feminism, Men, and Modern Love: Greenwich Village, 1900–1925," in Ann Snitow, Christine

Stansell, and Sharon Thompson, eds., *Powers of Desire: The Politics of Sexuality* (New York: Monthly Review Press, 1983), 131–152.

50. Anna Strunsky to Willoughby and Rosalind Walling, April 29, May 20, 1906, ASWP.

51. Elias Strunsky to Anna Strunsky, July 10, 1911, ASWP. A legal "matters of facts" [sic] statement [n.d] summarized the damage done to Elias Strunsky by his partner, Isaac Lipshitz: "It was not only that he cheat me out of my money, but he also deprived me of my family happiness, my very beloved wife gat to be an enemy to me and my dearly children who was always the pride of my life had forsaken me" (sic).

52. Anna Strunsky to Willoughby and Rosalind Walling, Feb. 16, 1908, WEWP; interviews with Rosamund (Walling) Tirana, May 15, 1991, by telephone, and Anna Walling Hamburger, Dec. 14, 1991, in New York City.

53. Anna Strunsky to William English Walling, Feb. 13, 1924, ASWP.

54. Anna Strunsky to Rosalind Walling, February 25, 1908, ASWP. Rosalind Walling to William English Walling [1908], WEWP.

55. Quoted in introduction to ASWP, Feb. 8, 1909; Hyman Strunsky to Anna Strunsky [1908], ASWP; Mary E. Haskell to Anna Strunsky [n.d.], ASWP.

56. Interview with Anna Walling Hamburger.

57. Anna Strunsky to Willoughby Walling, Feb. 26, 1908, ASWP.

58. Anna Walling Hamburger speculates that Anna had as many pregnancies as she did "because she wanted a son." Ms. Hamburger sets significance in the fact that Hayden was her parents' youngest child and speculates that Georgia, the third child, received her name as a transmutation of the intended name, George. Anna Walling Hamburger interview.

59. Ibid.; Anna Strunsky to William English, Dec. 6, 1917, ASWP.

60. Interview with Anna Walling Hamburger; Emma Goldman to Anna Strunsky, Feb. 27, 1916; Aug. 8, 1916, ASWP. Goldman's disappointment was heightened by her high regard for Anna's politics and agitational skills. In 1912, for example, Strunsky drew rave reviews for an address at a benefit for Alexander Berkman. Emma Goldman to Anna Strunsky, Nov. 2, 1912, ASWP. Goldman picked up this conversational thread years later in 1931, when she wrote to Anna on completion of her autobiography: "You see, my dear, . . . I had to deny myself a child in the flesh. *Living My Life* has taken its place." Quoted in Alice Wexler, *Emma Goldman in Exile: Fropm the Russian Revolution to the Spanish Civil War* (Boston: Beacon Press, 1989), 153.

61. Anna Strunsky to William English Walling, July 15, 1919, ASWP.

62. Interviews with Anna Walling Hamburger and Rosamund Walling Tirana.

63. Anna Strunsky to William English Walling, July 15, 1919, Jan. 10, 1919, ASWP.

64. Louise C. Howe to Anna Strunsky Walling [1917], ASWP.

65. Winifred Heath to Anna Strunsky, Aug. 22, 1915, ASWP.

66. Emma Goldman to Anna Strunsky, March 17, 1915, ASWP. Goldman had herself privately elaborated on this painful dilemma, calling herself "too much" a woman. "That's my tragedy. The great abyss between my woman nature and the nature of the relentless revolutionist is too great to allow

much happiness in my life. But then, who can boast of happiness?" quoted in Candace Serena Falk, *Love, Anarchy, and Emma Goldman* (New Brunswick, N.J.: Rutgers University Press, 1990), 43.

67. "Violence and the I.W.W.," address delivered in New York City, Nov. 22, 1914, ASWP.

68. *Los Angeles Record*, Aug. 28, 1917.

69. "Twilight Sleep II," *McClure's* (June 1922), 64.

70. Anna Strunsky to Rosalind Walling, Aug. 26, 1916, ASWP.

71. Dinner invitation, Jan. 14, 1926, ASWP.

72. Interview with Rosamund Walling Tirana.

73. Jessie Wallace Hughan to Anna Strunsky, June 25, 1943, ASWP.

74. See anonymous review in the *New Republic* 5 (Dec. 11, 1915), 155. In addition to its setting in the city of her daughter's death, the author refers in the early pages of *Violette* to "one other book—the story of the sufferings of a little child her own age," adding, "She was mistaken, this mother, to have let her baby go from her arms; she should have known that evil would befall her despite the love which from a distance she would send on, despite her prayers, her tears, the blood she would pour out for her—evil must befall a child separated from her mother!" Anna Strunsky Walling, *Violette of Pere Lachaise* (New York: Frederick A. Stokes, 1915), 29.

75. *Violette*, 24–25.

76. Ibid., 127, 156.

77. Ibid., 191, 195–196.

78. Anna Strunsky to William English Walling, Jan. 13, 1913, ASWP.

79. Norman Hapgood, *A Victorian in the Modern World* (New York: Harcourt Brace, 1939), 425.

80. William English Walling to Anna Strunsky, Jan. 4, 1914, ASWP.

81. Anna Strunsky to William English Walling [n.d.: 1911–12]; William English Walling to Anna Strunsky [n.d.: 1914], ASWP.

82. Mary V. Dearborn, *Love in the Promised Land: The Story of Anzia Yezierska and John Dewey* (New York: Free Press, 1988), 132.

83. William English Walling to Anna Strunsky, Feb. 22, 1916, WEWP.

84. William English Walling to Rosalind Walling [1917]; Woodrow Wilson to William English Walling, May 5, 1917; Walling to Woodrow Wilson, May 10, 1917; all in WEWP.

85. Anna Walling Hamburger interview.

86. William English Walling to Anna Strunsky [1917], WEWP.

87. Anna Strunsky to William English Walling, Jan. 27, 1917, ASWP. The source mentions only a "box of crackers," but metal packaging was common then, and the injury would seem to confirm the assumption. On the Wallings' domestic strains, see also Hapgood, *A Victorian*, 244–245.

88. Anna Strunsky to William English Walling, Jan. 27, 1917, March 21, 1917, ASWP.

89. Anna Strunsky to William English Walling, Dec. 15, 1916, ASWP.

90. Anna Strunsky to William English Walling, March 26, 1917, ASWP.

91. Zipser and Zipser, *Fire and Grace*, 176–198.

92. Ibid., 252–278. Troubled from early on, the Pastor-Stokes marriage ended in bitter divorce in 1925. He would soon remarry a woman from his own WASPish social circle, while Rose at forty-seven remarried twenty-nine-year-old Communist writer V. J. Jerome.

93. Anna Strunsky to Willoughby Walling, Nov. 4, 1916, WEWP.

94. Rosamund Walling to Anna Strunsky, Oct. 8, Oct. 18, 1916, WEWP.

95. *Chicago Record-American* [1911], clipping in WEWP.

96. Willoughby Walling (brother) to William English Walling, Oct. 8, 1917, WEWP.

97. Willoughby Walling (father) to William English Walling, Oct. 12, 1916, WEWP.

98. William English Walling to Willoughby Walling, Oct. 28, 1916, WEWP.

99. Anna Strunsky to William English Walling, Nov. 29, 1916, ASWP.

100. Thus, while Walling waited anxiously in 1906 for word that his parents accepted his wedding plans "at least without heart reserve," he wrote impatiently, "Of course you want to decide for yourself just how and why we love one another and how we are suited for a 'single' life [together]—you intellectuals!" William English Walling to Willoughby and Rosalind Walling [May 1906], WEWP.

101. Anna Walling Hamburger interview.

102. William English Walling to Anna Strunsky [1916], WEWP. Georges I. Gurdjieff (1877–1949) was a Russian-born mystic and occultist who attracted attention, and established institutes, in the West with his teachings of the "Fourth Way"—the attempt to awaken a higher consciousness through a combination of group movement, dance, manual labor, and a minimum of sleep. Strunsky's acquaintance with his writings may well have come via her friend Mary E. Haskell, a Boston schoolmistress and ardent admirer and secret confidante of Gurdjieff. See, e.g., Virginia Hilu, ed., *Beloved Prophet: The Love Letters of Kahlil Gibran and Mary Haskell and Her Private Journal* (New York: Knopf, 1972).

103. William English Walling to Anna Strunsky [1916–1917], WEWP. "System," admonished Walling, "means explicit instructions repeated over and over again with daily questions as to whether they have been carried out."

104. Anna Strunsky notes [1962], ASWP. For the most part, Walling apparently kept his rage hidden from his children. According to his daughter, his temper "was only directed at my mother." "He never raised his voice when speaking to his children . . . Because my mother explained away his 'tantrums' as being only caused by his bad stomach, my memory is of a happy, loving home until the appearance of Mrs. W in 1932." Letter from Anna Walling Hamburger to the author, Oct. 25, 1994.

105. William English Walling to Anna Strunsky, Jan. 12, 1921, WEWP.

106. William English Walling to Anna Strunsky, Nov. 23, 1922, ASWP.

107. William English Walling to Anna Strunsky, Nov. 24, 1922, ASWP.

108. William English Walling to Anna Strunsky, Nov. 24, 1922, ASWP.

109. William English Walling to Anna Strunsky, Dec. 2, 1922, ASWP.

110. Anna Strunsky Walling notes [1962], ASWP.

111. William English Walling to Anna Strunsky, July 13, 1923, WEWP.
112. William English Walling to Anna Strunsky, Feb. 25, 1923, WEWP. English, even Anna observed, appeared happiest away from the house and in his mother's company. As she confided to her mother-in-law, "It is perhaps a kind of transmutation of the suckling process of mother and child—throughout life he remains at your breast drawing from you the strength and the inspiration he needs to be most himself." Anna Strunsky to Rosamund Walling, May 8, 1921, ASWP.
113. Rosamund Walling to William English Walling, May 9, 1926, WEWP.
114. Anna Walling Hamburger interview.
115. William English Walling to Anna Strunsky, Feb. 15, 1924, Feb. 28, 1924; Anna Strunsky to William English Walling, Jan. 19, 1928, Feb. 25, 1929, July 3, 1929; all in WEWP.
116. William English Walling to Rosamund Walling [1929], WEWP.
117. Anna Walling Hamburger interview.
118. Anna Strunsky to Rosalind Walling, Sept. 4, 1929, ASWP.
119. Rosalind Walling to Anna Strunsky, Nov. 18, 1929, ASWP.
120. Anna Strunsky to William English Walling, Aug. 3, 1929, Aug. 21, 1929, ASWP.
121. Anna Strunsky to William English Walling, composed Aug. 2, 1929, sent Aug. 21, 1929, ASWP.
122. Anna Strunsky to William English Walling, Aug. 3, 1929, ASWP.
123. Anna Strunsky to William English Walling [1929], ASWP.
124. Ibid.; Anna Strunsky to William English Walling, Aug. 15, 1929, ASWP.
125. Anna Strunsky to William English Walling, Oct. 9, 1929; Anna Strunsky to William English Walling, May 21, 1932, ASWP.
126. Anna Strunsky to William English Walling, July 25, July 29, 1930, ASWP.
127. Anna's fears, like those of most parents, were no doubt part justified and part exaggerated. The daughters' automobile accident, for example, occurred through no fault of their own, when another car went through a red light and hit them broadside. Letter from Anna Walling Hamburger to author, July 28, 1994.
128. Anna Strunsky to William English Walling [1932], ASWP.
129. Anna Strunsky to William English Walling [1929–30], ASWP.
130. Anna Strunsky to William English Walling, Nov. 17, 1932, ASWP.
131. The child most affected by his parents' disaffection was undoubtedly young Hayden, who early on evidenced an extreme emotional dependency on his mother. Hayden, by age twenty, seemed to be "heading for disintegration" and talked "wildly about having no intention to develop himself further." His mother's fears proved only partially prescient. Turning to a life of service, Hayden completed conscientious objector work for the American Friends Service Committee during World War II and later distinguished himself in the employ of UNICEF and the World Health Organization before returning to the United States as a master builder. Yet he was never able entirely to shake off his early demons. Called English by his mother after William English Walling's death, Hayden struggled through three marriages and died

a suicide. Anna Strunsky to William English Walling, July 21, 1936; Aug. 14, 1936, ASWP; letter from Anna Walling Hamburger to author, July 28, 1994; Anna Strunsky to William English Walling (on word of his death), Nov. 22, 1936, ASWP.

132. Abbott's interest in Anna perhaps had begun even earlier. In 1926, he had confided in her, "Why does life get so sad as we grow older? I long for something which will involve my every energy, and instead I get just the dull daily round." Leonard D. Abbott to Anna Strunsky, Dec. 7, 1926, ASWP. Despite their mutual affection, the Victorian Anna Strunsky drew the limit at sexual intimacy with Abbott. As she told her daughter, "We would never think of doing anything [in private] that we couldn't do in Washington Square" (Anna Walling Hamburger interview). Similarly, she assured interviewer Hal Waters in 1963 and 1964, just before her death, that she "was never physically intimate with any man other than her husband, English." Waters, "Anna Strunsky and Jack London," 30.

133. Anna Strunsky to Leonard D. Abbott, June 24, 1933, ASWP.

134. Anna Strunsky to Leonard D. Abbott, July 26, 1933, ASWP.

135. Leonard D. Abbott to Anna Strunsky, June 30, 1936, ASWP.

136. Anna Strunsky notes to WEWP, 1962.

137. Jesse Jackson to Anna Strunsky [n.d.: 1963?], ASWP.

138. Irwin Suall to W. English Strunsky [sic], July 20, 1962, ASWP; Anna Strunsky, notes on reply to Suall, July 26, 196[2], ASWP.

139. Cameron King to Anna Strunsky, July 19, 1945, ASWP.

140. Steven Biel, *Independent Intellectuals in the United States, 1910–1945* (New York: New York University Press, 1992), 109–125, quotation 115. Biel's argument also recalls Lasch's central theme of the "cult of experience" in *The New Radicalism,* esp. 69–103.

141. Interview with Anna Walling Hamburger.

142. In his frustration to find in marriage the egalitarian romance he had once envisioned for himself and his bride, Walling was not alone. In a study of three of Walling's radical intellectual contemporaries—Max Eastman, Floyd Dell, and Hutchins Hapgood—Ellen Kay Trimberger finds a common pattern of "contradictions between their sexual desires and their need for intimacy with an intellectual woman . . . In their attempts at intimacy with talented women, [they] could not overcome a subtle form of inequality. Each wanted his woman to be passionately involved with him—a wife to whom he could confess all his deep emotional and psychological problems and conflicts. There is little evidence, however, that any of the men were willing to reciprocate. Although all three men sought a strong, intellectual woman, they seemed to desire a maternal figure—a woman who would subordinate her needs to their own rather than to insist on being an autonomous individual with interests and needs of equal worth." Trimberger, "Feminism, Men, and Modern Love," 140–141.

6. A Voice for the People: A. Philip Randolph

1. An earlier version of this chapter was delivered to the Eighth Southern Labor Studies Conference, Oct. 21–23, 1993, in Birmingham, Alabama. For three excellent overviews of Randolph's career—each written with a different emphasis—see Jervis Anderson, *A. Philip Randolph: A Biographical Portrait* (New York: Harcourt Brace Jovanovich, 1973); William H. Harris, *Keeping the Faith: A. Philip Randolph, Milton P. Webster, and the Brotherhood of Sleeping Car Porters, 1925–37* (Urbana: University of Illinois Press, 1977); and Paula Pfeffer, *A. Philip Randolph, Pioneer of the Civil Rights Movement* (Baton Rouge: Louisiana State University Press, 1990). For the best succinct evaluation of Randolph's career, see Benjamin Quarles, "A. Philip Randolph: Labor Leader at Large," in John Hope Franklin and August Meier, eds., *Black Leaders of the Twentieth Century* (Urbana: University of Illinois Press, 1982), 139–165. In addition, for Randolph's early radicalism, see Theodore Kornweibel, Jr., *No Crystal Stair: Black Life and the Messenger, 1917–1928* (Westport, Conn.: Greenwood Press, 1975).

2. Editorial, *Messenger* 1 (November 1917), 21; "Who's Who," *Messenger* 3 (May–June 1919), 26–27. If including the first name of Kelly Miller, Howard University sociologist and college dean, was not an editing error, "Kelly" perhaps referred to Douglas F. Kelly of Hampton Institute. Robert Russa Moton was longtime "commandant" of Hampton Institute, a key ally of Booker T. Washington, and principal of Tuskegee Institute after Washington's death in 1915. William Pickens, a classics and sociology professor, was serving as dean of Howard University before a later career (1920–1940) as NAACP field secretary. James Weldon Johnson, perhaps best known now for his *Black Manhattan* (1930), was the editor of the leading black newspaper, the *New York Age*. Fred Moore was publisher of the *Age* and an advocate of black capitalism on the National Urban League Board. T. Thomas Fortune served as first editor-owner of the *Age* in 1887 and remained loyal to Washington despite his more radical political ideology. Roscoe Conkling Simmons, a nephew of Mrs. Booker T. Washington, organized the Chicago black Republican vote. George Wesley Harris, founder and editor of the *New York News*, was New York City's first black alderman. Charles William Anderson, an important northern politician, rose through the patronage ranks of federal internal revenue collection and the New York State Department of Agriculture. Attorney William H. Lewis, a close Washington friend, became assistant U.S. attorney general under President Taft. Ralph Waldo Tyler, another Washington protégé, served as national organizer of the National Negro Business League and later as the only black journalist with the wartime Committee on Public Information. Emmet Scott served as Washington's private secretary, 1897–1915, and later as business manager of Howard University. George Edmund Haynes, founder of the National Urban League, 1910–1911, would serve as Special Assistant to the Secretary of Labor during World War I.

   To be sure, it was not only against black misleaders that Randolph and Owen vented their spleen. Evaluating President Woodrow Wilson's presidency in 1919, the editors wrote that "the chief beneficiaries of his public career are the combined manufacturers and capitalists and himself." Progressive forces, they continued, "would willingly witness the setting of his sun in public without grief. Unhonored, he will go down to the narrow, bigoted grave of private life from whence he sprang." Quoted in Quarles, "Labor Leader at Large," 144.

3. Nell Irvin Painter, *Exodusters: Black Migration to Kansas after Reconstruction* (New York: Norton, 1979), 26–30, 107.

4. I have benefited from discussions with James Epstein in particular on this point.

5. See, e.g., Nell Irvin Painter, "Malcolm X across the Genres," and Gerald Horne, "'Myth' and the Making of *Malcolm X*," *American Historical Review* 98 (April 1993), 432–439 and 440–450 respectively; Salim Muwakkil, "The X Files," *In These Times* 19, no. 6 (Feb. 6, 1995), 18–20.

6. Joseph Carpenter, Jr., "The Leadership Philosophy of Dr. Martin Luther King, Jr.: Its Educational Implications" (Ph.D. diss., Marquette University, 1970), 57.

7. Cornel West, *Race Matters* (New York: Vintage, 1993) 53.

8. Nathan Irvin Huggins, "Afro-Americans," in John Higham, ed., *Ethnic Leadership in America* (Baltimore: The Johns Hopkins University Press, 1978), 97, 99.

9. Wilson Jeremiah Moses, *Black Messiahs and Uncle Toms: Social and Literary Manipulations of a Religious Myth* (University Park: Pennsylvania State University Press, 1982), 86.

10. An independent Atlanta-based monthly published 1904–1907 with a reputation as the "most widely circulated journal published by Negroes," *The Voice of the Negro* self-consciously compiled the thoughts of the "doers and thinkers of the race" while also sharply protesting racial injustices. The paper was co-edited by Jesse Max Barber (a graduate of Virginia Union University in Richmond, who would later switch from journalism to dentistry) and John Wesley Edward Bowen (a Methodist clergyman who was the second black Ph.D.—Boston University in Philosophy in 1887—in the United States and held a chair in historical theology at Gammon Theological Seminary in Atlanta). Forced to suspend publication after the Atlanta race riot of 1906, *The Voice* relocated briefly to Chicago in its final year. Penelope L. Bullock, "Jesse Max Barber," and Richard Bardolph, "John Wesley Edward Bowen," in Rayford W. Logan and Michael R. Winston, eds., *Dictionary of American Negro Biography* (New York: Norton, 1982), 27–28, 52–53, quotation 52; Kevin K. Gaines, *Uplifting the Race: Black Leadership, Politics, and Culture in the Twentieth Century* (Chapel Hill: University of North Carolina Press, 1996), 60–66; [J W. E. Bowen,] "First Words," *Voice of the Negro* 1 (January 1904), 33–34.

11. W. S. Scarborough, "White vs. Black," *Voice of the Negro* 1 (January 1904), 26–27.

12. Kelly Miller, "Frederick Douglass," *Voice of the Negro* 1 (October 1904), 461.

13. Kelly Miller, *Race Adjustment: Essays on the Negro in America* (New York: Neale

Publishing Co., 1910), 264–265. On Washington's own attempts to advance native American interests, see Booker T. Washington, *Up from Slavery: An Autobiography* (Williamstown, Mass.: Corner House, 1989 [1900]), 97–99.

14. John R. L. Diggs, "Negro Church Life," *Voice of the Negro* 1 (February 1904), 48; Lewis B. Moore, "The Education of Negro Teachers," *Voice of the Negro* 1 (April 1904), 159.

15. Fannie Barrier Williams, "The Club Movement among the Colored Women," *Voice of the Negro* 1 (February 1904), 101.

16. Mary Church Terrell, "The Progress of Colored Women," *Voice of the Negro* 1 (July 1904), 294.

17. Emmett J. Scott, "The Tuskegee Negro Conference," *Voice of the Negro* 1 (May 1904), 179.

18. Evelyn Brooks Higginbotham, *Righteous Discontent: The Women's Movement in the Black Baptist Church, 1880–1920* (Cambridge, Mass.: Harvard University Press, 1993), 20–27, quotation 27.

19. David Levering Lewis, *W. E. B. Du Bois—Biography of a Race, 1868–1919* (New York: Henry Holt, 1993), 164.

20. W. E. B. Du Bois, *Souls of Black Folk* (Greenwich, Conn.: Fawcett Books, 1961 [1903]), 118. The famous section on Dougherty County, Georgia, in *Souls of Black Folk* (104–122) appears to reflect a synthetic refinement of Du Bois's earlier "Testimony before Industrial Commission" (1901), and his study "The Negro Landholder of Georgia" (1901), reprinted in Herbert Aptheker, ed., *Contributions of W. E. B. Du Bois in Government Publications and Proceedings* (Millwood, N.Y.: Kraus-Thomson, 1980), 65–228.

21. "The Talented Tenth," in Julius Lester, ed., *The Seventh Son: The Thought and Writings of W. E. B. Du Bois*, vol. 1 (New York: Random House, 1971), 385, 390.

22. Miller, *Race Adjustment*, 264; Du Bois, "The Talented Tenth," 395.

23. *Souls of Black Folk*, 54; "The Talented Tenth," 398.

24. *Souls of Black Folk*, 150–151. For elaboration on the political implications of the talented tenth idea, see Huggins, "Afro-Americans," 102–103, and Manning Marable, *W. E. B. Du Bois: Black Radical Democrat* (Boston: Twayne Publishers, 1986), 26, 50–51, 80.

25. Marcus Garvey, "Shall the Negro Be Exterminated?" in Amy Jacques-Garvey, ed., *Philosophy and Opinions of Marcus Garvey*, vol. 1 (New York: Atheneum, 1968 [1923], 64–67.

26. Ibid., 65; "Statement on Arrest," January 1922, in ibid., 101. For a sympathetic treatment of the UNIA as a democratic movement, see John Brown Childs, *Leadership, Conflict, and Cooperation in Afro-American Social Thought* (Philadelphia: Temple University Press, 1989), 115–122.

27. "W. E. B. Du Bois," *Messenger* 2 (July 1920), 27–28.

28. Kornweibel, *No Crystal Stair*, 137, 148; "Editorial," *Messenger* 4 (July 1922), 437.

29. *Messenger* 2 (May–June 1919), 26–27.

30. Allan H. Spear, "Introduction," in Alain Locke, ed., *The New Negro: An Interpretation* (New York: Johnson Reprint, 1968 [1925]), v. The term had earlier been appropriated with far less radical purposes in mind by William

Pickens in *The New Negro: His Political, Civil and Mental Status and Related Essays* (New York: Neale Publishing Co., 1916). For the contemporary tug of war over the term "New Negro," see Gaines, *Uplifting the Race*, 224.

31. Harris, *Keeping the Faith*, 26–36.

32. Anderson, *A. Philip Randolph*, 32–39, quotation 32. Among the literary staples in the Randolph household was the *Voice of the Negro*, mentioned earlier.

33. On Johnson in Jacksonville, see Bernard Eisenberg, "James Weldon Johnson and the NAACP, 1916–1934" (Ph.D. diss., Columbia University, 1968), 1–6. On Jacksonville, see Barbara Ann Richardson, "A History of Blacks in Jacksonville, Florida, 1860–1895: A Socio-Economic and Political Study," (D.A. diss., Carnegie-Mellon University, 1975), 221–234. "Reminiscences of Asa Philip Randolph," interview by Wendell Wray, Columbia University Oral History Research Office, 1972, transcript, 70–72.

34. Randolph, "Reminiscences," 76.

35. Ibid., 79.

36. Ibid., 76–77.

37. Anderson, *A. Philip Randolph*, 76, 80.

38. Pfeffer, *A. Philip Randolph, Pioneer*, 2; Anderson, *A. Philip Randolph*, 10–11.

39. Lawrence W. Levine, *Highbrow / Lowbrow: The Emergence of Cultural Hierarchy in America* (Cambridge, Mass.: Harvard University Press, 1988). Intriguingly, for the rough-hewn Lewis as well as the son of the black preacher, familiarity with classical texts served not only as a badge of self-acquired respectability, but also as evidence of "marrying up." Thus, the mineworkers' (and later CIO) chieftain acquired a love of reading and drama from a young schoolteacher, Myrta Edith Bell, the daughter of the town doctor in Lucas, Iowa, who subsequently became his wife. Cecil Carnes, *John L. Lewis: Leader of Labor* (New York: Robert Speller Publishing, 1936), 7, 10; and Melvyn Dubofsky and Warren Van Tine, *John L. Lewis: A Biography* (Urbana: University of Illinois Press, 1986), 16–17.

40. Anderson, *A. Philip Randolph*, 60–61.

41. Biography of Lucille Greene Randolph on her death, April 12, 1963. The cultural aspirations of the Randolphs are also suggested by Lucille's funeral program, which included printed selections from Longfellow, William Cullen Bryant, Alfred Lord Tennyson, and James Russell Whittier. (Randolph Personal Files, Brotherhood of Sleeping Car Porters Chicago Division Papers, Chicago Historical Society [hereafter cited as BSCPP]); George S. Schuyler, *Black and Conservative* (New Rochelle, N.Y.: Arlington House, 1966), 138; Cary D. Wintz, *Black Culture and the Harlem Renaissance* (Houston: Rice University Press, 1988), 90.

42. Randolph to P. T. W. Badger, April 19, 1957, BSCPP.

43. Quarles, "Labor Leader at Large," 142; Anderson, *A. Philip Randolph*, 7–8. Randolph's attire recalls a comment about another "imported" working-class leader, Ferdinand Lassalle: "[He] dressed with elegance for his working-men audiences, with the hope, he said, of reminding them that there was something better than their shabbiness." *The Kempton-Wace Letters* (New York: Haskell House, 1903), 26. See also Edmund Wilson, *To the Finland Station: A*

Study in the Writing and Acting of History (New York: Harcourt Brace, 1940), 228–259.

44. Pfeffer, *A. Philip Randolph, Pioneer,* 30. See, e.g., "The Porter's Duty to Pullman," *Black Worker* 2 (March 1, 1930), 1.

45. Jack Santino, *Miles of Smiles, Years of Struggle: Stories of Black Pullman Porters* (Urbana: University of Illinois Press, 1989), esp. 84.

46. Randolph to "Friends and Brothers," Dec. 21, 1926, BSCPP.

47. Randolph, "The Brotherhood and Our Struggle Today," *Black Worker* 1 (Nov. 15, 1929), 1, 3.

48. Joseph F. Wilson, *Tearing Down the Color Bar: A Documentary History and Analysis of the Brotherhood of Sleeping Car Porters* (New York: Columbia University Press, 1989), 269–270.

49. Higginbotham, *Righteous Discontent,* 192–197, 227.

50. Quarles, "Labor Leader at Large," 149.

51. M. Melinda Chateauvert, "Marching Together: Women of the Brotherhood of Sleeping Car Porters, 1925–1957" (Ph.D. diss., University of Pennsylvania, 1992), 162–163.

52. Childs, *Leadership,* 57–58.

53. Randolph to M. P. Webster, Sept. 21, 1926, and Dec. 22, 1926, BSCPP; Anderson, *A. Philip Randolph,* 69.

54. Randolph to W. G. Lee, June 14, 1928, BSCPP.

55. Harris, *Keeping the Faith,* 220–222.

56. Herbert Garfinkel, *When Negroes March: The March on Washington Movement in the Organizational Politics for FEPC* (Glencoe, Ill.: Free Press, 1959), 53–60; Anderson, *A. Philip Randolph,* 211.

57. Harris, *Keeping the Faith,* 222.

58. "To the Brotherhood Men," *Messenger* 8 (March 1926), 90.

59. As quoted in Harris, *Keeping the Faith,* 132.

60. Ibid., 220–225.

61. See ibid., 141–146, 222–223.

62. "A. Philip Randolph: The Seekers and the Sought," *Black Worker* 6 (June 1944), 3.

63. Arthur M. Powell to Randolph, June 27, 1974, and March 5, 1977, BSCPP.

64. Huggins, *"Afro-Americans,"* 106.

65. For the constraints that this expected social connectedness imposes on the individual intellectual, see John Hope Franklin, "The Dilemma of the American Negro Scholar," in *Race and History: Selected Essays, 1938–1988* (Baton Rouge: Louisiana State University Press, 1989), 295–308.

66. Moses, *Black Messiahs,* ix–xii, 1. Rev. Francis J. Grimké, "Victory for the Allies and the United States," *Negro Orators and Their Orations* (Washington, D.C.: Associated Publishers, 1925), 707–708.

67. Anderson, *A. Philip Randolph,* 11, 41; M. M. Ponton, *Life and Times of Henry M. Turner* (New York: Negro Universities Press, 1970), 102–103.

68. Anderson, *A. Philip Randolph,* 24–26; interview, 113.

69. E. Franklin Frazier, *The Negro Church in America* (New York: Schocken, 1974 [1963]), 90.

70. Pfeffer, *A. Philip Randolph, Pioneer,* 32, 66.
71. Quoted in William H. Harris, "A. Philip Randolph, Black Workers, and the Labor Movement," in Melvyn Dubofsky and Warren Van Tine, eds., *Labor Leaders in America* (Urbana: University of Illinois Press, 1987), 277. Schuyler, to be sure, as a black radical turned America Firster, was hardly an impartial observer. Still, his autobiography lists Randolph as "one of the finest, most engaging men I had ever met." *Black and Conservative* (New Rochelle, N.Y.: Arlington House, 1966), 135.
72. Anderson, *A. Philip Randolph,* 12. It is worth noting that Anderson did not see Randolph's "strange sort of cordiality" in gendered terms: Randolph tended to give the brush-off to anyone with whom he was not immediately dealing.
73. Pfeffer, *A. Philip Randolph, Pioneer,* 301–302.
74. Chateauvert, "Marching Together," esp. 38, 44, 135, 173, 214, 221–223, 229. See also David M. Colman, "On the Right Track: The Brotherhood of Sleeping Car Porters . . . Black Labor Organizing in St. Paul, 1937–1950" (Unpublished honors project, Macalester College, 1993).
75. Randolph to M. P. Webster, Aug. 17, 1926, BSCPP.
76. Quoted in Carol Mueller, "Ella Baker and the Origins of 'Participatory Democracy,'" in Vicki L. Crawford, Jacqueline Anne Rouse, and Barbara Woods, eds., *Women in the Civil Rights Movement, 1941–1965* (Brooklyn: Carlson Publishing, 1990), 51–69, quotation 64.
77. Clayborne Carson, *In Struggle: SNCC and the Black Awakening of the 1960s* (Cambridge, Mass.: Harvard University Press, 1981), 62. To be sure, SNCC itself proved notoriously resistant to concerns for gender equality: see ibid., 147–148.
78. See, e.g., James Miller, *Democracy Is in the Streets: From Port Huron to the Siege of Chicago* (New York: Simon and Schuster, 1987); Sara Evans, *Personal Politics: The Roots of Women's Liberation in the Civil Rights Movement and the New Left* (New York: Knopf, 1979); and Mueller, "Ella Baker."
79. Higginbotham, *Righteous Discontent;* Hazel V. Carby, *Reconstructing Womanhood: The Emergence of the Afro-American Woman Novelist* (New York: Oxford University Press, 1987), 84–85.
80. This fear was institutionalized in the German Greens through the principle (since abandoned) of enforced rotation of offices. On new democratic theory, see, e.g., Carole Pateman, *Participation and Democratic Theory* (Cambridge: Cambridge University Press, 1970), and Alan Scott, *Ideology and the New Social Movements* (Boston: Unwin Hyman, 1990).
81. For a good example of the exposure paradigm applied to African-American leaders, see Adolph L. Reed, Jr., *The Jesse Jackson Phenomenon: The Crisis of Purpose in Afro-American Politics* (New Haven: Yale University Press, 1986). For an example of characteristic recent discomfort in wrestling with the problem of leadership, see Leon Fink and Brian Greenberg, *Upheaval in the Quiet Zone* (Urbana: University of Illinois Press, 1989), esp. 181–208.
82. Santino, *Miles of Smiles,* 43, 61–67.
83. Ibid., 66.
84. Colman, "On the Right Track," 49–50.

85. McAlister Coleman, *Men and Coal* (New York: Farrar and Rinehart, 1943), 62 (reference courtesy of Andrew Arnold).

86. David Strand, "Social History and Power Politics: Agency, Interaction and Leadership," Wilder House Working Papers, no. 12, Center for the Study of Politics, History, and Culture, University of Chicago (unpublished paper, 1995), 16. On charismatic leadership, see Sonja M. Hunt, "The Role of Leadership in the Construction of Reality," in Barbara Kellerman, ed., *Leadership: Multidisciplinary Perspectives* (Englewood Cliffs: Prentice-Hall, 1984), 161.

87. Charles Bergquist, *Labor in Latin America: Comparative Essays on Chile, Argentina, Venezuela, and Columbia* (Stanford: Stanford University Press, 1986), 149–176, quotation 169. For elaboration on leader-crowd interactions within Perónism, see Daniel James, "October 17th and 18th, 1945: Mass Protest, Perónism and the Argentine Working Class," *Journal of Social History* 21 (Spring 1988), 441–462.

88. Richard J. Bernstein, "'The Banality of Evil' Reconsidered," paper presented at Hannah Arendt and the Meaning of Politics Conference, University of North Carolina at Chapel Hill, Feb. 17–18, 1995, 7–8. If leadership is relational and interactive, it apparently does not require live bodies at both ends of the relationship. Such, for example, was the power of the late Chinese leader that in a Beijing match factory in 1928, an organizer for the citywide Federation of Trade Unions "single-handedly overcame the factory management's opposition to unionization by entering the plant armed only with a portrait of Sun Yat-sen." David Strand, *Rickshaw Beijing: City People and Politics in the 1920s* (Berkeley: University of California Press, 1989), 231, 258–259.

89. *The Sociology of Georg Simmel,* trans. and ed. by Kurt H. Wolff (Glencoe, Ill.: Free Press, 1950), 185.

90. Nathan Irvin Huggins, *Black Odyssey: The African-American Ordeal in Slavery* (New York: Vintage, 1990), 78. For other historiographic references, see Sterling Stuckey's argument that "the authority of major religious leaders on the plantations owed much to the divine-kingship systems of West Africa." *Slave Culture: Nationalist Theory and the Foundations of Black America* (New York: Oxford University Press, 1987), 37–38; and Robert William Fogel, *Without Consent or Contract: The Rise and Fall of American Slavery* (New York: Norton, 1991), 170–171.

91. William Jeffrey Bolster, "African-American Seamen: Race, Seafaring Work, and Atlantic Maritime Culture, 1750–1860" (Ph.D. diss., Johns Hopkins University, 1992), esp. 185–187, 214–215, 219.

92. Edward L. Wheeler, *Uplifting the Race: The Black Minister in the New South, 1865–1902* (New York: New York University Press, 1986), 22.

93. As quoted in Gayraud S. Wilmore, *Black Religion and Black Radicalism: An Interpretation of the Religious History of Afro-American People* (Maryknoll, N.Y.: Orbis, 1983), 138, 169; Anderson, *A. Philip Randolph,* 20–22.

94. Stephen Ward Angell, *Bishop Henry McNeal Turner and African-American Religion in the South* (Knoxville: University of Tennessee Press, 1992), 37.

95. Theressa Hoover, "Black Women and the Churches: Triple Jeopardy," in

Gayraud S. Wilmore and James H. Cone, eds., *Black Theology: A Documentary History, 1966–1979* (Maryknoll, N.Y.: Orbis, 1979), 378. On the rise of a black feminist or "womanist" critique within black churches, see 363–444, and Delores S. Williams, "Womanist Theology: Black Women's Voices," *Christianity and Crisis* 47 (March 2, 1987), 66–70.

96. Michael Walzer, *Exodus and Revolution* (New York: Basic Books, 1985), 65–66.

97. Ken Post, *Arise Ye Starvelings: The Jamaican Labour Rebellion of 1938 and its Aftermath* (The Hague: Martinus Nijhoff, 1978), 238–265.

98. Lewis, *W. E. B. Du Bois*, 74–78; Arnold Rampersand, *The Art and Imagination of W. E. B. Du Bois* (Cambridge, Mass.: Harvard University Press, 1976), 28, 44–45.

99. Woodrow Wilson, *George Washington* (New York: Harper and Brothers, 1896), 313.

100. Charles Forcey, *The Crossroads of Liberalism: Croly, Weyl, Lippmann, and the Progressive Era, 1900–1925* (New York: Oxford University Press, 1961), 22–44.

101. For elaboration on the popular leadership theme, see Peter Karsten, *Patriot-Heroes in England and America: Political Symbolism and Changing Values over Three Centuries* (Madison: University of Wisconsin Press, 1978); James Epstein, *The Lion of Freedom: Feargus O'Connor and the Chartist Movement, 1832–1842* (London: Croom Helm, 1982); James Vernon, *Politics and the People: A Study in English Political Culture c. 1815–1867* (New York: Cambridge University Press, 1993), 251–294; and Eugenio F. Biagini, *Liberty, Retrenchment, and Reform: Popular Liberalism in the Age of Gladstone, 1860–1880* (New York: Cambridge University Press, 1992), 369–425. John Belchem and James Epstein offer an important caveat about the historical invocation of the gentleman-leader figure, particularly warning of its assimilation into a classless, and contextless, rhetorical-centered view of the political culture. "The Nineteenth Century Gentleman-Leader Revisited," *Social History* (May 1997), 174–193.

102. The *Oldham Standard*, 1860, quoted in Vernon, *Politics and the People*, 260.

103. Antonio Gramsci, *Letters from Prison*, ed. and with an introduction by Lynne Lawner (New York: Harper and Row, 1973), 41–44. Gramsci, of course, was skeptical of the detached persona of the traditional scholar—e.g., his influential contemporary Benedetto Croce, whose academic idealism masked connections to powerful Italian senators. Richard Bellamy and Darrow Schecter, *Gramsci and the Italian State* (New York: Manchester University Press, 1993), 130–131.

104. David Forgacs, ed., *An Antonio Gramsci Reader: Selected Writings, 1916–1935* (New York: Schocken, 1989), 309.

105. Ibid., 331.

106. Bellamy and Schecter, *Gramsci and the Italian State*, 131.

107. *Selections from the Prison Notebooks*, as quoted by Robert Bocock, *Hegemony* (Chichester, England: Ellis Horwood, 1986), 36–37.

108. See Bellamy and Schecter, *Gramsci and the Italian State*, 128–135.

109. Christopher Lasch, *Revolt of the Elites and the Betrayal of Democracy* (New York: W.W. Norton, 1995), 20.

110. In Randolph's own time, one thinks, for example, not only of Du Bois but also of James Weldon Johnson and Walter White, novelists and poets who served as executive secretaries of the NAACP from 1920 to 1955. No comparable legacy suggests itself for any other American community.

7. The People's Strategist: W. Jett Lauck

1. Gompers quoted in Louis S. Reed, *The Labor Philosophy of Samuel Gompers* (Port Washington, N.Y.: Kennikat Press, 1966), 12. On labor's late-nineteenth-century political culture, see Leon Fink, *Workingmen's Democracy: The Knights of Labor and American Politics* (Urbana: University of Illinois Press, 1983). The earlier ideological claims, to be sure, regularly reappeared in form of workplace-centered struggles for control and continuing calls for "industrial democracy," stoked by the influence of a strong socialist minority within the organized labor movement. See, e.g., David Montgomery, *Workers' Control in America: Studies in the History of Work, Technology, and Labor Struggles* (New York: Cambridge University Press, 1979), and Nelson Lichtenstein and Howell John Harris, eds., *Industrial Democracy in America: The Ambiguous Promise* (New York: Cambridge University Press, 1993).

2. I found no previous studies of Lauck's writing or larger work, and while several historians have made excellent use of fragments of the huge W. Jett Lauck Papers, Special Collections, Alderman Library, University of Virginia (hereafter cited as WJLP), none has focused squarely on Lauck himself. To date, the magisterial *John L. Lewis: A Biography* by Melvyn Dubofsky and Warren Van Tine (New York: Quadrangle / New York Times Book Co., 1977; abridged edition, Urbana: University of Illinois Press, 1986) offers the best available, albeit quite brief, assessment of Lauck's overall contribution, including his authorship of "most . . . of Lewis' speeches and publications in the 1930s" (556, n. 11). Even the biographical sketch at the front of the WJLP describes its subject as a "somewhat mysterious figure." His son, Peter B. Lauck, whom I contacted at age seventy-eight for an interview by telephone in 1995, had never previously been questioned about his father's role for scholarly purposes.

3. Cecil Carnes, *John L. Lewis: Leader of Labor* (New York: Robert Speller, 1936), 240; James A. Wechsler, *Labor Baron: A Portrait of John L. Lewis* (New York: William Morrow and Co., 1944), 46.

4. *Christian Science Monitor* quotation cited in Personal Diary, Nov. 17, 1936, WJLP.

5. In addition to some four hundred boxes of records, the WJLP include Lauck's Personal Diaries, 1935–1947, preserved on three reels of microfilm.

6. Peter Lauck interview, Oct. 30, 1995.

7. "Scrapbook," Box 29, WJLP.

8. "Testimony of W. J. Lauck, 1920," New York State Board of Arbitration on the Differences between the New York State Railways and the Employers' Associations, Box 12, WJLP.

9. Jeremiah W. Jenks and Lauck, *The Immigration Problem: A Study of American Immigration Conditions and Needs* (New York: Funk & Wagnalls Co., 1922 [1911]), 202.

10. Lauck to Frank Walsh, July 21, 1915, Frank Walsh Papers, New York Public Library.

11. Reed, *Labor Philosophy*, 11–53, quotation 12.

12. Daniel Horowitz, *The Morality of Spending: Attitudes yoward the Consumer Society in America, 1875–1940* (Baltimore: Johns Hopkins University Press, 1985), 16–18.

13. Lawrence Bennett Glickman, "A Living Wage: Political Economy, Gender, and Consumerism in American Culture, 1880–1925" (Ph.D. diss., University of California–Berkeley, 1992) provides the most sustained treatment of these issues.

14. Ibid., 323–335.

15. Horowitz, *The Morality of Spending*, 30–66.

16. Valerie Jean Conner, *The National War Labor Board: Stability, Social Justice, and the Voluntary State in World War I* (Chapel Hill: University of North Carolina Press, 1983), 50–67, quotation 66–67.

17. "Testimony of W. J. Lauck, 1920," New York State Board of Arbitration on the Differences between the New York State Railways and the Employers' Associations, Box 12, WJLP.

18. Conner, *The National War Labor Board*, 143–147, quotations 143, 146.

19. "Harmful Effects of Low Wages upon the Family, the Individual, and the Community," testimony on behalf of the Maintenance of Way Employees, Railroad Labor Board, 1922, Box 185, WJLP.

20. "The National Income and the Practicability of the Living Wage," memo prepared for hearings of the Maintenance of Way Employees case before the Railroad Labor Board, 1922, Box 180, WJLP.

21. Dubofsky and Van Tine, *John L. Lewis* (1986), 56.

22. Ibid., 56–71; James P. Johnson, *The Politics of Soft Coal: The Bituminous Industry from World War I through the New Deal* (Urbana: University of Illinois Press, 1979), 92–108.

23. Dubofsky and Van Tine, *John L. Lewis* (1986), 72–75.

24. Johnson, *The Politics of Soft Coal*, 118–123; see also David Brody, *In Labor's Cause: Main Themes on the History of the American Worker* (New York: Oxford University Press, 1993), 131–174.

25. John L. Lewis, *The Miners' Fight for American Standards* (Indianapolis: Bell Publishing, 1925), 24, 39–41, 130–131.

26. Lauck, *Political and Industrial Democracy, 1775–1926* (New York: Funk & Wagnalls, 1926), 25, 28–38, 42–43, 53–57, quotation 25.

27. Dubofsky and Van Tine, *John L. Lewis* (1986), 101–103.

28. Johnson, *The Politics of Soft Coal*, 95–98.

29. Dubofsky and Van Tine, *John L. Lewis* (1986), 110.

30. Ibid., 112.

31. Jett Lauck's son, Peter B. Lauck, remembers the Chevy Chase home as a "grand" white-framed mansion surrounded by two acres of gardens and a pond just at the end of the D.C. streetcar line. Interview Oct. 30, 1995.

32. Although he held a UMWA membership card, Lauck resisted entreaties to practice within the union headquarters, preferring to maintain his own independent Washington, D.C., office under the name William Jett Lauck and Associates, Consulting and Practicing Economists. (Peter Lauck interview; Personal Diaries, Feb. 22, 1937, and Aug. 25, 1938, both in WJLP.) In addition to UMWA and later special CIO-related projects, Lauck continued to advise other labor groups, particularly the New York Public Building Service Employees and the Brotherhood of Locomotive Firemen and Engineers.

33. Lauck to John L. Lewis, July 3, 1995, WJLP.

34. Lauck to John L. Lewis, Nov. 26, 1926, and Dec. 10, 1926, both in WJLP. For his part, Lewis was patient but not without limits in his responsiveness to Lauck's requests. While he regularly signed the requisite bank forms to extend the time frame for Lauck's debt repayments, he declined to cover further loans on grounds that his own personal financial standing did not warrant "added risk." Lewis to Lauck, Dec. 2, 1926, Nov. 29, 1928, May 5, 1929, all in WJLP.

35. Lauck to Lewis, May 2, 1929, and May 2, 1931, both in WJLP. By 1927, Lauck had exhausted his bank credit and was forced to turn to the "outrageous" rates of independent money-lenders. In desperation he appealed for loans to his active associates in the labor reform world, including attorney Morris L. Ernst and Pennsylvania governor Gifford Pinchot. Gifford Pinchot to Lauck, July 21, 1931; Lauck to Pinchot, Aug. 27, 1931; Lauck to Morris L. Ernst, Aug. 13, 1927; all in WJLP. In the end, according to his son, Lauck actually "traded down" his Chevy Chase home (to an officer of the virulently anti-union National Association of Manufacturers, no less!) for the lesser riverfront home plus $15,000 cash. (Peter Lauck interview.) By 1930, when Lauck's Lenox Building–related debt approached $75,000, even the usually gruff Lewis grew openly worried and counseled his friend not to "become melancholy or depressed by what I am sure is only momentary embarrassment." Lauck to Paul Brissenden, Oct. 13, 1938; John L. Lewis to Lauck, July 16, 1930; both in WJLP.

For the Lauck family, to be sure, the material deprivation involved in the move was only relative. Lauck estimated his average annual income during the 1920s (perhaps slightly inflated to reassure his creditors) at $32,000, a figure in 1925 dollars that economic historian Robert Gallman translates to a handsome $276,000 in 1995 prices, or effectively within the top one percent of family incomes of the day. Even when forced to economize, as Peter Lauck recalls, the family dropped to one servant in the Fredericksburg riverfront home called The Island. Meanwhile, Lauck maintained membership in both the Chevy Chase Country Club and the Cosmos Club in Washington, D.C., although, according to Peter Lauck, "my father hardly went there." Both his parents, Peter recalls, were rather "like children," unrealistic and always overextended when it came to money matters.

36. *Miners' Fight*, 130–131.

37. Ellis W. Hawley, *The New Deal and the Problem of Monopoly: A Study in Economic Ambivalence* (New York: Fordham University Press, 1995 [1966]), 28, makes

this point most succinctly. For an excellent, and largely parallel, treatment of the Hillman side of the equation, see Steve Fraser, *Labor Will Rule: Sidney Hillman and the Rise of American Labor* (New York: Free Press, 1991).

38. Robert H. Zieger, *Republicans and Labor, 1919–1929* (Lexington: University of Kentucky Press, 1969), 257; Johnson, *The Politics of Soft Coal,* 123.

39. Johnson, *The Politics of Soft Coal,* 132–133. Lauck himself rejoiced in the election of Franklin Roosevelt over Hoover. Lauck to Lewis, Nov. 10, 1932, WJLP.

40. Lauck to Lewis, May 13, 1930, WJLP.

41. Lauck to Lewis, July 8, 1930, WJLP.

42. Lewis to Lauck, Aug. 31, 1931, May 26, 1930, WJLP.

43. Dubofsky and Van Tine, *John L. Lewis* (1986), 131–133; Johnson, *The Politics of Soft Coal,* 142–144; Lauck draft, "Origin and History of the Recovery Act," Nov. 11, 1936, WJLP. For Lewis's recognition of Lauck's role in the creation of Section 7A of the NRA,see Saul Alinsky, *John L. Lewis: An Unauthorized Biography* (New York: G.P. Putnam's Sons, 1949), 65–66.

44. Dubofsky and Van Tine, *John L. Lewis* (1986), 133–135, 149.

45. Lauck notes headed "Socialization," 1934, Box 29, WJLP.

46. "Formula for the NRA," Oct. 18, 1934, Box 29, WJLP.

47. Lauck notes and memoranda, *New Republic* editorial, "Landon on Planning," Sept. 23, 1936, WJLP.

48. John L. Lewis, "What I Expect of Roosevelt," *The Nation* 143 (Nov. 14, 1936), 571–572.

49. Personal Diaries, Dec. 5, 1937, WJLP. Lauck here summarizes a conversation with *New York Times* reporter C. L. Sulzberger, who was researching his forthcoming *Sit Down with John L. Lewis* (New York: Random House, 1938).

50. Lauck memorandum to Lewis, Dec. 17, 1935, WJLP; Personal Diaries, Dec. 12, 1935, WJLP. Dr. Francis E. Townsend's Old Age Revolving Pension scheme (which helped to spur Roosevelt's Social Security Act of 1935) advocated payments of $200 per month to persons sixty years of age and older, the pensions to be drawn from a national 2 percent tax on commercial transactions.

51. Lauck memorandum to Lewis, "Objectives of Labor" [1936], WJLP.

52. J. Joseph Huthmacher, *Senator Robert F. Wagner and the Rise of Urban Liberalism* (New York: Atheneum, 1968), 167. Text of National Labor Relations Act as quoted in Charles J. Morris, ed., *The Developing Labor Law: The Board, the Courts, and the National Labor Relations Act* (Washington, D.C.: American Bar Association, 1971), Appendix A, 895.

53. Personal Diaries, Feb. 5, 1937, March 6, 1937, WJLP.

54. See James MacGregor Burns, *Roosevelt: The Lion and Fox* (New York: Harcourt, Brace, & World, 1956), 303–308; and William E. Leuchtenburg, *The Supreme Court Reborn: The Constitutional Revolution in the Age of Roosevelt* (New York: Oxford University Press, 1995), 213–236.

55. Perhaps Lauck's most explicit plan in this regard lay in his proposals for the Commonwealth of Pennsylvania based on his work as chairman of the state's Anthracite Industry Commission in 1937–38. The recommendations (which

proved a legislative nonstarter) included creation of a Public Service Commission to regulate prices of anthracite at the mine, public corporations to redirect coal bootleggers to legitimate operations under regulated prices and wages, cooperative marketing organizations among operators to reduce freight costs, and ultimately authority to reabsorb unemployed miners via TVA-like public development projects. *Report of the Anthracite Coal Industry Commission* (Harrisburg, July 30, 1938), reference courtesy of Thomas Dublin.

56. For reference to what they call the "Lauck-Lewis demonology" of the bankers, see Dubofsky and Van Tine, *John L. Lewis* (1977), 192, 197, 250, 252.

57. Personal Diaries, July 3, 1936, WJLP.

58. Ibid., Aug. 11, 1936, WJLP.

59. "Memo to Mr. Lewis on investment banking," Nov. 7, 1936, WJLP.

60. Personal Diaries, June 20, 1938, WJLP. See also Alan Brinkley, *The End of Reform: New Deal Liberalism in Recession and War* (New York: Alfred A. Knopf, 1995), 106–136.

61. Personal Diaries, June 23, 1938, WJLP.

62. "Memo to Mr. Lewis on investment banking," Nov. 7, 1936; Personal Diaries, Nov. 11, 1936; both in WJLP.

63. Personal Diaries, March 3, 1937, WJLP.

64. Most closely associated with union consultant Ray Rodgers, the corporate campaign became famous in the Farah and J.P. Stevens campaigns by the Amalgamated Clothing Workers in the 1970s and the Austin meatpackers' strike against Hormel in the mid-1980s. The idea involved "a combination of tactics such as consumer boycotts, legal appeals, attempts to broaden the issues from simple labor relations to moral or social matters, and pressure on interlocking sectors of the business and financial community in hopes of isolating the offending employer." Kim Moody, *An Injury to All: The Decline of American Unionism* (New York: Verso, 1988), 306–307, 317–319. See also Peter Rachleff, *Hard-Pressed in the Heartland: The Hormel Strike and the Future of the Labor Movement* (Boston: South End Press, 1993), 53, 109–110. Historical accounts of U.S. Steel's decision to recognize the union make no mention of the CIO's "bank war" as a possible influence on its action. But neither does the issue seem ever to have been researched. For the best existing account of these events, see Walter Galenson, *The CIO Challenge to the AFL: A History of the American Labor Movement, 1935–1941* (Cambridge, Mass.: Harvard University Press, 1960), 75–96. That Lewis, in particular, may have viewed the bank reform talk more as a negotiating posture than a serious political program is suggested by his willingness to meet, at President Roosevelt's request, with Thomas W. Lamont of the House of Morgan in 1938 in an effort to arrive at a "cooperative" recession-fighting program. Brinkley, *The End of Reform*, 88–90.

65. Originally funded at a rate of $800 per month from the union, the AAEF struggled to maintain an independent public posture. Personal Diaries, Sept. 30, 1938; Jul 5, 1939; WJLP.

66. Ibid., Jan. 26, 1938, WJLP.

67. Lauck to President Roosevelt, Jan. 30, 1940, WJLP. There is no sign that the AAEF received a positive reply to its request.
68. Lauck, "After the New Deal: A Program for America," *The New Republic* 99 (July 5, 1939), 243–246.
69. Personal Diaries, Aug. 29, 1938, WJLP.
70. Ibid., May 13, 1938, WJLP.
71. Ibid., April 30, 1938, WJLP.
72. The $35,000 realized from the sale went to the mortgage holders. Peter B. Lauck interview; Personal Diaries, May 17, 1939; June 6, 1939; WJLP.
73. Lauck, "After the New Deal," 243; Lauck to John L. Lewis, Nov. 5, 1937, WJLP.
74. On SWOC, see, e.g., Len De Caux, *Labor Radical: From the Wobblies to CIO, A Personal History* (Boston: Beacon Press, 1970), 280–281.
75. Personal Diaries, Feb. 29, 1936, WJLP.
76. Ibid., Dec. 17, 1935, WJLP; Robert H. Zieger, *The CIO, 1935–1955* (Chapel Hill: University of North Carolina Press, 1995), 36.
77. Lauck to John L. Lewis, July 5, 1937, WJLP.
78. For an extended discussion of these issues, see the definitive political biography by Nelson Lichtenstein, *The Most Dangerous Man in Detroit: Walter Reuther and the Fate of American Labor* (New York: Basic Books, 1995), esp. 116–118.
79. Personal Diaries, Aug. 14, 1937, WJLP.
80. Ibid., Nov. 15, Nov. 18, 1937, WJLP.
81. Lauck to John L. Lewis, Nov. 20, 1937; Personal Diaries, Jan. 16, 1938; both in WJLP. Lichtenstein, *The Most Dangerous Man in Detroit,* 117–118.
82. Personal Diaries, Feb. 26, 1938, WJLP.
83. "Ordway Tead," *Current Biography Yearbook* (New York: H. W. Wilson Co., 1942), 817–818; Personal Diaries, Oct. 25, 1939, WJLP.
84. Ordway Tead, *New Adventures in Democracy: Practical Applications of the Democratic Idea* (New York: Whittlesey House, 1939), 5, 92–93, 95, 142, 149. Tead, like Lauck, seemed to have little idea of what to do with workers' actual powers on the shop floor (let alone within their union). Along with the representation of different interests in industry, he suggested vaguely that "we should go further and create situations in which the working staff become virtual partners in the enterprise." But not only did Tead admit that there was "no easy formula to apply here," he tied such worker participation to considerations of "high output" as much as "democratic intention" (152).
85. On Lewis's growing conflicts with the administration, see Zieger, *The CIO,* 106–107, and Dubofsky and Van Tine, *John L. Lewis* (1986), 247–253.
86. Personal Diaries, Oct. 12, 1940, WJLP.
87. Rather sheepishly, Lauck confided to his diary that following Lewis's speech, he "decided not to do anything about it because I was economic and not political advisor to Lewis." Personal Diaries, Oct. 26, 1940, WJLP.
88. Ibid. Lewis' daughter Kathryn normally regulated official access to her father, but in this case even she (according to Lauck) expressed frustration at her father's self-isolation on the eve of a momentous decision. See also Zieger, *The CIO,* 96–97.

89. Personal Diaries, Nov. 6, 1940, WJLP.
90. Len De Caux, *Labor Radical: From the Wobblies to CIO, A Personal History* (Boston: Beacon Press, 1970), 386. Like many who worked with Lewis, De Caux viewed him with a mixture of awe and mystery: "Lewis usually knew which way the wind blew. He took account of the tides. He knew which was the safe and easy course. Yet sometimes he chose to chart a course against the wind, to follow it stubbornly, come shipwreck or glory. Only a fool, or a red, or a man like Lewis, does things like that" (390).
91. Personal Diaries, Oct 5, Nov. 19, 1943; quotation, Personal Diaries, Feb. 19, 1944; all in WJLP.
92. Ibid., Jan. 14, Jan. 22, Jan. 24, 1944, all in WJLP.
93. Ibid., Dec. 31, 1943, WJLP.
94. Peter B. Lauck interview.
95. Personal Diaries, July 6, Dec. 30, 1943, WJLP.
96. Peter B. Lauck interview. Peter Lauck himself served as a Navy airplane mechanic during World War II and settled later on a career as a small-town newspaper writer and editor.
97. Personal Diaries, Nov. 8, 1944, WJLP.
98. Ibid., Jan. 28, Jan. 29, Feb. l, 1944, all in WJLP.
99. Ibid., Nov. 4, 1944, WJLP.
100. Ibid., March 15, 1947, WJLP.
101. Brinkley, *The End of Reform*, esp. 128–136, 170–174, 198–200, 265–271.
102. Kennedy made the first of his oft-repeated references to the "rising tide" in an address in the Assembly Hall at Paulskirche, Frankfurt, West Germany, June 25, 1963. Suzy Platt, ed., *Respectfullly Quoted: A Dictionary of Quotations Requested from the Congressional Research Services* (Washington, D.C.: Library of Congress, 1989), 313.
103. Reuther and Green as quoted in Brinkley, *The End of Reform*, 224.
104. Ronald W. Schatz, *The Electrical Workers: A History of Labor at General Electric and Westinghouse, 1923–60* (Urbana: University of Illinois Press, 1983), 155.
105. Brinkley, *The End of Reform*, 4.

8. Teaching the People: Wil Lou Gray

The Cobbett quote is from the *Political Register*, 1833, in Richard Johnson, "'Really Useful Knowledge' 1790–1850: Memories for Education in the 1980s," in Tom Lovett, ed., *Radical Approaches to Adult Education: A Reader* (New York: Routledge, 1988), 13. The Jefferson quote is from his letter to Dupont De Nemours, April 24, 1816, in Paul Leicester Ford, ed., *The Writings of Thomas Jefferson*, 10 vols. (New York: G. P. Putnam's Sons, 1892–1899), vol. 10, 25. Reference courtesy of Robert McDonald.

1. Her parents—William LaFayette Gray, state legislator (1923–1924), gentleman farmer, and merchant (who was also a former teacher with a law degree), and Sarah Louise Dial, a college graduate and granddaughter of a Laurens bank president—gave their only daughter among three children the

first three letters of their own names. DaMaris E. Ayres, *Let My People Learn: The Biography of Wil Lou Gray* (Greenwood, S.C.: Attic Press, 1988), 5–17.

2. Joseph F. Kett, "Women and the Progressive Impulse in Southern Education," in Walter J. Fraser, Jr., R. Frank Saunders, Jr., and Jon Wakelyn, eds., *The Web of Southern Social Relations: Women, Family, and Education* (Athens: University of Georgia Press, 1985), 166.

3. Mabel Montgomery, *South Carolina's Wil Lou Gray: Pioneer in Adult Education, a Crusader, Modern Model* (Columbia, S.C.: Vogue Press, 1963), 19–20; Horace Coon, *Columbia: Colossus on the Hudson* (New York: E. P. Dutton, 1947), 123, 162; Gray, "The Political Philosophy of J. C. Hurd," (master's thesis, Columbia University, 1911); "John Codman Hurd," *Dictionary of American Biography*, vol. 5 (New York: Charles Scribner's Sons, 1961), 423.

4. Gray to "Family" [1960], letter in possession of Mary Mac Motley.

5. Montgomery, *South Carolina's Wil Lou Gray*, 21.

6. Ibid., 1–12, 17.

7. Ayres, *Let My People Learn*, 114.

8. Montgomery, *South Carolina's Wil Lou Gray*, 23–39.

9. Ibid., 32.

10. Kett, "Women and the Progressive Impulse," 166. For revisionist views that stress the radical edge and implications of women's progressive political culture, see esp. Kathryn Kish Sklar, *Florence Kelley and the Nation's Work: The Rise of Women's Political Culture, 1830–1900* (New Haven: Yale University Press, 1995), and Jacquelyn Dowd Hall, "O. Delight Smith's Progressive Era: Labor, Feminism, and Reform in the Urban South," in Nancy A. Hewitt and Suzanne Lebsock, eds., *Visible Women: New Essays on American Activism* (Urbana: University of Illinois Press, 1993), 166–198. For connections between female-centered progressive reforms and the later New Deal social welfarism, see Robyn Muncy, *Creating a Female Dominion in American Reform, 1890–1935* (New York: Oxford University Press, 1991).

11. See, e.g., J. Morgan Kousser, *The Shaping of Southern Politics: Suffrage Restriction and the Establishment of the One-Party South, 1880–1910* (New Haven: Yale University Press, 1974), 229–237.

12. Dewey W. Grantham, *Southern Progressivism: The Reconciliation of Progress and Tradition* (Knoxville: University of Tennessee Press, 1983), esp. xvii–xviii.

13. William A. Link, *The Paradox of Southern Progressivism, 1880–1930* (Chapel Hill: University of North Carolina Press, 1992), 323, 91; see also Kett, "Women and the Progressive Impulse," 172.

14. On the developmental strategies that reformers borrowed from black education, see William A. Link, *A Hard Country and a Lonely Place: Schooling, Society, and Reform in Rural Virginia, 1870–1920* (Chapel Hill: University of North Carolina Press, 1986), 83, 90, 173–189. On reformers' motives, see also David E. Whisnant, *All That Is Native and Fine: The Politics of Culture in an American Region* (Chapel Hill: University of North Carolina Press, 1983).

15. I. A. Newby, *Plain Folk in the New South: Social Change and Cultural Persistence, 1880–1915* (Baton Rouge: Lousiana State University Press, 1989), 420–421.

16. Ibid., 445; see also David Meek, "Public Welfare in North Carolina and the

Menace of the Feebleminded, 1911–1929," (master's thesis, University of North Carolina at Chapel Hill, 1994), 37–38.

17. Mary K. D. Cann, "The Morning After: South Carolina in the Jazz Age" (Ph.D. diss., University of South Carolina, 1984), 104; David L. Carlton, *Mill and Town in South Carolina, 1880–1920* (Baton Rouge: Louisiana State University Press, 1982), 7–8.

18. Carlton, *Mill and Town,* 134, 146–148; Cann, "The Morning After," 104.

19. Norfleet Hardy, *Farm, Mill, and Classroom: A History of Tax Supported Adult Education in South Carolina to 1960* (Columbia, S.C.: University of South Carolina Press, 1967), 36; Cann, "The Morning After," 290. The measurement of illiteracy by the U.S. census, of course, was at best a rough approximation, relying as it did on self-reported or "admitted" answers to various questions about the basic ability to read and write. On the general problems and changing definitions of literacy analysis, see Carl F. Kaestle, "The History of Literacy and the History of Readers," in Eugene R. Kintgen, Barry M. Knoll, and Mike Rose, eds., *Perspectives on Literacy* (Carbondale: Southern Illinois University Press, 1988), 95–126.

20. Wil Lou Gray, "Evolution of Adult Elementary Education in South Carolina" [1913], Wil Lou Gray Papers, South Caroliniana Library, Columbia, South Carolina (hereafter cited as WLGP).

21. Cann, "The Morning After," 135.

22. David English Camak, *Human Gold from Southern Hills* (Greer, S.C.: D. E. Camak, 1960), 139.

23. Samuel F. Stack, Jr., "A Critical Analysis of Welfare Capitalism as Educational Ideology" (Ph.D. diss., University of South Carolina, 1990).

24. Ronald Dantan Burnside, "The Governorship of Coleman Livingston Blease of South Carolina, 1911–1915," (Ph.D. diss., Indiana University, 1963), esp. 235–266, quotation 255.

25. Carlton, *Mill and Town,* 215–272.

26. Melton quoted in Cann, "The Morning After," 289; Carlton, *Mill and Town,* 263.

27. Carlton, *Mill and Town,* 175–185. Such measures were capped by the "6–0–1 Law" of 1924, which dramatically transformed South Carolina public education from a decentralized system based on local funding to a centralized administration that guaranteed all public schools a minimum of six months of state support, provided that the local district supported the school for the seventh month. Cann, "The Morning After," 314–318.

28. Rebecca Dial, *True to His Colors: A Story of South Carolina's Senator Nathaniel Barksdale Dial* (New York: Vantage Press, 1974), 144–145.

29. J. Truett Willis, "The First Fifty Years of the South Carolina Opportunity School," (Ph.D. diss., University of Georgia, 1973), 24.

30. The name "opportunity school" derived from an adult education institution in Denver called the Emily Griffith Opportunity School. Gray to Howard Johnson, April 16, 1952, WLGP; Ayres, *Let My People Learn,* 114; Montgomery, *South Carolina's Wil Lou Gray,* 46–47. Opportunity school sessions were held annually from 1921 to 1945 in summer quarters at the state's

small, religiously endowed colleges (except for the opening session, which was held at Tamassee's D.A.R. School, and the 1931–1942 sessions, which were held at Clemson), including Lander (Methodist), Anderson (Baptist), Erskine (Presbyterian), Woman's (Presbyterian, since defunct), and Columbia College (Methodist). Over five thousand students attended such summer sessions before a permanent home for the South Carolina Opportunity School was found at the Columbia Army Air Base in 1946. Gray served as director of the school until 1957, when she officially retired at age seventy-four (although her involvement continued for many more years as director emeritus). Gray died at the age of 100 in 1984. The South Carolina Wil Lou Gray Opportunity School continues, although in recent decades its emphasis has shifted from adult learners to at-risk adolescents.

31. Wil Lou Gray, "South Carolina's Program for Belated Learners," *AAUW Journal* 23 (January 1930), 82–85.
32. Montgomery, *South Carolina's Wil Lou Gray*, 46–58; see also Mary S. Hoffschwelle, "The Science of Domesticity: Home Economics at George Peabody College for Teachers, 1914–1939," *Journal of Southern History* 57 (November 1991), 659–680.
33. Gray, "Memo to County Organizers," July 19, 1920, WLGP.
34. *Elementary Studies in Civics* (Columbia, S.C.: The State Co., 1927), 3, 16.
35. Ibid., 16.
36. Ibid., 42–43.
37. Gray to Katherine Cooper, June 20, 1927, WLGP.
38. Montgomery, *South Carolina's Wil Lou Gray*, 37.
39. Ibid., 50.
40. Willis, "The First Fifty Years," 66.
41. On the historical role of manners as a means of negotiating social divisions, see John F. Kasson, *Rudeness and Civility: Manners in Nineteenth-Century Urban America* (New York: Hill & Wang, 1990).
42. Ayres, *Let My People Learn*, 107–113.
43. Gray to Col. Fred W. Bugbee, Feb. 23, 1928, WLGP.
44. Gray, "Introducing Charleston and Trip Plan," April 1928, WLGP.
45. John F. McClymer, "The Americanization Movement and the Education of the Foreign-Born Adult, 1914–25," in Bernard J. Weiss, ed., *American Education and the European Immigrant: 1840–1940* (Urbana: University of Illinois Press, 1982), 109.
46. Carlton, *Mill and Town*, 269.
47. Cann, "The Morning After," 297. As a banker and owner of textile mills in Williamston, Greenville, and Anderson, Gossett likely identified in an uncommon way with the educational needs of millworkers. Orphaned at age ten, he had struggled to attend school while supporting himself as an agricultural laborer and later attributed much of his future success to the inspiration of two high school teachers. Elizabeth D. Hutto, *The Story of a Good Citizen: James Pleasant Gossett, 1860–1937* (Columbia, S.C.: Works Progress Administration, [1937?]).
48. Cann, "The Morning After," 260–263.

49. Norfleet Hardy, *Farm, Mill, and Classroom: A History of Tax Supported Adult Education in South Carolina to 1960* (Columbia, S.C.: University of South Carolina Press, 1967), 54.
50. Gray, mailing to county organizers, South Carolina Illiteracy Commission, July 19, 1920, WLGP.
51. Illiteracy Commission of South Carolina, "A Speech for Our Four-Minute Men to be Used in Behalf of the Illiteracy Commission," 1918, WLGP.
52. Frank Evans to Gray, Nov. 8, 1918, WLGP.
53. Quoted in Ayres, *Let My People Learn*, 86–87.
54. Caroline V. Cuttino to Gray, Jan. 12, 1922, WLGP. The religious issue was one that Gray herself managed most delicately. Her own beliefs led her to describe her professional activity as one of "applied Christianity," and her curricula always set aside time for ecumenical chapel and vesper services, which all Opportunity School students were expected to attend. Even so, she had to defend her practices from some fundamentalist students who objected not only to community prayers but to Gray's tolerance of card-playing and dancing as part of the schools' recreational activities. Ayres, *Let My People Learn*, 212; Gray to Leila Freeman, Sept. 8, 1948, Opportunity School Papers, Student Correspondence, South Carolina Department of Archives and History, Columbia, South Carolina (hereafter cited as OSP).
55. Mrs. M. B. Hall to Gray, Feb. 5, 1935, WLGP.
56. Montgomery, *South Carolina's Wil Lou Gray*, 35.
57. See, e.g., William J. Reese, *Power and the Promise of School Reform: Grassroots Movements during the Progressive Era* (Boston: Routledge and Kegan Paul, 1986); and James R. Barrett, "Americanization from the Bottom Up: Immigration and the Remaking of the Working Class," *Journal of American History* 79 (December 1992), 996–1020.
58. "Call to the Illiteracy Conference of Southern States," April 10, 1923, WLGP. It is worth recalling here that establishment of such a discrete department did not come about until 1979, upon the reorganization of the Department of Health, Education and Welfare, itself only created in 1953.
59. Gray to Cora Casadeval, March 2, 1922, WLGP.
60. Leroy Springs to Gray, June 22, 1925, WLGP; advertisement of Cotton Manufacturers' Association of South Carolina in *The State* (Columbia, S.C.), Dec. 2, 1930, WLGP.
61. On conceptualizing progressivism, see, e.g., Daniel P. Rodgers, "In Search of Progressivism," *Reviews in American History* 10 (December 1982), 111–132.
62. *Elementary Studies in Civics*, 56–57.
63. Gray, quoted in Willis, "The First Fifty Years," 59.
64. Carlton, *Mill and Town*, 266–267.
65. James Harvey Robinson, *The Mind in the Making: The Relation of Intelligence to Social Reform* (New York: Harper & Bros., 1921), 20.
66. James Miles to Gray, Aug. 31, 1934, WLGP.
67. South Carolina was one of the first states to use federal aid for unemployed teachers. Ayres, *Let My People Learn*, 153–159.
68. Gray and Mary E. Frayser to "Club Women," Nov. 10, 1939, reprinted in

Eunice Ford Stackhouse, *Mary E. Frayser: Pioneer Social and Research Worker in the South* [n.p., 1944], Appendix A, 97–98 (reference courtesy of Cristina R. Nelson).

69. On Olin D. Johnston and his millworker constituency, see esp. Bryant Simon, "A Fabric of Defeat: The Politics of South Carolina Textile Workers in State and Nation, 1920–1938," (Ph.D. diss., University of North Carolina at Chapel Hill, 1992), 273–338, and Nadine Cohodas, *Strom Thurmond and the Politics of Southern Change* (New York: Simon & Schuster, 1993), 45. Johnston's daughter, Liz J. Patterson, herself a public servant elected to the U.S. Congress 1986–1992, remembers "Miss Wil Lou" as a close family friend, "almost like a cousin." In the late 1940s and early 1950s, Patterson recalls, her father (then a U.S. senator) even opened his Columbia home, with Gray's encouragement, to several Opportunity School students, who helped with the children and housework in exchange for room and board. Telephone interview with Liz J. Patterson by the author, Feb. 29, 1996. Sen. Johnston offered a public tribute to Gray in honor of her eightieth birthday in 1963. *Congressional Record*, 88th Cong., 1st Sess., Sept. 13, 1963, 16946–47.

70. The daughter of a wealthy Massachusetts manufacturer and a graduate of Mount Holyoke College and Columbia University, Frances Perkins entered the field of social work before taking on a host of public positions—including director of the Council on Immigration Education (1921)—and was ultimately appointed Secretary of Labor (1933–1945), the first woman Cabinet officer.

71. For help in placing Gray within both a state and national political context I am indebted to several conversations with Bryant Simon; Gray to Mrs. Smoak, Sept. 16, 1960, WLGP; Gray's attitude to Thurmond gleaned from family sources via Mary Mac Motley. A further, albeit indirect, indication is contained in a letter Gray received in 1965 from an old friend who expressed "shame" at "my native state going Republican" (for Goldwater in 1964). "I believe Kennedy was a very strong President and will go down in history as one of our greatest. I've been thoroughly disgusted with Strom Thurmond and Jimmy Byrnes." (As governor, 1951–1955, Byrnes, a former New Deal insider, so opposed moves towards racial desegregation that he backed Dwight Eisenhower for president in 1952.) S. Oliver O'Bryan to Gray, March 12, 1965, WLGP.

72. Gray to "Family" [1962].

73. Gray to Gertrude Maginnis, Jan. 29, 1929, WLGP.

74. Ayres, *Let My People Learn*, 116. Men's enrollment, begun in the third year of Opportunity School operations, was tied to separate facilities throughout the 1920s, then consolidated in coeducational programs at Clemson College in 1931. Hardy, *Farm, Mill, and Classroom*, 89.

75. Eleanor Roosevelt to Gray, Sept. 22, 1937, WLGP. In reply the First Lady thanked her South Carolina advocate but allowed that "the time has not yet come when a woman would have the support which is necessary to hold the position of President."

76. Hardy, *Farm, Mill, and Classroom*, 54–55. For an excellent account of the

Jeanes Fund and black schoolteachers in the South, see Glenda E. Gilmore, *Gender and Jim Crow: Women and the Politics of White Supremacy in North Carolina, 1896–1920* (Chapel Hill: University of North Carolina Press, 1996), 147–175.

77. Collin A. Embly to Gray [1930]; Susie F. Washington to Gray [1930], WLGP.

78. William Scott Gray served as Dean of the College of Education, University of Chicago, from 1917 to 1931. A pioneer innovator and developer of such measurements of reading skills and teaching effectiveness as the Gray Standardized Oral Reading Paragraphs and the Gray Silent Reading Test, he was known for his emphasis on the "sight method" and, most of all, for his creation of the "Dick and Jane" elementary school reading books, the basis for reading instruction in the United States for almost half a century. Jack J. Cardoso, "William Scott Gray," *Dictionary of American Biography* (New York: Scribner's, 1964), Supplement 6, 1885–1960, 248–249.

79. William S. Gray, Wil Lou Gray, J. W. Tilton, *The Opportunity Schools of South Carolina: An Experimental Study* (New York: American Association for Adult Education, 1932), 127, 136; Hardy, *Farm, Mill, and Classroom*, 92–93.

80. Ibid., 127–128. One discrepancy in the test results the educators recognized could not be scored as a right or wrong answer. This was a question on the Binet test where "a subject is given a setting and then is aked what the frightened man had seen hanging from the limb of a tree. In the course of the Binet testing, 13 whites and 16 negroes were asked this question. Only six of the whites answered "a man" but all of the negroes did. This difference cannot be expressed in terms of mental age or I.Q., but it serves to show the effect of background differences" (124).

81. Archie Vernon Huff, Jr., *Tried by Fire: Washington Street United Methodist Church* (Columbia, S.C.: R. L. Bryan Co., 1975), 99. Bethune's visit likely occurred sometime during 1937 or 1938. Local memory embellishes the Bethune visit with further drama. According to testimony that historian Huff chose not to publish, parishioner Cole Blease also attended church that day; but once aware of the visitor's presence, he slapped his cane on the church window and walked away, saying, "I refuse to worship with a goddam nigger in the pulpit." Interview of A. V. Huff, Jr., by Mary Mac Ogden, July 31, 1995 (transcript courtesy of the interviewer).

82. Columbia, S.C., *The State*, April 8, April 12, April 15, 1935; Ayres, *Let My People Learn*, 110.

83. Gray to Sam Latimer, April 30, 1948, WLGP; Harvey Neufeldt, "Wil Lou Gray: Adult Education, The Opportunity School, and the Problem of Race," (unpublished ms., Tennessee Technological University, 1996). Gray's "only regret," as she expressed it late in life to her biographer, was her inability to develop support for an Opportunity School for Negroes (no facility was established until long after the Brown v. Board of Education desegregation decision of 1954). Ayres, *Let My People Learn*, 199.

84. For elaboration on this theme, see Dorothy Ross, *The Origins of American Social Science* (New York: Cambridge University Press, 1991), esp. xvi–xvii, 28–30.

85. Harold W. Foght, *Rural Denmark and Its Schools* (New York: Macmillan, 1915), 199–203; E. F. Fain, "Grundtvig, Folk Education and Scandinavian Cultural

Nationalism," in Rolland G. Paulston, ed., *Other Dreams, Other Schools: Folk Colleges in Social and Ethnic Movements* (Pittsburgh: University Center for International Studies, 1980), 58, 66–67. On Southern attention to the Danish economic model, see *Mr. D. R.: A Biography of David R. Coker* (Hartsville, S.C.: Coker College Press, 1994), 163.

86. Edgar Wallace Knight, *Among the Danes* (Chapel Hill: University of North Carolina Press, 1927), 69, 226–227.

87. Olive Dame Campbell, *The Danish Folk School: Its Influence in the Life of Denmark and the North* (New York: Macmillan, 1928), viii, 179–180.

88. Willis, "The First Fifty Years," 65; Ayres, *Let My People Learn,* 114.

89. Eduard Lindeman, *The Meaning of Adult Education* (New York: New Republic, 1926), xvi; Stephen Brookfield, "Eduard Lindeman," in Peter Jarvis, ed., *Twentieth Century Thinkers in Adult Education: The Search for a Unifying Principle* (London: Croom Helm, 1988), 123.

90. Harold W. Stubblefield, *Towards a History of Adult Education in America: The Search for a Unifying Principle* (London: Crown Helm, 1988), 128–133; Joseph K. Hart, *Light from the North: The Danish Folk Highschools, Their Meanings for America* (New York: Henry Holt, 1926), 96, 98–99, 152. What Amerian education lacked, above all, argued Hart, was "the cultivation of personality and independence of mind" (xvii).

91. John M. Glen, *Highlander: No Ordinary School, 1932–1962* (Lexington: University Press of Kentucky, 1988), 14–19; F. Adams, "Highlander Folk School: Social Movements and Social Change in the American South," in Paulston, *Other Dreams,* 214–234. "Our task," Horton wrote future staff member Jim Dombrowsky in 1933, "is to make class-conscious workers who envision their roles in society, and to furnish motivation as well as technicians for the achievement of this goal" (230–231). Recurringly harassed by unsympathetic neighbors for its aid to labor and civil rights organizing campaigns and ultimately prosecuted by McCarthyite state authorities, Highlander Folk School lost its charter in 1959, forcing relocation to a site in Jefferson County, twenty miles east of Knoxville, where the Highlander Center remains today a vigorous exponent of environmental activism and continuing democratic educational experiment. Adams, "Highlander Folk School," 234.

92. Daniel Hinman-Smith, "'Does the Word Freedom Have a Meaning?': The Mississippi Freedom Schools, the Berkeley Free Speech Movement, and the Search For Freedom Through Education" (Ph.D. diss., University of North Carolina at Chapel Hill, 1993), 39.

93. Edmund L. Drago, *Initiative, Paternalism, and Race Relations* (Athens: University of Georgia Press, 1990), 272.

94. Paulo Freire, *The Politics of Education: Culture, Power and Liberation* (South Hadley, Mass.: Bergin and Garvey, 1985), 175–199.

95. Richard Shaull, "Introduction," in Paulo Freire, *Pedagogy of the Oppressed* (New York: Continuum, 1983), 15.

96. For Freire's basic concepts, see, e.g., *Pedagogy of the Oppressed,* esp. 58–59, 167; and Ira Shor and Paulo Freire, *A Pedagogy for Liberation: Dialogues on*

Transforming Education (South Hadley, Mass.: Bergin and Garvey, 1987), 30–38, 44–47, 103–105. An excellent overview of Freire's critical pedagogy is provided by Stephen T. Leonard, *Critical Theory in Political Practice* (Princeton: Princeton University Press, 1990), 136–166.

97. Paulo Freire, *Cultural Action for Freedom* (New York: Penguin Books, 1977 [1970]), 44–45. Freire is quoting here from a report by Dario Salas based on their joint work in Chile in the late 1960s; Shaull, "Introduction," 13–14.

98. Joe Gum to Gray, Aug. 30, 1919, WLGP.

99. D. J. Sanders to Gray, March 7, 1922, WLGP.

100. JoAnn Deakin Carpenter, "Olin D. Johnston, the New Deal, and the Politics of Class in South Carolina, 1934–1938" (Ph.D. diss., Emory University 1987), 33.

101. Anonymous alumnus of Opportunity School quoted in Willis, "The First Fifty Years," 117.

102. Freire as quoted in Lovett, *Radical Approaches,* 36.

103. Katherine F. Tinsley and Carl F. Kaestle, "Autobiographies and the History of Reading: The Meaning of Literacy in Individual Lives," in Carl F. Kaestle, ed., *Literacy in the United States: Readers and Reading since 1880* (New Haven: Yale University Press, 1991), 225.

104. J. D. Hill to Gray, Oct. 31, 1931; S. J. Adams to Gray, Oct. 11, 1931, WLGP.

105. A. C. Floyd to Gray [1951]; copy of letter from A. C. Floyd to Joe E. Berry, April 24, 1951, Director's File, OSP.

106. "Mary Moore" [a.k.a. Fannie Miles], Federal Writers' Project Life Stories, U.S. Works Project Administration A-3–14, Dec. 1, 1938, copy in James Franklin Miles Papers, South Caroliniana Library, Columbia, South Carolina (hereafter cited as JFMP).

107. Biographical reference sheet, 1960; Fannie Bell Miles (mother) to James F. Miles, Aug. 5, 1933; Gray to James F. Miles, Sept. 9, 1933, JFMP. A. C. Floyd and Miles were Opportunity School friends, so likely date to same year's session.

108. James F. Miles to Gray, June 17, 1933, WLGP. Perhaps out of classroom habit, Gray continued to annotate Miles's letters with her own corrections of his spelling and grammar.

109. Tinsley and Kaestle, "Autobiographies," 225. For development of the cultural capital concept, see Pierre Bourdieu, *Distinction: A Social Critique of the Judgment of Taste* (Cambridge, Mass.: Harvard University Press, 1984).

110. Verna Humphries to Gray, May 6, 1922, WLGP.

111. Ayres, *Let My People Learn,* 81.

112. Vernon Murphy to Gray, July 8, 1925, WLGP.

113. Holcome quoted in Ayres, *Let My People Learn,* 112.

114. Quoted in Carpenter, "Olin D. Johnston," 34.

115. Paul F. Armstrong, "The Long Search for the Working Class: Socialism and the Education of Adults, 1850–1930," in Tom Lovett, ed., *Radical Approaches to Adult Education: A Reader* (New York: Routledge, 1988), 37.

116. Quoted in Ayres, *Let My People Learn,* 116–117.

117. Morris Rosenfeld to Gray, Feb. 14, 1920, WLGP.

118. Mimie P. Temple to Gray [December 1934], WLGP. On the more general trend towards the feminine domestication of Christmas and other holidays, see Mary P. Ryan, *Women in Public: Between Banners and Ballots, 1825–1880* (Baltimore: Johns Hopkins University Press, 1990), 37–39.
119. Mrs. Ryan Atkins to Gray, Nov. 15, 1934, WLGP.
120. Paul Bumgarner to Gray, Feb. 5, 1927, WLGP.
121. To his unofficial biographer, Rudy Maxa, Turner cited as specific inspiration the message of "Think!" taped to every bulletin board in the school. *Dare to Be Great* (New York: William Morrow, 1977), 40; *New York Times*, Sept. 15, 1969; John Frasca, *Con Man or Saint* (Anderson, S.C.: Drake House, 1969), 27–29.
122. Turner sold sewing machines on commmission to poor whites and poor blacks before entering the cosmetics industry and mastering its high-pitched promotion techniques. The name Koscot (Interplanetary, Inc.) was an acronym for "Kosmetics for the communities of tomorrow." Founded in Orlando, Florida, where Turner was working at the time, Koscot drew self-consciously on the name Epcot ("experimental prototype community of tom-morow"), which was already in the planning stages as a centerpiece of Orlando's expanding Disney World. Maxa, *Dare to Be Great*, 46–48, 63–64; *New York Times*, May 27, 1979.
123. Maxa, *Dare to Be Great*, 26.
124. Ibid., 12.
125. Ibid., 13.
126. *New York Times*, Dec. 4, 1970; Jan. 6, 1972; March 29, 1972; Dec. 15, 1973; June 27, 1974; Nov. 27, 1975; Dec. 9, 1975; Aug. 29, 1978; May 27, 1979; Maxa, *Dare to Be Great*, 240–241.
127. Maxa, *Dare to Be Great*, 208. Turner underwrote only a $40,000–$50,000 summer program for the Opportunity School before the IRS impounded his assets. Telephone interview with Patrick Smith, Wil Lou Gray Opportunity School Director of Administration, Feb. 16, 1996. For all his faults, Turner's affection for Gray and her kind regard for him apparently never wavered. As late as 1980 he visited the Opportunity School to join the celebration of Gray's ninety-eighth birthday. Ayres, *Let My People Learn*, 225.
128. Septima Poinsette Clark, *Echo in My Soul* (New York: Dutton, 1962), 89, quotation 148–149.
129. Ibid., 150.
130. "Septima Poinsette Clark," interview conducted by Jacquelyn D. Hall (transcript), July 25, 1976, Southern Oral History Project, University of North Carolina at Chapel Hill; "Septima Clark," in Eliot Wigginton, ed., *Refuse to Stand Silently By: An Oral History of Grass Roots Social Activism in America, 1921–64* (New York: Doubleday, 1992), 21. Gray was also the first person to be acknowledged by Clark in her autobiography, *Echo in My Soul*, xi.
131. Quotations from Clark and Jenkins in Hinman-Smith, "'Does the Word Freedom Have a Meaning?'" 38. Clark, continued as late as 1962 to describe the illiterate Johns Island blacks with whom she worked as "unmoral" and "primitive" (ibid.).

Epilogue

1. Theodor W. Adorno, *Negative Dialectics* (New York: Seabury, 1973 [1966]), 265.

2. Patrick Brantlinger, *Bread and Circuses: Theories of Mass Culture as Social Decay* (Ithaca: Cornell University Press, 1983), 229.

3. Dewey, as quoted in Max Horkheimer, *Critical Theory: Selected Essays* (New York: Continuum, 1982 [1937]), 290.

4. Gerald Graff, *Professing Literature: An Institutional History* (Chicago: University of Chicago Press, 1987), 146–149.

5. Cleanth Brooks, "Irony as a Principle of Structure," (1949) in Hazard Adams, ed., *Critical Theory since Plato* (New York: Harcourt Brace, 1971), 1046–47.

6. Terry Eagleton, *Literary Theory: An Introduction* (Minneapolis: University of Minnesota Press, 1983), 45; cf. Brantlinger's concept of "negative classicism" here, a likening of "social decay" associated with contemporary mass culture to the "bread and circuses" of the decadent Roman Empire. *Bread and Circuses*, 17–52.

7. William M. Chace, *Lionel Trilling: Criticism and Politics* (Stanford: Stanford University Press, 1980), 31–63, 178, quotation p. 74.

8. Chace, *Lionel Trilling*, 79–97, 113–115.

9. Richard Hofstadter, *The American Political Tradition and the Men Who Made It* (New York: Knopf, 1948), viii; Hofstadter, *The Progressive Historians: Turner, Beard, Parrington* (New York: Knopf, 1968), 452, n. 9.

10. Hofstadter, *The Progressive Historians* 439.

11. See Hofstadter, *Anti-Intellectualism in American Life* (New York: Knopf, 1962); Susan Stout Baker, *Radical Beginnings: Richard Hofstadter and the 1930s* (Westport, Conn.: Greenwood Press, 1985), 191.

12. For an extended commentary on Hofstadter's *The Age of Reform* (New York: Knopf, 1955), see Baker, *Radical Beginnings*, 209–221.

13. Ibid., 216.

14. *Anti-Intellectualism in American Life*, 197–198.

15. Ibid., 227.

16. Joseph Schumpeter, *Capitalism, Socialism, and Democracy* (London: Unwin Paperbacks, 1989), 269. Instead of "government by the people," Schumpeter self-consciously proposed "government approved by the people" (246). See also Carole Pateman, *Participation and Democratic Theory* (Cambridge: Cambridge University Press, 1970), 1–21; and David M. Ricci, *The Tragedy of Political Science: Politics, Scholarship, and Democracy* (New Haven: Yale University Press, 1984), esp. 160–162.

17. Anthony Downs, *An Economic Theory of Democracy* (New York: Harper and Row, 1957), as cited in Terence Ball, "An Ambivalent Alliance: Political Science and American Democracy," in James Farr, John S. Dryzek, and Stephen T. Leonard, eds., *Political Science in History: Research Programs and Political Traditions* (New York: Cambridge University Press, 1995), 56–60, quotation 58. Cf. Robert H. Wiebe, *Self-Rule: A Cultural History of American Democracy* (Chicago: University of Chicago Press, 1995), 218–220.

18. Philip Rahv, 1939, quoted in Chace, *Lionel Trilling*, 51.

19. Sheldon S. Wolin, *Politics and Vision: Continuity and Innovation in Western Political Thought* (Boston: Little, Brown and Co., 1960), esp. 352–434, quotations 420–421.

20. Philip E. Converse, "The Nature of Belief Systems in Mass Publics," in David E. Apter, ed., *Ideology and Discontent* (New York: Free Press of Glencoe, 1964), 206–261, quotations 206, 213, 229–230, 255, 256. It is not, suggests Converse, that "poorly educated people have no systems of belief about politics" but rather that the "entities that might best be called folk ideologies" apparently fall outside the rubric of rational thought (255–256).

21. Ricci, *The Tragedy of Political Science*, 161.

22. "The Port Huron Statement," reprinted in James Miller, *"Democracy Is in the Streets": From Port Huron to the Seige of Chicago* (New York: Simon and Schuster, 1987), 329–374, quotation 332.

23. See, e.g., Clayborne Carson, *In Struggle: SNCC and the Black Awakening of the 1960s* (Cambridge, Mass.: Harvard University Press, 1981), 175–180.

24. "Port Huron Statement," 331–332; Miller, *"Democracy Is in the Streets,"* 148–150.

25. Miller, *"Democracy Is in the Streets,"* 80. C. Wright Mills, *Sociology and Pragmatism: The Higher Learning in America* (New York: Paine-Whitman, 1964).

26. Mills as quoted in Miller, *"Democracy Is in the Streets,"* 83. See Mills, *The New Men of Power, America's Labor Leaders* (New York: Harcourt, Brace, 1948), *The Power Elite* (New York: Oxford University Press, 1956), and *Power, Politics, and People: The Collected Essays of C. Wright Mills* (New York: Oxford University Press, 1963).

27. Miller, *"Democracy Is in the Streets,"* 90.

28. Peter Bachrach, *The Theory of Democratic Elitism: A Critique* (Boston: Little, Brown and Co., 1967), 99.

29. Ibid., 93–94.

30. Ibid.Bachrach, 103.

30. Miller, *"Democracy Is in the Streets,"* 152.

31. Nigel Young, *An Infantile Disorder? The Crisis and Decline of the New Left* (Boulder: Westview Press, 1977), 96–97; cf. Howard Machtinger, "Clearing Away the Debris: New Left Radicalism in 1960s America" (master's thesis, San Francisco State University, 1990), 69–70.

32. Marcuse, *Critique of Pure Tolerance*, 81, quoted in Young, *An Infantile Disorder,* 97.

33. Marcuse, *Essay on Liberation*, 64, quoted in ibid., 97.

34. Miller, *"Democracy Is in the Streets,"* 263.

35. Young, *An Infantile Disorder*, 344–345; see, e.g., Fanon, *The Wretched of the Earth* (New York: Grove Press, 1965).

36. For elaboration of this point, see Jean-Christophe Agnew, "A Touch of Class," *Democracy* 4 (1983), 59–72, esp. 68. The problem of defining "the people" vs. "the system" in the sixties also receives valuable attention in Michael Kazin, *The Populist Persuasion: An American History* (New York: Basic Books, 1995), 195–218. Defending the politics of resistance in 1967, Noam Chomsky as-

serted, "There is no basis for supposing that those who will make the major policy decisions are open to reason on the fundamental issues, in particular the issue of whether we, alone among the nations of the world, have the authority and the competence to determine the social and political institutions of Vietnam. What is more, there is little likelihood that the electoral process will bear on the major decisions." "On Resistance," reprinted in Chomsky, *American Power and the New Mandarins* (New York: Pantheon, 1969), 383. The problem recalls the old Puritan self-justifying ethic, which went something like this: "The land and its riches belong to the saints. We are the saints. Therefore, it is ours!"

37. Cornel West, *Keeping Faith: Philosophy and Race in America* (New York: Routledge, 1993), 108; see also West and John Rajchman, eds., *Post-Analytic Philosophy* (New York: Columbia University Press, 1985); and Robert S. Boynton, "The New Intellectuals," *Atlantic Monthly* 275 (March 1995), 53–70.

38. West, *Keeping Faith*, 82, 104–105.

39. Richard Rorty, "Method, Social Science, and Social Hope," in *Consequences of Pragmatism: Essays, 1972–1980* (Minneapolis: University of Minnesota Press, 1982), 203.

40. Richard Rorty, "Postmodernist Bourgeois Liberalism," in *Objectivity, Relativism, and Truth: Philosophical Papers*, vol. 1 (New York: Cambridge University Press, 1991), 197. In the interest of gender-neutral language, Rorty appears here to ignore the gender-specific (i.e., male) nature of the traits he is criticizing.

41. A rare exception to such neglect is George E. Marcus and Russell L. Hanson, eds., *Reconsidering the Democratic Public* (University Park: Pennslvania State University Press, 1993). See esp. Benjamin I. Page and Robert Y. Shapiro, "The Rational Public and Democracy" (35–64).

42. Nancy Fraser, "Rethinking the Public Sphere: A Contribution to the Critique of Actually Existing Democracy," in Craig Calhoun, ed., *Habermas and the Public Sphere* (Cambridge, Mass.: MIT Press, 1992), 109–142, quotations 109, 127.

43. John McGowan, *Postmodernism and Its Critics* (Ithaca: Cornell University Press, 1991), 276–277.

Index